INSIDE AUTOCAD® LT
FOR WINDOWS® 95

MICHAEL BEALL

HOWARD FULMER

FRANCIS SOEN

New Riders Publishing, Indianapolis, Indiana

Inside AutoCAD LT for Windows 95

By Michael Beall, Howard Fulmer, and Francis Soen

Published by:
New Riders Publishing
201 West 103rd Street
Indianapolis, IN 46290 USA

Printed in the United States of America 1 2 3 4 5 6 7 8 9 0

Library of Congress Cataloging-in-Publication Data

```
Beall,  Michael  E.,  1953-
    Inside  AutoCAD  LT  95  /  Michael
    Beall,  Howard  Fulmer,  Francis
    Soen.
        p.      cm.
    Includes  index.
    ISBN  1-56205-612-3
    1.  Computer  graphics.    2.  AutoCAD
    LT  for  Windows    3.  Computer-
    -aided  design.    I.  Fulmer,  Howard,
    1954-    .    II.  Soen,  Francis.
    III.  Title.
    T385.B423    1996
    604.2'0285'5369--dc20
                              96-12126
                                   CIP
```

Warning and Disclaimer

Publisher	Don Fowley
Publishing Manager	David Dwyer
Marketing Manager	Mary Foote
Managing Editor	Carla Hall

Product Director
Alicia Buckley

Development Editor
David Pitzer

Project Editor
Laura Frey

Copy Editors
Nancy Albright, Jill Bond,
Larry Frey, Carla Hall
Dayna Isley, Cliff Shubs

Technical Editor
Kevin McWhirter

Associate Marketing Manager
Tamara Apple

Acquisitions Coordinator
Stacey Beheler

Administrative Coordinator
Karen Opal

Cover Designer
Aren Howell

Cover Production
Aren Howell

Book Designer
Anne Jones

Production Manager
Kelly Dobbs

Production Team Supervisor
Laurie Casey

Graphics Image Specialist
Stephen Adams

Production Analysts
Jason Hand,
Bobbi Satterfield

Production Team
Heather Butler, David
Garratt, Aleata Howard,
Christine Tyner, Pamela
Volk, Megan Wade,
Christy Wagner

Indexer
John Hulse

About the Authors

Michael Beall is the owner of Computer Aided Management and Planning in Shelbyville, KY near Louisville. Mr. Beall offers contract services and professional training on AutoCAD as well as CAP and CAP.Spex from Sweets Group, a division of McGraw-Hill. He is the co-author of *AutoCAD Release 13 for Beginners* and *Inside AutoCAD LT for Windows 95* from New Riders Publishing. Mr. Beall has been presenting CAD training seminars to architects and engineers since 1982 and is currently an instructor at the University of Louisville ATC. As owner of the former Computer Training Services in San Jose, CA, Mr. Beall developed a highly successful six month Architecture and Facility Planning program for re-entry adults at The Copper Connection, and ATC in Santa Clara, CA. He received a Bachelor of Architecture degree from the University of Cincinnati and is an affiliate member of the International Facility Managers Association. Mr. Beall can be reached at 502-633-3994 or by CompuServe at 74632,701.

Howard Fulmer is the president of HMF Consulting, based in Norristown, Pennsylvania. His firm is a full-service computer consulting enterprise, specializing in all aspects of hardware and software installation, training, customization, and support. He regularly conducts seminars and lectures at Fortune 500 companies as well as local high schools, sharing his 20-plus years of computer expertise from PCs to mainframes. Mr. Fulmer is also a college faculty member and teaches mechanical engineering and AutoCAD-related courses at Villanova University, Penn State University, and Montgomery County Community College. He was Phi Beta Kappa at Temple University and also has studied at the University of Minnesota. He is one of the founders and long-standing members of the Philadelphia AutoCAD Users Group, having served as PAUG President, Vice President, Program Chairman, and on executive steering committees. He has intensively utilized and customized AutoCAD since v1.4 (1984), and is an ATC trainer. In addition, Mr. Fulmer has co-authored the best-selling book *Inside AutoCAD Release 13 for Windows and Windows NT* from New Riders Publishing.

Francis Soen is an independent AutoCAD consultant who resides in Pittsburgh, PA and covers the tristate area. He has more than 12 years of experience working with AutoCAD and has co-authored several books on the subject. Mr. Soen provides customized training, LISP programming and menu customization services, advice on network and drawing management, and database programming. He is also an instructor at the AutoCAD Authorized Training Center at the Community College of Allegheny County. With degrees in Civil Engineering, Mr. Soen has developed an expertise in using AutoCAD for civil engineering and AEC applications in general, and digital terrain modeling applications in particular. In addition to AutoCAD, he also provides training and support for Softdesk's Civil/Survey modules and IGS scanning/conversion software. Francis can be contacted through CompuServe at 73232,760, or by phone at 412-922-0412, and is always happy to hear from other local users.

Trademark Acknowledgments

All terms mentioned in this book that are known to be trademarks or service marks have been appropriately capitalized. New Riders Publishing cannot attest to the accuracy of this information. Use of a term in this book should not be regarded as affecting the validity of any trademark or service mark.

Dedication

I dedicate this book to my parents who have made it possible for me to work at what I enjoy doing. — Francis Soen

Acknowledgments

Thanks are extended to my wife, Joan, and father, Aaron, for their ongoing support during the writing of this book. —Howard Fulmer

I would like to thank New Riders for giving me the opportunity to work on their projects and to their staff who make my writing look so professional. —Francis Soen

Contents at a Glance

Part VII: Appendices

Glossary
Index

Table of Contents

INTRODUCTION

This version of AutoCAD LT is far from "lite." When first introduced, the product was dubbed with the LT moniker intending to refer to a product that could be used with a laptop. It was intended to have the *power* of standard AutoCAD without the additional weight of 3D objects and the AutoLISP "wiring" for the connectability of hordes of third-party products. Surprisingly to most users, this resulted in an extremely affordable and powerful, albeit slimmer, version of AutoCAD.

AutoCAD LT for Windows 95 is even more powerful by virtue of being blessed with many of the new features added to Release 13. And users of Release 13 for Windows will be hard-pressed to see a significant difference between the menus and tools available in the two products.

Hopefully, this effort on the part of the authors and New Riders will provide you with an effective means by which you can feel immediately comfortable with an extremely useful CAD tool.

LEARNING FROM THIS BOOK

Inside AutoCAD LT for Windows 95 is designed as a tutorial to help new users learn how to use AutoCAD LT. Concepts and exercises are organized to build your knowledge and understanding gradually. This section presents conventions and terms used to explain commands and concepts.

Terms Used with the Pointing Device

When using the Windows pointing device, referred to throughout the book as a mouse, you will encounter the following terms to describe the mouse actions:

- **Click:** Press and release the pick button, button 1.

- **Click on, click in:** Position the cursor on the appropriate user interface object (such as an icon, edit box, menu item tool, and so on), then click the pick button.

- **Double-click:** Press and release the pick button twice in rapid succession.

- **Pick:** Position the AutoCAD LT cursor or pointer on the appropriate object, then click the pick button.

- **Select:** Highlight an object in the AutoCAD drawing area by picking it or by using other object selection methods. Also, to highlight an item, word, or character in a drop-down list, dialog box, or edit box by clicking on it.

- **Choose:** Select an item in a menu or dialog box by either clicking on it or typing its hot key letter.

- **Drag:** Move the mouse and cursor, causing lines or objects in the drawing area to move with the cursor.

- **Press and drag:** Press and hold down the pick button of the mouse, drag the object across the drawing area, then release the mouse. This could also refer to the dragging of the scroll box in a scroll bar.

Notes, Tips, and Warnings

Inside AutoCAD LT for Windows 95 features three special types of sidebars that are shown apart from the normal text by icons: Notes, Tips, and Warnings. These notations provide you with extra help and information to supplement the general discussion.

NOTE

A Note gives you extra information that is not critical to the subject at hand, but can be useful. A Note can tell you how to avoid problems with your computer or describe situations that can occur under certain circumstances and might tell you what steps to take.

TIP

A Tip can tell you how to get the most out of AutoCAD LT for Windows 95 as you follow the discussion of a topic. A Tip might show how to make your system run a little faster, how to speed up a procedure, or how to perform a time-saving or system-enhancing technique within AutoCAD LT or the Windows 95 environment.

WARNING

A Warning alerts you to when a procedure might be disastrous (when you run the risk of losing data, locking your system, or even damaging the hardware). Warnings can tell you how to avoid these situations or describe steps to take to remedy such situations.

Toolbar Selection

New to AutoCAD LT for Windows 95 are command toolbars. When you rest your cursor on a tool, you are given a *tooltip* in a little yellow box. This is the name of the tool and oftentimes the name of the command issued by that tool. On some toolbars, choosing a tool will cause another set of tools to pop up either to the right or below the tool. These are know as *flyouts*. Tools are referred to by their name and the name of their corresponding toolbar (and flyout). If you are instructed to choose *Dtext (Draw, Text)*, for example, you would choose the Dtext tool located in the Draw toolbar on the Text flyout.

Pull-Down Menu Selections

When you see instructions such as Choose Draw, Line, this means to move the mouse to the pull-down menu item Draw and click the left mouse button. You can also use the accelerator key (a combination consisting of the Alt key and the letter under-lined in the menu bar item) to display the menu. In the previous example, you could either click on the Draw pull-down menu, then choose Line, or press Alt+D and then L.

Keyboard Entry

In some exercises, you will see *Press Enter* or the symbol ↵. Your computer will have a key labeled Enter, Return or ↵ that you should press when you see *Press Enter* or ↵ during the course of the steps in an exercise.

Some commands cannot be accessed through menus. Point coordinates, distances, and option keywords must be typed. The exercise will indicate when typed input is required by showing it in bold text following a prompt, such as Type **LIMITS** ↵ or To point: **5,30** ↵. You should type the bold text, then press Enter.

This book will present commands and their prompts in the exercise in which they are first introduced. Later, familiar or routine prompts will be omitted.

Most exercises finish with a step to save the drawing. Build the habit of saving your drawing at the end of each exercise. Some chapters can be finished in one or two sittings, or you might continue at a more leisurely pace, if you prefer. If you take a break and want to continue the drawing later, just save the drawing, then open it when you are ready to continue.

Sample Exercise

Exercises consist of numbered steps and one or more illustrations of what your computer screen should look like. When a new command is introduced, the prompt line will be shown in the appropriate step. The following sample exercise draws two lines and a circle as shown in figure I.1.

Figure I.1

A sample exercise figure.

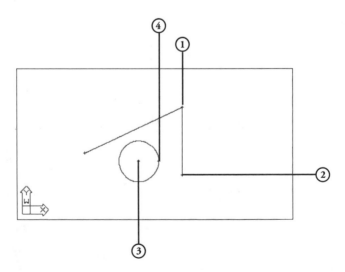

A QUICK SAMPLE EXERCISE

1. Begin a new drawing From Scratch, then choose File, Save As.

2. Enter **INTRO01** as the drawing File Name, then choose OK.

3. Choose Line from the Draw toolbar to invoke the LINE command and you see the following prompt:

```
_line  From point:
```

4. Type **4,4,** then press Enter and you will see the next prompt:

```
To point:
```

5. Pick the point at ① as shown in fig. I.1.

6. Before placing the next point, press F8 to turn on Ortho, then pick ②.

7. Press Enter to end the LINE command.

8. Choose Draw, Circle, Center, Radius and you see the following:

```
_circle 3P/TTR/<Center point>:
```

9. Pick the point at ③ as the center point and you see the next prompt:

```
Diameter/<Radius>:
```

10. Pick ④, to set the circle's radius and end the CIRCLE command.

11. Choose File, Save to save the drawing.

Exercises and the Graphics Display

This book's figures were created by capturing the screen displays during the process of performing the exercise. All screen displays were captured from systems using a resolution of 640×400-pixels, 256-color mode under Windows 95. If your display is set to a higher (or lower) resolution, your screen display might not match the figures. Menus and screen items can appear larger or smaller than they do in the figures, and you might want to zoom in or out farther than the exercise steps indicate. You should adjust your display according to the current task and the resources available. You might find that if you use colors that are different from those specified in the exercises, the objects are easier to see, especially if you are working with a white background rather than a black background.

The Command Glossary

As a new command is presented, the most frequently used options of that command will be explained in that chapter, often by way of an exercise. The Glossary at the end of this book contains all AutoCAD LT command definitions as well as the page(s) on which they are discussed.

Handling Problems

As you work through the exercises in *Inside AutoCAD LT for Windows 95*, you might experience some problems. These problems can occur for any number of reasons, from input errors to hardware failures. If you have trouble performing any step described in this book, take the following actions:

- Try again. Double-check the steps you performed in the previous exercise(s), as well as earlier steps in the current exercise.

- Check the settings of any AutoCAD system variables or dialog boxes modified in any previous exercise sequence.

- Check the AutoCAD LT for Windows 95 documentation or online help that came with your copy of AutoCAD LT.

If none of these suggestions helps, call your AutoCAD dealer or log on to the ACAD forum on CompuServe and ask or search for help.

CompuServe

The Autodesk Software Forum (GO ASOFT) on CompuServe is a terrific source of information and inspiration for users. Here you can get in touch with experienced AutoCAD users, developers, and Autodesk personnel, as well as find out about the latest software developments.

The Internet

Like many large companies, Autodesk now has a presence on the World Wide Web. To find it, set your Web browser (such as Netscape) to this URL:

```
http://www.autodesk.com
```

If you have an Internet newsreader, you can also access a number of Internet newsgroups that are devoted to CAD, 3D, graphics, multimedia, teaching, and other topics of interest. The list is too long (and changes too frequently) to mention here. For more information on these Internet sites, visit the New Riders World Wide Web site at this URL:

`http://www.mcp.com/newriders`

When you reach the New Riders home page, click on the CAD icon to find out more.

New Riders Publishing

The staff of New Riders Publishing is committed to bringing you the very best in computer reference material. Each New Riders book is the result of months of work by authors and staff who research and refine the information contained within its covers.

As part of this commitment to you, the NRP reader, New Riders invites your input. Please let us know if you enjoy this book, if you have trouble with the information and examples presented, or if you have a suggestion for the next edition.

Please note, though: New Riders staff cannot serve as a technical resource for AutoCAD LT or for questions about software- or hardware-related problems. Please refer to the documentation that accompanies AutoCAD LT or to the applications' Help systems.

If you have a question or comment about any New Riders book, there are several ways to contact New Riders Publishing. We will respond to as many readers as we can. Your name, address, or phone number will never become part of a mailing list or be used for any purpose other than to help us continue to bring you the best books possible. You can write us at the following address:

New Riders Publishing
Attn: Publisher
201 W. 103rd Street
Indianapolis, IN 46290

If you prefer, you can fax New Riders Publishing at (317) 581-4670.

You can also send electronic mail to New Riders at the following Internet address:

`ddwyer@newriders.mcp.com`

NRP is an imprint of Macmillan Computer Publishing. To obtain a catalog or information, or to purchase any Macmillan Computer Publishing book, call (800) 428-5331.

Thank you for selecting *Inside AutoCAD LT for Windows 95*!

AutoCAD LT for Windows 95 Basics

OPENING AUTOCAD LT 95

Chapter 1 serves as an orientation to the drawing environment of AutoCAD LT 95. Whether you are an existing LT user upgrading to LT 95 or are a new LT user, this chapter should prove informative. In this chapter, you learn the following:

■ *How to start AutoCAD LT 95*

■ *What drawing files are*

■ *How to begin new drawing files*

■ *How to open existing drawing files*

■ *The parts of the LT application window*

■ *How to issue commands*

■ *How to get help*

Starting LT

Following a standard installation from the AutoCAD LT 95 CD, a folder labeled AUTOCAD LT can be found in the Programs folder of the Start menu of the Windows 95 taskbar. To start an LT drawing session, select AutoCAD LT from the AutoCAD LT folder; the menu item starts LT and uses the directory (or folder) ACLTWIN as the working directory. The two other items in the AutoCAD LT folder are AutoCAD LT Readme and On-line Help. You should read the AutoCAD LT Readme file as it contains last-minute changes and additions to the program documentation. The On-line Help program is the same help facility that is accessible from within LT. The LT installation routine does not create a desktop shortcut for LT but you can, of course, add one yourself. LT is installed, configured to run and use the Win95 system drivers for the display, printer, and mouse. After LT completely loads, the initial drawing environment appears (see fig. 1.1).

Figure 1.1

The initial drawing environment of a new drawing session.

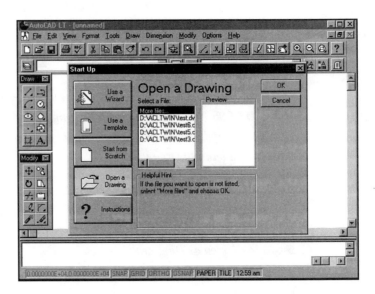

You can only work on one drawing at a time. You can, however, start and run multiple sessions of LT concurrently.

Beginning New Drawings

All work performed in LT is stored in drawing files. You either are working in a new drawing file or editing an existing drawing file. To prepare the drawing environment before creating a new drawing file, you must perform the following tasks:

- Choose a system of units

- Define the drawing area or limits

- Draw a title block

To aid you in these setup steps, LT displays the Start Up dialog box when LT is initially started (refer to figure 1.1). When you choose to begin a new drawing later in the drawing session by clicking the New button on the standard toolbar or choosing New from the File menu, the Create New Drawing dialog box (a variation of the Start Up dialog box) appears (see fig. 1.2). The only difference between the two dialog boxes is that the Start Up dialog box offers an option to open an existing drawing while the Create New Drawing dialog box does not. A new drawing is created with the aid of a wizard, a template, or is created from scratch.

Figure 1.2

The Create New Drawing dialog box.

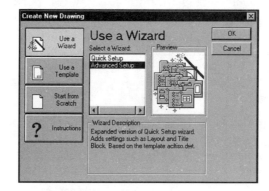

Using the Quick Setup Wizard

AutoCAD LT provides two wizards you can use to set up a new drawing: the Quick Setup wizard and the Advanced Setup wizard. To use the Quick Setup wizard, choose the Use a Wizard button and then choose the Quick Setup option from the list of wizards that appears. As a rule, you can choose an item from a list by double-clicking on the item or by clicking on the item once (thereby selecting it) and then choosing the OK button. After choosing the Quick Setup Wizard, the Quick Setup dialog box appears (see fig. 1.3).

Figure 1.3

The Quick Setup dialog box you use to create a new drawing.

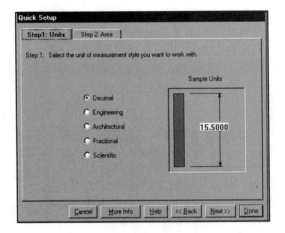

The Quick Setup wizard consists of two parts: choosing a system of units and precision for linear measurements and setting the drawing area. The following are the available choices for the system of units for linear measurements:

System of Units	Example
Decimal	25.2500
Engineering	2'-1.2500"
Architectural	2'-1 $^1/_4$"
Fractional	25 $^1/_4$
Scientific	2.525E+01

The basic unit of measure in an LT drawing is a *drawing unit*, which is dimensionless. When either engineering or architectural units are chosen, LT treats each drawing unit as representing an inch. For metric drawings, decimal units are used.

After you select the system of units you want, choose the Step 2: Area file tab or the Next button. In the Step 2 file tab, the limits of the area to be drawn on are set. LT has a near infinite drawing area. It is, however, useful to set limits in this infinite drawing area to accommodate the drawing you want to create. If you want to draw a floor plan of a 100 feet by 50 feet building, then you should set the limits to at least that size, if not larger.

After you set all the parameters, a new drawing can then be created. Initially, the new drawing has no assigned name and is referred to as an "unnamed" drawing; you assign the file name at the time you first save the drawing.

NOTE

> You can modify the units and limits of a drawing at any time by using the DDUNITS and LIMITS commands.

In the following exercise, you use the Quick Setup wizard to begin a new drawing.

CREATING A NEW DRAWING USING THE QUICK SETUP WIZARD

1. Start a session of LT by choosing AutoCAD LT from the Windows 95 taskbar.

2. From the Start Up dialog box, choose Use a Wizard and select the Quick Setup wizard, which displays the Quick Setup dialog box.

3. For the system of units, choose Decimal units.

4. Next, choose the Step 2: Area tab and enter 17 for the width and 11 for the height. Choose Done to end the wizard.

   A new drawing is created with decimal units in effect and a 17 by 11 drawing unit area defined.

   Because you will not be doing any work in this drawing, do not worry about saving it.

Using the Advanced Setup Wizard

Choosing the Advanced Setup wizard in the Start Up or Create New Drawing dialog boxes results in the display of the Advanced Setup dialog box (see fig. 1.4).

Figure 1.4

The Advanced Setup wizard dialog box.

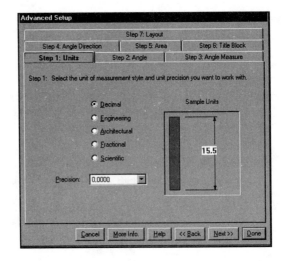

In addition to choosing the system of units for linear measurements and setting drawing limits (see "Using the Quick Setup Wizard"), the Advanced Setup dialog box also enables you to choose the following:

■   The precision of the linear units

■   The system of units and precision for angular measurements

■   The orientation of zero degrees

■   The direction that positive angles are measured

■   The title block to be drawn

■   Whether the title block is drawn in tiled model space or paper space

The precision chosen for the linear units of measurement only affect the display of coordinates and distances on the screen. The precision you choose does not affect the precision with which the coordinates and distances are recorded in the drawing file. Following are the available choices for the system of units for angular measurements.

System of Units	Example
Decimal Degrees	30.5000
Deg/Min/Sec	30d30'00"
Grads	33.8889g

System of Units	Example
Radians	0.5323r
Surveyor	N59d30'00"E

You set the angular system of units by choosing Step 2: Angle tab in the Advanced Setup dialog box (see fig. 1.5).

Figure 1.5

Setting the system of units for angular measurements.

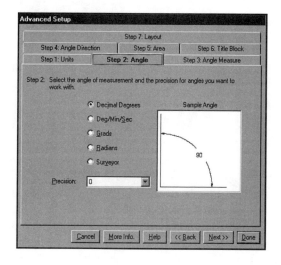

You also can set the precision with which angular measurements are displayed. This only affects the display of angles on-screen, not the precision with which angles are recorded in the drawing file.

The orientation of zero degrees normally is horizontal and to the right (see fig. 1.6).

Figure 1.6

The orientation of X and Y axes and 0 degrees.

This orientation corresponds to standard CAD practices; however, you can change this if necessary. For example, surveyors use zero degrees to represent north and drawings usually are drawn so that north is pointing up on the paper.

You set the orientation of zero degrees by choosing the Step 3: Angle Measure tab in the Advanced Setup dialog box (see fig. 1.7).

Figure 1.7

Setting the orientation
of zero degrees.

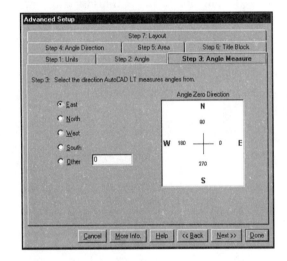

Choosing the Step 4: Angle Direction tab displays the screen shown in figure 1.8.

Figure 1.8

Setting the direction
of positive angles.

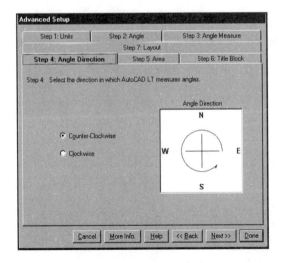

Positive angles are normally measured counter-clockwise from zero degrees, which corresponds to standard CAD practices. You can set LT, however, to measure positive angles clockwise, starting from zero degrees. Surveyors, for example, commonly measure positive angular values in a clockwise direction.

TIP

Unless you have a very good reason to do otherwise, leave the orientation of zero degrees and the direction of positive angles at the default values.

Choosing the Step 6: Title Block tab displays the screen shown in figure 1.9.

Figure 1.9

Choosing a title block.

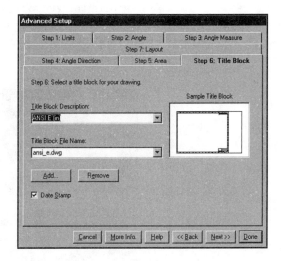

You can insert a predefined title block into the new drawing. Choose the title block from a drop-down list of predefined title blocks; access by choosing the top element of the list. You will see two lists: the top list provides descriptions of the title blocks and the bottom list provides the corresponding drawing file names.

You can add additional title blocks to the list by using the Add button. Title blocks no longer needed are deleted from the list with the Remove button.

NOTE

If the Date Stamp option is enabled, then the current user name (as entered during the installation of LT), the current drawing filename, and current time are recorded along the left edge of the title block. The date stamp information can be updated at any time by choosing Date and Time Stamp from the Tools menu.

The final step, the "Step 7: Layout" tab, enables you to determine whether the chosen title block is drawn in tiled model space or paper space (see fig. 1.10). Paper space is dealt with extensively in Chapter 16, "Working with Model and Paper Space," and Chapter 17, "Sheet Composition and Plotting." All the discussion and exercises in the coming chapters—up to Chapter 16—deal exclusively with tiled model space. So for now, always choose the No option to enable tiled model space when starting new drawings.

NOTE

When you choose to use a title block and enable the No option, the limits of the new drawing are automatically set to correspond to the edges of the title block and any values set in the Step 5: Area tab are ignored. If you want to set the limits of the new drawing to the area specified in the Step 5: Area tab and still enable the No option, choose No Title Block from the list of title block descriptions in the Step 6: Title Block tab.

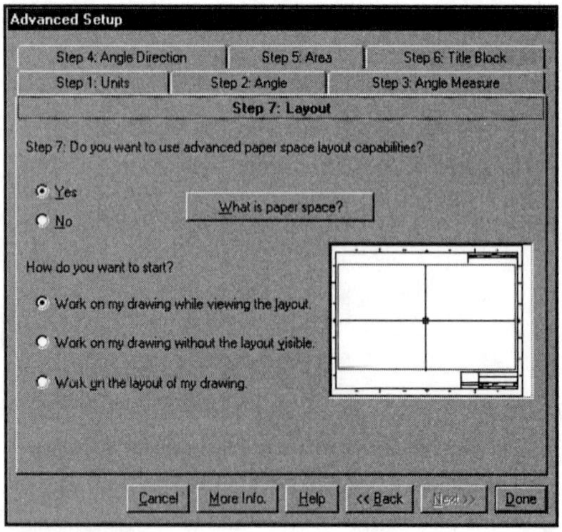

Figure 1.10

Choosing tiled model space or paper space.

When all the parameters are set, choose Done to create the new drawing.

In the following exercise, you abandon the current drawing and create a new drawing with the Advanced Setup wizard.

CREATING A NEW DRAWING USING THE ADVANCED SETUP WIZARD

1. Choose New from the File menu.

   If you are prompted to save the changes to the current drawing, answer No.

2. Choose Advanced Setup from the Create New Drawing dialog box.

3. Choose Architectural Units with 1/8" precision.

4. Choose the Step 6 tab and select ANSI D title block.

5. Choose the Step 7 tab and choose the No option.

6. Choose Done.

   A D-size title block is inserted into tiled model space and a new drawing is begun.

Using a Template

Another option for beginning a new drawing is to take a copy of an existing drawing and use the copy as the basis for the new drawing. The copied drawing is referred to as a *template*. The use of templates is enabled by choosing Use A Template in the Create New Drawing dialog box.

NOTE

> The advantage of using a template is that the new drawing will have everything that is already in the existing drawing, including layers, linetypes, objects, text styles, dimension styles, and so on. You will be learning in the following chapters to define and use all the items just mentioned.

Template files have a .DWT file extension rather than the normal .DWG file extension and must be stored in the directory \ACLTWIN\TEMPLATE. The specifics of creating new template files with the SAVEAS command are covered in Chapter 2, "Setting Up Your Drawing Environment."

Starting from Scratch

If the Start From Scratch option in the Start Up on Create Drawing dialog boxes is enabled, the new drawing is created from a set of standards defined internally in the LT program. This set of standards defines a completely new and empty drawing and is used to begin a new drawing. Use the Start From Scratch option when you want to ensure that the new drawing is completely empty.

TIP

You use the Start From Scratch option most often when importing a .DXF file into the drawing (see the IMPORT command).

The LT Drawing Environment

The LT drawing environment (the Graphical User Interface) consists of several distinct components (see fig. 1.11):

- Pull-down menus
- Toolbars
- The drawing
- Command and text windows
- Status and task bars
- Function and accelerator keys
- Pointing device
- Keyboard

You enter commands through several of these components, which enables you to use the medium most comfortable to you.

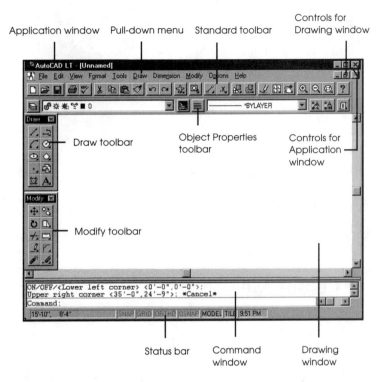

Figure 1.11

The components of the LT application window.

Application window   Pull-down menu   Standard toolbar   Controls for Drawing window

Draw toolbar   Object Properties toolbar   Controls for Application window

Modify toolbar

Status bar   Command window   Drawing window

Pull-down Menus

The pull-down menus contain menu items that either issue commands or display submenus. You select a pull-down menu and a menu item by using your pointing device or by pressing the Alt key along with the underlined letter in the menu item. For example, pressing Alt+V (do not press the + sign) displays the View menu (see fig. 1.12).

A menu item that has an arrowhead to the right of the item displays a *submenu* (also known as a *cascading menu*). A menu item that ends with three dots displays a dialog box. All other menu items issue commands. Some menu items may be disabled or dimmed (greyed out), indicating that under the current circumstances that command is not available.

After you select a menu item, the pull-down menu disappears. To close a pull-down menu without selecting a menu item, press the Esc key.

Figure 1.12

The View pull-down menu.

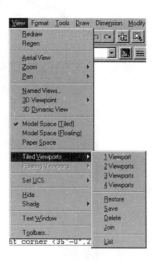

Cursor Menu

The Cursor menu is a menu that appears on-screen at the current location of the crosshairs (or cursor) (see fig. 1.13).

Figure 1.13

Displaying the Cursor menu.

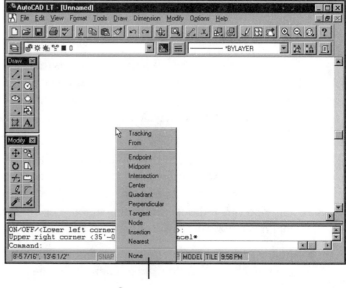

Cursor menu

If you have a two- or three-button mouse, you can display the Cursor menu by pressing Shift and clicking the right mouse button. With a three-button mouse, clicking the middle mouse button also displays the Cursor menu. If you are using a digitizer, pressing Shift and button 1, or pressing button 2 by itself, displays the Cursor menu.

After you display the cursor menu, simply select the menu item you want and the cursor automatically disappears. To close the Cursor menu without selecting a menu item, press Esc.

Toolbars

A *toolbar* is a collection of tools, represented by icons, that are grouped together. When you initially start LT, four toolbars are displayed on-screen: the Standard toolbar, the Object Properties toolbar, the Draw toolbar, and the Modify toolbar (refer to figure 1.11).

If you position the screen pointer over a tool and leave the pointer in that position, a word (Tool Tip) appears below that particular tool, giving you a description of the function of the tool (see fig. 1.14). Additionally, a more detailed explanation of the tool's function appears on the left side of the status bar.

Figure 1.14

Parts of a toolbar.

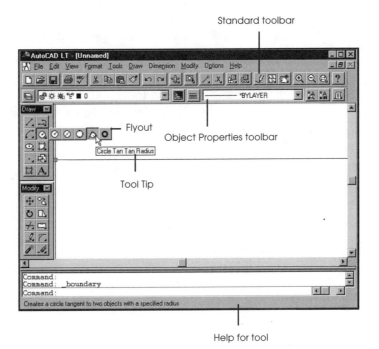

Each tool issues a command and some tools also display a flyout, or a submenu. Any tool that has an arrowhead in the lower right corner of the tile is a part of a flyout. To display the flyout, choose the tool representing the flyout and press and hold down your pick button. To select a tool from the flyout, drag the pointer to the tool you want and release the pick button. The command then is issued and the flyout closes. To close a flyout without selecting a tool, move the pointer completely outside the toolbar and release the pick button.

When you select a tool from a flyout, the tool is moved to the main toolbar and, from that point on, represents that flyout until another tool is chosen from the flyout. This way, the most recently used tool on the flyout becomes the "top" tool.

Notice that the Standard toolbar and Object Properties toolbar are different from the Draw and Modify toolbars. The Draw and Modify toolbars each have a title bar and a Close button while the Standard toolbar and Object Properties toolbar have neither.

The reason the two pairs of toolbars appear different is that the Draw and Modify toolbars are in an *undocked* state while the other two are in a *docked* state. When a toolbar is docked, it is made to appear as a single row or column of tools and its title bar is taken away to minimize the space the toolbar takes up.

You can dock a toolbar along any of the four edges of the application window. To dock a toolbar, drag the toolbar by its title bar to one of the four edges. Drag the toolbar to the edge you want and position it until the outline of the toolbar becomes thinner and dimmer. Then release the pick button. The toolbar then is docked at that location.

To undock a toolbar, drag the toolbar by choosing a point on the toolbar that is not on any of the tools. Drag the toolbar away from the edge until the outline of the toolbar becomes heavier and bolder. Release the pick button and the toolbar is undocked at that location.

You also can drag a toolbar to the edge of the application window and prevent it from docking by pressing Ctrl while dragging the toolbar into position. You can change the size of an undocked toolbar by moving the pointer to one of the edges of the toolbar. When the pointer changes to a double-headed arrow, drag that edge as desired and the shape of the toolbar changes accordingly.

To close a toolbar, click its close button. To open a toolbar, choose Toolbars from the View pulldown menu (which issues the VIEWTOOLBAR command) and then select the toolbar(s) you want to display. LT records the position of all toolbars so that the next time you start LT, the toolbars appear in the last known positions.

Drawing Window

Within the overall application window is the *drawing window*, which is where the drawing is displayed. Initially, the drawing window is displayed in a maximized state, with its controls displayed immediately below the controls the application window (refer to figure 1.11).

Unlike most other Window applications, LT can only display one drawing (or document) at a time. You are, however, allowed to start multiple sessions of LT and have each session display a different drawing. As such, minimizing the drawing window accomplishes nothing, so it is best to leave it maximized.

Command Window

The *command window* is the window that displays the command line prompt. When a command is issued by typing or by selecting a tool or menu item, the command word appears in this window. When a command displays options or other prompts, the options and prompts are displayed in the command window.

Initially, the command window is sized to display three lines of text. You can change the height of the window by moving the pointer to the splitter bar until the pointer is displayed as a double-headed arrow. You then drag the splitter bar until the height of the command window is the way you want.

TIP

> The default height of the command window is the ideal height for most drawing situations. Do not change the height to less than three lines. Increasing the height to display more lines usually is unnecessary and simply takes away space from the drawing window. The text within the window can be scrolled and is also displayed in the text window.

The command window initially is docked at the bottom of the application window and, if desired, can be undocked or even moved to the top of the application window. To undock the application window, move the pointer just below the splitter bar before the pointer changes to a text cursor, and then drag the window to the position you want. Docking the command window is similar to docking a toolbar.

Text Window

The *text window* is an enlarged version of the command window (see fig. 1.15).

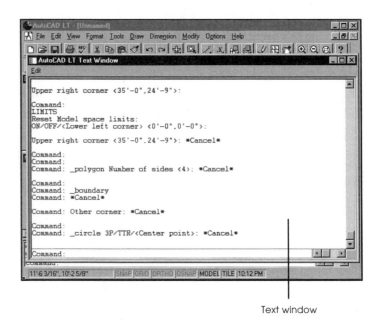

Text window

The text window automatically is displayed by certain LT commands that display text information. You can access the text window at any time simply by pressing F2. To switch back to the application window, press F2 again. Use the text window to review previous text display and to view lengthy displays of text. To copy a portion of the text (for a copy/paste or cut/paste operation), highlight the target text and use the commands in the Edit menu of the text window. Do not press Ctrl+C (COPYCLIP command) to make the copy as would be done in a word processing software or text editor because COPYCLIP copies the contents of the drawing window and not of the text window.

Status Bar

The *status bar* is displayed at the very bottom of the application window (refer to figure 1.11). On the left end of the bar, the current X and Y coordinates of the crosshairs are displayed. There are also several labeled buttons that issue commands that affect the drawing environment. When a particular option is enabled, the button representing that option appears bold. When the option is disabled, the button appears dimmed. To enable or disable an option represented by a button, double-click on the button. The rightmost button displays the current time. You can toggle the display of the status bar by pressing F10.

Buttons on the Mouse or Digitizer

On a two-button mouse, you use the left button to select menu items, tools, points, and objects. Pressing the right mouse button is equivalent to pressing the Enter key on the keyboard. Pressing the right mouse button while holding down the Shift key displays the Cursor menu. With a three-button mouse, pressing the additional middle button also displays the Cursor menu.

With a multi-button digitizer puck (or pad), the buttons usually are numbered. Button 0 typically is the pick button and the other buttons send out the commands shown in table 1.1.

Table 1.1

Buttons on a Multi-Button Digitizer Puck

Button #	Command Issued
1	Enter key
2	Displays the Cursor menu
3	Issues two cancels in a row
4	Toggles snap on/off
5	OPEN
6	Toggles grid on/off
7	Toggles coordinates display
8	Toggles current isoplane
9	Toggles tablet on/off

Function Keys

The *function keys* on the keyboard (shown in table 1.2) issue the following commands:

Table 1.2

Keyboard Function Commands

Function Key	Command Issued
F1	HELP
F2	Toggles between text and drawing windows
F3	DDOSNAP
F4	Toggles tablet on/off
F5	Toggles isoplanes
F6	Toggles coordinates
F7	Toggles grid on/off
F8	Toggles ortho on/off
F9	Toggles snap on/off
F10	Toggles status bar display on/off

Accelerator Keys

Accelerator keys are keyboard combinations that issue commands. Each sequence typically involves pressing the Ctrl key and another key. Table 1.3 shows the accelerator keys that are predefined for you. You can define additional accelerator keys.

Table 1.3

Accelerator Keys

Accelerator Key Sequence	Command Issued
Del	ERASE
Ctrl+A	SELECT with the All option specified
Ctrl+C	COPYCLIP
Ctrl+L	Toggles ortho on/off

Accelerator Key Sequence	Command Issued
Ctrl+N	NEW
Ctrl+O	OPEN
Ctrl+P	PLOT
Ctrl+R	Toggles viewports
Ctrl+S	QSAVE
Ctrl+V	PASTECLIP
Ctrl+X	CUTCLIP
Ctrl+Y	REDO
Ctrl+Z	UNDO

Typing Commands

Unlike many other Windows programs, you can enter AutoCAD LT commands using the keyboard. A command word that is typed must be terminated with the spacebar or the Enter key. A quick way to repeat the last command issued is to press the spacebar.

The labels on the pull-down menus and the tool tips that appear below the tools are not necessarily the command word that is issued by the menu item or tool. To find out what command word is actually being issued by a menu item or tool, just watch the command window as the menu item tool is selected. The command word that appears in the command window is what you would type to issue the command. An LT command is always a single word with no spaces.

Parts of a Dialog Box

Quite a number of LT commands display a dialog box. Many elements are incorporated into a dialog box and it is important to know how to access these elements. For example, the Running Object Snap dialog box contains check boxes, a slider bar, and buttons (see fig. 1.16).

Figure 1.16

Elements of the Running Object Snap dialog box.

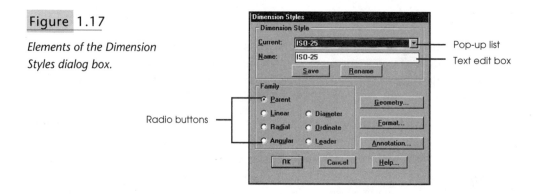

Toggles are options you either enable or disable by selecting the box next to the label. When an option is enabled, an X appears in the box. You use a slider to control the value of a setting that can range from a minimum to a maximum value. You activate buttons by selecting them. Another example of a dialog box is the Dimension Styles dialog box (see fig. 1.17).

Figure 1.17

Elements of the Dimension Styles dialog box.

Radio buttons are used to offer a series of options that are mutually exclusive of each other. This means that you can select only one of the group at a time. You select a radio button by choosing the button next to the label.

A *pop-up list*, in its condensed state, appears as a box with a down arrow on the right side. You activate the list by selecting the box. The list then expands to show the full list. If the list is longer or wider than the box can show, scroll bars appear on the edges of the list.

Text in a *text edit box* is edited by placing the cursor in the box at the point in the text. You use the Backspace and Delete keys to remove characters. You use Insert to toggle between insert and overwrite mode. You can highlight text by choosing a point at the beginning of the text and dragging to the end. The highlighted text can then be deleted by pressing Del or replaced with new text when you type.

Almost all dialog boxes contain OK, Cancel, and Help buttons. To close the box and carry out the command, click OK or press the Enter key when the OK button is highlighted. To abort the command and select Help to get help information, click Cancel or press the Esc key.

TIP

If you are editing the last text box in the dialog box, usually pressing the Enter key after typing the text is equivalent to clicking the OK button.

You can use the keyboard to move among elements in a dialog box. Press Tab to move to the next element or press Shift+Tab to move to the previous element. To move to a specific element, press Alt plus the underlined letter in the label next to the controls (buttons, sliders, lists, and so on).

In the next exercise, you practice accessing the various elements of the LT application window.

CONTROLLING THE LT DRAWING ENVIRONMENT

You can use your current drawing for this exercise.

1. Press F2 to display the text window. Press F2 again to return to the application window.

2. Press F1 to access the Help facility. Close the Help window.

3. Press F10 to hide the status bar. Press F10 again to redisplay the status bar.

4. Drag the Draw toolbar (by its title bar) to the right edge of the application window until the outline of the toolbar becomes thinner and dimmed, as shown in figure 1.18. Release the pick button. The Draw toolbar is now docked.

Figure 1.18

Docking the Draw toolbar.

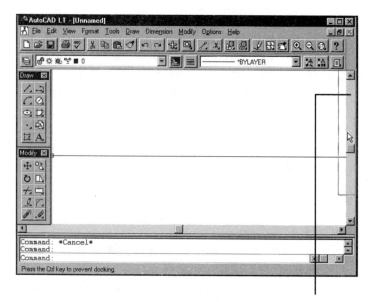

Drag the Draw
toolbar to this
position.

5. Drag the Modify toolbar to the right edge of the application window, to the
   left of the docked Draw toolbar, until the outline of the toolbar becomes
   thinner and dimmed, as shown in figure 1.19. Release the pick button.

Figure 1.19

*Docking the Modify
toolbar next to the Draw
toolbar.*

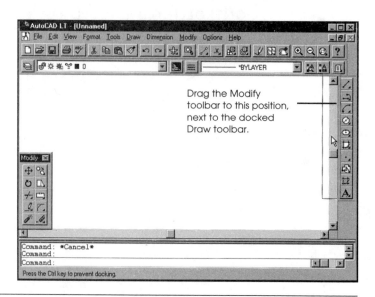

Drag the Modify
toolbar to this position,
next to the docked
Draw toolbar.

If you are left-handed, you may prefer to dock the toolbars on the left edge of the application window.

The arrangement of toolbars on the right side of the window is used throughout the remainder of this book.

Opening Existing Drawings

To open and view the contents of existing drawings, choose Open A Drawing from the Start Up dialog box (refer to figure 1.1). After selecting the Open A Drawing option, a list of the last four drawings on which you worked appears. (The drawings are also listed in the File pull-down menu.) If the drawing you want to open is not one of the four in the list, choose More Files from the list; the Select File dialog box appears (see fig. 1.20).

Figure 1.20

The Select File dialog box.

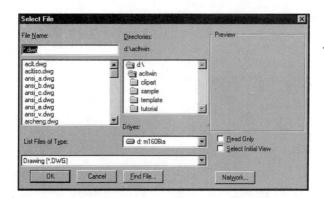

Choosing Open from the File pull-down menu or clicking the Open button on the Standard toolbar also displays the Select File dialog box. You can issue the OPEN command at any time during a drawing session to open the next existing drawing you want to edit.

Selecting a File

You use the Select File dialog box to select a drawing file to open (refer to figure 1.20). Select from the Directories list the directory you want. Choose the drawing file from the File Name list. A preview picture of the file you select appears in the Preview box. If the drawing is a pre-LT 3.0 drawing, then it will not have a preview picture. If need be, select the Drives list to choose the drive you want. If the drive is a network drive, select the Network button.

If.the list of drawings is too long to appear in the list, you can narrow down the list by setting a file specification in the text edit box above the list of files. The default file specification is *.DWG, which results in all drawing files in the specified directory being listed.

Normally, a drawing is opened for both read and write operations, which means that you can make and save changes in the drawing file. If you want to guarantee that a drawing file is not inadvertently changed, however, enable the Read Only option. The file opens, but changes you make are not saved when you close the drawing.

When a drawing opens, the initial view that appears is the current view at the time you last closed the file. If you have a particular view you want to see when you open the file, click the Select Initial View button to choose the view. For more information on saving and restoring views, see Chapter 2, "Setting Up Your Drawing Environment."

After you select the parameters, choose OK to open the file. Another way to select a file and close the dialog box is to double-click on the file you want from the list of file names (refer to figure 1.20).

Browsing for a File

If you need help finding a particular drawing file to open and do not know the directory in which the file is located, choose the Find File button in the Select File dialog box. The Browse/Search dialog box appears (see fig. 1.21).

Figure 1.21

The Browse/Search dialog box with Browse mode active.

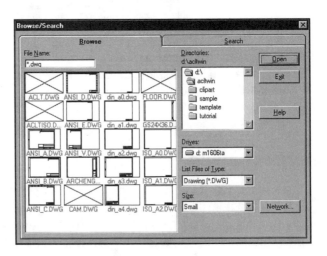

The Browse/Search dialog box contains two components: Browse and Search. Each component is represented by a file folder tab and is activated by selecting the tab. By default, the mode that was last used is displayed as the dominant mode.

In Browse mode, preview pictures of all the drawing files in the current directory on the current drive appear in the preview area. If the file is a pre-LT 3.0 drawing, then its preview picture is of a rectangle with an X drawn through it. The size of the preview picture is set through the size list. Choose a file by selecting a preview and then choose Open or double-click the preview you want.

Searching for a File

If you select the Search tab, the Search tab of the Browse/Search dialog box appears (see fig. 1.22).

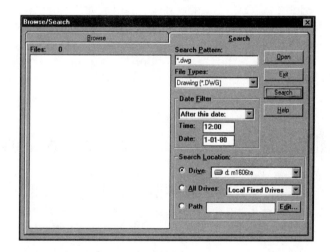

You use Search to find a file or group of files that meet the specified search criteria. The specified criteria can consist of three parts: a file specification, a date filter, and a search location.

You use the date filter to find files with file dates before or after a date you specify. You can perform a search on an entire drive, all local drives, all drives including network drives, and even a specific directory (including the directories below the specified directory).

All files that fit the criteria appear in the preview area. To open the file for which you searched, select that file from the list and choose the Open button or double-click on the filename.

Getting Help and Running the Tutorials

LT includes an extensive help facility that you can access by selecting On-Line Help from the AutoCAD LT program group (Start menu on the taskbar) by choosing Help from the Standard toolbar, by choosing AutoCAD LT Help from the Help pull-down menu, or by pressing F1. If Help is started while an LT command is active, then help information for that command is displayed; otherwise, general help information is displayed.

Three tutorials are also available from the Help pull-down menu: Orientation, Tutorial, and What's New. The Orientation tutorial is designed to give some helpful hints to a new CAD user. The Tutorial tutorial is designed to give some basic lessons to the new LT user. The What's New tutorial serves as a guide to the new features of LT 3.0.

Normally as soon as you move the system pointer from the Command Reference window (HELP Command) to the LT application window and pick a point, the window containing HELP information is sent to the background. If you want to have the information in the Command Reference window visible at all times (like a cue card), enable the On Top option by choosing Keep Help on Top from the Options menu of the Command Reference window. The same can be done with tutorial windows.

Ending LT and Saving the Drawing

To end your LT drawing session, choose Exit from the File menu. If LT detects that changes have been made in the current drawing, you are prompted to save the changes. If you answer Yes, the changes are saved to the drawing file and LT is terminated. If you answer No, the changes are *not* saved and LT is terminated.

If you choose to save your drawing and the drawing has yet to be named, the Save Drawing As dialog box appears, enabling you to assign a name and directory location to the drawing (see fig. 1.23). When naming the drawing, keep in mind that the .DWG file name extension automatically is appended to the name you specify.

When working on a drawing, you can save your work by choosing the Save button on the Standard toolbar or by choosing Save from the File menu.

You also can save the changes to a different filename by choosing Save As from the File menu, which issues the SAVEAS command (see fig. 1.23). After saving the changes to the specified file, LT immediately abandons the current drawing and open the drawing containing the recently saved changes.

Figure 1.23

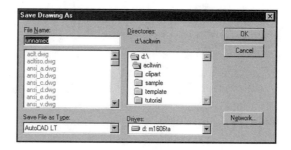

The Save Drawing As
dialog box.

NOTE

The SAVEAS command also is used to create new template drawings to be used with the
Template option of the NEW command.

Summary

Now you know how to start LT and are familiar with the various components of the
LT drawing environment. In the next chapter, you learn how to customize the
drawing environment and to control the view of the drawing.

RELATED SYSTEM VARIABLES

DDUNITS, UNITS, and LIMITS	LUNITS
DATE	LPREC
DWGNAME	AUNITS
DWGPREFIX	APREC
DWGTITLED	ACCTPREFIX
DWGWRITE	LIMMAX
CDATE	LIMMIN

2

SETTING UP YOUR DRAWING ENVIRONMENT

After you start a new drawing or open an existing drawing, you can make certain adjustments to the drawing environment as you work on the drawing. In this chapter, you learn how to do the following:

- *Use the PREFERENCES command to set the display colors and other settings*

- *Modify the units and limits of the drawing after the drawing has been started*

- *Set the current object properties*

- *Create new layers*

- *Control the display*

Setting Your Preferences

The PREFERENCES command is issued when you choose Preferences from the Tool menu. PREFERENCES enables you to set a variety of settings that are used to customize LT to your particular needs. The settings are divided into five categories: Work Space, User, Color, Font, and the File System.

Setting Up the Work Space

The Work Space settings are the first settings to be discussed (see fig. 2.1).

Figure 2.1

Setting the work space settings of PREFERENCES.

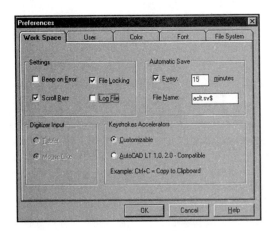

Enabling the Beep on Error option causes LT to beep every time an error is made when entering a command or responding to a command. By default, it is not enabled, although it is a useful option to enable when first learning LT.

Enabling the Scroll Bars option causes scroll bars to appear along the right and bottom edges. You use these bars to scroll the display left/right and up/down. There are, however, other commands that accomplish the equivalent results, so you can disable the scroll bars, thereby freeing up more space for the display of the drawing itself.

By default, file locking is enabled. As you access a drawing file, LT creates a special "lock" file that prevents anyone else from opening the same file. If someone else does try to access a drawing you have open, that person is informed that the desired file is open and then is given the option to open the file with the Read-only option enabled. This facility prevents multiple users from editing the same drawing file and over-writing each other's work.

The lock file normally is automatically removed when a drawing file is closed; however, should an unexpected termination of the LT session occur (such as a power interruption), then LT does not have a chance to remove the lock file. The next time you go to edit that drawing file, you are informed that the file is still locked and you are only allowed to open it with the Read-only option enabled. To remove the lock file manually, use the UNLOCK command, which is issued by choosing Management from the File menu and then choosing Unlock Files.

In addition to drawing files, lock files are created for other types of LT files, such as menu files. File locking is important for network environments. For a single user station, file locking can safely be disabled. Disabling file locking relieves you of ever having to worry about unlocking files manually.

The Log File option is disabled by default. When enabled, LT records all the text displayed in the text window in the file ACLT.LOG (located in \ACLTWIN directory). ACLT.LOG is a simple text file that you can view with any text editor or word processor. The log file is updated continuously from one LT session to another. The start date and time of each session also is recorded in the log file.

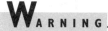

WARNING

If you enable the Log File option, periodically erase the file; otherwise, the file size will eventually get out of hand.

The Automatic Save feature is a backup feature to help prevent the loss of changes made to the current drawing should LT terminate unexpectedly (such as with a power interruption). When Every is enabled, LT saves the current drawing at the specified time interval to the specified file (default file name is ACLT.SV$). Should a failure occur and you want to recover the contents of ACLT.SV$, rename the file with a new drawing name (with a .DWG extension) prior to starting LT. You then can open the renamed drawing file.

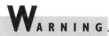

WARNING

It is important for you to fully understand that the Automatic Save feature does not save to the drawing file. To save the changes to the drawing file, use the SAVE command (choose SAVE from the standard toolbar).

If you are using a digitizer, you can choose to use the digitizer as a tablet or a mouse by enabling either the Tablet or Mouse Like options. With the Tablet option enabled, you can trace over (or digitize) a drawing into LT. Pressing F4 is another way to enable/disable the Tablet option. In addition to enabling the Tablet mode, you must use the TABLET command to calibrate the digitizer.

The Keystroke Accelerators options enable you to choose whether to use the current LT version's keystrokes or the keystrokes of version 1.0 and 2.0. Because the two systems are quite different, enabling the use of the older keystroke system can facilitate the transition to LT version 3.0 for the user upgrading from 1.0 or 2.0.

WARNING

The keystrokes used in LT 95 are fully compliant with Windows 95 standards, whereas the keystrokes implemented in older versions were not 100 percent compliant with the older versions of windows. It is better for the user upgrading from an older version of LT to just use the new keystrokes rather than try to stick to an older and outdated system.

Setting Up User Settings

By enabling the User tab of the Preferences dialog box, you can set the User Name (set at the time of installation), the spelling dictionary you will use with the SPELL command, and the units of measurement (English or Metric) you want (see fig. 2.2).

Figure 2.2

Setting the user settings of PREFERENCES.

Preferences				☒
Work Space	**User**	Color	Font	File System

User Name: `Francis Soen, Soen Inc.`

Spelling Dialects: `American English` ▼

Measurement: `English` ▼

| OK | Cancel | Help |

The User Name is used in the Date/Time stamp option of the Advanced Setup wizard and in the REVDATE command.

The selection of English or Metric units in the Measurement field affects the default values that are used in the Quick and Advanced Setup wizards and sets some of the other default settings (such as the dimension settings) for a new drawing. Be sure to choose the appropriate system prior to beginning any new drawings.

Setting Your Colors

With the settings found in the Color tab of the Preferences dialog box, you can change the colors used for the various elements of the drawing, and also change the command and text windows (see fig. 2.3).

Figure 2.3

Setting the color settings of
PREFERENCES.

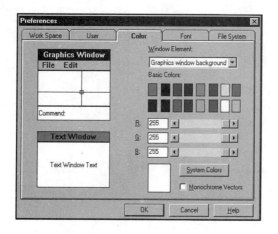

To change a window element, choose the element you want to change by selecting it from the Window Element drop-down list (the box expands to display all choices). You can modify the background color of the drawing window, the background and text colors of the text window, the color of the crosshair, and the background and text colors of the command window. After you choose the element you want to modify, choose the color you want by selecting one of the colors in the 16 Basic Colors section or create your own color by mixing a combination of red, green, and blue with the sliders. To revert back to the default colors, choose the System Colors option.

By enabling the Monochrome Vectors option, you also can instruct LT to display all drawing objects with the same color, regardless of the objects' assigned color.

Enable this option only when you want a screen capture of the drawing window and will not be using colors.

Choosing Fonts

You change the fonts and text size in the Font tab. As you change the settings, a sample of the resulting text appears (see fig. 2.4).

Figure 2.4

Setting the font settings of PREFERENCES.

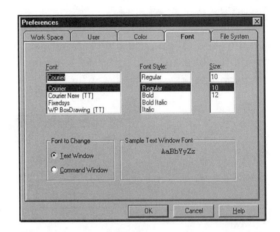

Setting Up the File System

Changes you make in the File System tab affect those files with which LT interacts (see fig. 2.5).

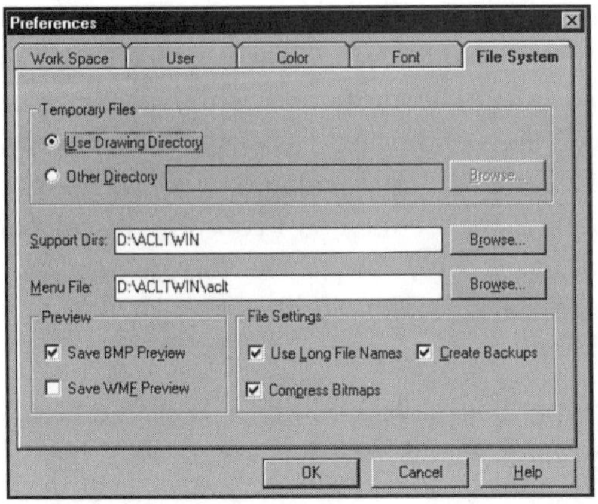

Figure 2.5

Setting the file system settings of PREFERENCES.

As you work on a drawing, LT maintains several temporary files that are reset automatically when you open another drawing end LT. By default, these temporary files are created in the same location in which the drawing is stored. If you choose to edit a drawing on a floppy disk, the temporary files are located on the floppy disk. Because a floppy disk has a very limited storage capacity, you run the risk of the temporary files consuming the available space, thus resulting in a disk error.

If the drawing file you are going to edit is on a slow network drive, LT itself could be slowed down due to the network traffic. To solve both problems, enable the Other Directory option and specify a directory on your local hard drive. Another reason to enable the Other Directory option is to ensure that the temporary files LT creates are located in one location that can be found easily if you ever need to clean up the files after an unexpected shutdown.

Support directories are where you can find various files used by LT commands, such as BHATCH or DDINSERT. By default, the support directory is the same as the program directory, Program Files\AutoCAD LT. If necessary, you can add additional directories to the list of support directories by editing the Support Dirs text box. You should use a semicolon to separate each directory pathname from the previous pathname. The list of directories then is automatically searched, should an LT command require a particular file.

TI P

LT searches the directories in the order they are placed in the list, so place first the directories you reference most often.

The pulldown menus and toolbars are defined in a type of file called a *menu file*. By changing menu files, you can change the commands presented in the menus and toolbars. By default, the menu file used is ACLT.MNU. If you want to use an alternative menu file, specify the filename in the Menu File edit box.

The preview picture that appears when you select a file in the Select File dialog box of the OPEN command is referred to as a *BMP Preview*. By default, the creation of the BMP Preview is enabled. The preview expands the drawing size, so if your goal is to minimize the file size, disable the Save BMP Preview option. By default, the Compress Bitmaps option is enabled and all previews are compressed to save file space.

You also can save a preview in the WMF (Windows MetaFile) format. A preview is saved in this format when the Save WMF Preview option is enabled.

Windows 95 allows the use of long filenames, so by default, the Use Long File Names option is enabled. If compatibility with other operating systems, such as DOS, is required, disable this option. Filenames then are restricted to the standard DOS format of an eight character length name with an optional three character filename extension.

By default, the Create Backups option is enabled. When you save changes to an existing drawing file, the previous version of the drawing file is saved as a backup file. The backup file is renamed with a .BAK filename extension. To open the backup file in LT, rename the file to a name that uses a .DWG extension, and then you can access the renamed file using the OPEN command.

TIP

> Disable the Create Backups option only if you are running out of hard drive space. The backup file will come in handy should the primary drawing file get corrupted or otherwise destroyed.

Setting the Units

As mentioned in Chapter 1, "Opening AutoCAD LT 95," one of the tasks you perform when using the Quick or Advanced Setup wizards is to choose the units of measurement. In the Quick Setup, the only option available is to set the units for length measurements. In the Advanced Setup, the options to set the units and precision for length and angular measurements, the direction of 0 degrees, and the direction of positive angles, are available.

After you begin a drawing, you can change the units of the drawing at any time by choosing Units from the Format menu, which issues the DDUNITS command (see fig. 2.6).

Figure 2.6

The Units Control dialog box of DDUNITS.

The Units Control dialog box is where you choose the units and precision used for linear and angular measurements. To set the direction of 0 degrees and the direction that positive angles are measured, choose the Direction button. The Direction Control dialog box appears (see fig. 2.7).

Figure 2.7

The Direction Control dialog box of DDUNITS.

Changing the Drawing Limits

As mentioned previously, an LT drawing has a near infinite drawing area; however, setting limits on the drawing area and drawing within the defined area is a desirable practice. In both the Quick and Advanced Setup wizards, the option to set the width and length of the drawing area is available. After the initial setup of the drawing, you can change the drawing limits at any time by choosing Drawing Limits from the Format menu (issues the LIMITS command).

You use LIMITS to set the coordinates of the lower left corner and upper right corners of the rectangular drawing area. LIMITS also has two other options: On and Off. If the LIMITS are turned on, then you are prevented from drawing beyond the drawing limits. If the LIMITS are turned off, which is the default setting, then you are not prevented from drawing beyond the drawing limits.

TIP

It is quite a common practice to use the area beyond the drawing limits as a scratch pad or as an area to write miscellaneous notes to other members of the design team, thus, the On option of LIMITS often is not enabled.

When setting up the units and drawing limits, you must take into consideration the final plot scale of the drawing. As far as scale is concerned, drawings fall into two categories: paper-size drawings and full-size drawings.

Paper-Size Drawings

Paper-size drawings are not drawn to scale. Examples of such drawings include sketches, P&ID diagrams, electronic schematics, and so on. Setting up for a paper-size drawing is quite simple—you simply treat the LT drawing as a sheet of paper. For example, if you are going to create a sketch on a sheet of paper that has physical dimensions of 11" by 17" and the maximum usable area (the area within the title block and including the title block) is 10" by 16", then set the units to decimal and treat each drawing unit as representing 1 inch. You then set the width and length of the drawing area to 16 and 10 drawing units (landscape orientation) or to 10 and 16 drawing units (portrait orientation).

If you use the Quick Setup, set the units to decimal and enter the appropriate values for the width and length of the drawing area. If you use the Advanced Setup, set the units, choose the appropriate title block, and then enable the No option in the Layout section. The Advanced Setup wizard sets up a new drawing with the specified title block drawn at a 1=1 scale.

With paper-size drawings, all objects are sized as they are to appear on the final plot. If a line is to be 6" long on the plot, you draw it so that it is 6 drawing units long. If the text is to be $1/4$" in height on the plot, you draw the text $1/4$ drawing unit in height in the drawing. The drawing is just treated as an electronic version of a physical sheet of paper.

The final step you take with paper-size drawings occurs when you plot the drawing. You must make sure that the drawing is plotted at a 1=1 scale, which specifies that 1" on the paper is equal to 1 drawing unit in the drawing.

If you use templates to set up new paper-size drawings, the templates should themselves be drawn as paper-size drawings.

Full-Size Drawings

The opposite of drawings drawn with no scale are drawings drawn to scale. Drawings drawn to scale are set up differently from paper-size drawings. In CAD, drawings (also referred to as models) of real world objects, such as buildings or machinery, typically are drawn full size. The lengths in full-size drawings are not scaled down at the time the lengths are drawn; the scaling occurs at plotting.

The first step in setting up full-size drawings is to choose a system of units. The second step then is to choose a scale for the drawing. The process for choosing a scale for a full size CAD drawing is very similar to the process used to set up a drawing at the drafting board, as in the following:

1. Examine the overall dimensions of the object you want to draw.

2. Examine the area on the paper in which you want to fit the object.

3. Select a scale that enables you to fit the object in the available space.

Suppose that a model to be drawn is a building of 100' by 150' and the model must fit in the maximum usable area of a 24" by 36"piece of paper. Assuming that the maximum usable area is 23" by 35", then a scale of $^1/_8$" equals 1' allows the model to be drawn in the available space with enough empty space around the model for additional annotations. Now that you have selected a scale, you can set up a new drawing.

If you are using the Quick Setup wizard, set the units. Then set the area to the real world area that is represented by the maximum usable area of the sheet at the chosen drawing scale. For example, if the maximum usable area is 23" by 35", then the length and width of the drawing area is set to a 184' length (23" by 8' per inch) and a 280' (35" by 8' per inch) width. Now you can model the 100' by 150' building full size within the drawing area. At plot time, you then scale the model to fit on the physical sheet of paper by specifying a plot scale of $^1/_8$" equals 1', which defines that $^1/_8$" on the paper is to equal 1' in the drawing.

Currently, using the Advanced Setup wizard to set up a full-size drawing without utilizing paper space is not supported. Because paper space is not covered until Chapter 16, "Working with Model and Paper Space," and Chapter 17, "Sheet Composition and Plotting," the Advanced Setup wizard is not to be used to set up full-size drawings until then.

If you are using the Advanced Setup wizard, first set the units in the Step 1: Units tab. Then set the width and length in the Step 5: Area tab to the desired area (such as 280' and 184'). Then from the Step 6: Title Block tab, choose No title block from the Title Block description list. Finally, enable the NO option in the Step 7: Layout tab. This last step ensures that the new drawing is set up in model space rather than in paper space. Setting up drawings in paper space is covered in detail in Chapter 17, "Sheet Composition and Plotting."

Use table 2.1 as an aid in calculating the corresponding drawing area for various scales.

Table 2.1

Scale Functions for Typical Architectural Drawing Scales

Drawing Scale	Scale Factor
1"=1"	1
1"=1'	12
1/2"=1'	24
1/4"=1'	48
1/8"=1'	96
1/16"=1'	192
1/32"=1'	384

In the following exercise, you use the Quick Setup wizard to set up a new drawing for 1 $\frac{1}{4}$" equals 1' scale for a maximum usable area on the final plot of 23" by 35".

SETTING UP A FULL-SIZE DRAWING

1. Start LT or click the New button on the Standard toolbar. Choose to use the Quick Setup wizard.

2. Choose architectural units.

3. Set the width to **140'** (35" by 4' per inch) and the length to **92'** (23" by 4' per inch).

4. Choose Units from the Format menu to display the Units Control dialog box. You use this dialog box to change the units and precision of the drawing if needed.

    Choose Cancel because the units you chose in the setup wizard are fine.

5. Choose Drawing Limits from the Format menu. You use this command to set the drawing limits and to turn on and off the limits.

    Press Esc to cancel the command because the Limits set through the setup wizard are fine.

Setting Up Drawing Aids

Drawing aids are a group of commands and system variables (system settings) that make drawing objects easier and quicker. You can issue the commands individually or using the Drawing Aids dialog box, which you access by choosing Drawing Aids from the Option menu (see fig. 2.8).

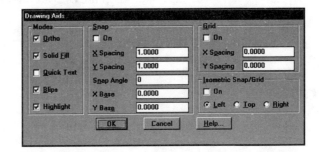

The Drawing Aids dialog box of DDEMODES.

The options in the Drawing Aids dialog box are divided into four groups: Modes, Snap, Grid, and Isometric Snap/Grid.

Modes

In the Modes section are the Ortho, Solid Fill, Quick Text, Blips, and Highlight options. The Ortho mode is helpful in drawing orthogonal lines. By default, Ortho mode is disabled. The Solid Fill mode controls whether certain objects such as solids and polylines, are drawn filled in or in outline form only. By default, the Solid Fill mode is enabled. You use the Quick Text option to speed up the display of text in a drawing by displaying text in outline form only. The Quick Text option is by default, turned off. The Blips mode determines whether temporary blips are drawn when points are selected. By default, the Blips mode is on. The Highlight option determines whether objects are highlighted when selected. By default, the Highlight mode is enabled.

The options are not explained in detail in this chapter but are explained fully in later chapters.

Snap

The options in the Snap section of the Drawing Aids dialog box control the snap grid. When the snap grid is enabled (the On option), the movement of the crosshair is restricted to a grid of invisible points, enabling you to select points with precision. You can change the exact X and Y spacings of the snap points at any time to any positive value other than zero.

You use the other options, Snap Angle, X Base, and Y Base, to set the origination point and angle of the snap grid. A much better method for setting the origination point and angle of the snap grid is to use the UCS command. Refer to Chapter 4, "Drawing Accuracy," for more information on the UCS command.

You also can enable/disable the snap grid by using the F9 function key, the SNAP button on the status bar, or button #4 on a digitizer puck.

Grid

In addition to the grid of invisible snap points, you can use the grid of visible points when specifying points. The options found in the Grid portion of the Drawing Aids dialog box control the grid of visible points. When the On option is enabled, grid points are made visible with the spacing specified in the X Spacing and Y Spacing text edit boxes.

It often is useful to link the spacing of the grid of visible points with the spacing of the grid of invisible snap points. To establish the link, the X and Y spacings of the grid points is set to 0 (the default value), which instructs LT to use the X and Y spacings of the snap points. Regardless of the spacing set for the grid points, the origin point and angle of the grid points is always kept the same as the origin point and angle of the snap points.

One point that must be made clear is that the grid points are visible onscreen but are not part of the drawing and can never be plotted. You also can enable/disable the grid points with the F7 function key, the GRID button on the status bar, or with button #6 on a digitizer puck.

Isometric Snap/Grid

You use the options in the Isometric Snap/Grid section of the Drawing Aids dialog box to draw a two-dimensional isometric drawing. Isometric drawings are covered in detail in Chapter 18, "Drawing 2D Isometric Views."

Setting Current Object Properties

When you draw an object such as a line or circle, you draw it using the current object properties, such as layer, color, and linetype. You establish the current object properties using the Current Properties dialog box, which you access by choosing Current Properties from the Format menu or clicking the Object button on the Object Properties toolbar (see fig. 2.9).

Figure 2.9

The Current Properties dialog box of DDEMODES.

Setting the Current Color

The current color is the color with which you draw new objects. By default, the current color is set to BYLAYER, which instructs LT to draw an object in the color assigned to the layer on which the object resides. To change the color, choose the Color button to display the Select Color dialog box (see fig. 2.10).

Figure 2.10

Choosing a color in the Select Color dialog box.

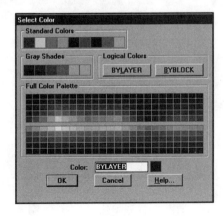

When the Select Color dialog box appears, select the color you want. Note that two colors, BYBLOCK and BYLAYER, are not true colors but are referred to as *logical colors*. You use the BYBLOCK color specifically for creating blocks; it is discussed in detail in Chapter 9, "Drawing with Basic Blocks."

Another command that is used to set the current color is the DDCOLOR command, which is issued by choosing Color from the Format menu or Object Properties toolbar. DDCOLOR displays the same Select Color dialog box that is displayed when you choose the Color button in the Current Properties dialog box.

Setting the Current Layer

The current layer is the layer that new objects are drawn on. By default, the current layer is set to 0. Layers are discussed in detail in the section "Setting Layers and Their Properties."

Setting the Current Linetype

The current linetype is the linetype with which new objects are drawn. By default, the current linetype is set to BYLAYER, which instructs LT to draw an object in the linetype assigned to the layer on which the object resides. To change the linetype, choose the Linetype button in the Current Properties dialog box to display the Select Linetype dialog box (see fig. 2.11).

Figure 2.11

Choosing a linetype in the Select Linetype dialog box.

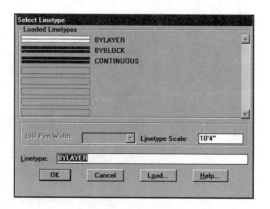

When the Select Linetype dialog box appears, select the linetype you want. Note that two linetypes, BYBLOCK and BYLAYER, are not true linetypes but are referred to as *logical linetypes*. You use the BYBLOCK linetype specifically for creating blocks. This linetype is discussed in detail in Chapter 9, "Drawing with Basic Blocks."

Another command you can use to set the current linetype is the DDLTYPE command, which is issued by choosing Linetype from the Format menu or from the Object Properties toolbar. DDLTYPE displays the same Select Linetype dialog box as is displayed when you choose the Linetype button in the Current Properties dialog box.

Linetypes are discussed in detail later in this chapter in the section "Setting Layers and Their Properties."

Setting the Current Text Style

The drawing of text is controlled by a set of settings that collectively, are referred to as a *text style*. The creation of text styles in association with the drawing of text, is covered in Chapter 3, "Creating and Printing a Simple Drawing."

Setting the Current Linetype Scale

The generation of linetypes is affected by the current linetype scale (also referred to as the *object linetype scale*). The default value is 1. The scaling of linetypes is discussed in detail later in this chapter in the section "Setting Layers and Their Properties."

Setting the Current Elevation and Thickness

By default, the current Elevation and Thickness are set to 0. Both properties relate to the generation of 3D objects and are covered in detail in Chapter 19, "Drawing in 3D."

Setting Layers and Their Properties

Layers act like transparent overlays. You draw objects on various layers and by displaying the layers in varying combinations, different information is communicated to the viewer. AutoCAD LT provides two basic tools used to manipulate layers.

One tool, the Layer Control dialog box, is displayed by choosing Layers from the Format menu or from the Object Properties toolbar (see fig. 2.12).

Figure 2.12

The Layer Control dialog box of DDLMODES.

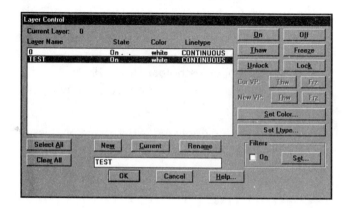

The other tool is the Layer Control drop-down list found on the Object Properties toolbar (see fig. 2.13).

Figure 2.13

The Layer Control drop-down list on the Object Properties toolbar.

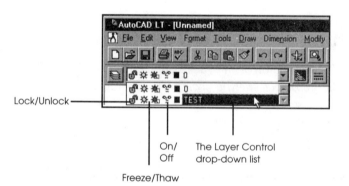

A layer has certain properties: its states, a color, and a linetype. All the properties of a layer are assigned by you and can be changed at any time.

Creating New Layers

Every LT drawing has at least one layer that is named 0. You create any other needed layers using the Layer Control dialog box (choose Layers from the Format menu or the Object Properties Toolbar) (refer to figure 2.12). To create a new layer, type the name of the new layer in the text edit box and then select the New button. A layer name can be up to 31 characters in length and consist of alphanumeric characters and the dollar sign ($), hyphen (-), and underscore (_). You can create more than one layer at a time by entering in the text edit box the multiple layer names, separated by commas.

By default, new layers initially are assigned a white color and a continuous linetype. You can change the assigned color and linetype at any time. New layers appear at the end of the list of layers. The next time you display the Layer Control dialog box, the layer list is resorted into an alphabetical order. By default, lists of any type, less than or equal to 200 in length, are sorted by LT. Any lists longer than 200 in length are not sorted. You can raise or lower the limit of 200 by changing the value of the system variable MAXSORT. You access any system variable by typing its name at the command prompt.

T_{IP}

Use a specific naming convention when naming new layers. Select a naming convention that helps you to keep track of the layers and the contents of the layers. For example, for an architectural drawing, you might use layers named WALLS, DOORS, WINDOWS, DIMENSIONS, and TEXT. Try to keep the names short and descriptive.

Assigning Colors

You can change the color assigned to a layer by selecting the layer from the layer list in the Layer Control dialog box and then choosing the Set Color button. The Select Color dialog box appears from which you select the color you want (refer to figure 2.10). To change the color of more than one layer at a time, select all the target layers from the layer list and then choose the Set Color button.

Assigning Linetypes

An LT linetype consists of a series of spaces, dashes, dots, text, or symbols (see fig. 2.14).

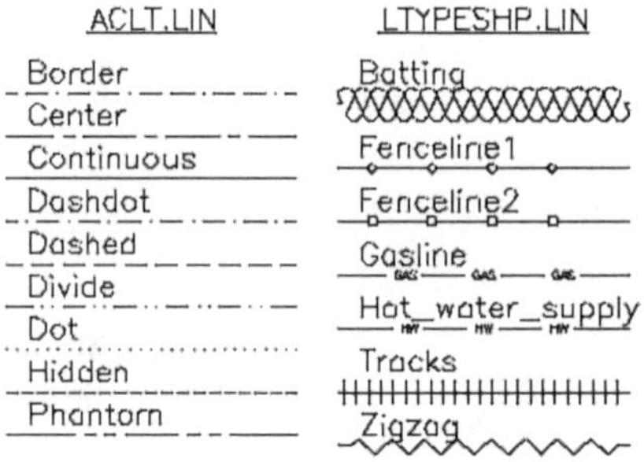

Figure 2.14

The linetypes stored in the files ACLT.LIN and LTYPESHP.LIN.

The default linetype assigned to a new layer is CONTINUOUS. To change the linetype assigned to a layer, select the layer from the layer list in the Layer Control dialog box and then choose the Set Ltype button. The Select Linetype dialog box appears (refer to figure 2.11) from which you choose the linetype you want. If the linetype you want is not listed, choose the Load button and load the needed linetypes.

The code that defines the linetypes is stored in several files and must be loaded into the drawing before you can use the linetypes in the drawing. Click the Load button to display the Load or Reload Linetype dialog box, which you use to select the file and the specific linetypes in the file you want to load (see fig. 2.15).

Figure 2.15

Using the Load or Reload Linetypes dialog box to load linetypes.

To choose the linetype file you want to load, select the File button. If the measurement field in the Preferences dialog box is set to English, then the default file is ACLT.LIN; however, if the measurement field is set to Metric, the default file is ACLTISO.LIN. ACLT.LIN contains mostly linetypes designed for drawings set up for English units. There are, however, some linetypes in ACLT.LIN designed for metric work and should only be loaded into metric drawings. The names of the metric linetypes begin with the prefix ACAD_ISO.

If the drawing on which you are working is a metric drawing, use the metric linetypes in ACLT.LIN or any of the linetypes in ACLTISO.LIN. The lengths of dashes and spaces in the English and Metric linetypes are defined in terms of drawing units. For English linetypes, however, the assumption is that a drawing unit is equal to 1", whereas for metric linetypes, a drawing unit is equal to 1 mm.

A third linetype file, LTYPESHP.SHP, also is provided. This file contains several linetype definitions that use text and symbols. The linetype definitions are designed for English drawings and would have to be scaled up for use in Metric drawings.

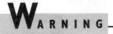

WARNING

When using linetypes with text, be sure to draw the lines from left to right; otherwise, the text will be upside down.

Linetype definitions are scaled up or down using a combination of the following two factors:

```
Final Linetype Scale = Object Linetype Scale X Global Linetype
➥Scale
```

You use the global linetype scale to scale all linetypes in a drawing proportionately and you set it by choosing Global Linetype Scale from the Linetypes menu of the Options menu. The linetype definitions are designed for use in a 1=1 scale drawing. Using the linetypes in a drawing setup for any other scale requires that the linetypes be scaled up by the reciprocal of the drawing scale. If the drawing is set up for a scale of 1/4" equals 1', for example, the value of the global linetype scale factor should be 48 (refer to table 2.1).

You set the object linetype scale using the Object Properties dialog box or the Select Linetype dialog box. The object linetype factor scales the linetype used for each object as the object is drawn. Typically, you use the object linetype scale to generate variations in a standard linetype definition. If you want a dashed linetype with the dashes 3/4 as long as the normal DASHED linetype, for example, set the object linetype scale to 0.75 when drawing with the DASHED linetype.

NOTE

AutoCAD LT provides three variations of each linetype defined for use with English units: for example, the DASHED, DASHED2, and DASHEDX2 linetypes. Consider DASHED as the standard dashed linetype. DASHED2 is the same as DASHED, except that the lengths of the dashes and spaces are half as long. DASHEDX2 is the same as DASHED, except that the lengths of the dashes and spaces are twice as long.

The linetypes supplied in the file LTYPESHP.LIN are designed to be used in English drawings. You can, however, use the linetypes in Metric drawings by setting the object linetype scale factor to 25.4.

Creating a Layer Current

LT can support a near infinite number of layers but only one layer can be current at any one time. The current layer is the layer on which you draw new objects. To set the current layer with the Layer Control dialog box, select the layer you want and then choose the Current button. Be sure only one layer is selected, otherwise, the Current button is not active.

You also can use the Layer Control drop-down list of the Object Properties toolbar to set the current layer. Select the Layer control drop-down list box to expand the list. Then choose the layer name you want and that layer becomes the current layer.

Turning On/Off a Layer

When you turn off a layer, all objects residing on that layer become invisible. You cannot select invisible objects (except with the All selection option). You also cannot plot invisible objects. You turn off layers for a variety of reasons, such as the following:

■ To protect the information on the layer from accidental changes

■ To clarify the display by removing unneeded information from the screen

■ To emphasize the remaining visible information for a plot

To turn off or on a layer using the Layer Control dialog box, select the layer or layers to be affected and then choose the On or Off button. When you turn off a layer, the word On is removed from the State column. To use the Layer Control drop-down list of the Object Properties toolbar, choose the facial expression corresponding to the target layer to turn on or off that layer. When the face has open eyes, the layer is on. When the face has closed eyes, the layer is off.

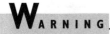

> While it is possible to turn off the current layer, it is not advisable to do so for a long period of time. Eventually, you will forget you have the current layer turned off and start drawing. As the objects are drawn, the objects immediately become invisible as the current layer is turned off. The objects become visible as soon as you turn on the current layer again.

Freezing/Thawing a Layer

Freezing a layer makes the objects on the layer invisible. *Thawing* the layer makes the objects visible again. To freeze or thaw a layer using the Layer Control dialog box, select the layer or layers to be affected and then choose the Freeze or Thaw button. When you freeze a layer, the letter F is placed in the State column.

To freeze a layer using the Layer Control drop-down list of the Object Properties toolbar, choose the sun symbol that corresponds to the target layer. The sun symbol then is replaced with a snowflake symbol. To thaw a frozen layer, choose the snowflake symbol of the target layer. The visual effects of freezing a layer are identical to that of turning off a layer, however, there are some other differences, such as the following:

- You cannot select objects on a frozen layer (even with the ALL option).

- A multi-layer block behaves differently (see Chapter 9, "Drawing with Basic Blocks," for more information).

- Freezing a layer speeds up the responsiveness of the drawing whereas turning a layer off does not.

- Freezing a layer can affect the drawing extents whereas turning off a layer does not.

- The current layer can never be frozen.

Freezing layers improves the responsiveness of a crowded drawing because LT completely ignores the objects on a frozen layer. With a layer that is turned off, LT still performs all the work needed to display and keep track of the objects on that layer, but does not take the final step of displaying the objects.

Locking/Unlocking a Layer

Another option you can use to protect information on a layer is to *lock* the layer. Locking a layer leaves the objects on the layer visible but prevents changes from being made to the objects. To lock or unlock a layer using the Layer Control dialog box, select the layer or layers to be affected and then choose the Lock or Unlock button. When a layer is locked, the letter L is placed in the State column.

To lock or unlock the layer using the Layer Control list of the Object Properties toolbar, choose the padlock symbol that corresponds to the target layer. When a layer is locked, the padlock appears closed and when the layer is unlocked, the padlock appears open.

In the following exercise, you create several new layers and assign colors and linetypes to the layers.

CREATING NEW LAYERS

For this exercise, continue to use the drawing from the previous exercise.

1. Choose the Layers button on the Standard toolbar.

2. Enter **LINES,TEXT** in the text edit box and choose the New button. You have just created two new layers.

3. Select LINES from the layer list in the Layer Controls dialog box.

4. Choose Set Color and choose the color red. Then choose OK.

5. Choose Set Ltype and choose the Load button. Make sure to specify the ACLT.LIN file, and then select the BORDER and CENTER linetypes. Choose the OK button.

   The linetypes BORDER and CENTER now are loaded in the drawing and available for assignment to layers.

6. Choose the linetype BORDER from the list of available linetypes and choose OK. To choose the linetype, select the linetype by its sample picture (not the text label).

7. Deselect the layer LINES and select the layer TEXT.

8. Choose the Set Color button, choose the color blue, and then choose OK.

You now have two new layers with the assigned colors and linetypes.

9. Choose OK to close the Layer Controls dialog box.

Controlling the Display

You can use a variety of commands to determine the portion of the drawing area displayed onscreen. These "display" commands enable you to view and work with the tiniest detail on the drawing or to view the overall drawing area. As a general rule, you issue display commands at the command prompt and even while running another command. When it is possible to issue a command from within another command and not disturb the first command, that second command is referred to as a *transparent* command. DDRMODES and DDEMODES also are transparent commands.

Redrawing the View

At times, you might want to refresh or clean up the display, in which case, choose Redraw from the View menu or click the Redraw View button on the Standard toolbar. The REDRAW command replaces all missing grid dots, removes all blip marks, and refreshes the display of all objects.

Regenerating the Drawing

You sometimes need to force LT to redo all the calculations used to display the drawing. To do this, choose Regen from the View menu to issue the REGEN command. Regen is short for "regeneration" and is performed whenever the drawing extents have been shrunk or when a setting that affects the display of existing objects is changed. When the latter occurs, a regen usually is performed automatically. A REGEN command is not a transparent command and cannot be issued while another command is running.

Using the Aerial View

With the Aerial View Window open, an overall view of the drawing area is visible at all times on the screen. Furthermore, the window is used to choose the area to be displayed in the drawing window. You open the Aerial View window by choosing Aerial View from the View menu or from the Standard toolbar (see fig. 2.16).

Figure 2.16

The Aerial View window of DSVIEWER.

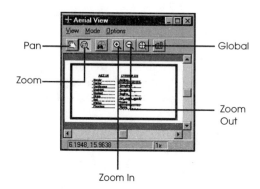

To change the area displayed in the drawing window, move the crosshair into the Aerial View window and choose two points to define the rectangular area you want to display. The two points define a diagonal of the rectangular area to be displayed. Defining a rectangular area by picking two points also is referred to as *windowing an area*. The area currently displayed in the drawing window is outlined in the Aerial View with a rectangle with thick lines.

To pan the view in the drawing window, choose the Pan tool in the Aerial View window. The cursor then is replaced with a rectangle with dimensions that correspond to the area currently displayed in the drawing window. Position the rectangle over the area you want to pan and click the Pick button to complete the panning operation.

You use the Zoom In, Zoom Out, and Global tools to control the view in the Aerial View window itself. Zoom In magnifies the view by a factor of 2 while Zoom Out shrinks the view by a factor of 0.5. The Global tool displays the overall drawing area in the Aerial View window.

The Locator tool is another method you can use to determine the portion of the drawing window you want to magnify. To use the Locator, use the following procedure:

1. Drag the Locator tool to the drawing window. The normal crosshair is replaced by a rectangular box (or window) that corresponds in size and shape to the display area of the Aerial View window.

2. Position the window over the desired area of the drawing window. As you move the window over an area of the drawing window, that area is displayed in the Aerial View window.

3. After you position the window, release the Pick button. The view of the windowed area in the drawing window is magnified.

The magnification factor, by default, is set to 1; however, you can change it by choosing Locator Magnification from the Options menu of the Aerial View window.

There are two other options in the Options menu that, by default, are enabled and should be left enabled: Auto Viewport and Dynamic Update. When Dynamic Update is enabled, the display in the Aerial View window constantly is updated as the drawing changes. The Auto Viewport option works with viewports and is explained in the section "Using Multiple Viewports."

The one drawback to using the Aerial View window is that it takes up precious room on the display. Although you can move and size the window, just like any other window, you may conclude that it takes up too much space. If that is your decision, then use the ZOOM and PAN commands, and scroll bars (all of which are discussed in the following sections) to control the display.

Using the Zoom Options

The ZOOM command contains a variety of options that enable you to magnify or shrink the view in the drawing window. You specify the ZOOM options by choosing the corresponding menu item from the Zoom submenu of the View menu, the corresponding tool on the Standard toolbar, or from the Zoom flyout of the Standard toolbar (all tools representing the ZOOM command use a magnifying glass symbol). Following are the available options:

■   **All:** Choosing All from the View menu or Zoom All from the Zoom flyout causes LT to display the entire drawing area or the area actually occupied by objects (the drawing extents), whichever is greater.

■   **Center:** Choosing Center from the View menu or Zoom Center from the Zoom flyout enables you to specify the point you want at the center of the new display and the height of the area you want to display.

■ **Extents:** Choosing Extents from the View menu or Zoom Extents from the Zoom flyout causes LT to display the drawing area actually occupied by objects.

■ **Previous:** Choosing Previous from the View menu or Zoom Previous from the Zoom flyout causes LT to restore the previous display. LT records the last 10 displays.

■ **Scale:** Choosing Scale from the View menu or Zoom Scale from the Zoom flyout enables you to magnify or shrink the current view by a certain scale factor. The scale option is the default option and you enter the scale as a number followed by an X. 2X, for example, results in the current view being magnified by a factor of 2. To shrink the current view, enter a factor less than 1 (such as 0.5x). The Zoom In and Zoom Out menu items on the View submenu and the Zoom In and Zoom Out tools on the Standard toolbar issue the ZOOM command with a pre-set scale factor of 2X (Zoom In) and 0.5X (Zoom Out).

You also can enter a scale factor without an X suffix, in which case the factor is applied relative to the full view, not the current view.

■ **Window:** Choosing Window from the View menu or Zoom Window from the Zoom toolbar enables you to specify the rectangular area you want to magnify.

With the exceptions of All and Extents, you can perform all other ZOOM options transparently.

Performing a Real-Time Zoom

The RTZOOM command is a real time version of the ZOOM command and is issued by choosing Real-Time Zoom from the Zoom submenu of the View menu or from the View flyout of the Standard Toolbar. After you issue RTZOOM, the normal crosshair is replaced with a magnifying glass symbol. Place the magnifying glass in the center of the screen and then click the Pick button. As you drag the magnifying glass upwards, the view becomes magnified. As you drag the magnifying glass downwards, the view shrinks. When you achieve the view you want, release the Pick button and press Esc or Enter to end RTZOOM.

Using the PAN Command

You use the PAN command to pan the view. You invoke PAN by choosing Pan Point from the Pan submenu of the View menu or from the PAN flyout of the Standard toolbar. You use the PAN command in two ways. With the first method, you pick two points. The first point is the point on the current display that is to be moved and then the second point is the new location of the first point.

The second method involves typing a displacement. A *displacement* is a set of coordinates that instructs LT to pan the view a certain distance in the X and Y directions. Coordinates are covered in more detail in Chapter 3, "Creating and Printing a Simple Drawing."

Performing a Real-Time Pan

The RTPAN command is a real time version of the PAN command that you invoke by choosing Real-Time Pan from the Pan submenu of the View menu or from the PAN flyout of the Standard toolbar. After you issue the RTPAN command, the normal crosshair is replaced with a hand symbol. Position the hand symbol over the point in the drawing you want to move, and then click the Pick button. As you drag the hand, the view also moves. After you achieve the view you want, release the Pick button and press Esc or Enter to end RTPAN.

Using the Scroll Bars

As an alternative to using the PAN command, you can pan the drawing using the scroll bars that appear on the right and bottom edges of the drawing window.

TIP

To enlarge the area displayed in the drawing window, disable the scroll bars using the PREFERENCES command. You can still pan the drawing with the PAN and RTPAN commands or Aerial View window.

Using Named Views

You can name the view displayed in the drawing window. After you name the view, you can restore it at anytime using a single command. The command you use to name and manage named views is DDVIEW, which is issued by choosing Named Views from the View menu or from the View flyout of the Standard toolbar. When you issue the DDVIEW command, the View Control dialog box appears (see fig. 2.17).

Figure 2.17

The View Control dialog box of DDVIEW.

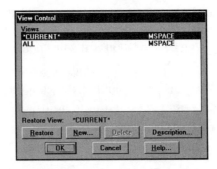

A list of the currently named views is displayed in the dialog box. To restore a view, select the name of that view from the list and choose the Restore button. To delete a named view, select the target view name from the list and choose the Delete button. To make a new view, choose the New button, which then displays the Define New View dialog box (see fig. 2.18).

Figure 2.18

The Define New View dialog box.

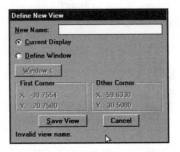

To name the current display, make sure the Current Display option is enabled and then type the name in the New Name text edit box. The name can be up to 31 characters in length and consist of any combination of alpha-numeric characters and the special characters dollar sign ($), dash (-), and underscore (_). Finally, choose the Save View button to complete the naming process.

If the Define Window option rather than the Current Display option is enabled, then the dialog box disappears temporarily while you window the area you want to name. Otherwise, the process is the same as for the Current Display option.

TIP

Giving a name to a view is very useful when dealing with areas that are referred to repeatedly, especially when dealing with large drawings.

Using Multiple Viewports

By default, the drawing window displays a single view in a single viewport. LT is, however, capable of displaying multiple viewports and displaying a different portion of the drawing area in each viewport (see fig. 2.19).

Figure 2.19

The Drawing window split into two viewports.

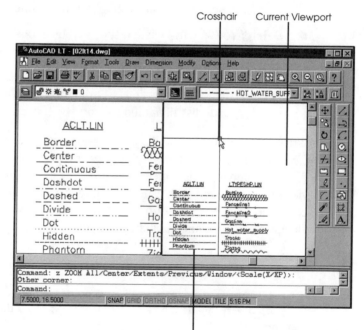

Crosshair   Current Viewport

Heavier Border Line

You use the VPORTS command to set up multiple viewports. VPORTS has several options and each option is specified by choosing the corresponding menu item from the Tiled Viewports submenu of the View menu, as in the following:

- **Single:** You specify Single by choosing 1 from the Tiled Viewports submenu. The display in the drawing window is restored to a single viewport.

- **2:** You specify 2 by choosing 2 from the Tiled Viewports submenu. The current viewport is divided into 2 viewports.

- **3:** You specify 3 by choosing 3 from the Tiled Viewports submenu. The current viewport is divided into 3 viewports.

- **4:** You specify 4 by choosing 4 from the Tiled Viewports submenu. The current viewport is divided into 4 viewports.

- **Save:** You specify Save by choosing Save from the Tiled Viewports submenu. Save enables you to name the current viewport configuration for later restoration.

- **Restore:** You specify Restore by choosing Restore from the Tiled Viewports submenu. Restore enables you to restore a named viewport configuration.

- **Delete:** You specify Delete is specified by choosing Delete from the Tiled Viewports submenu. Delete enables you to delete a named viewport configuration.

- **?:** You specify ? by choosing List from the Tiled Viewports submenu. ? enables you to list all named viewport configurations.

While you can display multiple viewports, only one can be current. The *current viewport* is the viewport in which points are specified and objects are selected. The display commands also affect only the view in the current viewport. The current viewport is outlined with a heavier border and is the only one that displays the crosshair. To change the current viewport, simply move the system pointer to the viewport you want and click the Pick button once.

TI P

While it is possible to divide the single viewport into as many as 45 viewports, the result is a group of very tiny viewports. Two to four viewports is the practical limit for most monitors.

VPORTS is not a transparent command and can only be used in tiled model space. Later on, when paper space is covered in Chapter 16, "Working with Model and Paper Space," a command equivalent to VPORTS but usable in paper space, is covered.

If you use the Aerial View window with the multiple viewports, the display in the Aerial View window reflects the view in the current viewport so long as the Auto Viewport option in the Options menu of the Aerial View window is enabled. So as you make another viewport current, the display in that Aerial View window is updated. Furthermore with Auto Viewport enabled, the ZOOM and PAN operations carried out in the Aerial View window affect the current viewport.

Summary

In this chapter, you learned how to set up drawings, change the drawing environment and control the view. These are all tasks that you will be performing repeatedly in the chapters and exercises that follow.

DRAWING BASICS

CREATING AND PRINTING A SIMPLE DRAWING

Now that you've learned how to start AutoCAD LT for Windows 95 and set up the initial drawing environment, it's time to apply the concepts in a drawing session. When you complete the design, you can plot or print the final drawing, which is shown in figure 3.1.

This chapter develops a drawing from scratch, and covers the following topics:

- *Assigning new drawing settings*
- *Drawing straight-edged objects*
- *Drawing curved objects*
- *Placing text*
- *Deleting and undeleting objects*
- *Printing and Plotting*

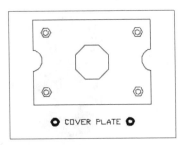

Figure 3.1

The final cover plate drawing.

Assigning New Drawing Settings

Before you construct your first line in a new drawing, you should confirm some initial settings. These values assist you in creating your model geometry with greater ease and accuracy.

Table 3.1 lists the more common settings you should verify and their initial values for the target drawing. These settings will be made during the following exercise.

Table 3.1

Initial Settings for the Cover Plate Drawing

Setting	Value
UNITS	Decimal, 2 places accuracy
LIMITS	ON, from 0,0 to 10,7.5
SNAP	0.25
GRID	0 (updates with SNAP change)
LAYERS	BORDER (red)
	PART (white)
	NOTES (blue)

ASSIGNING INITIAL DRAWING VALUES

1. Start AutoCAD LT for Windows 95, choose Start from Scratch from the Create New Drawing dialog box, choose English, and then choose OK.

2. Choose Format, Units, and select Decimal for Units, 2 decimal places from the drop-down Precision list box, and Decimal Degrees for Angles. Then choose OK.

3. Enter the LIMITS command. Type **On** and press enter. Press Enter again to repeat the LIMITS command. This time, leave the lower left corner at 0,0 but change the upper right corner to **10,7.5**.

4. Enter the SNAP command and type **0.25** in response.

5. Similarly, enter the GRID command and type **0**. AutoCAD LT turns the grid on whenever you change the current grid value.

6. To see the grid and limits more clearly, enter the **ZOOM** command and type **0.75X** in response.

7. Click the Layers tool on the Object Properties toolbar and create new layers: BORDER, PART, and NOTES. Make BORDER red, PART white, and NOTES blue. Set the current layer to BORDER.

8. Choose File, Save (or Ctrl+S), and enter the name **COVRPLAT**.

Figure 3.2 shows a section of the current screen with the Layers drop-down list active.

Figure 3.2

Initial drawing values in effect.

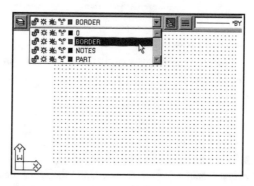

In the next section, you use basic Draw commands to construct a rectangular border around the limits of the drawing.

Drawing Straight-Edged Objects

As you continue with the exercise drawing, you add straight-edged objects including the sheet border (a rectangle), the cover plate (lines), and the mounting bolts (polygons).

CONSTRUCTING THE SHEET BORDER

Continue the COVRPLAT drawing, and check that BORDER is the current layer.

1. Choose Draw, Polygon, Rectangle. You see the following prompt:

```
First corner:
```

With SNAP On, pick 0,0 at ① and 10,7.5 at ②. Figure 3.3 shows the completed border.

2. Choose View, Zoom, Extents to maximize the drawing on the screen.

3. Use Ctrl+S to save your work in progress.

Figure 3.3

The completed sheet border.

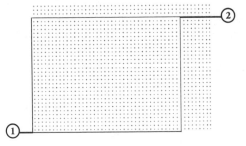

Tɪ ᴘ

Zooming to the extents is a good way to check whether you inadvertently placed objects outside the border.

Nᴏ ᴛ ᴇ

The RECTANG command creates a special object type called a polyline (PLINE). See Chapter 7, "Creating Advanced Lines, Curves, and Points," for details.

For the next step, refer back to figure 3.1. You will note that the cover plate boundary comprises both straight and curved sections. Although Modify tools are available in AutoCAD LT to generate this model quicker (covered in Chapter 6, "Editing Drawings"), the exercise will be restricted to Draw tools only. You use lines and polygons to create the straight edges, and arcs and circles to generate the curves.

CONSTRUCTING THE COVER PLATE BOUNDARY

Continue the COVRPLAT drawing. Drop down the Layer Control list on the Object Properties toolbar and choose layer PART to make it current.

1. Choose Draw, Line. You see the following prompt:

   ```
   From point:
   ```

   Enter the following sequence of points: **1.5,4** at ①, **1.5,2** at ②, **8.5,2** at ③, **8.5,4** at ④, and then enter.

   You now have completed the lower part of the cover plate.

2. Press Enter to start a new LINE sequence.

   Enter the following sequence of points: **1.5,5.25** at ⑤, **1.5,7** at ⑥, **8.5,7** at ⑦, **8.5,5.25** at ⑧, and then press Enter.

   ```
   Command:
   ```

   Your model should appear as shown in figure 3.4.

3. Use Ctrl+S to save your work in progress.

Figure 3.4

Straight edges of cover plate.

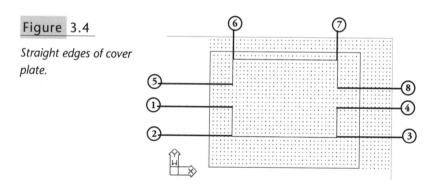

So far, you have explored a few AutoCAD LT commands that generate straight edges. In the next section, you work with drawing tools that create curves, such as circles and arcs.

Drawing Curved Objects

AutoCAD LT uses various construction methods to create circles and arcs, based on the quantities that are known to the user. Three points that are non-collinear, for example, determine a plane, and in particular, a circle. As a practical application of this geometric fact, did you know that a three-legged stool can never wobble, but a four-legged table might? You can draw a circle, therefore, using this three-point method.

Other methods also exist for circle construction, such as center point and radius. Figure 3.5 shows the various ways AutoCAD LT can make a circle, and figure 3.6 illustrates the techniques to generate an arc.

Figure 3.5

Circle construction methods.

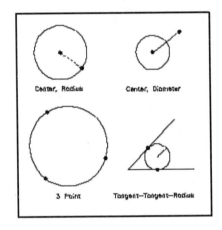

Figure 3.6

Arc construction methods.

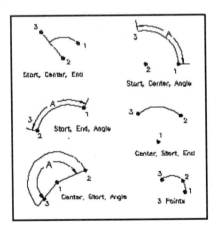

Continue the chapter exercise by completing the cover plate boundary and adding the bolt locations.

COMPLETING THE BOUNDARY AND ADDING BOLT LOCATIONS

Continue the COVRPLAT drawing. Ensure PART is the current layer and SNAP is On.

1. Choose Draw, Arc, Start, End, Angle. You see the following prompt:

```
Center/<Start point>:
```

Figure 3.7 shows the pick points and results of completing this exercise.

2. When prompted for the arc start point, pick 1.5,4 at ①.

The arc end point is 1.5,5.25 at ②. Enter **180** for the included angle to complete the semicircular arc on the left side.

3. To create the semicircular arc on the right side, use the same arc method and pick 8.5, 5.25 at ③ for the start point, 8.5, 4 at ④ for the end point, and enter **180** for the included angle. Again, you have described a semicircular arc in a counterclockwise fashion.

4. To add the bolt locations, you construct four circles. Choose Draw, Circle, Center, Radius and pick the first circle's center point 2.25, 2.75 at ⑤. The radius is 0.15.

5. The center points of the other three bolts (same radius) are 2.25,6.25 at ⑥, 7.75,2.75 at ⑦ and 7.75,6.25 at ⑧.

6. Use Ctrl+S to save your work in progress.

Figure 3.7

Completed boundary and bolt locations.

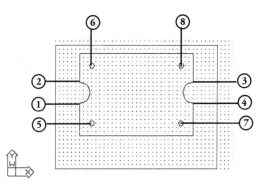

To add the center opening and bolt heads, draw hexagons, which are really special cases of AutoCAD LT's POLYGON command. Polygons are regular, multisided figures where the number of sides can be between 3 and 1,024.

Figure 3.8 shows the center-radius and edge methods used to construct regular polygons.

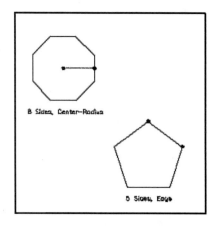

Figure 3.8

Polygon construction methods.

ADDING THE CENTER OPENING AND BOLT HEADS

Continue the COVRPLAT drawing. Ensure PART is the current layer and SNAP is On.

1. Choose Draw, Polygon, Polygon. You see the following prompt (the default value may differ):

       Number of sides <4>:

   Enter **8** as the number of sides. Enter **5.0,4.625** at ① for the polygon center, and **1.0** for the radius.

2. Add the bolt heads by placing four hexagons (6-sided figures) around the bolt circles. Use 0.25 radius, and center them at the following four points: 2.25, 2.75 at ②, 2.25, 6.25 at ③, 7.75, 2.75 at ④, and 7.75, 6.25 at ⑤. The drawing should appear as shown in figure 3.9.

3. Use Ctrl+S to save your work in progress.

Figure 3.9

Cover plate with added polygons.

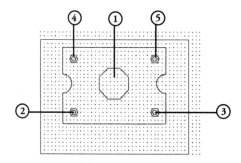

Placing Text

The model now needs a text label that identifies the part. In the next exercise, you draw a string of text using the DTEXT command.

N OTE

AutoCAD LT includes three types of text entry commands. TEXT creates a single line of text, DTEXT generates multiple lines of text, and MTEXT (new Release 3 feature) inserts paragraph-style text. See Chapter 12, "Advanced Text Concepts," for details.

ADDING THE TEXT LABEL

Continue the COVRPLAT drawing. Switch the current layer to NOTES using the drop-down layer list on the Object Properties toolbar. Ensure that SNAP is On. Refer to figure 3.10.

1. Choose Draw, Text, Line Text, and you see the following prompt:

    `Justify/Style/<Start point>:`

    Enter **J** to see the justification options, then enter **M** to specify Middle alignment. Pick 5,1 at ① for the alignment point. The text will be middle justified about this point.

2. Specify **0.3** at the `Height:` prompt, and **0** at the `Rotation angle:` prompt. A small cursor box appears on-screen, denoting the approximate shape of the lettering to be applied.

3. In uppercase characters, type **COVER PLATE**, then press Enter. The text will not appear middle justified yet. Press Enter on a separate line to realign the text.

4. Use Ctrl+S to save your work in progress.

Figure 3.10

Cover plate with text label.

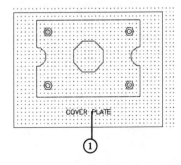

To highlight this label, surround it with fancy endpoints. Use the DONUT command to obtain this effect. A *donut* is a filled circle or a ring. Some applications of donuts include drilling locations on a civil site plan and solder points on an electrical schematic.

Figure 3.11 shows the two flavors of AutoCAD LT donuts.

Figure 3.11

Donut construction methods.

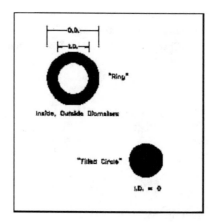

ADDING THE TEXT ENDPOINTS

Continue the COVRPLAT drawing. Ensure the current layer is NOTES and SNAP is On. Refer to figure 3.12.

1. Choose Draw, Circle, Donut, and you see the following prompt (the default value may differ):

   ```
   Inside diameter <0.5000>:
   ```

   Enter **0.25** and **0.5** for the inside and outside diameters, respectively. You see an image of the donut to be placed.

2. Pick 2.75, 1 at ① and 7.25, 1 at ②. Note that you must press Esc or return to end the placement of subsequent donuts.

3. Choose the Zoom Window tool from the Standard toolbar and place a window from ③ to ④ around the cover plate label. Figure 3.13 shows the results of this magnification.

4. Use Ctrl+S to save your work in progress.

Figure 3.12

Adding the label endpoints.

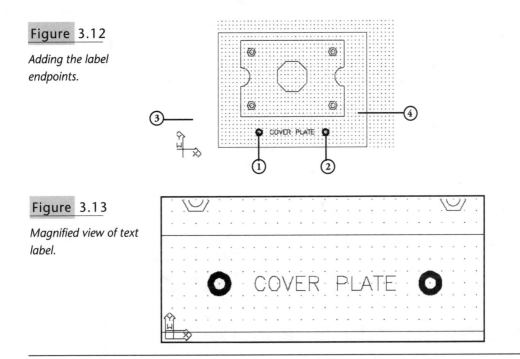

Figure 3.13

Magnified view of text label.

Deleting and Undeleting Objects

In this chapter, you have added objects to the drawing and saved your work as you made progress. Occasionally, however, you need to delete objects. Construction lines, for example, are often temporary in nature and do not need to be shown in the final model geometry.

The ERASE command deletes a selection of objects from the drawing database. Are they gone forever? Not necessarily; AutoCAD LT also offers the convenient OOPS command that restores the most recent set of erased objects.

In the next exercise, you erase the last object drawn and then restore it.

DELETING AND UNDELETING OBJECTS

Continue the COVRPLAT drawing. Ensure all layers are visible.

1. Enter **ERASE** and you see the following prompt:

```
Select objects:
```

Enter **L** and the most recently (or Last) drawn object highlights. AutoCAD LT gives you instant visual feedback on the currently selected objects.

2. The `Select objects:` prompt is still active, so pick another object on the screen. Note that the command line informs you of this additional selection by displaying 1 found.

3. Press Enter and AutoCAD LT deletes the selected objects.

4. Enter **OOPS** and the objects reappear.

5. Use Ctrl+S to save your work in progress.

NOTE

In the preceding exercise, you used L (Last) to automatically select the most recently drawn object. AutoCAD LT offers many other object selection options to expedite drawing modifications. See Chapter 5, "Selecting Objects," for details.

Printing and Plotting

At some point in the development of a drawing, you usually need to produce a hard-copy output. This sheet can be either a quick check plot that is unscaled, or a final production print suitable for boardroom presentations or inclusion in a bid and proposal document.

NOTE

AutoCAD LT provides many plotting selections, adjustments, settings, and parameters. Chapter 17, "Sheet Composition and Plotting," discusses the printing and plotting methods and procedures in greater detail.

In the next exercise, you generate a check plot of the COVRPLAT drawing.

PRODUCING A CHECK PLOT

Continue the COVRPLAT drawing. Ensure all layers are visible.

1. Choose View, Zoom, Extents to make the drawing appear on-screen as large as possible.

2. Choose File, Print (or Ctrl+P) and you obtain the Plot Configuration dialog box shown in figure 3.14.

3. Make sure the Setup and Default Information group is set to System Printer ①, the Additional Parameters group is set to Extents ②, the Paper Size and Orientation group is set to Inches ③, the Plot Rotation is set to 90 ④, the Plot Scale is set to 1=1 ⑤, and the Plot Preview group is set to Full ⑥. Then, choose the Preview button ⑦, and you obtain the Plot Preview shown in figure 3.15.

4. In Full Plot Preview, you cannot edit the drawing, only pan and zoom. If your printer is on and ready, choose the OK button and your drawing will print.

Figure 3.14

The Plot Configuration dialog box.

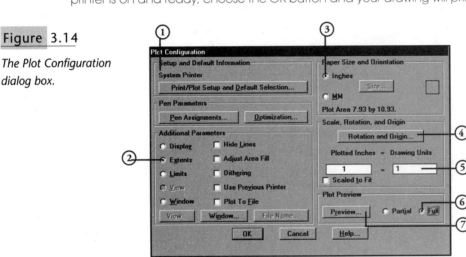

Figure 3.15

Previewing the Check Plot.

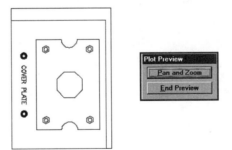

Summary

In this chapter, you explored some of AutoCAD LT's drawing commands to create and print a small mechanical design. In Chapter 4, you work with the program's techniques of obtaining as much accuracy as your more complex models require.

DRAWING ACCURACY

AutoCAD LT is an extremely precise drawing and design package, accurate to 16 decimal places. Behind every object drawn lies a sophisticated database. Although a line on the screen may appear as a series of connected dots, for example, AutoCAD LT knows about (and you can quickly work with) the relevant geometry: the endpoints, midpoint, and even the angle of the line.

As you develop your computerized drafting skills, you incorporate your manual drafting standards with this newer technology, still ensuring that lines do not overlap and intersections are clean. To achieve this kind of drawing accuracy, you need to understand concepts of a rectangular coordinate system.

In this chapter, you learn the following ways that AutoCAD LT maintains drawing precision:

■ *Coordinate entry modes*

■ *User coordinate systems*

■ *Object snaps*

■ *Point filters*

Understanding Coordinates and Points

You create AutoCAD LT drawings within a three-dimensional Cartesian (rectangular) coordinate system. The program locates a point in 3D space by specifying its distance from an *origin*, measured along three perpendicular axes: the X, Y, and Z axes. The origin is the point 0,0,0. Only the X and Y axes are used for 2D drawings (0,0). Figure 4.1 shows the coordinate system you use to create 2D drawings.

Figure 4.1

The X and Y axes in a 2D coordinate system.

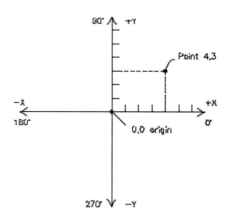

In the standard AutoCAD LT coordinate system, the X axis is horizontal, the Y axis is vertical, and the Z axis is perpendicular to both the X and Y axes. The axes intersect at the origin. X values increase to the right of the origin; Y values increase above the origin.

As you have seen, points can be picked or entered from the keyboard. AutoCAD LT reads the point as a set of numbers in the form X,Y,Z. Each number represents the distance from the origin along the specified axis. For 2D drawings, the Z-value defaults to 0 and can be omitted. The coordinates 4,3, for example, specify a point four units in the positive X axis and three units in the positive Y axis measured from the 0,0 origin, as illustrated in figure 4.1.

In most drawings, the origin is at the lower left corner of the drawing area, but its location can vary. You can change your view to relocate the origin anywhere by using the UCS command, explained later in this chapter.

Specifying coordinate locations accurately is a critical part of AutoCAD LT. As a general rule, any prompt that includes the word "point" requires some form of location or coordinate input. AutoCAD LT provides a handy way of keeping track of the current cursor location—the coordinate display.

Using the Coordinate Display

The coordinate display is located at the left edge of the status bar. Figure 4.2 shows the coordinate display with the cursor positioned at 3.5839,2.5494. In its default mode, the coordinate display provides a constant readout of the cursor location.

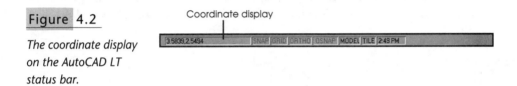

Coordinate display

3.5839,2.5494   SNAP GRID ORTHO OSNAP MODEL TILE 2:49 PM

Figure 4.2

The coordinate display on the AutoCAD LT status bar.

In the chapter exercises, you explore coordinate entry methods by creating simple drawings. With experience, you will develop tips, tricks, and shortcuts to perform the exercises with alternate solution methods.

NOTE

Chapter 17, "Sheet Composition and Plotting," discusses the printing and plotting methods and All of the exercises in this chapter are 2D; therefore, the Z-coordinate value is omitted (and assumed to be 0).

Coordinate Entry Modes

AutoCAD LT recognizes the X,Y coordinates of drawing objects. You need methods of entering these points, therefore, that are acceptable to the program. One method is to use the pointing device to pick points from the screen. This method would be sufficient if a single snap and grid combination existed (see Chapter 2, "Setting Up Your Drawing Environment") for the entire duration of drawing development. To account for design deviations, non-uniform measurements, odd angles, and other methods must be employed.

The method that yields the greatest accuracy is the keyboard. Although you can control the precision for *display* purposes (refer to the UNITS command in Chapter 2), the drawing database always stores the accuracy that was entered from the keyboard.

AutoCAD LT uses three modes of keyboard coordinate entry: *absolute*, *relative*, and *polar*. In the next section, you explore the three different entry schemes.

Using Absolute Coordinates

Absolute coordinates are always measured from the 0,0 origin. The input format is as follows:

X,Y ↵

You type an ordered pair of numbers, separated by a comma. The points 4.2,-1.5 and -3.1,2.0, for example, are valid absolute coordinates, as shown in figure 4.3.

Figure 4.3

Absolute coordinate format.

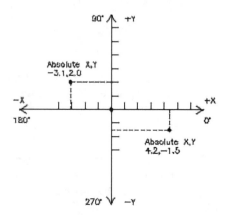

Absolute coordinate entry is useful only if the X and Y distances from the origin are known. In practical applications, however, you often obtain the next point from its horizontal and vertical distances (or displacements) from the previous point, not the origin. That is, you seek a coordinate *relative* to the previous point. This is the second method of coordinate entry.

Using Relative Coordinates

Relative coordinates are always measured from the previously referenced point. The input format is very similar to absolute mode, as follows:

@Xdisp, Ydisp ↵

In this case, the X and Y values represent displacement distances. To distinguish relative mode from absolute mode, you prefix the two values with the @ symbol. @5,2 and @-1,-3 are valid relative coordinates, for example, as shown in figure 4.4.

Figure 4.4

Relative coordinate
format.

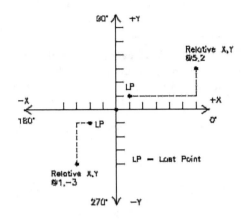

WARNING

If you forget to include the @ symbol during relative coordinate entry, the input will still be valid, but AutoCAD LT will interpret the value as an absolute coordinate—not what was intended.

TIP

If you enter the @ symbol by itself in response to any command asking for a point, AutoCAD LT will use the last point. Entering @ alone is the same as entering @0,0.

Relative coordinates are quite useful, but there is still one drawback; the displacements must be measured parallel (*orthogonal*) to the X and Y axes. What if these distances are not known? Fortunately, there is a third method of keyboard coordinate entry—one that employs distances and angles.

Using Polar Coordinates

Polar coordinates require the entry of a distance and an angle. The input format is as follows:

```
@Distance<Angle ↵
```

The components of this entry are: the @ symbol, the distance (in the current units), the less than sign, the desired angle (in the current units), and the Enter key.

NOTE

> The standard angle orientation is 0 degrees east, with angles increasing counterclockwise, corresponding to classic trigonometric calculations. The UNITS command can override these settings. Refer to figure 4.1 for the default coordinate system measurements

@3<30 and @5<135 are valid polar coordinates, for example, as shown in figure 4.5.

Figure 4.5

Polar coordinate format.

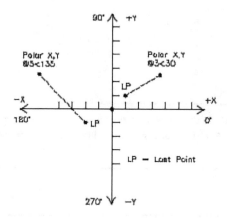

NOTE

> AutoCAD LT also accepts *absolute polar* coordinates, which are offset from the 0,0 origin instead of the last point. (The @ prefix is omitted.) This type of polar coordinate is seldom used in production drafting.

Figure 4.6 shows a north arrow comprised of a series of line segments. Note that each endpoint is labeled with a letter. Table 4.1 shows the LINE command sequence that generates this north arrow, using all three types of coordinate entries. Point A is shown in absolute coordinates *only.*

Figure 4.6

A north arrow comprised of line segments.

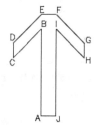

Table 4.1

Keyboard Coordinate Entry Using the LINE Command

Point	Absolute X,Y	Relative @Xdisp,Ydisp	Polar @Distance<Angle
A	2,2		
B	2,3.5	@0,1.5	@1.5<90
C	1.5,3	@-.5,-.5	@.7071<225
D	1.5,3.25	@0,.25	@.25<90
E	2,3.75	@.5,.5	@.7071<45
F	2.25,3.75	@.25,0	@.25<0
G	2.75,3.25	@.5,-.5	@.7071<315
H	2.75,3	@0,-.25	@.25<270
I	2.25,3.5	@-.5,.5	@.7071<135
J	2.25,2	@0,-1.5	@1.5<270
A	2,2	@-.25,0	@.25<180

The sequence in the preceding table describes an enclosed figure; the last specified point coincides with the first point. Enter **C** at the LINE command To point: prompt to close two or more line segments.

TIP

You can abbreviate distances, points, and other numbers by omitting insignificant leading zeros, trailing zeros following the decimal point, and trailing decimal points. Enter 0.25,75.0000 as .25,75, for example, to save typing.

Experiment with keyboard coordinate input in the following exercise by drawing the north arrow shown in figure 4.6.

DRAWING A NORTH ARROW

1. Begin a new AutoCAD LT drawing. Use table 4.1 as your guide.

2. At each point, enter its coordinate using one of the three listed modes. Note that you can "mix-n-match" the inputs as you develop the figure.

3. Save the drawing as **N-ARROW**.

Relative and polar coordinates are efficient for entering a sequence of known points, but they don't help much when you want to enter several points relative to a single known point. As mentioned earlier in the chapter, the UCS command resets the location of the 0,0 origin. Then, you can use absolute coordinates relative to the new origin.

TIP

The latest version of AutoCAD LT supports *direct distance entry*, a quicker alternative to using relative or polar coordinates. At any prompt for a point location, move the cursor in the desired direction, then enter a distance.

Changing the Origin and Axes with UCS

The UCS command enables you to establish your own coordinate system. You can change the origin point by changing the position of the coordinate system, and you can rotate the axes by changing the angle of the coordinate system. The default coordinate system is called the *WCS* (*World Coordinate System*), and a user-defined coordinate system is called a *UCS* (*User Coordinate System*). Although the drawing has only one "real" origin (0,0,0 of the WCS), the UCS options permit you to locate alternate origin points and rotate the X,Y,Z reference plane in 3D space to accommodate your design needs. By default, all 2D points you specify are placed in the plane of the X,Y axes.

NOTE

Although the UCS command was developed to address 3D drawing (see Chapter 19, "Drawing in 3D"), it is quite useful in 2D drafting.

Showing the Origin and Axes with the UCS Icon

If you look at the UCS icon in figure 4.7, you see the X arrow points along the positive X axis, and the Y arrow points along the positive Y axis. The "W" on the Y arrow means that the current UCS is the default World Coordinate System (WCS). The "+" on the UCS icon indicates that the icon is displayed at the origin of the current UCS (0,0).

Figure 4.7

The UCS icon at the WCS origin.

The UCS icon reflects any rotation of the X,Y axes. If the icon is set to display at the origin, it also can indicate the location of the origin of the current UCS. The UCS icon shown in figure 4.8 has been rotated to a 45-degree angle and set to display at the origin. The grid, axes, and crosshairs are also offset and rotated with any changes to the UCS. You will duplicate these effects in the next exercise.

Figure 4.8

Rotated UCS icon, grid, and crosshairs.

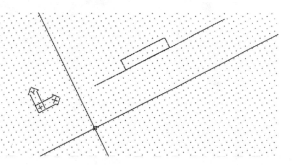

In the following exercise, you define new User Coordinate Systems; first, by relocating the UCS origin and second, by rotating the UCS to a specified angle about one of the axes.

ADJUSTING THE UCS ORIGIN

Continue from the previous exercise. Zoom a window around the north arrow so that it nearly fills the screen. Ensure that GRID is set to 0, and SNAP is set to .25. Also check that both SNAP and GRID are on.

1. Choose Options, UCS, On to verify that the UCSICON is on. You see the following prompt at the command line:

```
ON/OFF/All/Noorigin/ORigin <ON>:
```

If the check mark does not appear to the left of the menu item, choose On; otherwise, it already is on.

2. Relocate the UCS origin by using the UCS command. Choose View, Set UCS, Origin and pick the point G (2.75,3.25) at ① in figure 4.9. Notice that the UCS icon no longer displays "W"; the new UCS has been defined.

Figure 4.9

Establishing a new UCS origin.

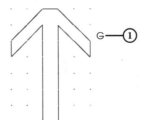

3. Enter UCSICON at the **Command:** prompt, and enter **OR** to relocate the icon at the new origin. Your screen should resemble figure 4.10. Notice that the UCS icon has now moved to the new UCS origin. When the crosshairs are positioned at the point G, the coordinate display reads 0.0000,0.0000 in absolute coordinates, confirming the new UCS origin.

4. To rotate the coordinate system 45 degrees about the Z axis, choose View, Set UCS, Z Axis Rotate, then enter **45**. Figure 4.11 shows the results of this operation.

5. To reestablish the World Coordinate System (WCS), press Enter at the **Command:** prompt. Press Enter again to accept the default response <World>, and the UCS icon jumps back to its former position.

Figure 4.10

Moving the UCS icon to the new origin.

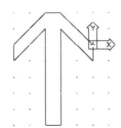

Figure 4.11

Rotating the UCS.

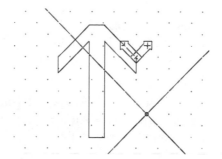

NOTE

Manipulating various UCSs facilitates drafting and design in 3D. See Chapter 19, "Drawing in 3D," for details.

To recap, you have seen how to place objects when a convenient snap and grid system is active. You have also explored ways to precisely locate model elements by absolute, relative, and polar coordinates. Additionally, you worked with some simple operations to define a new user coordinate system. Perhaps the most powerful tools available in AutoCAD LT for accurately defining relationships between objects, however, are the object snap modes.

Understanding Object Snap

CAD provides many new tools to assist the application of graphical methods to geometric construction problems, such as bisecting an angle (see fig. 4.12). These tools yield three clear benefits: Construction is simpler and therefore easier to perform; the geometry is more accurate, as are the points derived from the geometry; and the results can be consistently maintained with far more precision than was possible with manual drafting methods.

Figure 4.12

*The classic angle
bisection problem.*

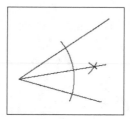

The Object Snap modes in AutoCAD LT are a set of tools for creating accurate geometric constructions. These tools are used to directly identify key points within objects. Figure 4.13 shows the Object Snap toolbar and corresponding pop-up cursor menu. You also can access the Object Snap modes from the keyboard by entering their first three letters.

You can open the pop-up cursor menu in two ways. If you use a three-button mouse, click the middle button. If you use a two-button mouse, press Shift while clicking the Enter button, hereafter referred to as Shift+Enter.

Figure 4.13

*Object Snap toolbar and
pop-up cursor menu.*

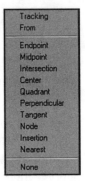

In the following exercise, you use some of AutoCAD LT's object snap functions to solve the classic angle bisection problem shown in figure 4.12. Note how AutoCAD LT simplifies the procedure.

BISECTING AN ANGLE USING ENDPOINT, NEAREST, AND MIDPOINT

1. Begin a new drawing and name it OSNAP.

2. Use the LINE command to draw two lines, from ① to ② to ③ (see fig. 4.14).

3. To activate the Object Snap toolbar, choose View, Toolbars, then check Object Snap, then click OK.

4. Choose Draw, Arc, Center, Start, End. You see the following prompt:

   ```
   arc Center/<Start point>:
   Center/End/<Second point>: _c Center:
   ```

5. Click on the Snap to Endpoint tool. Pick the upper line at ④ (see fig. 4.14).

6. At the `Start point:` prompt, click on the Snap to Nearest tool, and pick the lower line at ⑤.

7. At the `Angle/<End point>:` prompt, enter **ENDP** and pick the upper line at ⑥. AutoCAD LT draws the arc shown in figure 4.15.

8. Choose Draw, Line and Shift+Enter. The pop-up cursor menu appears, and then choose Endpoint. Pick the lower line at ⑦.

9. At the `To point:` prompt, click on the Snap to Midpoint tool, and pick any point on the arc. Press Enter in response to the `To point:` prompt, and the angle bisection is complete.

Figure 4.14

Creating an arc using object snap modes.

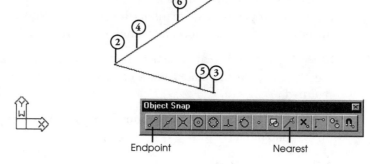

Endpoint   Nearest

Figure 4.15

Bisecting an angle using the midpoint of an included arc.

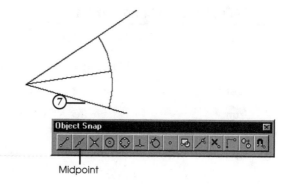

Midpoint

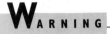

WARNING

As seen in the previous exercise, you can activate the Snap to Endpoint mode by entering END. To avoid this entry being interpreted as an END command and accidentally ending your AutoCAD LT session, enter four characters (ENDP). All other object snap modes can be typed safely with three characters.

During object snap mode, the cursor changes to a larger box at the intersection of the crosshairs, called the target box or *aperture*. You can change the size of the aperture box, as you will see later in this section.

When you are seeking an object's endpoint, for example, you do not need to have the endpoint physically within the aperture box; you need only have a portion of the object within the aperture box. Just pick near the endpoint you want, and AutoCAD LT snaps to the object's endpoint that is closest to the point you pick. Most of the object snaps operate in this manner (the exception is the Intersection object snap—the desired intersection must be within the aperture box).

Several object modes can be active concurrently (running mode, discussed later in the chapter); the calculated point closest to the picked point is the one that is returned.

AutoCAD LT has 13 object snap modes. Table 4.2 gives a simple description of each object snap mode.

Table 4.2

AutoCAD LT Object Snap Modes

Mode	Description
Center	Finds the center of a circle or an arc
Endpoint	Finds the endpoint of a line or an arc
From	Establishes a temporary reference point as a basis for specifying subsequent points
Insert	Returns the insertion point of text objects and block references
Intersection	Locates the intersection of two lines, arcs, or circles or the intersection of any combination of these objects

Mode	Description
Midpoint	Finds the midpoint of a line or an arc
Nearest	Returns a point (on an object) that is nearest to the point you pick
Node	Returns the location of a point object
None	Instructs AutoCAD LT not to use any object snap modes
Perpendicular	Returns a point at the intersection of the object selected and a line perpendicular to that object from either the last or the next point picked
Quadrant	Finds the closest 0-, 90-, 180-, or 270-degree point (relative to the current UCS) on a circle or an arc
Tangent	Locates a point that is tangent to the selected circle or arc from either the last or the next point picked
Tracking	Specifies a point that is relative to other points, using orthogonal displacements

The Snap From and Tracking object snap modes are new in AutoCAD LT Release 3.

In the next exercise, you use the Snap From feature to draw a door swing in a floor plan. Figure 4.16 shows the completed exercise.

Figure 4.16

Completed door swing in floor plan.

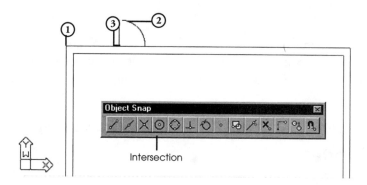

USING SNAP FROM, INTERSECTION, AND ENDPOINT OBJECT SNAP MODES

Open drawing FLOOR4 from the companion CD. Make DOORS the current layer. Activate the Object Snap toolbar. Refer to figure 4.16.

1. Start a LINE command and in response to the **From point:** prompt, click the Snap From tool on the Object Snap toolbar. Then click the Snap to Intersection tool, and pick the upper left wall corner at ①.

2. At the **<Offset>** prompt, enter **@5'<0**.

3. The door width is 2'6" wide. Double-click SNAP on the status bar to turn it on and drag the rubberband cursor up until the coordinate display shows 2'6"<90 in relative polar coordinates. Pick this point at ②.

4. Choose Draw, Arc, Start, Center, Angle and in response to the **Start point:** prompt, enter **@30",-30"**

5. At the **Center:** prompt, Shift+Enter, and pick Intersection from the cursor menu. Pick point ③.

6. At the **Included angle:** prompt, click the Snap to Endpoint tool and respecify 2.

As you have seen in the preceding exercises, AutoCAD LT has no object snap modes enabled by default. Thus your point picks are constrained only by a snap grid (if Snap is on) and an orthogonal direction (if Ortho is on). Selecting an object snap only when needed is called an object snap override. This term is used because the mode overrides Snap, Ortho, and any running mode currently set, including None.

Another method of using object snaps is to set running object snap modes that apply to every point picked until you change the mode setting or specify an override. The next section explains the use of running object snap modes.

Setting and Applying Running Object Snap Modes

If you need to snap to many similar points or if you want more than one object snap active at the same time, you should use a running object snap. You set these running object snap modes by using the Running Object Snap dialog box (see fig. 4.17). You can access this dialog box by clicking the Running Object Snap tool, or choosing Options, Running Object Snap from the pull-down menu, or by entering **DDOSNAP** (OS for short) at the command line. You can temporarily turn running object snaps on or off without losing the defined settings by clicking OSNAP on the status bar.

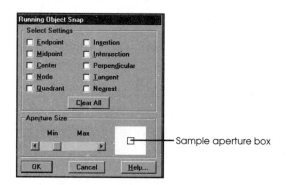

Figure 4.17

*The Running Object
Snap dialog box.*

Sample aperture box

Tıp

A smaller object snap aperture enables you to more accurately pick the desired object or objects in crowded drawings, but it requires a steady hand. To change the aperture size, enter APERTURE at the Command: prompt. An alternate way to handle crowded drawings is to use object cycling techniques, covered in Chapter 5, "Editing with Grips."

There are many methods that AutoCAD LT uses to locate points with total geometric precision. In fact, there is yet another technique available: Point filters.

Using Point Filters

Point filtering is a method of snapping to a location based on partial X, Y, and Z coordinates of other points. The term "filtering" is unfortunate—the method does not deliver a single coordinate value; it actually builds additional points by collecting and assembling the required coordinates. The method is perhaps underutilized by even the most "savvy" AutoCAD LT users.

Tıp

Under many circumstances, point filtering techniques make construction lines unnecessary.

In the following exercise, you use point filtering techniques to place a circle exactly in the middle of a rectangle. This method can easily be extended to 3D to place a sphere in the center of a box.

USING POINT FILTERS

Start a new drawing. To realize the full impact of this exercise, turn off all drawing modes (such as Snap, Grid, Ortho, and Osnap).

1. Use the RECTANG command to describe a randomly sized rectangle.

2. Choose View, Toolbars, and ensure Object Snap and Point Filters toolbars are checked. Then click OK. Figure 4.18 shows the completed drawing.

3. Enter **C** (circle). At the `Center point:` prompt, click the X Coordinate tool on the Point Filters toolbar.

4. To specify the X value of the circle's center point, click the Snap to Midpoint tool on the Object Snap toolbar, then click the bottom rectangle line at ②. The X value is now "locked in."

5. AutoCAD LT now prompts for the Y and Z values. Because you are working in 2D, only the Y value is needed. Enter **MID** and click the left side rectangle line at ②. The Y value is now set, and you can specify any radius size.

Figure 4.18

Point filtering to locate the circle.

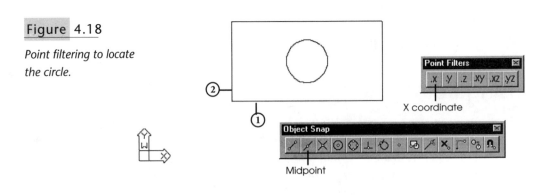

X coordinate

Midpoint

Summary

This chapter provided several techniques to ensure drawing accuracy, such as keyboard coordinate entry and the use of object snaps. In the next chapter, you explore various ways of selecting objects.

Remember, AutoCAD LT offers several ways of accomplishing a task. Choose the method that works for you.

CHAPTER 5

EDITING WITH GRIPS

As your skills with AutoCAD LT develop, you will start using an increasing number of editing commands. For example, you might use the Line and Arc commands to represent a chair, but to fully utilize the chair in the drawing you must choose from editing commands such as Move, Copy, Rotate, or Array.

Before you can perform any editing operations, however, AutoCAD LT must know upon which objects you want to perform the operation. There are several ways to do this. In this chapter you learn the following object selection methods:

- *Using grips and the autoediting modes*

- *Understanding object selection order*

- *Controlling grips and selection parameters*

- *Object cycling*

NOTE

Chapter 6, "Editing Drawings," continues the discussion of editing techniques and selection options in more depth.

One of the most effective methods of selecting objects for editing is by the use of grips. When grips are enabled, choosing an object at the Command: prompt causes grips to appear. A *grip* is a convenient location on the object to help control and manipulate that object, much like a modern suitcase with wheels has a couple of handles. Each AutoCAD LT object has several grip points that can be chosen accurately (without specifying object snap modes) by picking the point in the grip box. Figure 5.1 shows the grip locations of common objects.

Figure 5.1

Common object
grip locations.

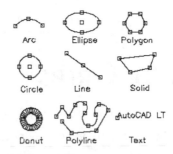

The grip points on a line, for example, are the endpoints and the midpoint. When grips are enabled (the default), the grips appear on an object when you select that object at the Command: prompt.

When you click on a visible grip, it becomes *hot* (selected) and appears highlighted. A hot grip becomes a base point for one of the autoediting modes to manipulate the object.

NOTE

Selecting objects for editing with the use of grips is also known as *autoediting*. Autoediting is covered in the next section of this chapter.

In the following exercise, you experiment with grips to select and edit some basic objects.

GRIPPING AND EDITING OBJECTS

1. Begin a new AutoCAD LT drawing. Draw a line, circle, and polygon, as shown in figure 5.2 (the objects won't yet appear highlighted or display grips). Ensure that SNAP is off.

2. Select a window around all the objects by picking two points. Click at ①, and then drag the pointing device and click ②. AutoCAD LT displays the grips.

3. Choose an endpoint of the line. The grip highlights, and you see the following prompt:

```
** STRETCH **
<Stretch to point>/Base point/Copy/Undo/eXit:
```

4. Move the cursor around, and then click the Enter button. Each time you move the cursor and click the Enter button, AutoCAD LT switches the autoediting mode, as listed in table 5.1. Cycle to the SCALE operation.

5. Enter **0.8** and all AutoCAD LT scales all objects 80 percent of their original size, based from the selected grip point.

6. Choose an arc endpoint and cycle the autoediting modes to the MIRROR operation. Drag the cursor away from the hot grip and AutoCAD LT temporarily displays object images reflected about the rubberband cursor location. Click a second point.

7. Press Esc twice; once to remove the object highlighting, and a second time to deselect all grips.

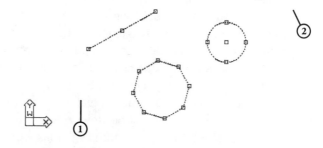

<u>**Figure** 5.2</u>

Selected objects with grip points.

The next section explains the important features of grips and shows how proper grip usage can make editing tasks less tedious.

Introducing Autoediting Modes

Autoediting modes are a special group of common editing methods that are available when you choose a base grip. Table 5.1 briefly explains these modes.

Table 5.1

AutoCAD LT Autoediting Modes

Mode	Description
STRETCH	Modifies objects by moving one or more grips to another location while leaving the other part of the object intact. This can easily change the size or shape of an object or a group of objects. In some cases, the STRETCH mode moves an object.
MOVE	Relocates objects from a base point to another specified location. The size and orientation do not change.
ROTATE	Revolves objects around a specified base point. The angle can be entered or dragged.
SCALE	Resizes objects up or down by a given scale factor about a specified base point. Scale factors can be entered, dragged, or shown using the Reference option.
MIRROR	Reflects selected objects about a line described by the base point grip and another chosen point.

All these autoediting modes have common properties. First, when objects are selected and a base grip is chosen to issue the command, you can choose the desired mode by entering the first two letters of the mode (SC for scale, for example) or by pressing Enter, the spacebar, or the pointing device Enter button. Pressing Enter repeatedly, as you saw in the last exercise, cycles through the autoediting modes in the order shown in the preceding table. Each mode displays a set of options, such as the Copy option. If you want to make a copy while executing any autoediting mode, use the Copy option or hold down the Shift key while making multiple second point picks. The Undo option undoes the last edit, and the eXit option exits the autoediting modes. These modes and their options are similar to the corresponding commands, such as STRETCH and MOVE, which are discussed in Chapter 6, "Editing Drawings."

WARNING

> If you are new to the Microsoft Windows 95 environment, you might be tempted to move and copy objects using the Edit Cut, Edit Copy, and Edit Paste options. These options access the Windows Clipboard mechanism, discussed fully in Chapter 23, "Using OLE and the Windows 95 Editing Features."

If, by mistake, you select objects and activate grips, press Esc *twice*. The first Esc deselects the objects, and the second Esc removes the grips.

NOTE

> If you miss the object when picking, a rubberband box (a window) appears from the pick point. Pick again at the same point, and then try again. Window selection is covered later in this chapter in the section "Controlling Press and Drag."

The cursor automatically snaps to grip points as though they are magnetized. This convenient feature greatly reduces the need for object snaps while grip editing.

TIP

> You can grip-edit objects with the minimal use of object snaps. First, select object geometry and the objects to edit to snap to (displaying all grips). Then, click on the grips of the objects to edit (making those grips hot). Finally, snap to any of the displayed grips, eliminating the need for most (but not all) object snap modes. All grips remain displayed until you enter a command or press Esc at the Command: prompt.

To better control editing with grips, you must understand AutoCAD LT's grip and selection settings and methods. You can create a selection set of objects before or after you choose the editing command. The next section explains how.

Understanding Object Selection Order

AutoCAD LT supports two methods of object editing—verb/noun selection and noun/verb selection. To illustrate the distinction grammatically, consider the active-voice sentence "John threw the ball." Here, the verb (throw, an action) precedes the noun (ball, an object). The passive-voice sentence "The ball was thrown by John." places the noun before the verb. Both sentence variations convey the same meaning.

As an AutoCAD LT user you have a choice of which method to use. You can choose an editing operation first, and then choose the objects to be acted on (verb/noun), or you can choose objects first, and then apply an editing command (noun/verb). The method you choose is purely a personal preference. The result is the same—object editing occurs. The next section compares these two methods.

Verb/Noun Selection

This selection method is analogous to a scientist verbally ordering a robot to perform some movement: "Push chair!" or "drop package!" The robot applies the commands (verbs) to the appropriate set of objects (nouns). These directives are simple yet effective.

Historically, this command sequence was the sole means of editing AutoCAD objects. More recently, AutoCAD and AutoCAD LT provided an alternate method of object editing called noun/verb selection.

Noun/Verb Selection

In most Microsoft Windows 95 applications, you can edit objects by creating a selection set (noun) first, and then choosing the desired operation (verb). AutoCAD LT for Windows 95 is no different.

To use noun/verb selection, make sure the mode is checked in the Object Selection Settings dialog box. You can display this dialog box by using the DDSELECT command or by choosing Options, Selection from the pull-down menu.

Controlling GRIPS and Selection Parameters

Grips must be on for autoediting modes to function. You can display the Grips dialog box (see fig. 5.3) by using the DDGRIPS command or by choosing Grips from the Options menu.

Putting a check mark in the Enable Grips check box turns on the GRIPS system variable; clearing the box turns it off. You can easily adjust the grip size, which works similarly to object snap aperture size, with the slider bar. You also can specify the color of both displayed and selected grips in this dialog box by choosing the Unselected and Selected buttons.

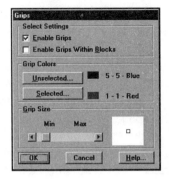

Figure 5.3

The Grips dialog box.

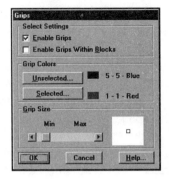

T_{IP}

The GRIPS system variable stores the grips on/off setting. On is 1 and off is 0. To check *all* the AutoCAD LT system variables related to grips, enter SETVAR at the `Command:` prompt, then ?, and then GRIP*. See Appendix A, "System Variable Tables," or use online help for the details on the corresponding values.

Controlling Selection with DDSELECT

Two other selection settings, Use Shift to Add and Press and Drag, improve the versatility and interaction of editing with grips. They are found in the Object Selection Settings dialog box that you can access through the DDSELECT command or by choosing Selection from the Options menu (see fig. 5.4). The other settings in the Object Selection Settings dialog box are covered in Chapter 6, "Editing Drawings."

Figure 5.4

The Object Selection Settings dialog box.

AutoCAD LT editing modes and commands operate on a selection set of objects that you select. The current selection generally is indicated by highlighting the objects. The Use Shift to Add setting controls the way in which objects are added to the selection set. When this setting is off (the default), objects are added to the selection set as you select them. When this setting is on, newly selected objects replace the existing selection set unless you hold down Shift as you select them. Holding down Shift and selecting (Shift+pick) currently highlighted objects removes those objects from the selection set, independent of the Use Shift to Add setting. To add objects when Use Shift to Add is on, hold down Shift while selecting objects. After you remove a selected object from the selection set, its grips still appear until you clear them, as described later in this section. Experiment with Use Shift to Add in the following exercise.

CONTROLLING SELECTION

Continue from the preceding exercise, or begin a new AutoCAD LT drawing session by drawing the objects shown in figure 5.2 (the objects won't yet appear highlighted or display grips). Ensure that SNAP is off.

1. Choose Selection from the Options menu. Choose Default, and then click OK.

2. Select any object, and note that AutoCAD LT highlights the object and starts a selection set.

3. Select the two other objects, and note that AutoCAD LT adds them to the selection set.

4. Shift+pick one of the highlighted objects. AutoCAD LT removes the object from the set, but leaves the grips intact.

5. Choose Selection from the Options menu. AutoCAD LT clears the selection set, and displays the Object Selection Settings dialog box.

6. Put a check mark in the Use Shift to Add check box, and then click OK.

7. Pick any object to start a new selection set. Pick any other object, and note that AutoCAD LT clears the selection set (leaving grips on) and starts a new set.

8. Shift+pick the two other objects, and AutoCAD LT adds the objects to the selection set.

9. Shift+pick a highlighted object. AutoCAD LT removes the object from the set.

As an alternative to pressing Esc to clear a selection set or to clear grips (press Esc twice to clear both), you also can select in a clear area to accomplish the same result. When you do so, you actually are selecting to clear the selection set. If Press and Drag is off (the default), you must pick twice. (Press and drag is discussed in the next section.)

If your first pick finds an object, AutoCAD LT selects it. If, however, the first pick misses, it sets the base corner of a rubber-banded window or crossing box. A second pick completed the window or crossing selection. A window selects all objects totally enclosed in its box; a crossing selects all objects in the box or that cross its box. When you pick window points left-to-right, the rubberband box is shown solid. When you pick crossing points right-to-left, the rubberband box is dashed. If the selection set is already empty, or if you just emptied it with a window or crossing selection of empty space, making another empty window or crossing selection removes all grips from the drawing window. The following exercise demonstrates this technique.

CLEARING THE SELECTION SET AND GRIPS

Continue with the drawing from the preceding exercise. Turn on Use Shift to Add and select some objects.

1. Pick points ① and ② (see fig. 5.5). AutoCAD LT clears the selection set.

2. Pick points ① and ② again and AutoCAD LT clears the grip markers.

Figure 5.5

Picking empty space to clear selection and grips.

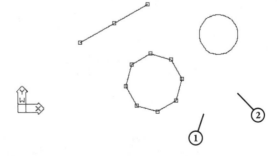

Window and crossing selections, including clearing a selection set and grips using the preceding method, are easier if you change the way AutoCAD LT makes window and crossing selections. The next section explains how and why.

Controlling Press and Drag

In most software with a graphical interface, you can make a window selection by pressing and holding the button at the first point, dragging to the second point, and then releasing the button. When the Press and Drag box is checked in the Object Selection Settings dialog box, AutoCAD LT creates a window by pressing the Pick button, moving to the other corner of the window, and releasing. Even if you are accustomed to the old two-pick method, once you get used to Press and Drag you will find it faster and more efficient.

Tip

Keeping Press and Drag on avoids the nuisance of starting a selection window by mistake. If you inadvertently pick a clear area of the drawing without moving the pointing device, no damage is done.

Press and Drag also behaves the same as other software you might use and enables you to clear selection sets or grips with a single pick. Try this technique in the next exercise.

CONTROLLING PRESS AND DRAG

Continue with the drawing from the preceding exercise. Ensure that Use Shift to Add is turned on.

1. At the **Command:** prompt, enter DDSELECT. AutoCAD LT displays the Object Selection Settings dialog box. Put a check mark in the Press and Drag checkbox, and then click OK.

2. Press and hold the pick button at ① (see fig. 5.6), drag to ②, and release the Pick button. AutoCAD LT creates a crossing window selection.

3. Press and hold the Pick button at ③, drag to ④, and release. AutoCAD LT creates a window selection, clears the previous selection set, and starts a new set.

4. Click once in empty space to clear the selection set.

5. Click again in empty space to remove the grip markers.

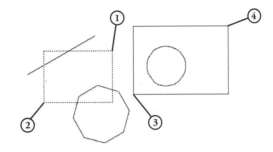

Figure 5.6

*Selection points for press
and drag windows.*

NOTE

Autodesk provides these object selection features for users migrating from other CAD
systems that utilized them. In the remainder of the book exercises, Press and Drag and Use
Shift to Add should be turned off, unless instructed otherwise.

Controlling the Pick Box Sizes

The *pick box* is a small box that enables you to select objects. Unless both Noun/Verb
selection in the Object Selection Settings dialog box and grips are disabled, the pick
box appears on the crosshairs at the Command: prompt. The pick box also appears
without the crosshairs at the Select objects: prompt during editing commands
such as ERASE, MOVE, and COPY. The pick box size is controlled by a system
variable. You can easily adjust the size by clicking and dragging a horizontal slider
in the Object Selection Settings dialog box. The size units are in pixels, and usually
range between 1 and 15, depending on your graphics resolution. Use whatever is
comfortable for your display and pointing device, but be sure to set it to a different
size than the aperture (refer to Chapter 4, "Drawing Accuracy").

NOTE

A large pick box size can either increase the time required to select objects, or increase
the likelihood of picking an object in a crowded area by mistake. Conversely, a small pick
box can be difficult to manage. Experiment with pick box and aperture sizes to find a "happy
medium."

To set the values transparently, enter either **'PICKBOX** or **'APERTURE**.

Rather than repeatedly zooming your drawing or adjusting the pick box size to select a particular object within a crowded area, AutoCAD LT provides another method to select just the object you want—object cycling. The next section explains this technique.

Using Object Cycling

Occasionally during an editing session, you need to pick a single object within a dense area of a drawing. If the pick box is large, other objects may lie inside it, making it tricky to select objects that are close together or lie directly on top of one another.

AutoCAD LT provides a cyclical mode of selecting objects. Holding down the Ctrl key while clicking an object with the pick box (Ctrl+pick) activates Cycle mode. You can continue the process until the desired object is selected.

For the next exercise, see figure 5.7. Here, you use object cycling to remove the center of the flower petals without zooming into the drawing.

USING OBJECT CYCLING

1. Open the FLOWER1 drawing from the PROJECTS/CH05 directory on the companion CD.

2. At the Command: prompt, enter **PICKBOX**. For the now value, enter **8**.

3. Position the cursor crosshairs over the center of the flower petals, as shown in figure 5.7. Hold down the Ctrl key and click the pointing device pick button. Repeatedly pick with the Ctrl key pressed until the center donut highlights. Then, release the Ctrl key and click the Enter button. AutoCAD LT also displays the donut grip markers.

4. Type **E** and AutoCAD LT erases the center donut.

5. Choose the Undo button on the Standard toolbar to restore the center donut.

6. Repeatedly choose the Undo button until the pick box reverts to its original size.

Figure 5.7

Cycling through selected objects.

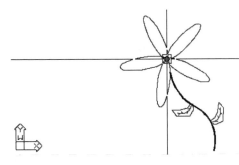

NOTE

Object cycling is a new feature with this version.

Summary

This chapter emphasized the procedures to create and modify objects from existing geometry, using the techniques of grip editing and object selection cycling. When you complete a drawing, think of ways to draw it more efficiently the next time.

In the following chapter, you'll discover many more AutoCAD LT editing commands that will expedite the drawing development process.

EDITING DRAWINGS

*A wise man once said, "the only thing constant in this world is change."
How true that is with engineering drawings—a change request invariably will occur before the drawing is issued. Therefore, to use AutoCAD
LT successfully, you must become familiar with the program's editing
functions. The benefits of electronic drawing editing are clear—as you
master the commands and their options, you stay ahead of project
changes without falling behind in your drawings.*

In this chapter, you learn the following editing techniques:

■ *Building a selection set of objects*

■ *Recovering from mistakes (UNDO)*

■ *Relocating objects (MOVE, ROTATE)*

■ *Duplicating objects (COPY, ARRAY, OFFSET)*

■ *Resizing objects (SCALE, STRETCH, LENGTHEN)*

■ *Finishing edges (TRIM, EXTEND, BREAK)*

■ *Finishing corners (FILLET, CHAMFER)*

■ *Checking your work (LIST, DIST, AREA)*

■ *Changing object properties (DDCHPROP, DDMODIFY)*

In the exercises in previous chapters, you spent most of the time creating new drawing objects. Chapter 5, "Editing with Grips," explored the grip editing methods of accessing several commands. AutoCAD LT, however, includes many more powerful and versatile modification commands and options. Figures 6.1 and 6.2 identify commands used to develop and refine the main exercise drawing for this chapter.

Figure 6.1

The CHAP06 drawing before editing.

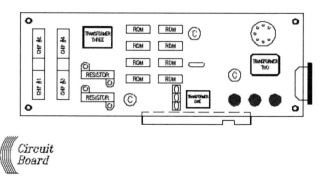

Figure 6.2

The CHAP06 drawing after editing.

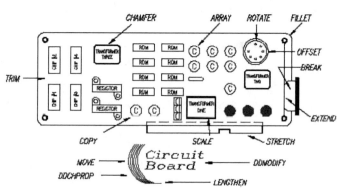

You perform three basic kinds of edits to drawings: changing, copying, and erasing objects. You can change an existing object's location, layer, and visual properties, such as color and linetype. You also can break objects by deleting portions of line and arc segments. Breaking an object reduces its length or divides it into multiple objects. You can copy objects, singly or in a regular pattern. You also can erase objects to get rid of mistakes.

NOTE

When you edit a set of objects, the newly created geometry inherits the corresponding layers of the original objects, not the current layer.

Most of AutoCAD LT's editing commands are gathered on the Modify toolbar. In addition, the Select Objects flyout on the Standard toolbar contains tools for picking objects. Figure 6.3 shows these important toolbars and flyouts for editing.

Figure 6.3

The Modify toolbar and the Select Objects flyout.

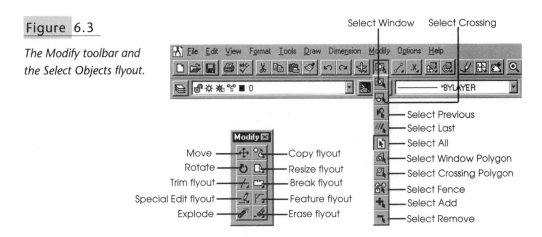

The remaining exercises for this chapter show you how to change the spatial (location) properties of existing objects. Only a few basic editing commands are required to perform these simple functions.

TIP

If you want to practice individual editing commands as you work through the chapter, create a layer named SCRATCH. Create some objects on this layer, try out some editing variations, freeze your SCRATCH layer, and then pick up again with the exercise sequences.

Building a Selection Set of Objects

AutoCAD LT offers more than a dozen ways to collect objects for editing. You can, for example, pick individual objects or enclose multiple objects within a window. As you select objects, AutoCAD LT sets up a temporary selection set and highlights the objects by temporarily changing their colors, making them blink, or giving them dotted lines. This highlighting confirms the objects that you have selected. You can enter any valid selection or option at the `Select objects:` prompt. If you enter invalid input, AutoCAD LT prompts you with all the available modes and reissues the

`Select objects:` prompt, as follows:

Expects a point or one (or more) of the following:

```
Window/Last/Crossing/BOX/ALL/Fence/WPolygon/CPolygon/Add/
Remove/Multiple/Previous/Undo/AUto/SIngle
Select objects:
```

After you select all the objects you want, press Enter to end object selection and continue with the editing command.

The Select Object Options and Methods

AutoCAD LT provides many ways to add objects to a selection set, as follows:

- **Object pick:** Enables you to pick individual objects.

- **Window:** Selects objects within a window you specify.

- **Last:** Selects the last object created that is visible in the drawing window.

- **Crossing:** Works the same as Window, except that Crossing also selects any objects that are partially within, crossing, or touching the window.

- **BOX:** Combines Window and Crossing into a single selection. Picking the points of your box from left to right produces a Window selection; picking from right to left produces a Crossing selection.

- **ALL:** Selects all objects in the drawing that are not on locked or frozen layers.

- **Fence:** Enables you to draw an open, multiple-point fence with which to select objects. All objects touched by the fence line are selected.

- **Wpolygon:** This method is similar to Window selection but enables you to draw an irregular closed polygon to select objects. All objects completely within the polygon are selected.

- **Cpolygon:** This method is similar to the Crossing selection but enables you to draw an irregular closed polygon to select objects. All objects inside or crossed by the polygon are selected.

- **Add:** Switches from Remove mode back to Normal so that you again can add objects to the selection set.

- **Remove:** Switches to Remove mode so that you can remove selected objects from the selection set (not from the drawing).

- **Multiple:** Enables you to pick multiple objects in close proximity and speeds up selection by enabling multiple selections without highlighting or prompting. Pressing Enter an extra time is required to complete the multiple selection and return to normal object selection.

- **Previous:** Selects the entire preceding selection set (from a previous command) as the current selection set.

- **Undo:** Undoes or reverses the last selection operation. Each U undoes one selection operation.

- **AUto:** Combines individual selection with the BOX selection. This selection performs the same as BOX, except that if the first pick point finds an object, that single object is selected and the BOX mode is aborted.

- **SIngle:** Works in conjunction with the other selection options. If you precede a selection with SIngle, object selection automatically ends as soon as an object is detected; pressing Enter to confirm is not required.

When do you use which mode? The default option, picking objects, is fast and simple, even for picking three or four objects, and it requires no mode setting. Previous is great for repeated operations on the same set of objects, like a copy and rotate operation. A Fence selection is ideal in a crowded area. The selection set options BOX, AUto, and SIngle are designed primarily for use in menus. They offer no real advantages over the other options discussed in the preceding list when specifying modes via the keyboard. Some of these options and others will be explored in the exercises that follow.

TIP

Another method of picking objects in a crowded area is known as *object cycling*, covered in Chapter 5, "Editing with Grips."

Recovering from Mistakes

Occasionally, you discover after performing several operations that your drawing is not turning out the way you want. In such cases, you can back up in your drawing session to the point where you made an error using AutoCAD LT's U (single-step undo) command. U enables you to step back in your drawing one command at a time. The U command is more flexible than ERASE and OOPS because it reverses almost all commands, including settings that you might have changed or objects that you might have moved or otherwise edited. To reverse a U operation immediately, issue REDO.

Figure 6.4 shows these tools on the Standard toolbar.

Figure 6.4

The Undo and Redo tools on the Standard toolbar.

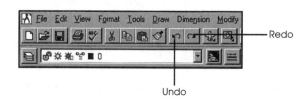

TIP

AutoCAD LT also has a more full-featured UNDO command, with more flexible options. The UNDO Mark and Back options provide an excellent way to perform a "what if" scenario in your drawing. If you later determine the changes are not workable, simply undo back to the mark. UNDO resembles an "electronic bookmark" or even a "time machine" in your drawing!

Relocating Objects (MOVE, ROTATE)

The MOVE command is one of the simplest editing commands to use. To move an object, you select it and issue the MOVE command (or vice versa), and then specify the object's new location. After the object is repositioned, you may need to ROTATE it to a new angle.

In the following exercise, you use the MOVE and ROTATE commands to reposition the circuit board logo, and then pivot the contact plate.

MOVING AND ROTATING OBJECTS

Using the CIRCUITB drawing in the PROJECTS/CH06 directory of the CD-ROM as a prototype, create a new drawing called CHAP06. Zoom to the view shown in figure 6.5.

1. Pick at ① and ② around the logo to display the grip markers, and then pick the grip on the word Board to start grip autoediting mode.

2. Press the spacebar once to switch to MOVE mode. At the `Command:` prompt, type **@3<0** and press Enter to move the logo three inches to the right. Press Esc twice to clear the grip markers.

3. For the next edit, choose the Rotate tool on the Modify toolbar. At the `Select objects:` prompt, pick at ③ and ④ around the contact plate. AutoCAD LT reports eight objects selected. Press Enter to complete the selection set.

4. At the `Base point:` prompt, you choose the center of the outer circle. Select Snap to Center from the Object Snap flyout on the Object Properties toolbar, and then pick at ⑤.

5. At the `Rotation angle:` prompt, type **135** and then press Enter. Your drawing should appear as shown in figure 6.6.

6. Save the drawing.

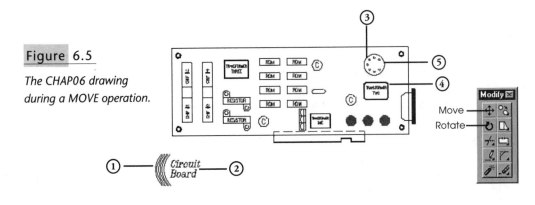

Figure 6.5

The CHAP06 drawing during a MOVE operation.

Figure 6.6

The CHAP06 drawing after relocating objects.

In the preceding exercise, AutoCAD LT gives visual confirmation of the edit opera-tions by showing a temporary rubber-band line trailing the crosshairs from the first point to the second. As you moved the logo, an image of the selection set also followed the crosshairs. Again, AutoCAD LT provides a visual aid to help you pick your second displacement point. This action is called *dragging*. Without dragging, it can be difficult to see if the selection set fits where you want it.

An alternate way to specify an angle during a ROTATE operation is to use the "reference" method. You can change the angle of an object by giving AutoCAD LT a reference angle that should equal the desired angle. You can say, for example, "Put a handle on 237 degrees and turn it to 165." This often is easier than calculating the difference (72 degrees clockwise) and entering that number at the prompt. You do not need to know the actual angles—pick points to instruct AutoCAD LT to calculate them. To align with existing objects, use object snaps when picking the points of the angle(s).

TI P

When you set a base point, try to pick one that is easy to visualize (and remember). Use a corner point for rectangular objects, a center point for circular objects, and appropriate object snap points for all other types of geometry. Otherwise, you appear to be carrying the selection set around without touching it.

Duplicating Objects (COPY, ARRAY, OFFSET)

The COPY command is very similar to the MOVE command, except for one important difference—COPY creates the selected set of objects at another location and *retains* the original set, whereas MOVE *deletes* the original set.

The ARRAY command also duplicates objects, but results in a rectangular or circular arrangement, as illustrated in figure 6.7.

Figure 6.7

Rectangular and polar (circular) arrays.

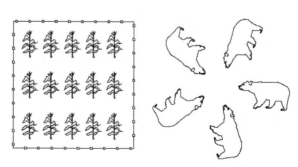

The OFFSET command generates parallel lines and curves. Some applications of OFFSET include topographic maps, pool aprons, and parking stalls.

In the following exercise, you use the COPY and ARRAY commands to duplicate capacitors on the circuit board, and the OFFSET command to generate the fastener surrounding the contact plate.

DUPLICATING OBJECTS

Continue with the CHAP06 drawing, and zoom to the view shown in figure 6.8.

1. Pick at ① and ② to describe a Crossing window at the indicated capacitor, and then choose the Copy tool on the Modify toolbar.

2. At the default `Base point or displacement:` prompt, pick any point near the capacitor (see fig. 6.8). For the second point of displacement, type **@0.5<0** and then press Enter. AutoCAD LT creates another copy of the capacitor to the right.

3. For the next edit, choose the Rectangular Array tool on the Modify toolbar, and then pick at ③ and ④ to describe a Window at the indicated capacitor (see fig. 6.9). Specify **2** ↵ for the number of rows (which includes the original), and 3, and then press Enter for the number of columns. Specify the row distance as **-0.4** and then press Enter (generates downward, the negative Y direction). Specify the column distance as **0.5** and then press Enter (generates to the right, the positive X direction).

4. Finally, choose the Offset tool on the Modify toolbar, type **0.05**, and then press Enter to establish the default offset distance (see fig. 6.9). Pick the contact plate circle at ⑤ and then show AutoCAD LT at ⑥ that the offset goes outside. Press Enter to complete the offset operation, and your drawing should appear as shown in figure 6.10.

5. Save the drawing.

Figure 6.8

The CHAP06 drawing during a COPY operation.

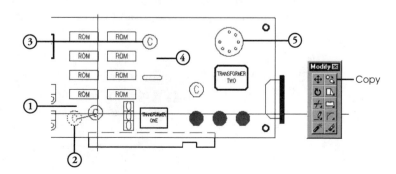

Figure 6.9

The Duplicate Objects flyout on the Modify toolbar.

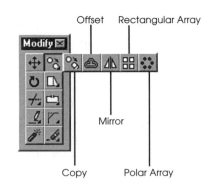

Figure 6.10

The CHAP06 drawing after duplicating objects.

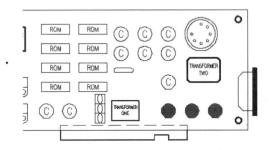

TIP

You also can employ a unit cell method to generate rectangular arrays by picking two points of a rectangle. AutoCAD LT uses these points to establish the directed row and column distances.

To create rotated arrays, first use the SNAP Rotate option.

You can use advanced editing commands, such as EXTEND, STRETCH, and TRIM, for more than copying and moving objects. These commands build on AutoCAD LT's capability to recognize drawing geometry. By combining these commands with construction techniques, you can make a rough draft of a drawing quickly, and then finish it perfectly.

The trick to using SCALE, STRETCH, and LENGTHEN (for resizing) and TRIM, EXTEND, and BREAK (for finishing edges) in the next pair of exercises is to plan ahead. The operational details of the commands can involve several objects, so think about the ways you will use these commands in production drawings.

Resizing Objects (SCALE, STRETCH, LENGTHEN)

Occasionally, as you develop a drawing, you use the wrong symbol and text scale or need to change an object's size. The SCALE command shrinks or enlarges existing objects. During a scaling operation, you use a scale factor or reference length to change the size of objects around a given base point. The base point remains constant; everything around it grows or shrinks by your scale factor. You can enter an explicit scale factor, pick two points to have AutoCAD LT compute the distance, or specify a reference length. To use the reference method, define a current length (generally on an object), and then specify its new length.

The STRETCH command moves or stretches objects along a displacement vector. You can lengthen objects, shorten them, and alter their shapes. However, the results of stretching depend on the object types selected.

In a stretch operation, you normally select your objects with a crossing window and then indicate a displacement from a base point. Everything selected inside the crossing window moves, and objects crossing the window are stretched.

Another editing task that you are often required to perform is to alter the length of a line or arc by a specified amount. In prior versions of AutoCAD LT, you had to select a line, extend it to a boundary, offset that boundary, and finally, trim the line accordingly—quite a few steps. For arcs, the construction tasks were even more involved!

OTE

> The LENGTHEN command is new in this version.

The LENGTHEN command presents the following options:

```
DElta/Percent/Total/DYnamic/<Select object>:
```

- **DElta:** Lengthens or shortens an object by a specified increment. You also can alter the angle of an arc.

- **Percent:** Specifies a percentage change for the object.

- **Total:** Sets a new, total absolute length of an object from a fixed endpoint. For an arc, this option determines the total included angle of the arc.

- **DYnamic:** Drags the length of the selected object dynamically. AutoCAD LT uses the endpoint closest to the pick point of the object to drag the desired length or included angle (for an arc), while the other endpoint remains fixed.

■ **Select object:** Displays the length of the object if applicable. This option does not necessarily define the selection set to be lengthened.

In the following exercise, you explore three edit commands to further develop your drawing. Use SCALE to enlarge a transformer, STRETCH to elongate the right side of the slot connector (along the circuit board's bottom edge), and LENGTHEN to increase all arc lengths within the circuit board logo.

SIZING OBJECTS

Continue with the CHAP06 drawing, and zoom to the view shown in figure 6.11.

1. Select a window from ① to ② and then pick the grip at the lower left corner of the transformer. Press the spacebar three times and AutoCAD LT activates the SCALE autoediting mode.

2. You need to scale the transformer so that its length is exactly 0.8". Without measuring the current length, you can use the Reference option. Type **R**, and AutoCAD LT prompts for the Reference length.

3. Pick both the lower left and lower right grips, type **0.8"**, and press Enter for the new length. AutoCAD LT enlarges the transformer to the proper length, and proportionally scales its width.

4. For the next edit, choose the Stretch tool on the Modify toolbar and select a crossing window from ③ to ④ around the right edge of the slot connector (see fig. 6.12). Use Snap to Intersection object snap and pick the connector's bottom right corner for the base point. Then, type **0.49"<0** and press Enter for the second point of displacement. AutoCAD LT stretches the smaller, notched edge by 0.49".

5. Choose the Lengthen tool on the Modify toolbar. At the initial prompt, pick the rightmost arc at ⑤. AutoCAD LT reports its current length as 0'-1.01" and included angle as 7'-11.85".

NOTE

In early versions of AutoCAD LT for Windows 95, the included angle measurement is incorrectly reported when the units are not set to decimal.

6. Specify **T** to change the total length of the selected arc to 1.5 and then press Enter. Pick all arcs in sequence, right to left, to apply the new length to all

arcs. Press Enter to complete the lengthen operation, and your drawing should appear as shown in figure 6.13.

7. Save the drawing.

Figure 6.11

The CHAP06 drawing during a SCALE operation.

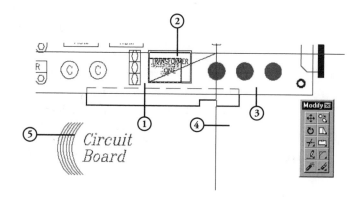

Figure 6.12

The Resize Objects flyout on the Modify toolbar.

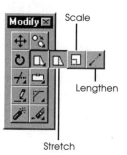

Figure 6.13

The CHAP06 drawing after resizing objects.

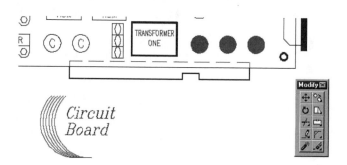

In the previous exercise, you also selected the bottom edge of the circuit board with the crossing window. However, it was not stretched because neither endpoint fell within the crossing window. Don't confuse SCALE and STRETCH. Although both commands resize objects, SCALE alters both X and Y directional axes proportionally. STRETCH (with ortho on) alters either X or Y, not both. For further details on subtleties of STRETCH command usage, consult the online help.

The Reference option of the SCALE command is an excellent way to create prototype titleblock drawings. By maintaining a single background sheet, you can easily define additional drawings for various intended sheet sizes and plot scales by entering appropriate new lengths.

Finishing Edges (TRIM, EXTEND, BREAK)

Frequently, you need to cut existing lines in a drawing. If you are working with a large number of objects, breaking individual objects is time-consuming. You can get the same results faster by using TRIM. The TRIM command uses boundary objects that include lines, arcs, circles, polylines (covered in Chapter 7, "Creating Advanced Lines, Curves, and Points"), and, in paper space, viewports. The objects that you select as your boundary edge become your cutting edge(s). After you select your cutting edge, you pick the individual objects that you want to trim. You can trim lines, arcs, circles, and polylines. Other object types are ignored by the TRIM command; therefore, you can select extra objects that are in the area.

The EXTEND command is analogous to the TRIM command. Whereas TRIM uses cutting edges, EXTEND uses boundary edges. In both cases, you either cut or project objects to an edge.

The boundary edge(s) can be lines, polylines, arcs, circles, and viewport objects (when in paper space). Use normal object selection to select the boundary edge(s) to which you want to extend, and then pick the objects that you want to extend. You must individually pick each object to extend—you cannot use other modes to fill a selection set of objects to extend simultaneously.

Note

> The TRIM and EXTEND commands have a new option in the latest version. If Edge Extend is active (off by default), you can trim or extend objects without the object actually intersecting the cutting (trim) or boundary (extend) edge. In this case, AutoCAD LT follows the natural path of the edge to perform the corresponding operation. Figure 6.14 shows both operations with edge extend active.

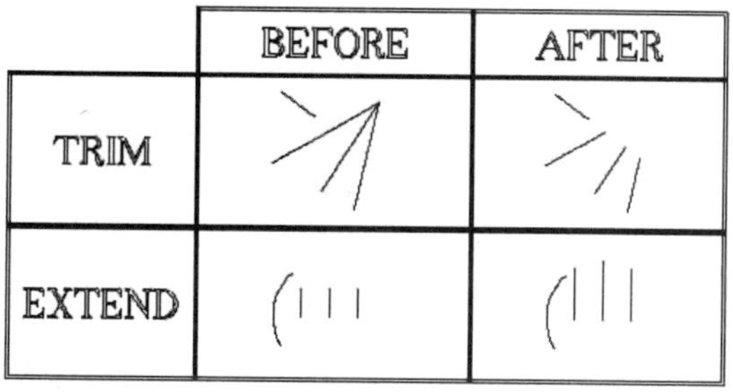

Figure 6.14

TRIM and EXTEND operations using Edge Extend mode.

	BEFORE	AFTER
TRIM		
EXTEND		

Often, you will erase only a portion of an object. If no cutting edge exists for a trim operation, you can use the BREAK command.

During a break operation, you pick one or two breakpoints. With the one-point method, AutoCAD LT creates two objects with a common point of intersection. With the two-point method, AutoCAD LT creates a gap between the disjoint objects.

Tip

> The order of picking the breakpoints is important on curved objects—AutoCAD LT breaks circles and arcs in a counterclockwise direction.

In the following exercise, you use TRIM to finish edges of the chipset on the left side of the circuit board. You then use EXTEND and BREAK to modify the geometry near the port connector. The port connector is located at the lower-right corner of the circuit board.

FINISHING OBJECT EDGES

Continue with the CHAP06 drawing, and zoom to the view shown in figure 6.15.

1. Choose the Trim tool on the Modify toolbar, and pick a window from ① to ②. Press Enter to complete the set of cutting edges.

Figure 6.15

The CHAP06 drawing before the TRIM operation.

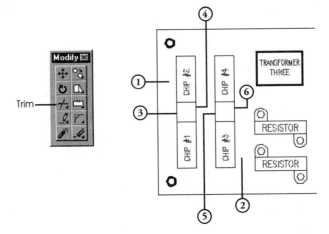

2. Pick the vertical lines at ③, ④, ⑤, and ⑥. Press Enter to complete the trim operations. Your drawing should resemble figure 6.16.

3. Save the drawing and then zoom to the view shown in figure 6.17.

Figure 6.16

The CHAP06 drawing after trimming the chip edges.

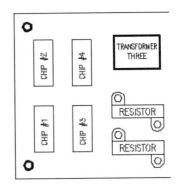

Figure 6.17

The port connector of the circuit board.

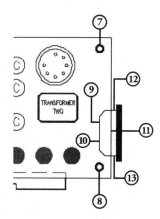

4. For the next edit, choose the Extend tool on the Modify toolbar. Pick the grommets at ⑦ and ⑧. Press Enter to complete the set of boundary edges.

5. Pick the rear of the port connector at ⑨ and ⑩. Press Enter to complete the extend operations.

6. Finally, choose the Break 2 Points Select tool on the Modify toolbar (see fig. 6.18). Pick the vertical line ⑪ in the middle of the port connector. Then, use Snap to Intersection to pick the two points ⑫ and ⑬. Your drawing should resemble figure 6.19.

7. Save the drawing.

Figure 6.18

The BREAK tools on the Modify toolbar.

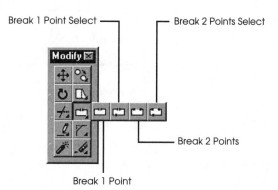

Figure 6.19

Figure 6.19

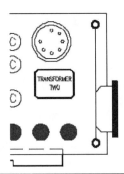

The CHAP06 drawing after
the EXTEND and BREAK
operations.

In the previous exercise, you used editing commands to clean up the edges of objects. Occasionally, you need to adjust the geometry at the corner of objects. AutoCAD LT supports two types of corner editing, as shown in the next section.

Finishing Corners (FILLET, CHAMFER)

AutoCAD LT enables you to finish off a corner of an object by applying two types of geometry: a *fillet* (smooth arc) and a *chamfer* (bevel cut). Figure 6.20 illustrates these corner editing operations.

Figure   6.20

The FILLET and CHAMFER
corner editing operations.

	BEFORE	AFTER
FILLET		
CHAMFER		

In the following exercise, you continue to modify the circuit board geometry. You use FILLET to round the outermost corners of the board. You then use CHAMFER to apply angled cuts to one of the transformers.

FINISHING OBJECT CORNERS

Continue with the CHAP06 drawing. Set the current layer to BOARD, and freeze all layers except BOARD, TRANS, and TRANS-TEXT. Zoom to the drawing extents and then Zoom 0.8X. Figure 6.21 shows the results of this exercise.

1. Choose the Fillet tool on the Modify toolbar. AutoCAD LT presents the following prompt:

```
Polyline/Radius/Trim/<Select first object>:
```

2. Type **R** and enter **0.2**. AutoCAD LT repeats the default prompt and pick the adjacent lines at ① and ②.

3. Similarly, pick adjacent pairs of lines and repeat the FILLET operation at the remaining three corners.

In the next part of this exercise, you apply a chamfer to all four corners of a transformer. In this case, however, you indicate the transformer (a wide polyline) once, and AutoCAD LT edits all four vertices simultaneously.

4. Choose the Chamfer tool on the Modify toolbar. AutoCAD LT presents the following prompt:

```
Polyline/Distance/Angle/Trim/Method/<Select first line>:
```

5. Type **D** to establish the first chamfer distance, and enter **0.05**. AutoCAD LT defaults the second distance equal to the first; press Enter to accept it.

6. Press Enter to repeat the CHAMFER command, and type **P**. AutoCAD LT requests a 2D polyline to edit. Pick the boundary of the transformer at ③, and AutoCAD LT cuts all the corners.

7. Save the drawing.

Figure 6.21

The CHAP06 drawing after the FILLET and CHAMFER operations.

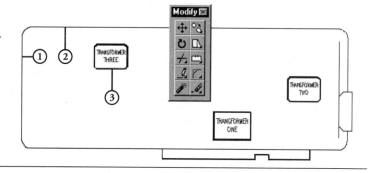

NOTE

The FILLET and CHAMFER commands have a new option in the latest version. If No trim is active (off by default), AutoCAD LT will retain the original edges at the fillet or chamfer endpoints.

You can perform a chamfer operation by specifying two distances, or a length and an angle. Use the method that is more convenient for a given application.

In the course of editing, you need to verify your results. Because AutoCAD LT maintains about 16 decimal places of accuracy, linework can be, and should be, extremely precise.

In the next section, you explore some commands that inspect the database "behind" your drawing.

Checking Your Work (LIST, DIST, AREA)

AutoCAD LT is a *vector-based* graphics program—each drawing has an associated database, and each object has recordable geometry. For example, a LINE command displays a straight line segment on the screen, but AutoCAD LT records information in addition to its graphical display.

Use the LIST command to display the database information for selected objects. The information that AutoCAD LT reports depends on the object type. Figure 6.22 shows the results of a LIST command applied to a line and a circle.

TIP

The DDMODIFY command, covered in the next section, is more dynamic than the LIST command. DDMODIFY not only enables you to inspect the information like LIST, but you also can edit the information.

The DIST command measures the distance and angle between two points.

The AREA command calculates the area and perimeter of objects or defined areas.

Figure 6.22

LIST command results for a LINE and CIRCLE.

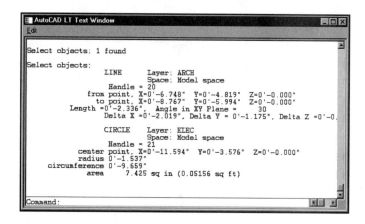

> ### TIP
>
> Use the LIST command on a closed polyline to report the total area and perimeter, in addition to its vertices. Chapter 7, "Creating Advanced Lines, Curves, and Points," covers polylines in greater detail.

AutoCAD LT provides a convenient method of using these measurement-related commands. See figure 6.23 for the location of the Inquiry flyout on the Object Properties toolbar.

An application that involves electrical circuitry usually demands very accurate measurements. In the following exercise, you investigate some dimensions of the circuit board. You use LIST to inspect a capacitor, DIST to find the length of the slot connector, and AREA to report the surface area of a transformer.

CHECKING YOUR WORK

Continue with the CHAP06 drawing, and thaw all layers. See figure 6.23 for the pick points.

1. Choose the List tool on the Inquiry flyout on the Object Properties toolbar. AutoCAD LT requests a set of objects to list.

2. Choose ① to inspect a capacitor. Press Enter and notice the radius of the circle is 0.15".

3. Choose the Distance tool on the Inquiry flyout and snap to the intersections at ② and ③. At the **Command:** prompt, AutoCAD LT reports the length of the longer slot connector is 2.0". Check the distance from ④ to ⑤. AutoCAD LT informs you the length of the shorter edge is 0.89".

4. Choose the Area tool and AutoCAD LT issues the following prompt:

    `<First point>/Object/Add/Subtract:`

5. Type **O** and choose transformer three at ⑥. AutoCAD LT reports the area is 0.34 square inches and the perimeter is 2.28".

6. Save the drawing.

Figure 6.23

Checking your work with the Inquiry flyout.

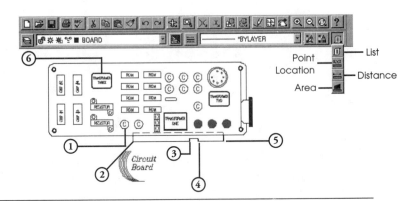

As you saw in the last exercise, every object in the AutoCAD LT drawing database has an associated property list. Until now, you explored editing commands, which change the on-screen geometry. The question arises, is it possible to alter object properties (such as layer, color, and linetype) *without* changing the on-screen geometry? The answer is yes—the next section shows how.

Changing Object Properties (DDCHPROP, DDMODIFY)

Every object in the AutoCAD LT drawing database has at least five properties: color, layer, linetype, linetype scale, and thickness (for details on wireframes, see Chapter 19, "Drawing in 3D"). There are two primary commands available for manipulating object properties:

■ **DDCHPROP:** Changes the color, layer, linetype, linetype scale, and thickness of a set of selected objects.

■ **DDMODIFY:** Similar to DDCHPROP, but allows the selection of a single object only. Depending on the object selected, however, you can change more than the basic five properties and AutoCAD LT will present an appropriate dialog box. For example, you can change the width factor of TEXT, the radius of a CIRCLE, the start and end angle of an ARC, and so on.

In this chapter's final exercise, you use DDCHPROP to change the color of the logo arcs and DDMODIFY to change the width factor of the logo text.

CHANGING OBJECT PROPERTIES

Continue with the CHAP06 drawing, and zoom your drawing to the view shown in figure 6.28, which shows the results of this exercise.

1. Using any of the object selection methods discussed earlier in this chapter, choose all of the logo arcs. AutoCAD LT displays the grip markers.

2. Choose the Properties tool on the Object Properties toolbar. (Note that this tool issues the DDCHPROP command to *backedit* existing objects. If you want to change the properties of objects yet to be drawn, use the Current Properties tool, which issues the DDEMODES command. See figure 6.24 for the tool locations on the toolbar.)

Figure 6.24

The Current Properties and Properties tools.

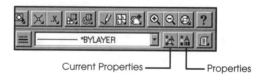

Current Properties ———— Properties

3. Click the Color button in the Change Properties dialog box and choose any color from the Full Color Palette on the Select Color dialog box (see figures 6.25 and 6.26). Click OK twice and AutoCAD LT changes the arc colors to the desired selection.

Figure 6.25

The Change Properties dialog box.

Change Properties	
Color...	BYLAYER (red)
Layer...	TEXT
Linetype...	BYLAYER
Linetype Scale:	1.00"
Thickness:	0.00"

OK   Cancel   Help...

Figure 6.26

Figure 6.26

*The Select Color
dialog box.*

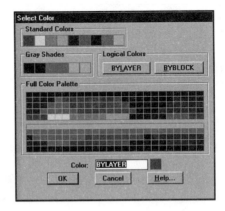

4. To change the width factor of the logo text, click the word Circuit. Then type **DDMODIFY** and AutoCAD LT presents the Modify Text dialog box (see fig. 6.27). Change the Width factor value to **1.50** and click OK. Perform the same modification to the word Board.

   Ensure that your logo resembles the drawing shown in figure 6.28, and save your work.

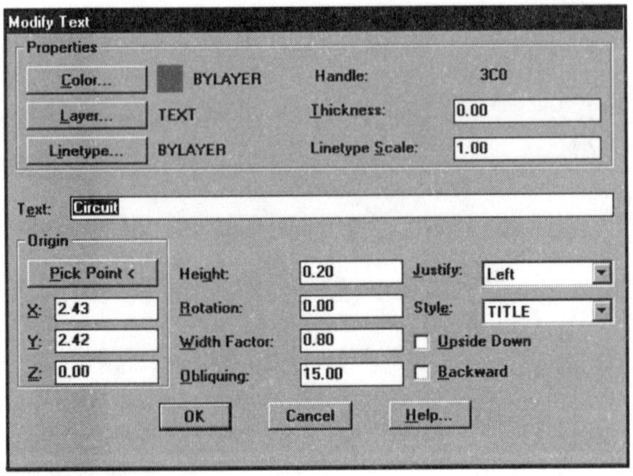

Figure 6.27

*The Modify Text
dialog box.*

Figure 6.28

The Circuit Board logo after property modifications.

As you conclude this chapter, you might want to experiment with these modification commands in other applications. Understanding the extensive editing toolkit that AutoCAD LT provides is critical to increasing your expertise level and drawing proficiency.

Summary

From this chapter, you have seen the importance of editing during drawing development. Your job is to produce high-quality drawings in an efficient manner, so learning valuable techniques and adopting good work habits are key steps toward achieving your goal.

ADVANCED DRAWING FEATURES

CHAPTER 7

CREATING ADVANCED LINES, CURVES, AND POINTS

In Chapter 3, "Creating and Printing a Simple Drawing," you worked with some basic drawing commands, such as LINE, CIRCLE, and ARC. In Chapter 6, "Editing Drawings," you investigated some convenient methods of editing these objects, including SCALE, TRIM, and FILLET. In this chapter, you learn the following advanced drawing and editing techniques in the AutoCAD LT toolkit:

- *Drawing points*

- *Changing point styles*

- *Dividing and measuring objects*

- *Drawing polylines*

- *Editing polylines*

- *Using ellipses and splines*

- *Using xlines and rays*

Someone once asked, "If points don't have any moving parts or hinges, how do they connect to form a line?" While you ponder that point, let's make a few more.

Drawing Points

The most basic drawing command is POINT. POINT is the simplest of drawing commands because it is used solely to create its namesake. *Points* are dimensionless and abstract representations of a single location in 3D coordinate space. The default point object plots as a dot and as such, has little value as a graphic element.

In manual drafting, you often draw temporary points as reference marks to which you later measure or align, or use points to stipple surfaces or sections. As you will discover shortly in this chapter, AutoCAD LT has some versatile commands for measuring discrete lengths along a path, and in Chapter 8, "Drawing and Editing Hatch Patterns," you will work with methods of filling a closed area with patterns.

In the following exercise, you use the POINT command to draw several points and the DDPTYPE command to change the point styles.

USING THE **POINT** COMMAND

Using the TRANSFER drawing in the PROJECTS/CH07 folder of the CD-ROM as a prototype, create a new drawing called CHAP07A. Zoom to the view shown in figure 7.1.

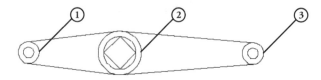

Figure 7.1

The initial view of the CHAP07A drawing.

1. Set a running Object Snap to Center. Choose the Point tool on the Draw toolbar and pick ① (see fig. 7.2). Reissue the POINT command and pick the centers ② and ③. AutoCAD LT displays the usual blip markers at the specified coordinates.

Figure 7.2

The Point tools on the Draw toolbar.

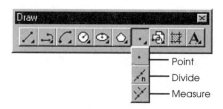

2. You must redraw the screen to see the points that AutoCAD LT generates. Type **R** and AutoCAD LT erases the blip markers. Notice that the default point style is a dot, which is barely noticeable.

3. From the Format pull-down menu, choose Point Style and AutoCAD LT displays the Point Style dialog box (see fig. 7.3). Choose the style indicated in the figure (an X), and click OK. This sets the point style for newly created points.

4. You must regenerate the screen to see the new point style immediately. Type **REGEN** and your drawing should appear as shown in figure 7.4.

5. Save the drawing.

Figure 7.3

The Point Style dialog box.

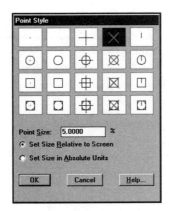

Figure 7.4

The CHAP07A drawing with modified point styles.

Changing Point Styles

As shown in figure 7.3, AutoCAD LT provides 20 different *styles* of point objects. If you prefer to set the point style at the Command: prompt rather than using the dialog box, alter one or both of the following system variables:

- PDMODE (Point Display Mode) controls the shape of a point object. The Point Style dialog box shows the corresponding images in four rows. The first row has the values 0 through 4. Add 32 to obtain the values on the second row, 64 to obtain the values on the third row, and 96 to obtain the values on the fourth row. Note that PDMODE 1 generates a blank style.

- PDSIZE (Point Display Size) controls the size of the point figures, except for PDMODE values 0 and 1. The value 0 instructs AutoCAD LT to show the point at five percent of the graphics screen height. A positive value specifies an absolute size for the points; a negative value yields the corresponding percentage of the current viewport.

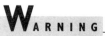

> Use an easily noticeable point style when drawing, but remember to set it to the default dot (PDMODE 0) before plotting. If you don't want points to plot, set them to the blank point style (PDMODE 1). You also can place construction points on their own layer and turn off or freeze the layer before plotting.

If you change PDMODE or PDSIZE, AutoCAD LT updates the point display at the next drawing regeneration.

You can use point objects as construction or marker points, and snap them with the NODE object snap mode.

WARNING

> It actually is considered rude and impolite to pick your nodes.

Dividing and Measuring Objects

As mentioned earlier in this chapter, AutoCAD LT has some versatile commands for measuring discrete lengths along a path: DIVIDE and MEASURE. The next section explores these commands in detail.

Using the DIVIDE Command

Sometimes you need to divide an object into an equal number of segments while laying out a drawing. For example, a mechanical design might call for equally spaced holes along a part, or a landscape designer might want to plant shrubs at equal intervals along a pathway. The DIVIDE command provides a method by which you can do this automatically. You can accurately divide lines, circles, arcs, ellipses, polylines (covered later in this chapter), donuts, polygons, and rectangles into equal intervals.

The DIVIDE command does not break these objects into separate segments. Instead, it places a point object at equal intervals along the divided object. You also can specify a block rather than a point for AutoCAD LT to insert at these intervals (for more information on blocks, see Chapter 9, "Drawing with Basic Blocks").

Figure 7.5 shows objects with divisional variations.

Figure 7.5

DIVIDE command options.

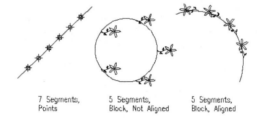

7 Segments,   5 Segments,   5 Segments,
Points   Block, Not Aligned   Block, Aligned

Using the MEASURE Command

Placing objects at a set distance apart is another common necessity in drafting— placing a 2-inch-by-6-inch stud every 24 inches along a wall in an architectural floor plan, for example, or thread spaced 18-per-inch in a mechanical drawing. AutoCAD LT provides the MEASURE command for this situation.

The MEASURE command works like DIVIDE, but rather than dividing an object into equal parts, MEASURE enables you to specify the segment length.

In the following exercise, you use the DIVIDE command to place shrubs along the fence perimeter and benches along the path. You then use the MEASURE command to place lightpoles along the pathway opposite the benches. See figure 7.6 for the pick points.

DIVIDING AND MEASURING OBJECTS

Using the CITYPARK drawing in the PROJECTS/CH07 folder of the CD-ROM as a prototype, create a new drawing called CHAP07B. Zoom to the view shown in figure 7.6.

A zoomed view of the CHAP07B drawing.

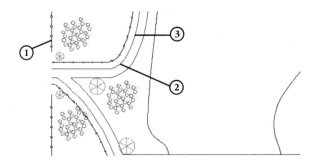

1. Set the current layer to SHRUBS. Choose the Divide tool on the Draw toolbar (refer to figure 7.2) and pick ①. AutoCAD LT issues the following prompt:

   ```
   <Number of segments>/Block:
   ```

2. Type **200**. AutoCAD LT divides the perimeter fence by adding 199 points (PDMODE 3). This is not what was intended; you meant to add shrubbery along the fence, so choose the Undo button on the Standard toolbar. AutoCAD LT reverses the operation.

3. Again choose the Divide tool, and pick the same location. This time, type **B** to indicate a block to insert. Type **SHRUBS**. Accept the default block alignment with the object. Enter **200** for the number of segments.

4. Press Enter to repeat the DIVIDE command. This time, pick ②, type **B** and then **BENCH**. Accept the default alignment, and enter 20 for the number of segments.

5. Choose the Measure tool on the Draw toolbar and pick ③. AutoCAD LT issues the following prompt:

   ```
   <Segment length>/Block:
   ```

6. Type **B** and then type **LIGHTPOLE**. Accept the default alignment and enter **100'** for the segment length. Your drawing should appear as shown in figure 7.7.

7. Choose the Zoom Out tool to see the shrubs, benches, and lights along the complete fence and path.

8. Save the drawing.

Figure 7.7

CHAP07B drawing with shrubs, benches, and lightpoles.

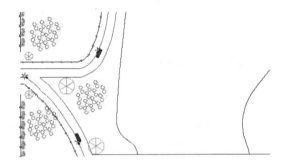

T_{IP}

DIVIDE and MEASURE create a Previous selection set, which enables easy selection of inserted blocks for editing.

In the next section, you learn the benefits of using polylines over simple lines and arcs.

Drawing Polylines

A polyline is a connected series of lines and arcs that comprise a single object. Figure 7.8 shows samples of polylines.

Figure 7.8

Several types of polylines.

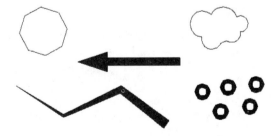

AutoCAD LT stores information such as tangent direction and line width at each vertex (endpoint) along the polyline path. Polylines offer two distinct advantages over lines. First, versatility: they can be straight or curved, thin or wide, one width or tapered. Second, editing operations are easier; because each segment is connected, you need only select one of the segments to work with the entire polyline.

The PLINE Command

The PLINE command draws polylines (plines). You can switch between line and arc modes while you add polyline vertices. After you pick the first point of a new polyline, AutoCAD LT issues the default line-mode prompt:

```
Arc/Close/Halfwidth/Length/Undo/Width/<Endpoint of line>:
```

The following list briefly describes each option:

- **Arc:** Switches from line mode to arc mode.

- **Close:** Closes the polyline by drawing a segment from the last endpoint to the initial start point, and exits.

- **Halfwidth:** Prompts for the distance from the center to the polyline's edges (half the actual width).

- **Length:** Prompts for the length of a new polyline segment. AutoCAD LT then draws the new segment at the same angle as the last line segment or tangent to the last arc segment.

- **Undo:** Undoes the last drawn segment. It also undoes any line option that immediately preceded drawing the segment, but will not undo arc options.

- **Width:** Prompts for a width (default 0) for the next segment. Tapered segments have different starting and ending widths. The ending width becomes the new default width.

- **Endpoint of line:** This default option prompts for the endpoint of the current line segment.

If you switch to Arc mode, AutoCAD LT issues the following prompt:

```
Angle/CEnter/CLose/Direction/Halfwidth/Line/Radius/
Second pt/Undo/Width/<Endpoint of arc>:
```

The following list briefly describes each option:

- **Angle:** Prompts for the included angle (a negative value draws the arc clockwise).

- **CEnter:** Prompts for the arc's center.

- **Close:** Same as line mode.

- **Direction:** Prompts for a tangent direction for the segment.

- **Halfwidth:** Same as line mode.

- **Line:** Switches from arc mode to line mode.

- **Radius:** Prompts for the arc's radius.

- **Second pt:** Selects the second point of a three-point arc.

- **Undo:** Same as line mode.

- **Width:** Same as line mode.

- **Endpoint of arc:** This default option prompts for the endpoint of the current arc segment.

In the following exercise, you use a single PLINE command to draw the partial floor plan shown in figure 7.9. Chapter 13, "Dimensioning Styles," discusses dimensioning techniques.

DRAWING POLYLINES

Using the PFLOOR drawing in the PROJECTS/CH07 folder of the CD-ROM as a prototype, create a new drawing called CHAP07C. Zoom to the view shown in figure 7.9. Make sure WALLS is the current layer, and that SNAP and GRID are on.

1. Choose the Polyline tool on the Draw toolbar and AutoCAD LT issues the `From point:` prompt. Pick the following points in sequence. If you make a mistake, type **U** and continue the exercise from the previously entered point.

```
From point: ①
Current line-width is 0'-0"
Arc/Close/Halfwidth/Length/Undo/Width/<Endpoint of line>: ②
Arc/Close/Halfwidth/Length/Undo/Width/<Endpoint of line>: A ↵
Angle/CEnter/CLose/Direction/Halfwidth/Line/Radius/Second pt/
➥Undo/Width/<Endpoint of arc>: S ↵
Second point: ③
```

```
End point: ④
Angle/CEnter/CLose/Direction/Halfwidth/Line/Radius/Second pt/
➥Undo/Width/<Endpoint of arc>: L ↵
Arc/Close/Halfwidth/Length/Undo/Width/<Endpoint of line>: ⑤
Arc/Close/Halfwidth/Length/Undo/Width/<Endpoint of line>: ⑥
Arc/Close/Halfwidth/Length/Undo/Width/<Endpoint of line>: ⑦
Arc/Close/Halfwidth/Length/Undo/Width/<Endpoint of line>: ⑧
Arc/Close/Halfwidth/Length/Undo/Width/<Endpoint of line>: ⑨
Arc/Close/Halfwidth/Length/Undo/Width/<Endpoint of line>: A ↵
Angle/CEnter/CLose/Direction/Halfwidth/Line/Radius/Second pt/
➥Undo/Width/<Endpoint of arc>: S ↵
Second point: ⑩
End point: ⑪
Angle/CEnter/CLose/Direction/Halfwidth/Line/Radius/Second pt/
➥Undo/Width/<Endpoint of arc>: L ↵
Arc/Close/Halfwidth/Length/Undo/Width/<Endpoint of line>: ⑫
Arc/Close/Halfwidth/Length/Undo/Width/<Endpoint of line>: ↵
Command:
```

2. Save the drawing.

AutoCAD LT treats the wall lines you drew in the previous exercise as a single polyline object. In the next section's exercise, you learn how to edit these wall lines by joining two polylines together and assigning a uniform width.

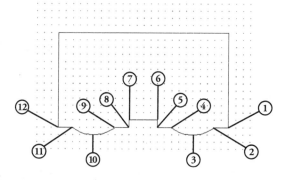

Figure 7.9

Completing the partial floor plan.

Editing Polylines

Polylines can contain a complex continuous series of line and arc segments, so AutoCAD LT provides the PEDIT command, which you use only to edit polylines.

PEDIT also contains a large list of subcommands for polyline properties. To manage this list, AutoCAD LT divides PEDIT into two groups of editing functions. The primary group of functions works on the entire polyline that you edit, and the second group works on the vertices that connect segments within the polyline.

The PEDIT command prompts for a polyline to edit. When you choose an open polyline, AutoCAD LT issues the following prompt:

```
Close/Join/Width/Edit vertex/Fit/Spline/Decurve/Ltype gen/Undo/eXit
➥<X>:
```

The following list briefly describes each option:

- **Close/Open:** Adds a segment (if needed) and joins the first and last vertices to create a continuous polyline. When the polyline is open, the prompt shows Close; when closed, the prompt shows Open.

- **Join:** (2D only) Enables you to add selected arcs, lines, and other polylines to an existing polyline. Endpoints must coincide exactly to be joined.

- **Width:** (2D only) Prompts for a single width for all polyline segments. The new width overrides any individual segment widths already stored. You also can edit individual segment widths by using a suboption of the Edit vertex option.

- **Edit vertex:** Presents suboptions that enable you to edit vertices and their adjoining segments.

- **Fit:** (2D only) Creates a smooth curve through the polyline vertices.

- **Spline curve:** Creates a curve controlled by, but not usually passing through, a framework of polyline vertices. AutoCAD LT controls the spline type and resolution by system variables.

- **Decurve:** Undoes a Fit or Spline curve back to its original definition.

- **Ltype gen:** (2D only) Controls whether linetypes are generated between vertices (Ltype gen OFF) or between the polylines' endpoints (Ltype gen ON), spanning vertices. This is ignored for polylines with tapered segments.

- **Undo:** Undoes the most recent editing function.

- **eXit:** This default option <x> exits PEDIT and returns to the Command: prompt.

In the following exercise, you join all wall lines together and change their width.

EDITING POLYLINES

Continue with the CHAP07C drawing.

1. Choose the Edit Polyline tool on the Draw toolbar and AutoCAD LT prompts for a polyline to edit. As shown in figure 7.10, pick ①.

2. At the next prompt, type **J**, pick ②, and then press Enter. AutoCAD LT informs you that three segments were added to the polyline.

3. Type **W** and enter **6"** as the new width for all segments. AutoCAD LT immediately updates the display to show the wide polyline.

4. Type **U** to undo the width modification, then **X** to exit the PEDIT command. The polylines are still joined.

5. Choose the Offset tool from the Modify toolbar. Enter **6"** for the offset distance, pick the polyline at ③. Select any interior point for the side to offset. AutoCAD LT creates the interior wall perimeter. Finally, press Enter to exit the OFFSET command. Your drawing should appear as shown in figure 7.10.

6. Save the drawing.

Figure 7.10

Joining and generating parallel wall lines.

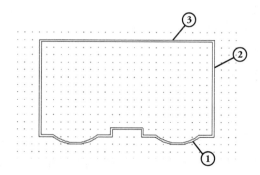

In the preceding exercise, you experimented with a 6" wall thickness using two methods. In the first method, you applied PEDIT to a single polyline and used the Width option. In the second method, you used OFFSET to generate a parallel polyline wall 6" apart.

Which method is correct? Your intended measurement technique determines the drawing procedure. If you measure distances from centers of walls, use the first method; if you measure distances from interior walls, use the second method.

TIP

You also can draw double (parallel) lines directly by using the DLINE command, which provides additional features including end cap styles and dragline alignment.

In the next section's exercise, you change the wall thickness on three sides of the building using a technique known as *vertex editing*.

Editing Polyline Vertices with PEDIT

Each polyline segment belongs to, and is controlled by, the preceding vertex. The PEDIT Edit vertex option provides another prompt with a separate set of suboptions, as follows:

```
Next/Previous/Break/Insert/Move/Regen/Straighten/Tangent/Width/eXit
➥<N>:
```

When you use these options, the current vertex is marked with an X. Move the X until you mark the vertex you want to edit.

The following list briefly describes each option:

- **Next/Previous:** Moves the X marker to a new current vertex. Next is the initial default.

- **Break:** Splits the polyline in two, or removes segments of a polyline at existing vertices.

- **Insert:** Adds a vertex at a point you specify.

- **Move:** Changes the location of the current (X-marked) vertex to a point you specify.

- **Regen:** Forces a regeneration of the polyline to see effects such as width changes or spline frame visibility.

- **Straighten:** Removes all intervening vertices between the two you select and replaces them with one straight segment.

- **Tangent:** Sets a tangent to the direction you specify at the currently marked vertex to control curve fitting. You can see the tangent angle at the vertex with an arrow, and you can drag it with the cursor or assign it from the keyboard.

- **Width:** Sets the starting and ending width of an individual polyline segment to the values you specify.

- **eXit:** Exits vertex editing and returns you to the Command: prompt.

In the following exercise, you increase the width of the two side walls to 12", leaving the top and bottom wall widths unchanged.

EDITING POLYLINE VERTICES

Continue with the CHAP07C drawing, and refer to figure 7.11 for the pick points.

1. Choose the Edit Polyline tool and pick the interior wall polyline at ①. Type **E** and AutoCAD LT enters vertex editing mode.

2. Type **M**. For the new vertex location, type **@6"<180** and then press Enter. Notice the X marker has moved 6 inches to the left. The default prompt response is now N, which will move the marker along the polyline path.

3. Press Enter repeatedly until AutoCAD LT locates the marker at the lower-left interior wall at ② (see fig. 7.11). Type **M**, followed by **@6"<0**, and then press Enter to move the marker 6" to the right.

4. Move the next vertex ③ 6" to the right, and the next vertex ④ 6" to the left. Your drawing should appear as shown in figure 7.12.

5. Type **X** to exit vertex editing. Type **X** again to exit the PEDIT command.

6. Save the drawing.

Figure 7.11

Using PEDIT Edit vertex to adjust wall boundaries.

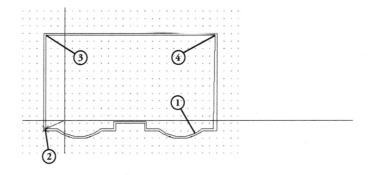

Figure 7.12

The CHAP07C drawing with modified wall boundaries.

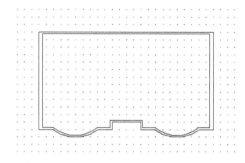

WARNING

Choosing Undo at the main PEDIT prompt undoes an entire vertex editing session.

In the preceding exercise, you adjusted the location of polyline vertices. You also can use grips with Stretch autoediting mode as an alternative method to accomplish the same task.

In the next section, you explore some drawing objects that possess a high degree of precision—ellipses and splines.

Using Ellipses and Splines

In AutoCAD LT, you can create full ellipses as well as elliptical arcs. Both use true mathematical representations of ellipses. Ellipses created in this manner have both center object snap points and might have quadrant object snap points.

NOTE

True mathematical ELLIPSEs and SPLINEs are new object types in the latest software version.

In previous releases of AutoCAD LT, ellipses were created using polyline approximations. True ellipses and elliptical arcs were not possible. The same ellipse approximations are supported in the current version, although true representations are more accurate. If the system variable PELLIPSE is set to 0 (the default), true ellipses are drawn.

A circle projected in isometric view appears as an ellipse, as figure 7.13 illustrates.

Figure 7.13

Isometric circles appear as ellipses.

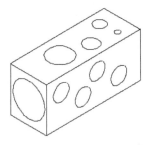

Another new object type is the *spline*, or more properly, a NURBS (Non-Uniform Rational Bézier Spline) curve. The SPLINE command uses higher-order polynomial curve-fitting techniques to draw a spline governed by control points, and results in a more versatile object than a spline-fit polyline. Splines often are used in shipbuilding and airfoil construction to optimize the hydraulic and aerodynamic design.

NOTE

Spline manipulations, although extremely versatile, can become overly technical. Consult the online help screens for details of the SPLINE and SPLINEDIT commands.

In the following exercise, you design a sailing regatta course. The labeled points in figure 7.14 represent buoys. You will use the ELLIPSE command to draw an elliptical arc (the sail) and the SPLINE command to lay out the course.

USING THE **ELLIPSE** AND **SPLINE** COMMANDS

Using the REGATTA drawing in the PROJECTS/CH07 folder of the CD-ROM as a prototype, create a new drawing called CHAP07D. Zoom to the view shown in figure 7.14.

Figure 7.14

Adding the boat sail with ELLIPSE Arc.

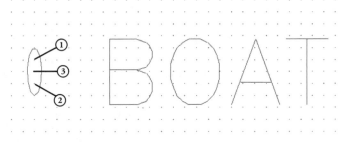

1. Set the current layer to BOAT. Choose the Ellipse Arc tool on the Draw toolbar. AutoCAD LT issues the following prompts:

    ```
    Arc/Center/<Axis endpoint 1>: _a
    <Axis endpoint 1>/Center: (1)
    Axis endpoint 2: (2)
    <Other axis distance>/Rotation:
    ```

    Turn SNAP off and drag to (3)

    ```
    Parameter/<start angle>: 0 ↵
    Parameter/Included/<end angle>: 180 ↵
    ```

2. Zoom to the drawing extents. Set the current layer to COURSE.

3. Set the Running Object Snap to Center. Choose the Spline tool on the Draw toolbar. Using figure 7.15 as a guide, pick the circles sequentially along the path of the course, in a "connect-the-dots" fashion. After you pick the last circle, type **C** to close the spline and press Enter to default the Tangent information.

Figure 7.15

Laying out the course with SPLINE.

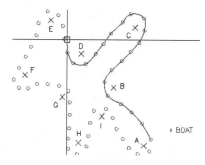

4. You decide that the path around buoy #3 is a little wide, so you will adjust the path closer to the buoy. Freeze layer PATH, and then zoom a window around buoy #3, as shown in figure 7.16. Next, pick the spline at (4) to display the grip markers. Pick the marker at (5) to move it closer (Stretch autoediting mode), and then pick the marker at (6) to adjust it as well.

5. Save the drawing.

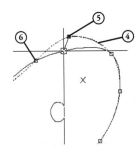

Figure 7.16

Grip-editing to adjust the course path.

TI P

Relocating spline points (as seen in the previous exercise) is much more easily accomplished through grip editing than using the SPLINEDIT command.

Manual drafting methods often employ light construction lines to lay out a drawing. They usually are erased before the final production drawing is issued, but are helpful in establishing centers, intersections, and projection lines of a multiview drawing.

In the next section, you learn about the new drawing objects that mimic manual construction lines.

NO T E

XLINEs and RAYs are new object types in the latest software version.

Using Xlines and Rays

An *xline* is a line with no starting point and extends to infinity in both directions. A *ray* has a finite starting point and extends from that point to infinity. Although both objects have infinite length, they do not affect the drawing limits or extents.

The name of the tool that issues the XLINE command is Construction Line; however, the object it creates is called an xline. In discussing xlines and rays, the term construction line is used to mean both objects.

TI P

Place all construction lines (xlines or rays) on a separate layer to facilitate subsequent plotting.

Figure 7.17 shows an isometric view of a block. In the next exercise, you use rays as construction lines to develop a multiview drawing of the block.

Figure 7.17

An isometric view of a block.

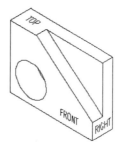

USING CONSTRUCTION LINES FOR MULTIVIEW DRAWINGS

Using the BLOCK3V drawing in the PROJECTS/CH07 folder of the CD-ROM as a prototype, create a new drawing called CHAP07E. The front and right-side views are drawn; you will develop the top view. Refer to figure 7.18 for the pick points.

Figure 7.18

Using construction lines in the CHAP07E multiview drawing.

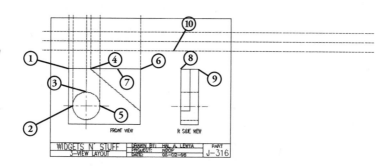

1. Set the current layer to CONST (which uses the HIDDEN linetype). Turn Ortho on and set the running object snap to intersection.

2. Choose the Ray tool on the Draw toolbar, and then pick ①. AutoCAD LT issues the **Through point:** prompt.

3. Pick any point above ①, and AutoCAD LT draws an infinite dashed ray from the intersection. Press Enter to exit the RAY command.

4. Following the same procedure in steps 2 and 3, draw a ray from ②, ③, ④, ⑤, and ⑥.

5. Choose the Construction Line tool (XLINE) on the Draw toolbar. Enter 1.0 for the offset distance, and then pick the top object line at ⑦. Pick any point above ⑦, and AutoCAD LT draws an xline in the top view. Press Enter to exit the XLINE command.

6. Press Enter to repeat the XLINE command, but this time, you show AutoCAD LT the offset distance by picking the intersections ⑧ and ⑨ on the side view. Next, pick ⑩ followed by any point above 10. To continue the next xline, pick the new line then a point above it. Press Enter to exit.

7. Use the TRIM command to cut back the new xlines and rays and change the properties (TRIM and DDCHPROP are covered in Chapter 6, "Editing Drawings") of the remaining top-view lines. Place lines on layer OBJ, HID, and CEN, according to the geometry legend shown in figure 7.19.

8. Save the drawing.

Figure 7.19

The completed top view of the CHAP07E drawing.

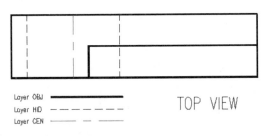

NOTE

Trimming an xline at one point results in a ray object; trimming an xline at two points (or a ray at one point) results in a line object.

Summary

In this chapter, you explored the use of polylines and splines to "broaden your horizons" with AutoCAD LT. In fact, using xlines and rays, you extended them all the way to infinity! As you continue to work with these commands, you will no doubt discover innovative ways to apply them. Don't be afraid to experiment—help is only a keystroke away.

DRAWING AND EDITING HATCH PATTERNS

In this chapter, you experiment with various hatching techniques. A hatch is a closed area filled with a pattern. As an example, a mechanical engineering drawing uses section lining (or poché) to depict the material composition of a sectioned object (see fig. 8.1). A business pie chart uses different shading methods and a legend to graphically explain the highlighted features (see fig. 8.2).

AutoCAD LT provides many options that enable you to accurately pattern-fill an enclosed area. In this chapter, you work with the following topics:

■ *Defining simple hatch areas*

■ *Selecting the hatch pattern*

■ *Previewing and applying the hatch*

■ *Inheriting hatch properties*

■ *Detecting boundaries and islands*

■ *Editing hatches*

■ *Direct hatching*

In general, hatching is a three-step process: define the boundary, select and preview the pattern, and then apply the hatch.

Sectioning an application.

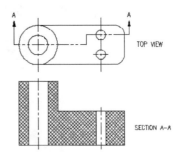

A pie chart application.

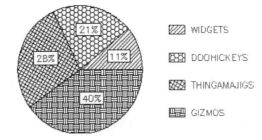

To begin a hatch operation, choose the Hatch tool on the Draw toolbar (see fig. 8.3). AutoCAD LT then issues the BHATCH command and presents the Boundary Hatch dialog box, shown in figure 8.4.

The Hatch tool.

Figure 8.4

*The Boundary Hatch
dialog box.*

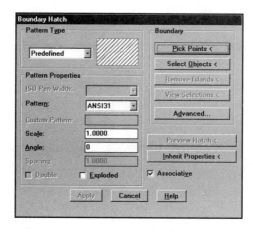

T
IP

To avoid editing a cluttered drawing, define one or more layers for hatching. You then can turn the layers on and off, as needed. As an added benefit, a separate layer (and color) enables you to control the line weight of the hatch at plot time.

Defining Simple Hatch Areas

The key to working with hatches successfully is to ensure that the boundary is closed. If intersections are not clean, the pattern can "bleed through" and begin to fill an unwanted region.

W
ARNING

If the hatch generates too slowly or is undesirable for any reason, press Esc as soon as possible. AutoCAD LT will terminate the pattern fill. If you press any other key, you must sit and wait! If the hatch is dense or drawn at a small scale, the size of the drawing can increase very quickly.

AutoCAD LT's hatching procedure provides a tremendous boost in your productivity. As the program quickly generates a pattern, you avoid the time otherwise spent to manually draw a specific line arrangement.

TI P

Save your drawing before starting a hatch operation. If the system locks up, you can recover your work.

The boundary itself can be simple or complex, as shown in figure 8.5.

Figure 8.5

Simple and complex hatch boundaries.

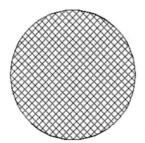 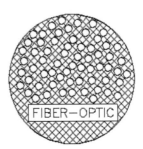

The objects that form a boundary are referred to as *boundary objects*. One method to obtain the hatch area is to select the boundary object(s) by choosing the Select Objects button in the Boundary Hatch dialog box (refer to figure 8.4). An alternate method to define the area to be hatched is to choose the Pick Points button. When you pick a point within the area to be hatched, BHATCH calculates and defines a closed boundary surrounding the selected point. If no boundary exists, a definition error occurs.

Depending on the situation, you most likely will find one method more convenient than the other for selecting the hatch area.

Selecting the Hatch Pattern

The next step to a successful hatch operation is to define the pattern parameters you want to apply. You can choose from three types of patterns, described in the following list:

- **Predefined:** This category refers to the patterns defined in the file ACLT.PAT, the hatch pattern file supplied with AutoCAD LT. (See figure 8.6 for examples.)

- **User-defined:** This category refers to patterns you can define using the BHATCH command. These patterns consist of one or two sets of parallel lines (see fig. 8.7). You can choose the angle and spacing of the lines in the first set, and optionally choose to have a second set of lines generated perpendicular to the first set, using the same spacing.

■ **Custom:** This category refers to hatch patterns defined in a file other than ACLT.PAT. For more information on customizing hatch patterns, see the AutoCAD LT user's guide.

Figure 8.6

Sample hatch patterns.

ANSI34   AR—BRELM   CORK

ESCHER   HOUND   STARS

Figure 8.7

Two user-defined hatch patterns.

Angle=30°
Spacing=0.25

Angle=60°
Spacing=0.75
Double

Setting Parameters for a Predefined Pattern

After you select the hatch pattern name from the drop-down list, you assign the parameters that control its generation. For a predefined pattern, the parameters are scale and angle (see fig. 8.8).

Figure 8.8

The Boundary Hatch dialog box for a predefined pattern.

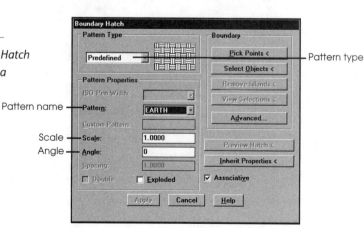

A pattern with the scale value set to 1 (default) appears with the exact lengths specified in the hatch definition. If the scale is greater than 1, AutoCAD LT enlarges the pattern; a value less than 1 reduces the pattern. This value changes the HPSCALE system variable (similar to the LTSCALE value with linetypes).

The angle value affects the pattern rotation. The default value of 0 results in no change; any other angle value yields a corresponding rotation of the pattern (although the ANSI patterns look as if they have a built-in 45° rotation).

TIP

> The hatch patterns that AutoCAD LT supplies are designed to be used with the continuous linetype. You can generate variations of the basic patterns, however, by using other linetypes and varying linetype scales. This especially is useful when you want a particular pattern to appear "lighter" than it would using a continuous line type.

Setting Parameters for a User-Defined Pattern

The parameters that specify a user-defined pattern are *angle*, *spacing*, and *double-hatching* (see fig. 8.9).

Figure 8.9

The Boundary Hatch dialog box for a user-defined pattern.

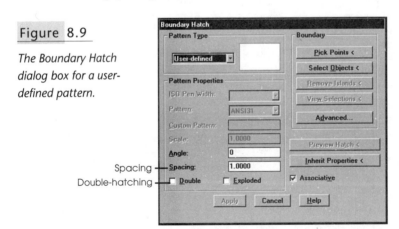

A user-defined pattern consists of one or two sets of parallel lines. The Angle value (default 0) defines the angle of the lines in the first set. The Spacing value (default 1 unit) defines the distance between the parallel lines. Enable the Double option to generate a second set of lines perpendicular to the first set.

TIP

You might be tempted to solid-fill a region by using a hatch pattern with a very small spacing value. Unfortunately, this method generates a substantial amount of vectors and wastes storage space. A better technique involves the use of solids or wide polylines.

Previewing and Applying the Hatch

After setting the pattern parameters, you are given the opportunity to "try before you buy." Choose the Preview Hatch button to view the resulting pattern without actually drawing it. If the result is unacceptable, go back and change the parameters. Continue to preview until satisfied, and then choose the Apply button.

Inheriting Hatch Properties

As you have seen, a hatch pattern contains properties such as pattern name, angle, scale, and spacing. If you want to match an existing pattern at another drawing location, a quick way is to choose the Inherit Properties button. You select the hatch you want to duplicate, and the BHATCH parameters are set to reproduce that hatch.

In the following exercise, you use BHATCH to hatch several rectangular areas.

HATCHING SIMPLE AREAS

Using the PIECHART drawing in the PROJECTS/CH08 directory of the CD-ROM as a prototype, create a new drawing called CHAP08A as shown in figure 8.10. Set the PATTERNS layer current.

1. Choose the Hatch tool from the Draw toolbar to display the Boundary Hatch dialog box. Ensure the pattern name is Predefined, ANSI31, Scale=1.0, and Angle=0.

2. Notice the default button is Pick Points. Press Enter and AutoCAD LT displays the following message:

   `Select internal point:`

   Pick the point inside the WIDGETS rectangle at ①. AutoCAD LT checks the surrounding area and displays the following messages:

```
Selecting everything...
Selecting everything visible...
Analyzing the selected data...
Analyzing internal islands...
```

and prompts for another internal point. Press Enter.

3. Choose the Preview Hatch button. The scale is too large, so choose the Continue button, reduce the scale to **0.6**, and then preview again. Choose the Apply button to complete the hatch operation.

4. For the DOOHICKEYS rectangle, assign the following hatch parameters: Predefined, HONEY, Scale=0.6, and Angle=0. Use the Select Objects method and pick the rectangle at ② and apply the hatch.

5. For the THINGAMAJIGS rectangle, choose User-defined in the Pattern type drop-down list. Assign Angle=60 and Spacing=0.09, and check the Double option. Use either of the previous methods to select the boundary, and then apply the hatch.

6. For the GIZMOS rectangle, choose the Inherit Properties button, and choose the existing pattern in the DOOHICKEYS rectangle. Then choose the Pattern drop-down list, select EARTH, and apply the hatch. Your drawing should appear as shown in figure 8.11.

7. Save the drawing.

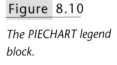

Figure 8.10

The PIECHART legend block.

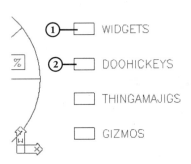

TI P

In the Boundary Hatch dialog box, you can change the current predefined pattern by choosing from the drop-down list or repeatedly clicking the image tile.

Figure 8.11

The legend block with
hatch patterns.

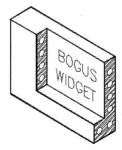

WIDGETS

DOOHICKEYS

THINGAMAJIGS

GIZMOS

Detecting Boundaries and Islands

A simple closed region is relatively easy to hatch. If an overall area contains individual subareas (called *islands*), however, the results might not be obvious. An island must be a closed area defined by one or more objects. Figure 8.12 shows a complex area with islands.

Figure 8.12

A complex area with
islands.

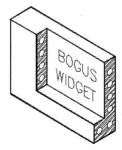

NOTE

> AutoCAD LT treats TEXT and MTEXT objects within a closed area as islands. Under default operating conditions, hatch patterns will not obscure the lettering.

In the following exercise, you hatch areas with islands—the individual segments of the pie.

HATCHING AREAS WITH ISLANDS

Continue with the CHAP08A drawing, and zoom to the view shown in figure 8.13. Set the PATTERNS layer current.

1. Choose the Hatch tool from the Draw toolbar to display the Boundary Hatch dialog box. Choose Inherit Properties and select ①.

2. Choose Pick Points and select ②. Press Enter and then choose Preview Hatch. Choose Continue, and then choose Apply. AutoCAD LT fills the WIDGETS segment with a pattern that matches its corresponding legend entry.

3. Repeating steps 1 and 2, inherit the properties from ③ and apply the pattern at ④. Similarly, inherit properties from ⑤ to ⑥ and from ⑦ to ⑧.

Your completed drawing should resemble figure 8.14.

4. Save the drawing.

Figure 8.13

Choosing pick points for hatching.

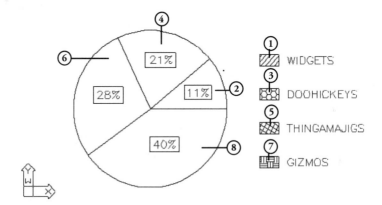

Figure 8.14

CHAP08A.DWG with hatched areas.

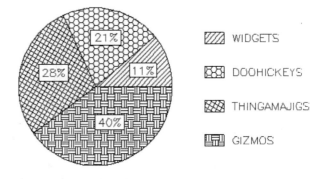

Editing Hatches

After you draw a hatch, you might find that you want to change either the pattern or its boundaries. AutoCAD LT makes it very easy to do both because by default, BHATCH objects are *associative*. This means that the hatch parameters, including the objects defining the hatch area, are recorded with the hatch object.

You use the HATCHEDIT command to edit hatch objects. In the next exercise, you alter one of the pie segments by assigning a new pattern.

CHANGING AN EXISTING HATCH PATTERN

Continue with the CHAP08A drawing, and zoom to the view shown in figure 8.15.

1. Choose the Edit Hatch tool from the Modify toolbar to display the Hatch Edit dialog box (see fig. 8.16). This dialog box is the same as the Boundary Hatch dialog box, with many of the options disabled (see fig. 8.17). You see the following prompt:

   ```
   Select hatch object:
   ```

2. Refer to figure 8.15 and choose ①. In the Pattern drop-down list, choose ANSI38, and then choose Apply.

3. To ensure the corresponding legend entry reflects this new pattern assignment, press Enter. The HATCHEDIT command repeats, and you choose ②. Choose Inherit Properties, rechoose ①, and then select Apply.

4. Save the drawing.

Figure 8.15

Altering the hatch pattern of the WIDGETS segment.

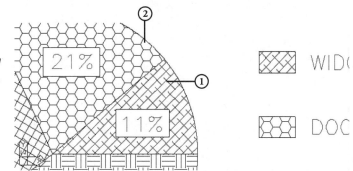

Figure 8.16

The Edit Hatch tool.

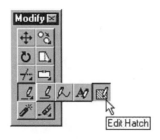

Figure 8.17

The Hatch Edit dialog box.

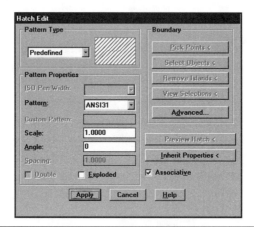

In the previous exercise, you changed the hatch pattern in one of the pie segments. As mentioned earlier, you also can change the boundary of an associative hatch and the AutoCAD LT regenerates the pattern to its new boundary.

In the next exercise, you change the boundary edge of the WIDGETS segment. You *increase* the pie segment percentage to 16 percent (from 11 percent), thereby decreasing the DOOHICKEYS segment to 16 percent (from 21 percent). Note that 5 percent of 360° equals 18°. Therefore, you will rotate the dividing line by this amount. Because the underlying hatches are associative, the two patterns automatically will update without further modifications.

CHANGING EXISTING HATCH BOUNDARIES

Continue with the CHAP08A drawing, and zoom to the view shown in figure 8.18. Set the current layer to PIE and turn off the PATTERNS layer.

1. Choose the dividing line at ① to display its grip markers (see fig. 8.18). Then choose the marker ② at the center of the circle.

2. Press the spacebar twice to display the ROTATE autoediting mode. Enter **18** for the angle. AutoCAD LT rotates the line, and analyzes the associative hatch. Press Esc twice to clear the grip markers.

3. Use DDMODIFY (covered in Chapter 6, "Editing Drawings") to change both segment text labels to 16 percent.

4. Use MOVE to relocate these text labels and surrounding boxes (the islands) within the modified segments. Note that once again AutoCAD LT analyzes the associative hatch at the completion of the edit operation.

5. Turn on the PATTERNS layer, and your drawing should resemble figure 8.19.

6. Save the drawing.

Figure 8.18

Altering the text, boundaries, and islands of adjacent segments.

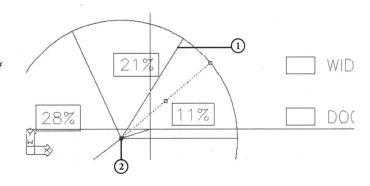

Figure 8.19

The updated hatches of adjacent segments.

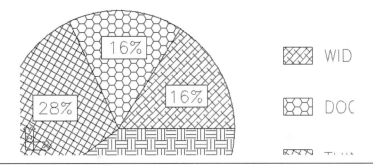

WARNING

If you freeze a layer that contains hatch patterns, you risk losing the hatch associativity. To prevent this from occurring, turn off the layer.

TIP

Chapter 12, "Advanced Text Concepts," introduces you to the DDEDIT command—a faster way of changing a text string.

All the exercises so far involved existing hatch boundaries. However, AutoCAD LT enables the placement of a pattern in an area that does not contain a boundary (see fig. 8.20). This method is called *direct hatching*.

Figure 8.20

Direct hatches without existing boundaries.

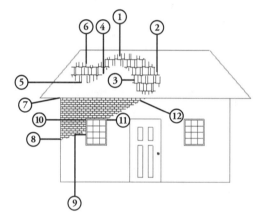

Direct Hatching

The HATCH command was the command-line predecessor of the BHATCH command in prior AutoCAD LT releases. Although the HATCH command is still included for upward compatibility, a new option (not available with BHATCH) enables you to define the area to be hatched by picking points that outline the intended boundary. As an added feature, you can choose to retain the generated polyline.

In the next exercise, you apply two representative samples of material composition to a house: cedar-shake shingles on the roof and brickwork on a wall.

HATCHING WITHOUT EXISTING BOUNDARIES

Using the MATHOUSE drawing in the PROJECTS/CH08 directory of the CD-ROM as a prototype, create a new drawing called CHAP08B as shown in figure 8.20. Set the MATERIALS layer current.

NOTE

> As you work the exercise, note the boundary for the roof material consists of arcs, whereas the boundary for the brickwork consists of straight lines.

1. To apply the pattern that represents cedar-shake shingles, type **HATCH** and then press Enter.

2. AutoCAD LT responds with the following command sequence:

```
Pattern (? or name/U,style) <ANSI31>: ARRSHKE ↵
Scale for pattern <1.0000>: 0.75 ↵
Angle for pattern <0>: ↵
Select hatch boundaries or RETURN for direct hatch option,
Select objects: ↵
Retain polyline? <N> ↵
From point: ①
Arc/Close/Length/Undo/<Next point>: A ↵
Angle/CEnter/CLose/...<Endpoint of arc>: ②
Angle/CEnter/CLose/...<Endpoint of arc>: ③
Angle/CEnter/CLose/...<Endpoint of arc>: ④
Angle/CEnter/CLose/...<Endpoint of arc>: ⑤
Angle/CEnter/CLose/...<Endpoint of arc>: ⑥
Angle/CEnter/CLose/...<Endpoint of arc>: CL ↵
From point or RETURN to apply hatch: ↵
Command:
```

3. To apply the pattern that represents brickwork, press Enter. The HATCH command repeats.

4. AutoCAD LT responds with the following command sequence:

```
Pattern (? or name/U,style) <AR-RSHKE>: BRICK ↵
Scale for pattern <1.0000>: 10.0 ↵
Angle for pattern <0>: ↵
Select hatch boundaries or RETURN for direct hatch option,
Select objects: ↵
Retain polyline? <N> ↵
From point: INT Enter of ⑦
Arc/Close/Length/Undo/<Next point>: MID Enter of ⑧
Arc/Close/Length/Undo/<Next point>: MID Enter of ⑨
Arc/Close/Length/Undo/<Next point>: INT Enter of ①, ⑩
Arc/Close/Length/Undo/<Next point>: INT Enter of ①, ①
Arc/Close/Length/Undo/<Next point>: MID Enter of ①, ②
```

```
Arc/Close/Length/Undo/<Next point>: C ↵
From point or RETURN to apply hatch: ↵
Command:
```

Your drawing should resemble figure 8.20.

5. Save the drawing.

WARNING

> A major drawback of the HATCH command is that it always generates nonassociative hatches. These hatches do not work with HATCHEDIT nor do they update automatically when you edit the boundary objects.

The direct hatch option of the HATCH command, in some situations, can be a timesaver. This single operation avoids the usual three-step process of drawing a boundary, using the BHATCH command, and finally, erasing objects.

TIP

> The BOUNDARY (or BPOLY) command is a great way to create a closed polyline boundary from existing objects without generating the interior hatch pattern. The resulting boundary can be used, for example, to determine the usable area of a room in a floor plan.

Summary

In this chapter, you worked with AutoCAD LT commands to draw and edit hatch patterns. As you discovered from the chapter exercises, you can employ hatches in a variety of applications, and with a speed boost unmatched in traditional hand drafting.

9

DRAWING WITH BASIC BLOCKS

In this chapter, you learn how to create and use objects called blocks to draw repetitive portions of a drawing quickly and accurately. Blocks are especially useful when drawing symbols, such as doors, windows, furniture, and so on. In this chapter, you learn to do the following:

- *Define basic blocks with the BMAKE command*

- *Draw defined blocks with the DDINSERT command*

- *The significance of layer 0 in defining blocks*

- *The significance of the BYBLOCK color and linetype setting*

- *Edit existing block definitions and insertions*

- *Insert drawings into the current drawing*

- *Exchange block definitions between drawings*

- *The approaches to create a symbol library*

- *Use blocks to create drawings consisting of details at multiple scales*

Creating a Block

The act of creating a block is often referred to as "defining the block" or "block definition." Whichever phrase you prefer, the procedure itself is quite simple:

1. First, draw the objects that are to be associated together as a block, using the appropriate LT drawing and editing commands.

2. Then, using the BMAKE command, create a block definition by assigning a name to the definition, choosing an insertion point, and selecting the objects to be included in the definition.

BMAKE (see fig. 9.1) is issued by choosing Make Block from the Draw pulldown menu or from the Block flyout of the Draw Toolbar.

Figure 9.1

The Block Definition dialog box displayed by BMAKE.

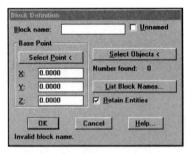

In the Block name field, enter the name to be assigned to the definition. The name cannot be longer than 31 characters and can consist of any combination of letters; digits; and the "$", "-", and "_" characters.

TIP

> Because spaces are not allowed in a block name, use a hyphen or an underscore in place of the space character to delineate words in a complex block name. Try to keep the names as short as possible, especially if you are planning to use the blocks in a drawing that might be used as an external reference (see Chapter 11, "External References").

If you cannot remember which blocks already exist in the drawing, choose the List Block Names button and a list of the block definitions already in the drawing is displayed.

WARNING

> Do not use the name of the current drawing as the name of a block definition. Doing so will prevent you from opening the drawing successfully. Unfortunately, LT does not prevent you from entering the drawing name as the block name. If you ever find yourself unable to open a drawing because a block in the drawing shares the drawing name, rename the drawing prior to opening it.

The Unnamed option is normally not enabled. If it is enabled, LT assigns an arbitrary name to the block definition. After entering a valid block name, use the Select Point button to select an insertion point for the block definition. The insertion point is the reference point that is used to position the objects making up the block definition.

TIP

> Pick a point that is useful in positioning the block. If the block includes a circle, for example, useful insertion points include the quadrant points or center point of the circle. When picking an insertion point, use object snap whenever possible to pick the point precisely.

After picking the insertion point, choose the Select Objects button and select the objects to be included in the block definition (from this point on in the book, the objects included in a block definition are referred to as the block's *component objects*). After you are finished selecting the objects, choose the OK button and the definition is completed. If you want visual confirmation of the objects included in the definition, disable the Retain Entities option and the selected objects are removed from the drawing. To retrieve the erased objects, issue the OOPS command.

WARNING

> Using the U or UNDO command not only retrieves the erased objects, but also deletes the newly defined block definition.

In the following exercise, you create a block definition to represent an office chair.

DRAWING A CHAIR SYMBOL

1. Begin a new drawing. Use the Quick Setup wizard. Choose architectural units and enter an area of 20' x 20'. Save the drawing with the name FURN.

2. Choose Standard Toolbar, Zoom Flyout, Zoom Window and enter the points 0',0' and 5',5'. Make sure the current layer is layer 0.

3. Choose Draw, Polygon Flyout, Rectangle. Enter the following points:

First corner: **2',2'** ⏎

Other corner: **@1'6,1'6** ⏎ **(see fig. 9.2)**

Figure 9.2

Creating a symbol for a chair.

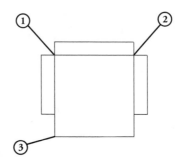

4. Choose the OSNAP button from the status bar. Enable Endpoint.

5. Repeat the Rectangle command and enter the following points:

First corner: **Pick ①**

Other corner: **@1'6,3** ⏎

6. Repeat the Rectangle command and enter the following points:

First corner: **Pick ①**

Other corner: **@-3,-1'1** ⏎

7. Repeat the Rectangle command and enter the following points:

First corner: **Pick ②**

Other corner: **@3,-1'1** ⏎

8. Choose Draw, Make Block. Enter CHAIR1 as the block name. Pick ③ as the insertion point. Select the four rectangles drawn.

The block definition CHAIR1 is now complete and ready to use. You may now turn off running object snap. Save the drawing.

Inserting a Block

Drawing a block definition is referred to as "inserting" the block. Each occurrence of a block is subsequently referred to as an "insertion" of the block or "block insertion." Use DDINSERT (see fig. 9.3) to draw insertions of a block definition. DDINSERT is issued by choosing Insert Block from the Draw pulldown menu or from the Block flyout of the Draw toolbar.

Figure 9.3

The Insert dialog box displayed by DDINSERT.

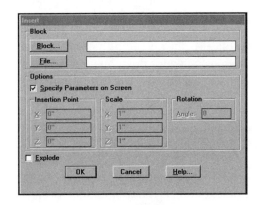

The procedure for inserting a block is straight forward.

- ■ Invoke DDINSERT and specify the name of the desired block definition.

- ■ Specify the insertion point and then choose scale factors and rotation angle.

Specify the name of the block to be inserted in the first field of the dialog box. Either type the name in the text edit box or choose the Block button and select the block name from the Defined Blocks dialog box (see fig. 9.4).

Figure 9.4

The Defined Blocks dialog box displayed by the Block button.

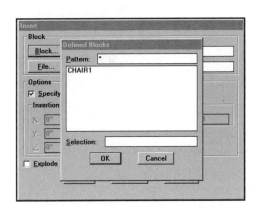

The second field, the File field, is used when inserting a drawing file as a block. This topic is discussed in detail in a later section in this chapter, "Inserting Drawings As Blocks." For now, leave this field blank.

When inserting a block, you specify an insertion point; the X, Y, and Z scale factors; and the rotation angle of the insertion. The insertion point is the point at which you want to place the block and it corresponds to the insertion point chosen when defining the block definition. The scale factors enable you to enlarge or shrink the original block definition, whereas the rotation angle enables you to rotate the insertion about its insertion point.

By default all of the preceding parameters are specified on screen, which means that you are prompted for the remaining information at the command line rather than through the dialog box. The first prompt you see asks for the insertion point:

```
Insertion point:
```

Next, you are prompted for a scale factor:

```
X scale factor <1> / Corner / XYZ:
```

Enter the X scale factor or accept the default value of 1 for the X scale factor. Use the Corner option if you want to specify the X and Y scale factors via a window, the width and height of which correspond to the X and Y scale factors, respectively. The XYZ option is chosen if you want to type the X, Y, and Z scale factors. The XYZ option must be specified if you want to enter a Z scale factor explicitly, otherwise, the Z scale factor is made equal to the X scale factor.

As you choose an insertion point, an image of the block is dragged on the screen. The image being dragged can be adjusted to reflect the final scale and or rotation angle by entering any of the following parameters:

Parameter	Associated Value
R	Rotation angle of insertion
S	Uniform scale of insertion
X	X scale factor of insertion
Y	Y scale factor of insertion
Z	Z scale factor of insertion

TIP

Unless you are dealing with 3D drawings, you only have to specify the X and Y scale factors.

Alternatively, set the insertion point and scale factors through the Options portion of the dialog box by disabling the Specify Parameters on Screen option.

The last option in the Insert dialog box is the Explode option. Normally, this option is not enabled and the insertion is drawn as a single object. When it is enabled, the insertion is drawn as a collection of its component objects rather than as a single block object. Enable this option only when you intend to change the objects making up the block insertion.

In the following exercise, you insert the block created in the previous exercise.

INSERTING SOME CHAIRS

1. Continue to use the drawing FURN. Choose Zoom Out from the Standard Toolbar.

2. From the Modify toolbar, choose Erase and erase the rectangles you drew in the previous exercise.

3. Choose Draw, Circle flyout, Center, Radius and enter the following:

    ```
    CIRCLE 3P/TTR/<Center point>: 5',3' ↵
    Diameter/<Radius>: 2'6 ↵
    ```

4. Choose Draw, Insert Block. Enter CHAIR1 as the block name. Choose the OK button and enter the following:

    ```
    Insertion point: 8',3' ↵
    X scale factor <1> / Corner / XYZ: ↵
    Y scale factor (default=X): ↵
    Rotation angle <0>: -90 ↵
    ```

5. Select the chair to display its grip point. Select the grip point and enter the following:

    ```
    ** STRETCH **
    <Stretch to point>/Base point/Copy/Undo/eXit: @0,7.5 ↵
    ```

NOTE

If the midpoint of the front edge of the chain had been chosen as the insertion point, the preceding stretch operation would have been unnecessary. The moral is choose the insertion point carefully.

6. The chair should still be highlighted. Select its grip point and press the Enter key until you see the ROTATE command. Enter the following:

```
** ROTATE **
<Rotation angle>/Base point/Copy/Undo/Reference/eXit: C ↵
** ROTATE (multiple) **
<Rotation angle>/Base point/Copy/Undo/Reference/eXit: B ↵
Base point: Using CEN object snap, pick ① (see fig. 9.5)
** ROTATE (multiple) **
<Rotation angle>/Base point/Copy/Undo/Reference/eXit: Turn ORTHO on and
pick ②
** ROTATE (multiple) **
<Rotation angle>/Base point/Copy/Undo/Reference/eXit: Pick ③
** ROTATE (multiple) **
<Rotation angle>/Base point/Copy/Undo/Reference/eXit: Pick ④
** ROTATE (multiple) **
<Rotation angle>/Base point/Copy/Undo/Reference/eXit: ↵
```

You now have an arrangement of a 5' round table and four chairs. Save the drawing.

Figure 9.5

Inserting chairs around a table.

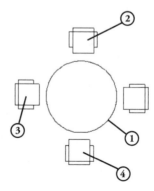

Nested Blocks and Levels

Block insertions also may be selected for inclusion in other block definitions. Including block insertions in a block definition is referred to as "nesting" blocks and the depth of the nesting is referred to as "levels." Suppose, for example, that you create a block consisting of lines and name it A1. Then, you create another block definition named B1 and include an insertion of A1. A1 is nested within B1 and is referred to as being nested at level 1 of B1. If you create a new block named C1 and include an insertion of B1, then C1 will have B1 and A1 nested within it. A1 is nested at level 1 of C1 and B1 is nested at level 2 of C1.

TIP

> Nesting can continue forever; however, having too many levels of nesting can make managing blocks cumbersome and is not recommended. Limit nesting to 1 or 2 levels.

In the next exercise, you create a nested block using the chairs you just drew.

CREATING A NESTED BLOCK

1. Continue to use the drawing FURN. Choose Draw, Block flyout, Make Block.

2. Enter SET1 as the block name. Choose the Select Point button and use center object snap to select the circle. Choose the Select Objects button and select the circle and 4 chairs. Choose the OK button.

3. Choose Draw, Block flyout, Insert Block and insert the block SET1.

SET1 is a nested block containing four insertions of CHAIR1.

Insertions, Object Snaps, and Grips

An insertion of a block behaves like a single object and has a unique object snap point—its insertion point. You can select this point by using the Insert object snap. You also can continue to select the relevant object snap points of the component objects of the insertion.

Just as you have a unique insertion point for a block insertion, you also have a unique grip point at the insertion point of the block. If you want, you can also reference the grip points of the component objects by enabling the Enable Grips Within Blocks option in the Grips dialog box (see fig. 9.6).

Figure 9.6

The Grips dialog box.

Blocks and Layers

Objects drawn for inclusion in a block definition, the component objects, may be drawn on a single common layer or spread over several layers. When the objects are associated together in a block definition, the layer information is preserved in the definition and is used when the block is inserted.

If you draw a component object on layer 0, the object is drawn on the current layer, or *insertion layer,* upon insertion. If the component object is drawn on any other layer other than layer 0, then upon insertion, that object is drawn on its original layer. You draw the object on a layer other than layer 0 when you want that object to be drawn on that particular layer regardless of the current layer.

While you can draw the component objects on multiple layers, you should only do so when you want the ability to control the visibility of a portion of the block insertion. A good example is a block definition that includes some hatching. At times, you might want the hatching to be visible and at other times you might want the hatching to be invisible with the rest of the insertion visible. You accomplish this by drawing the component hatch object on a layer separate from the layers inhabited by the other component objects. This gives you the option of turning off the layer containing the hatching independently of the layers containing the remainder of the block.

Freezing Versus Turning Off Layers

To make any object invisible, you either turn off or freeze the layer the object resides on. With blocks, there are three distinct cases, and the effect of freezing or turning off a layer can differ.

- A block definition that has all its component objects drawn on layer 0.

  Upon insertion of such a block, all the component objects are drawn on the block's insertion layer. Whether you turn off or freeze the insertion layer, the entire insertion becomes invisible.

- A block definition that has all its components drawn on a layer or group of layers, other than layer 0.

  Upon insertion of such a block, all the component objects are drawn on their original layers, which may be different from the insertion layer. If you turn off or freeze a layer other than a block's insertion layer, only the objects residing on that layer become invisible. If you turn off the insertion layer, only the component objects residing on that layer are affected, and the remainder of the insertion remains visible. If, however, you freeze the insertion layer, the entire block insertion becomes invisible, including the component objects residing on layers that are thawed and on.

- A block definition that has all its component objects drawn on multiple layers, including layer 0.

  Upon insertion of such a block, all the component objects that were originally drawn on layer 0 are drawn on the current layer, while the component objects that were originally drawn on layers other than layer 0 are drawn on their original layers. If the insertion layer is turned off, only the component objects residing on that layer becomes invisible, leaving the remainder of the block insertion visible. If the insertion layer is frozen, then the entire block insertion becomes invisible even if parts of the insertion reside on layers that are thawed and on.

In the following exercise, you observe the effects of turning off layers versus freezing the layers by drawing a new table/chair arrangement using two layers and define a new block with them.

BLOCKS AND LAYERS

1. Continue to use the drawing FURN. Make sure layer 0 is current. Choose Zoom Flyout, then Zoom Window from the Standard Toolbar, and enter the following points:

```
ZOOM All/Center/Extents/Previous/Window/<Scale(X/XP)>: 10',10' ↵
Other corner: 20',20' ↵
```

In the next step, you draw a table.

2. Choose Draw, Polygon flyout, Rectangle and enter the following points:

```
First corner: 12',11' ↵
Other corner: @5',3' ↵
```

Next, draw the chair on a new layer.

3. Choose Format, Layers and make a new layer named CHAIRS. Assign the color red to CHAIRS and make it current.

4. Choose Draw, Block flyout, Insert Block and enter CHAIR1 as the block name. Choose the OK button and enter the following:

```
Insertion point: 13'9,14'6 ↵
X scale factor <1> / Corner / XYZ: ↵
Y scale factor (default=X): ↵
Rotation angle <0>: ↵
```

5. Choose Draw, Make Block and enter SET2 as the name of the block. Choose Select Point and select ① (see fig. 9.7) using endpoint object snap. Choose Select Objects and select the table and chair. Choose OK.

Figure 9.7

Creating a multi-layer block definition.

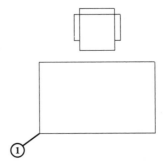

Next, you insert the newly defined block.

6. Choose Layers from the Standard Toolbar and make a new layer named FURNITURE. Assign the color green to FURNITURE and make it current.

7. Choose Draw, Block, Insert Block and insert SET1 anywhere on your drawing. Use scale factors of 1 and a rotation angle of 0.

   Notice that SET1 is drawn in green because it is on layer FURNITURE.

8. Insert the block SET2 anywhere on your drawing. Use scale factors of 1 and a rotation angle of 0.

   Notice that the table is drawn in green because it is on layer FURNITURE, but the chair is red because it is on layer CHAIRS.

9. Make layer 0 current. Turn off layer FURNITURE. Notice that the table in the SET2 insertion disappears, leaving the chair visible. The SET1 insertion disappears completely because all the component objects were drawn on layer FURNITURE.

10. Now, freeze layer FURNITURE. SET2 disappears completely, even though layer CHAIRS is still thawed and on.

11. Save the drawing.

Colors, Linetypes, and BYBLOCK

The colors with which the block's original component objects were drawn determines the colors that insertions are drawn with. There are three options for assigning a color to an object: BYLAYER, a specific color (such as red or green), or BYBLOCK. If a component object was drawn on layer 0 with a BYLAYER color, then the object is drawn with the color assigned to the insertion layer upon insertion, regardless of the value of the current object color (see DDEMODES). If a component object of a block was drawn with a specific color assignment, the object is drawn in its original color upon insertion, regardless of the layer the object is drawn on or the value of the current object color.

When the current object color is set to BYBLOCK, objects are drawn in white, no matter what color is assigned to the layer the object is drawn on. If you draw a block's component objects with a BYBLOCK color setting, the objects are drawn with the current object color setting upon insertion. If the current object color is BYLAYER, then the component objects are drawn with the color assigned to the insertion layer. If the current object color is set to a specific color, then the insertion is drawn in that color.

Insertions that have composed objects drawn with a BYBLOCK color assignment are more flexible in changing colors. When a component object is drawn with a BYLAYER color setting, the only way its color can be changed is to change the color assigned to the layer the object is drawn on. If a component object is drawn with a specific color assignment, then its color cannot be changed. With a component object drawn with BYBLOCK color, its color may be changed just like any other object.

The current object linetype also may be set to BYLAYER, BYBLOCK, or a specific linetype. When the current linetype is set to BYBLOCK, objects are drawn with the continuous linetype until they are included in a block definition and subsequently inserted. The preceding discussion about color assignments also applies to linetypes.

Editing Block Insertions and Definitions

At times, you might need to edit a block insertion or even to change the block definition itself. In both cases, a specific procedure has to be used to affect the change.

Editing Insertions

An insertion of a block is treated as a single object. As such, you cannot edit any of the component object other than changing colors or linetypes. Even then, you can only change the color and linetype of the component objects if they were originally drawn with a BYLAYER or BYBLOCK setting.

If the component objects of an insertion are to be edited, the EXPLODE command must first be applied. The EXPLODE command replaces an insertion of a block with its original component objects. Once an insertion is exploded, its component objects may be edited since they are no longer associated together as a single object.

If you know at the time of insertion that the insertion is to be edited, the Explode option in the Insert dialog box can be enabled. Enabling the Explode option causes the insertion to be drawn in an exploded state. One side effect of enabling this option is that only a uniform scale factor can be specified instead of having the usual option of specifying different X,Y,Z scale factors.

WARNING

When an insertion is exploded, all its component objects that were originally drawn on layer 0 are redrawn on layer 0, not the insertion layer. All component objects that were drawn with a BYBLOCK color or linetype assignment, are redrawn in white or with a continuous linetype.

Editing Block Definitions

To revise a block definition, you must first draw the revised component objects. Then you issue the BMAKE command specifying the name of the block you wish to redefine. Because the block definition already exists, you are asked if you really want to redefine the block. If the answer is "Yes," then you can proceed to define a new insertion point and select the revised components objects. Upon completion of the BMAKE command, LT automatically goes through the drawing and updates all insertions of the block to reflect the new block definition.

Block definitions are stored in the drawing file. Revising a block definition in one drawing does not automatically cause a change in that same block definition stored in other drawings. To revise the same block definition in multiple drawings, you have to export the revised block definition (see "Transferring Blocks Between Drawings) and then insert it into the other drawings (see "Inserting Drawings As Blocks").

In the following exercise, you revise the SET2 block.

REVISING THE BLOCK SET2

1. Continue to use the drawing FURN. Choose View Flyout, then Zoom Window from the Standard Toolbar, and enter the following points:

```
ZOOM All/Center/Extents/Previous/Window/<Scale(X/XP)>: 0,10' ↵
Other corner: 10',20' ↵
```

Make sure FURNITURE is thawed and current.

2. Choose Draw, Block Flyout, Insert Block, Insert Block. Enter the name SET2 and the following:

```
Insertion point: 5',14' ↵
X scale factor <1> / Corner / XYZ: ↵
Y scale factor (default=X): ↵
Rotation angle <0>: ↵
```

3. Choose Modify, Explode and select the SET2 insertion that you just drew. The insertion is replaced with its original component objects.

4. Explode one of the chairs. Magnify the view of the exploded chair. The chair has to be exploded before it can be modified because it is an insertion of the block CHAIR1.

5. Choose Modify, Fillet and set the radius to 1". Repeat the FILLET command and specify the Polyline option. Pick ① (see fig. 9.8).

Figure 9.8

Changing the chair block.

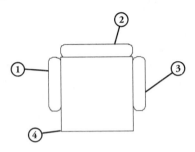

6. Repeat the FILLET command. Specify the Polyline option and pick ②.

7. Repeat the FILLET command. Specify the Polyline option and pick ③.

8. Choose Draw, Block Flyout, Make Block and enter CHAIR1 as the block name. Using endpoint object snap, pick ④ as the base point and select the four rectangles. When you choose the OK button, a warning message is displayed telling you that the block already exists. Choose the Redefine button.

    Adjust the view so that you can see the rest of the drawing. Examine all the other insertions. Notice that the chairs in all of them have been modified. Save the drawing.

Inserting Drawings as Blocks

DDINSERT is also used to insert other drawings into the current drawing as blocks. When a drawing filename is specified in the File text edit box of the INSERT dialog box (refer to figure 9.3), LT retrieves a copy of the drawing and imports the copy into the current drawing as a block definition. By default, the name of the new block is the same as the name of the drawing file being imported. The block name can, of course, be changed prior to choosing OK to complete the command.

By default, the insertion point of the new block is the point 0,0 in the drawing being imported. The insertion point can be changed by opening the drawing to be imported and issuing the BASE command. BASE enables the user to change the base insertion point of the current drawing, which is the point that is used as the insertion point should the drawing be imported into another drawing as a block. BASE is not listed in any of the pulldown menus or toolbars so it must be typed.

Once the copy of the drawing is imported into the current drawing as a block, LT does not maintain any links between the block definition and the original drawing file. If the drawing file is subsequently changed, the block version of the drawing is not affected; a copy of the revised drawing file would have to be re-imported via the DDINSERT command if the block definition is to be updated.

Transferring Blocks Between Drawings

Block definitions are stored in the drawing file in which they are defined. To use a block definition created in one drawing in another drawing, one of two procedures must be utilized. One procedure involves using the EXPORT and DDINSERT commands, while the other procedure utilizes Windows 95's Cut/Copy & Paste commands.

Using EXPORT and INSERT

First, the block is exported with the EXPORT command (see fig. 9.9). EXPORT enables you to export a portion of the drawing, or even the entire drawing, to a new file using one of several formats. You will find the EXPORT command in the File pull-down menu.

Figure 9.9

The Export Data dialog box.

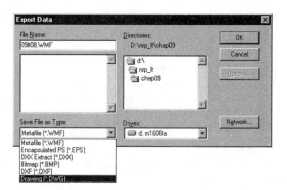

Because the EXPORT command can create files in a variety of formats, the filename must be typed with the .DWG file-name extension thus forcing EXPORT to create a drawing file. As an alternative, choose Drawing from the Save File as Type list and the .DWG file-name extension is automatically appended to the filename you type. Proceed with the rest of the command by choosing OK, after which you are prompted for a block name.

If the name of an existing block is entered, the block definition is exported to the new drawing file and inserted at 0,0. In the process, the insertion is exploded. The resulting file is just another drawing file, which can be opened for viewing or editing. Because DDINSERT can be used to import drawings as blocks (using the File button), any drawings created by EXPORT can be imported into other drawings as a block definition. EXPORT also can be used to export portions of the current drawing other than block definitions.

If you enter nothing and press Enter at the block name prompt, you are prompted to select an insertion point and objects. These prompts are similar to the actions taken when BMAKE is used to create new blocks. Instead of creating a block definition, the selected objects are exported to the new drawing file. The selected insertion point becomes the base point of the new drawing file. As a means of visual confirmation, the selected objects are erased from the current drawing and may be retrieved with the OOPS or U commands.

If * is entered as the block name, the entire drawing is exported to the new drawing file; however, all unreferenced objects, such as a layer with no objects drawn on it, are deleted from the new drawing file.

TIP

Specifying * as the block name is a handy way to clean up and decrease the file size of a drawing file since all unreferenced objects, such as unused layers or block definitions, are deleted.

Using Cut/Copy & Paste

The Cut or Copy commands of Windows 95 (found in the Edit pull-down menu) can be used to copy portions of the current drawing onto the Clipboard. Then, Paste (also found in the Edit pull-down menu) can be used to import the contents of the Clipboard into another drawing. If a block insertion is copied onto the Clipboard, that block is brought in but another block definition is also created. This second definition is what is actually inserted by Paste. Paste assigns an arbitrary name to this second block definition and nests the original block within this second definition. The arbitrary name always begins with A$ and the block is referred to as an anonymous block. Because of the arbitrary naming and the nesting of the block, it is better to explode the insertion drawn by Paste.

In the following exercise, you use both of the aforementioned techniques to transfer block definitions from one drawing to another.

TRANSFERRING THE BLOCKS

1. Continue to use the drawing FURN. Choose File, Export. Set the Save File as Type field to Drawing (*.dwg). Enter **CHAIR1** as the filename and choose OK. At the prompt for the block name, enter **CHAIR1**.

   A copy of the block CHAIR1 is written to the drawing file CHAIR1 and exploded.

2. Repeat the EXPORT command. Set the Save File as Type to "Drawing(*.DWG)" and enter **SET1.DWG** as the drawing name. Choose OK and enter **SET1** as the block name to be exported.

3. Using DDINSERT, insert SET2 somewhere in your drawing.

4. Choose Edit, Copy and select the SET2 insertion. This command copies selected objects to the Windows Clipboard.

5. Choose Open from the Standard Toolbar and save your changes. Open the drawing CHAIR1. This is the drawing file you created with the EXPORT command. The base insertion point of the drawing CHAIR1 corresponds to the insertion point of the block CHAIR1. If you want, type the command **BASE** but be sure not to change the default value.

6. From the Object Properties Toolbar, choose List from the Inquiry flyout. Select the parts of the chair and verify that the chair is not a block. EXPORT explodes the block that is exported.

7. Choose New from the Standard Toolbar and discard your changes. Begin a new drawing and use the Quick Setup wizard. Choose architectural units and set the area to 20'×20'. Save the drawing as LAYOUT.

8. Choose Draw, Block Flyout, Insert Block and set the filename to CHAIR1. Choose OK and insert the block anywhere in the drawing. A copy of the drawing CHAIR1 is made and brought into LAYOUT as the block CHAIR1. Notice that the block name is automatically set to the filename.

9. Choose Edit, Paste and insert the contents of the Clipboard.

10. From the Object Properties toolbar, choose List from the Inquiry flyout. Select the last insertion. Notice the name of the block begins with A$ (an anonymous block) and not SET2.

11. Choose Modify, Explode and select the last insertion.

12. From the Object Properties toolbar, choose List from the Inquiry flyout. Select the last insertion. Notice the block name is now SET2. SET2 was nested within the anonymous block.

Creating Symbol Libraries

One of the biggest boons to CAD productivity is the use of standard symbol libraries. There are quite a number of cost effective add-on products available that provide industry standard symbol libraries for a variety of applications. The best sources for information on such products is your LT dealer, Autodesk, or the publications that cover Autodesk products.

If you find yourself having to create your own symbol libraries, there are two basic approaches you can take. In the first approach, a drawing (the library drawing) is created for every symbol library to be created. In each library drawing, all the symbols for that library are drawn and defined as blocks. When a particular symbol is needed in another drawing, the library drawing is inserted. The desired symbol is inserted into the current drawing, along with all the other blocks in that particular library drawing. The advantage to this approach is that all related symbols are stored in a single library drawing which makes finding the symbols easy. The disadvantage is that even though only a couple of the symbols may be needed, the entire library of symbols must be imported, which in turn expands the size of your current drawing.

The second approach involves creating a symbol library consisting of a group of drawings where each drawing contains a single symbol. When a symbol is to be added to the library, a new drawing is created to hold the symbol. If a block definition is in the current drawing and is to be added to the symbol library, use the EXPORT command to export the block definition to a new drawing file in the library. The advantage to this approach is that only the symbols that are needed at any given time are imported, not necessarily the whole library. The disadvantage is that the symbol library might finally consist of a multitude of drawing files making it difficult to manage.

Tɪ P

If the second approach is chosen, use directories to group related symbols. Give some thought to the naming convention of the drawing files so that related symbols share some common prefix or suffix in their drawing filenames.

Using Blocks for Multi-Scale Drawings

DDINSERT can be used to create a complex drawing consisting of multiple details at varying scales (see fig. 9.10).

Figure 9.10

Composing a multi-scale layout.

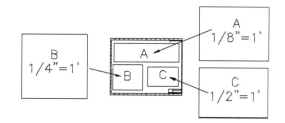

In the previous example, drawing D is to consist of three details—A, B and C—at different scales. First, each of the details is drawn at full size in separate drawing files. Detail A, for example, would be drawn in drawing A, which would be set up for $^1/_8$"=1' scale. Drawing D would be set up as a 1=1 scale drawing and would act as a host drawing for A, B and C. Drawing D is treated as the image of the final plot. Drafting details such as the title block, scale bars, and labels, are drawn in D. Drawings A, B, and C are then inserted into D as blocks and reduced by the appropriate scale factors. Drawing B, for example is inserted with a $^1/_{48}$ scale factor ($^1/_4$" = 1' scale). Drawing D would subsequently be plotted at a 1=1 scale.

How would the details be edited? Suppose Detail C needed some changes. The changes would be made in Drawing C. Then Drawing D would be opened and drawing C would be re-inserted. The latest version of Drawing C would replace the old version.

An alternate approach is to use the external references discussed in Chapter 11. Another approach to constructing a multi-scale drawing is to use paper space, which is discussed in Part IV, "Compositions & Plotting."

Summary

Blocks are a very useful tool for drawing repetitive symbols. In this chapter, you learned how to define, insert and revise blocks. In the next chapter, you learn how to make blocks a little more "intelligent" by including attribute definitions.

RELATED COMMANDS

BLOCK

SEE ALSO

INSERT

10

DRAWING WITH ADVANCED BLOCKS

In the previous chapter, you learned to create and insert basic blocks. In this chapter, you go one step further and learn to make blocks "intelligent" by incorporating attributes into block definitions. Attributes are objects that enable you to store text information with special characteristics in a block definition. In this chapter, you learn the following:

- *Defining and drawing attributes*

- *Incorporating attributes into a block definition*

- *Entering attribute values*

- *Controlling the display of attributes*

- *Editing inserted attributes*

- *Extracting attribute information*

Drawing Attribute Objects

An attribute is a special type of object designed to be incorporated into a block definition. DDATTDEF (see fig. 10.1) is used to draw attribute objects and is issued by choosing Define Attribute from the Draw pull-down menu or from the Attribute toolbar.

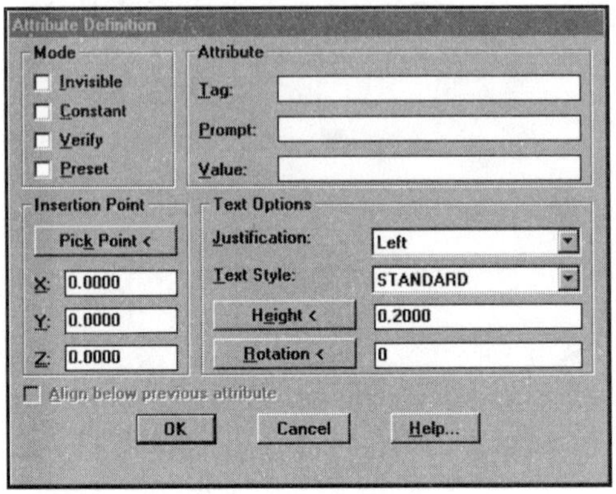

Figure 10.1

The Attribute Definition dialog box.

An attribute object is designed to store a text value. The attributes for a door symbol, for example, could describe its manufacturer, model number, and dimensions. There are two types of attributes: constant and variable attributes. The text value of a variable attribute can be changed at any time, whereas the text value of a constant attribute cannot be changed once it is defined. By default, DDATTDEF defines a variable attribute unless the Constant option in the Mode portion of the dialog box is enabled.

Every variable attribute object has a name that you assign called a tag name, an optional prompt (the text that is used to prompt the user to enter a value), and an optional value (the default value for the attribute). Every constant attribute object also has a tag name and a value (required for constant attributes), but not a prompt. A tag name can be up to 31 characters long and consist of letters, digits, and the characters "$", "-", and "_". The tag name is what actually appears on your drawing when the attribute is drawn.

TIP

Although assigning prompt and default values are optional when defining a variable attribute, it is always best to define them.

All attribute objects are visible when drawn. When the attribute is inserted as part of a block definition, however, the attribute can be drawn as a visible or invisible object. By default, attributes are defined to be inserted as visible objects. To have the attributes inserted as invisible objects, the Invisible mode must be enabled.

Tı p

Making an attribute invisible is useful when you want to attach text information to an insertion but do not want the text to clutter up the drawing. Whether visible or not, all attribute information can still be edited and extracted.

The Verify and Preset options affect the way an attribute is inserted only when a dialog box is not used to enter the attribute values (see the following section "Inserting Blocks with Attributes"), and the values are entered at the command prompt instead. By default, a dialog box is used to enter attribute values upon insertion; therefore, enabling these options has no affect until you choose not to use a dialog box to enter attribute values. When entering attribute values at the command prompt, the Verify option causes LT to prompt the user to confirm the attribute value typed. The Preset option causes the attributes to be inserted without any prompting for values (the default values are automatically used). Verify and Preset are only available for variable attributes and not for constant attributes.

Tı p

Using a dialog box is the easiest method for entering the attribute values. Therefore, do not disable the dialog box. Consequently, do not worry about enabling the Verify or Preset options.

Other than the special considerations discussed in the preceding paragraphs, drawing an attribute object is just like drawing a line of text (DTEXT command). A justification style, a text style, a text height (if the style is not a fixed height style), a rotation angle, and an insertion point have to be defined for each attribute. When defining multiple attributes, the Align below previous attribute option (bottom of dialog box) may be enabled. This option places the attribute immediately below the previously drawn attribute and with the same text parameters (such as justification and text height) as the previous attribute.

In the next exercise, you draw the component objects that are to be used to create two block definitions.

CREATING A REVISION SYMBOL

1. Begin a new drawing. Use the Quick Setup wizard. Choose decimal units and a 12×9 drawing area.

2. Choose Draw, Polygon flyout, Polygon and enter the following:

```
Number of sides <4>: 3 ↵
Edge/<Center of polygon>: 5,5 ↵
Radius of circle: 0.25 ↵
```

3. Choose Standard Toolbar, View flyout, Zoom window and zoom in on the triangle. Make a new layer named **REV_INFO**. Assign the color blue to REV_INFO and make it current.

4. Choose Draw, Define Attribute. Make sure all the modes are disabled. Enter **REV_NO** for the tag name. Enter **Revision number** for the prompt. Enter **1** for the value. Set 5,5 as the insertion point. Choose middle justification, the standard text style, a height of 0.15, and a rotation angle of 0. Choose OK.

You have just drawn your first attribute object.

5. Repeat the DDATTDEF command. Enable the Invisible mode while leaving all other modes disabled. Enter **REV_BY** for the tag name. Enter **Revised by** for the prompt. Enter **Nobody** for the value. Enable the Align below previous attribute option and choose OK.

6. Repeat the DDATTDEF command. Invisible mode should still be enabled. Enter **REV_DATE** for the tag name. Enter **Revision date** for the prompt. Enter **01/01/96** for the value. Make sure the Align below previous attribute option is enabled and choose OK.

7. Repeat the DDATTDEF command. In addition to the Invisible mode, enable the Constant mode. Enter **COMPANY** for the tag name and enter **NRP** for the value. Make sure the Align below previous attribute option is enabled and choose OK.

8. Choose Standard Toolbar, View flyout, Named views and name the current view **ORIGINALS**.

9. Save the drawing as **ATTRIB**.

Your drawing should look like figure 10.2.

Figure 10.2

Component objects for block creation.

Including Attributes in Blocks

After attribute objects are drawn, the objects must be incorporated into a block definition before they can be activated. A block can consist of attribute objects alone or attributes with other objects. Just as before, BMAKE is used to define blocks. Now, however, a new type of object is included in the object selection—the attribute object.

When multiple attribute objects are selected for the BMAKE command, the attributes should be selected in the order that they are to appear in the dialog box. The dialog box appears when the block is inserted. If a window is used to select the multiple attributes, the attributes usually will appear in the dialog box in the reverse order in which they were drawn.

In the next exercise, two blocks are created from the objects drawn in the previous exercise.

MAKING THE BLOCK DEFINITIONS

1. Continue to use the drawing ATTRIB.

2. Choose Draw, Block Flyout, Make Block. Enter **REV1** for the block name. Enter **5,5** for the base point. Select all the objects with a window. Choose OK to exit the dialog box.

3. Repeat the BMAKE command. Enter **REV2** for the block name. Enter **5,5** for the base point. Select the triangle first, then the attributes REV_NO, REV_BY, REV_DATE and COMPANY, in that order. *Do Not* use a window. Choose OK to exit the dialog box.

4. Save the drawing.

Inserting Blocks with Attributes

Attributes are active only when the block definition they are a part of is inserted. With variable attributes, you are prompted (with the prompt specified in DDATTDEF) to enter a value at the time of insertion. Constant attributes do not require any entry of text and are inserted with the value defined in DDATTDEF. A dialog box is used to solicit text values for variable attributes when the system variable ATTDIA is set to 1. The dialog box appears after the standard DDINSERT prompts for the insertion point, scale factors, and rotation angle.

Rather than using the dialog box, you can set the system variable ATTDIA to 0 (off) instead of the default value of 1 (on)to make the prompts appear at the command line. With ATTDIA off, the Verify and Preset options become active. If a variable attribute is defined with Verify enabled, then the user is asked to verify the entered text value. A variable attribute defined with Preset enabled is inserted with its default text value.

NOTE

As of this writing, the default value of ATTDIA is 0. In order to enable the usage of dialog boxes, set ATTDIA to 1.

There might be times when it is more convenient to have the variable attributes inserted with their assigned default values rather than having the user enter the values. To use the default values, turn off the system variable ATTREQ (set it to 0) to suppress all attribute prompting.

In the next exercise, you use the blocks created previously to see how attributes work.

INSERTING BLOCKS WITH ATTRIBUTES

1. Continue to use the drawing ATTRIB. Make a new layer named **REVISIONS**. Assign the color RED to REVISIONS and make it current. Zoom out to view the entire drawing area. Type **ATTDIA** at the Command: prompt. Set the value of ATTDIA to 1.

2. Choose Draw, Block flyout, Insert Block and insert the block REV1 anywhere on your drawing. Enter any values you want for the attribute values.

Notice that the constant attribute does not appear in the dialog box because no text entry for its value is required. Also note that the attributes appear in the dialog box in the reverse order in which they are drawn. This is a result of using a window to select the attributes for BMAKE.

3. Choose Draw, Block flyout, Insert Block and insert the block REV2 anywhere in the drawing. Enter any values you want for the attribute values.

In this case, the attributes appear in the dialog box in the order they were selected for BMAKE.

4. Type **ATTREQ** at the command prompt. Set the value of this system variable to 0.

5. Choose Draw, Block flyout, Insert Block and insert the block REV2 anywhere in the drawing.

Notice that no prompts appear; the attributes are drawn with their assigned default values when ATTREQ is off.

6. Save the drawing.

Attributes are not only useful for storing text data, but also for ensuring that the text values are drawn in a constant manner and position relative to the rest of the component objects of the block.

Controlling the Display of Inserted Attributes

The visibility mode, which originally defined the attributes, controls the visibility of inserted attributes. Additionally, you can control attribute visibility by using layers and the command ATTDISP.

To use layers to control attribute visibility, the attribute objects must be drawn on a layer separate from the rest of the component objects of a block definition. Then, visible attribute objects can be made visible or invisible simply by freezing/thawing or turning off/on the layer the attributes reside on. In extreme cases of blocks having multiple attributes, each attribute object can be drawn on its own layer so that the visibility of each attribute can be determined independently.

Use the command ATTDISP to control the display of attribute values throughout the drawing. ATTDISP is issued by choosing an option from the Attribute Display submenu. To display the Attribute Display submenu, choose Display from the Options menu. ATTDISP has three options:

■ **Normal:** The mode that defined the attribute object controls the attribute visibility.

- **ON:** All attributes are displayed even if the attributes are defined to be invisible.

- **OFF:** Attribute display is suppressed even if the attributes are defined to be visible.

As long as the layers the attributes reside on are thawed and on, ATTDISP will affect the attributes; otherwise, ATTDISP will have no effect.

In the next exercise, you make the invisible attributes visible.

VIEWING INVISIBLE ATTRIBUTES

1. Continue to use the drawing ATTRIB.

2. Choose Options, Display, Attribute Display, On. All attributes on layers that are thawed and on should now be visible.

3. Turn off layer REV_INFO. All attributes are now invisible.

4. Turn on layer REV_INFO and choose Options, Display, Attribute Display, Normal.

With ATTDISP, even attributes defined with the Invisible mode enabled can be viewed at any time.

Editing Attribute Objects and Values

Attribute objects can be edited before and after inclusion into block definitions. Even attributes in insertions can be edited to a certain degree. For each situation, there is a command or procedure that is used, and these are described in the following sections.

Revising Attribute Objects Not in Blocks

DDMODIFY (see fig. 10.3) is the best command to use to change any of the parameters defining an attribute object. Even parameters that are normally associated with text objects and not attribute objects, such as the Backward or Upside Down options, can be changed in the Modify Attribute Definition dialog box.

Figure 10.3

*The Modify Attribute
Definition dialog box.*

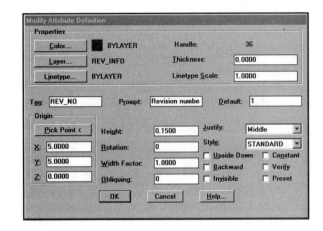

Although there are other commands, such as CHANGE or DDEDIT, that can be used to modify an attribute object, DDMODIFY gives you the most options for making changes. Furthermore, do not forget that editing commands such as COPY, MOVE, and SCALE also work on attributes.

Revising Attribute Objects in Block Definitions

You can also edit attribute objects that are already part of a block, but only with the following procedure:

1. An exploded version of the block definition must be available. If one is not available, then insert the block to be revised and explode the insertion. Alternatively, insert the block with the Explode option enabled.

2. Use DDMODIFY to make the desired changes in the attribute objects.

3. Revise the original block definition by using BMAKE with the original name of the block being revised. The new block definition replaces the old block definition.

Revising the attribute in a block definition does not affect the attributes of existing insertions. If you want the revisions to apply to existing insertions, you will have to erase the insertions and reinsert the block.

Editing Attributes in Insertions

Limited changes can be made to attributes in block insertions. If only the attribute values of a single insertion are to be edited, use the DDATTE command. DDATTE is issued by choosing Modify, Objects, Attribute, Single or by choosing Edit Attribute from the Attribute toolbar.

Selecting a single insertion with DDATTE results in all the attribute prompts and values being displayed in a dialog box. The attribute values can then be easily viewed and changed.

To edit multiple insertions, use ATTEDIT. ATTEDIT is issued by choosing Modify, Objects, Attribute, Global or by choosing Edit Attribute Globally from the Attribute toolbar. ATTEDIT can be used either to perform a text search and replace operations on selected attributes or to change certain properties of selected attributes, depending on how the first prompt, which follows, is answered.

```
Edit attributes one at a time? <Y>
```

To perform a text search and replace, answer "**No**" to this prompt. After entering "**No**," the next prompt appears.

```
Edit only attributes visible on screen? <Y>
```

If the response is "No," then all attributes in the drawing are automatically selected, as long as the attributes pass the Block name, attribute tag name, and attribute value specifications.

```
Block name specification <*>:
Attribute tag specification <*>:
Attribute value specification <*>:
```

Use the specifications to specify insertions with specific block names or attribute tag names or attribute values. The default value for each of these specifications is "*," which means "any and all." If you choose to edit only attributes visible on the screen, you are prompted to select the attributes to be changed after the specification prompts. In either case, the following prompts are displayed:

```
String to change:
New string:
```

First, enter the text that ATTEDIT is to search for and then the text that is to replace the found text.

To change selected properties of attributes, choose to edit attributes one at a time. After entering the block names, attribute tag names, and attribute value specifications, select the attributes to be edited. The following prompt is displayed and the attribute being edited is marked on the screen with a temporary "X":

```
Value/Position/Height/Angle/Style/Layer/Color/Next <N>:
```

- **Value:** Used to change the text value

- **Position:** Used to reposition the attribute

- **Height:** Used to change the height of the attribute

- **Angle:** Used to change the rotation angle of the attribute

- **Style:** Used to change the text style the attribute is drawn with

- **Layer:** Used to change the layer the attribute resides on

- **Color:** Used to change the color of the attribute

- **Next:** Used to move on to the next selected attribute. The current attribute— the attribute that is to be affected—is marked with a temporary "X" on the screen.

Remember, the attribute is part of a block insertion and normally cannot be edited. ATTEDIT, however, is designed to enable you to edit component attribute objects of insertions.

WARNING

ATTEDIT is supposed to allow the selection of one or more attributes when you choose to edit attributes one at a time or when you choose to edit only visible attributes. As of the time of this publication, a bug exists that restricts the user to selecting only one attribute.

In the next exercise, you change the text values of insertions and also change the attribute objects in the block definitions.

CHANGING ATTRIBUTES

1. Continue to use the drawing ATTRIB. Choose View, Named Views and restore the view ORIGINALS.

2. Choose Modify, Feature flyout, Fillet and set the radius to 0.1

3. Using the Polyline option of FILLET, round the corners of the triangle.

4. Choose Standard Toolbar, Properties and select the attribute object REV_NO. Change the height to 0.20 and choose OK. The results should be similar to that shown in figure 10.4.

5. Choose Draw, Block, Make Block. Enter the block name **REV2**. Select the modified triangle and the 4 attribute definitions. Choose OK to exit the dialog box and this time, you get a warning message indicating that the block TEST already exists. Choose the Redefine button.

   Note that the triangle in the existing insertions of REV2 change but not the visible attribute.

6. Choose Draw, Block, Insert Block and insert the block REV2 to verify that indeed, the height of the visible attribute has changed.

7. Choose Attribute, Edit Attribute and select one of the insertions. Change the attribute values and choose OK.

8. Save the drawing.

Figure 10.4

Modified component objects.

Extracting Attributes

The process of recording the attribute values of inserted blocks in an external text file is referred to as "extracting attribute values." Typically, attribute values are extracted from a drawing so that the values can be transferred to another software program to generate items, such as a bill of materials. The process of extraction is straightforward.

1. First, create an attribute template file. The template file contains the instructions that determine which block insertions are examined, what information is recorded for each insertion, and the format the data is written in.

2. Use the command DDATTEXT to extract the information.

Creating the Template File

The template file is an ASCII text file that you create. Windows 95 comes with the three editors Notepad, WordPad, and Edit (DOS). You can use any other editor (such as WordPerfect or Word) as long as the resulting file is a text file. The filename must end with ".txt."

T_I **P**

If you use WordPad or Notebook, press Enter after typing the last line. If you save the file with the cursor at the end of the last line of text, DDATTEXT will not read the file correctly. If you use the DOS Edit program, you need to save the file with the cursor at the end of the last line of text. If you press Enter at the end of the last line of text, DDATTEXT will not read the file correctly.

The template file consists of one or more lines of instructions. Each line of instruction consists of two items: the data type (or field name) to be extracted and the format the data type is to be recorded in.

    Data_type Data_format

The two items are separated by one or more spaces. The data format specification consists of seven characters.

    Cwww000 or Nwwwddd

The first character is either a C or N and determines whether the data is written as a character or numeric value. Next is a three-digit number (www) that specifies the total number of characters the data is to be allocated (also referred to as the field width). Finally, another three-digit number (ddd) specifies the number of decimal places that numeric data is to be recorded with. If the data is to be recorded as character data, then this last three-digit number is always "000." If the data is to be recorded as numeric data, then be sure that the field width includes the decimal point. The valid field names are detailed in the following table.

Table 10.1

Valid Field Names for Use in Extract Files

Field Name	Format	Description
attribute tag	Cwww000	Attribute value to be recorded as character data

continues

Field Name	Format	Description
attribute tag	Nwwwddd	Attribute value to be recorded as numeric data
BL:NAME	Cwww000	Block name
BL:X	Nwwwddd	X coordinate of block insertion point
BL:Y	Nwwwddd	Y coordinate of block insertion point
BL:Z	Nwwwddd	Z coordinate of block insertion point
BL:NUMBER	Nwww000	Block counter
BL:HANDLE	Cwww000	Block's handle
BL:LAYER	Cwww000	Block insertion layer name
BL:ORIENT	Nwwwddd	Block rotation angle
BL:XSCALE	Nwwwddd	X scale factor of block insertion
BL:YSCALE	Nwwwddd	Y scale factor of block insertion
BL:ZSCALE	Nwwwddd	Z scale factor of block insertion
BL:XEXTRUDE	Nwwwddd	X component of block's extrusion direction
BL:YEXTRUDE	Nwwwddd	Y component of block's extrusion direction
BL:ZEXTRUDE	Nwwwddd	Z component of block's extrusion direction
BL:LEVEL	Nwww000	Block nesting level
C:DELIM	c	For comma-delimited files, specifies the character used to separate fields, which by default, is ","
C:QUOTE	c	For comma-delimited files, specifies the character used to delimit text strings, which by default, is ""

In the extraction process, one line of data is recorded for every block insertion that contains at least one of the attribute tag names. For a tag name that is in the template file but is not part of a particular insertion, an empty or blank field is recorded for that attribute value.

Extracting the Data

Once the template file is created, the command DDATTEXT can be used to extract the attribute data. DDATTEXT cannot be found on any of the menus or toolbars, so type it (see fig. 10.5).

Figure 10.5

The Attribute Extraction dialog box.

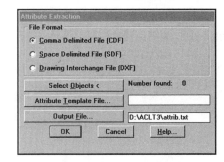

First, choose the file format. There are three options:

- **CDF:** Comma Delimited Format results in the data being separated by commas and text data enclosed with quotes:

  ```
  123,"test",0.2,"value"
  ```

- **SDF:** Space Delimited Format results in the data being separated by spaces:

  ```
  123    test0.2   value
  ```

  Each piece of data is written with enough blanks to fill out the field width specified in the template file. Numeric values are left justified and character values are right justified.

- **DXF:** Drawing eXchange Format results in the data being written in a DXF format.

The program that the data is to be transferred to determines the format needed. Check the documentation of the program receiving the data to see what format the data has to be in.

Choose the Select Objects button to select the insertions to be examined. Specify the template file to use with the Attribute Template File button. Specify the name of the output file to be created with the Output File button. When all the parameters are set, choose the OK button and the extraction is completed.

In the following exercise, you create a template file and extract the attributes for all insertions of REV1 and REV2.

EXTRACTING ATTRIBUTE DATA

1. Continue to use the drawing ATTRIB. Make sure that you have several insertions of REV1 and REV2.

2. Using the Start button on the taskbar, start Notepad from the accessories folder. Enter the following text:

BL:NAME   C010000
REV_NO   N010000
REV_BY   C015000
COMPANY   C015000

Be sure to press Enter at the end of the last line. Save the file as **EXTRACT.TXT** in the LT program directory. (The default is \ACLTWIN.)

3. Type the DDATTEXT at the `Command:` prompt of LT.

4. Specify the CDF format. Select all the objects in the drawing. Choose Attribute Template File and select the file EXTRACT.TXT. Accept the default extract file of EXTRACT.TXT and choose OK.

If the operation is carried out successfully, there will be a message in the command window indicating how many lines (records) were written in the extract file.

5. Using Notepad, view the contents of the extract file, ATTRIB.TXT.

The data file is now ready to be transferred to another program.

You are done with this drawing and can end the drawing.

Summary

Attributes are a very useful tool for recording text information in blocks such that the appearance of the text is consistent from one insertion to another. Attributes are also useful for recording text information with a symbol for later transference to another software package. Although it takes a little more thought, you will find using attributes is a superior method over using standard text objects for drawing text in a block.

RELATED COMMANDS

ATTDEF CHANGE   CHPROP
DDCHPROP   DDEDIT

11

EXTERNAL REFERENCES

The term "external reference" defines how one AutoCAD LT drawing relates to another drawing. An external reference is a standard AutoCAD LT drawing that is referenced to another drawing. An externally referenced drawing file (Xref) bears strong similarity to an inserted drawing file or block, in that you are prompted for a name (by way of a dialog box), an insertion point, the scale factors, and a rotation value.

The Xref drawing, however, is either overlaid or attached to the current drawing rather than inserted. Another similarity is that the Xref cannot be edited within what the "host" drawing—its primary intent is for "reference."

The word external is used because the referenced file is not physically a part of the host drawing when it is attached. When the host drawing is saved, AutoCAD LT simply makes note of the insertion point and file name of the Xref. The next time the host drawing is opened, LT loads the referenced file and attaches it at the insertion point. In addition to these issues, this chapter presents the benefits of using external references—more efficient drawings due to smaller drawings as well as the time-saving benefits of revising a single drawing rather than many.

- *Benefits of using Xrefs*
- *External references at work*
- *When to use XREF*
- *Utility features of the XREF command*

Benefits of Using External References

One of the primary benefits of using Xrefs is that the file size of the host drawing is minimized because it does not contain the entirety of the drawing, just a reference point.

Figure 11.1 shows a hospital drawing with a title block. The table that follows presents the individual file sizes of the two drawings, then compares the resulting file size if the hospital is *externally referenced* into the title block (the host) using the XREF command versus *inserting* the hospital drawing into the title block.

Figure 11.1

Benefits of XREF by comparison of file sizes.

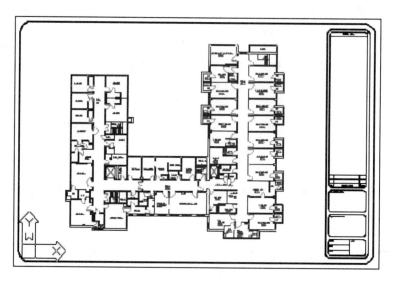

Title block drawing file size:	39,468 bytes
Hospital floorplan file size:	480,765 bytes
Final drawing size w/ floorplan externally referenced:	19,589 bytes
Final drawing size w/ floorplan INSERTed:	502,857 bytes

Another benefit of the resulting linkage between the Xref and the host is that if the externally referenced file has been changed, the next time the host drawing is opened, you will see the change. Figure 11.2 illustrates this concept.

Figure 11.2

Linkage benefits of using Xrefs.

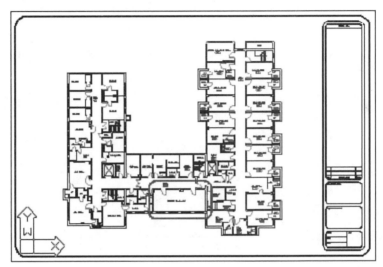

How Xrefs Work

This section presents exercises in which you encounter the fundamental principles involved in working with Xrefs. The Edit pull-down menu provides the method by which you can choose an XREF command option.

Attaching an External Reference File

The default option of Attach from the XREF command enables you to choose the drawing to be externally referenced from the Select File to Attach dialog box. In the following exercise, you begin a new drawing with a title block template, then insert and attach drawings.

ATTACHING EXTERNAL REFERENCE FILES

1. Begin a New drawing using the ANSI_A template, then make a new layer named PEN and set it to current.

2. Choose Draw, Insert Block, then the File button; then choose P-BODY.DWG from the PROJECTS/CH11 directory on the accompanying CD-ROM, then OK.

3. Enter **0,0** for the Insertion point and press Enter to accept the defaults for X scale factor, Y scale factor, and Rotation.

4. Choose Edit, External Reference, Attach; then choose P-CAP from the PROJECTS/CH11 directory on the accompanying CD-ROM, then OK and you see the following familiar prompt:

```
Insertion point:
```

5. Enter **0,0** and press Enter for the remaining prompts for scale factors and rotation.

6. Press the spacebar to reissue the XREF command, then press Enter for the Attach option.

7. Choose P-TIP from the PROJECTS/CH11 directory on the accompanying CD-ROM and attach the insertion point to 0,0. Your drawing should look like that shown in figure 11.3.

8. Choose Save and name the drawing **PEN01**.

Figure 11.3

The pen drawing created using INSERT and XREF.

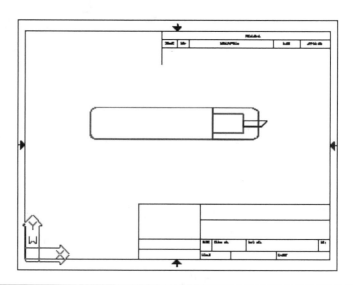

Making Changes to an External Reference File

Because an externally referenced file cannot be edited within the host (similar to a block), the drawing file itself must be edited. Then the host drawing will reflect the changes because a link exists between the Xref drawing and a host. In the next exercise, you edit the size of the pen cap drawing, then reopen the PEN01 drawing to see the change.

MODIFYING THE EXTERNAL REFERENCE FILE

1. Choose Open and save any changes to the PEN01 drawing; then choose the P-CAP drawing from the sample directory.

2. Zoom around the drawing so that your display resembles that shown in figure 11.4, then enter **S** to begin the STRETCH command.

3. Pick ① and ② as shown in figure 11.4, then press Enter.

4. When prompted for base point or displacement, enter **.5,0** and press Enter twice.

Figure 11.4

Editing the pen cap reference drawing.

5. Open the drawing PEN01 and save the changes to the P-CAP drawing.

6. The following messages should appear as the PEN01 is opened and the external reference drawings are resolved:

```
Resolve Xref P-CAP: P-CAP.DWG
P-CAP loaded.
Resolve Xref P-TIP: P-TIP.DWG
P-TIP loaded. Regenerating drawing.
```

Differences between Inserted and Attached Files

As mentioned at the beginning of this chapter, files that have been attached are similar to files that have been inserted. There are many commands that you can use to get information about the blocks and external references in a drawing.

Because an external reference file does not become an integral part of the host drawing, the layer names belonging to the Xref display the Xref name. In the following exercise, you view information about the Xrefs.

LISTING AND INQUIRING **XREF** SPECIFICS

1. Choose Edit, External Reference, List and you see the following:

```
?/Bind/Detach/Path/Reload/Overlay/<Attach>: _?
Xref(s) to list <*>:
```

2. Press Enter to accept the default for all Xrefs and you see the following table:

```
Xref name                      Path               Xref type
......................         ....               ..........
P-CAP                          P-CAP.DWG          Attach
P-TIP                          P-TIP.DWG          Attach

Total Xref(s): 2
```

3. Enter **BLOCK** at the Command: line, then type **?**, and press Enter twice. You will see the following table with information regarding blocks as well as external references:

```
Defined blocks.
P-BODY
P-CAP          Xref: resolved
P-TIP          Xref: resolved
REVDATE
TITLEBLOCK

User      External      Dependent    Unnamed
Blocks    References    Blocks       Blocks
  3          2            0            2
```

4. Enter **LIST** and pick the pen body and the pen cap; then press Enter, and you see the following information regarding the block and Xref:

```
BLOCK REFERENCE  Layer: PEN
Space: Model space
Handle = 103
P-BODY
at point, X=   0.0000  Y=   0.0000  Z=   0.0000
X scale factor    1.0000
Y scale factor    1.0000
rotation angle      0
Z scale factor    1.0000

BLOCK REFERENCE  Layer: PEN
Space: Model space
Handle = 109
P-CAP
External Reference
```

```
at point, X=   0.0000  Y=   0.0000  Z=   0.0000
X scale factor   1.0000
Y scale factor   1.0000
rotation angle      0
Z scale factor   1.0000
```

5. Choose Layers from the Standard toolbar to display the Layer Control dialog box as shown in figure 11.5. Notice that the P-CAP layer belongs to the CAP drawing, and the P-TIP layer is associated with the TIP drawing.

Figure 11.5

The layers associated with Xref files.

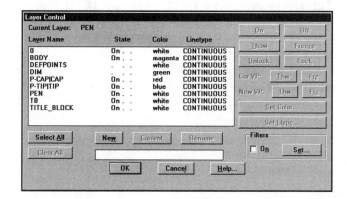

Detaching the Xref

As you learned in Chapter 10, "Drawing with Advanced Blocks," even when you erase a block from a drawing, the drawing still retains a definition to that block.

Detaching an externally referenced file is a more complete operation than erasing the attached Xref. By using the Detach option, you not only erase the Xref from the host drawing but also remove it from the block reference table. In the following exercise, you detach the Xref file P-CAP.

DETACHING THE PEN CAP XREF

1. Choose Edit, External Reference, Detach, and you see the following:

   ```
   ?/Bind/Detach/Path/Reload/Overlay/<Attach>: _d
   Xref(s) to detach:
   ```

2. Enter **P-CAP**, after which AutoCAD LT scans the drawing and detaches the pen cap Xref.

3. Now choose Edit, External Reference, List and press Enter to accept the default for all Xrefs. You see the following table:

```
Xref name                         Path          Xref type
----------------------            ----          ----------
P-TIP                             P-TIP.DWG     Attach

Total Xref(s): 1
```

Binding an Xref to the Host Drawing

If you want to save the Xref file with the host drawing so that it is not externally referenced when the host is opened, use the Bind option. The Bind option severs the external linkage, at which time the Xref is treated as an inserted block.

Once an Xref has been bound, LT changes the names of all layers associated with the Xref by replacing the pipe (|), which previously separated the filename from the layer name, with the character set 0. In the next exercise, you bind the pen tip to the PEN01 drawing and confirm the changes.

TIP

> You can rename the newly modified layer name from a bound Xref by entering the new name in the New Layer Name edit box and choosing Rename or by using the Rename dialog box presented when you use the DDRENAME command.

BINDING THE PEN TIP TO THE DRAWING

1. Choose Edit, External Reference, Bind, and you see the following:

```
?/Bind/Detach/Path/Reload/Overlay/<Attach>: _b
Xref(s) to bind:
```

2. Enter **P-TIP**, after which AutoCAD LT scans the drawing for the requested Xref and severs the external linkage.

3. Choose List from the Object Properties toolbar, then select the pen tip and press Enter to see the following information confirming its recognition as a block:

```
BLOCK REFERENCE  Layer: PEN
Space: Model space
Handle = 10F
P-TIP
```

```
at point, X=   0.0000  Y=   0.0000  Z=   0.0000
X scale factor    1.0000
Y scale factor    1.0000
rotation angle       0
Z scale factor    1.0000
```

4. Choose Layers and notice that the layer name formerly associated with the Xref of P-TIP is now selectable and has a different name.

N O T E

> Because a bound Xref is recognized as a block reference, you need to EXPLODE the block if you want to edit the objects.

The Option of Overlay

As you have seen, you can have more than one Xref attached to a host drawing. The second tier of working with Xrefs involves attaching a file that contains Xrefs to another host drawing. This results in a second level of hierarchy of attached Xrefs. If the Attach option is used, the external reference files will be displayed in the host drawings at either level in the hierarchy as is illustrated in figure 11.6.

Figure 11.6

*Attaching Xrefs at
multiple levels.*

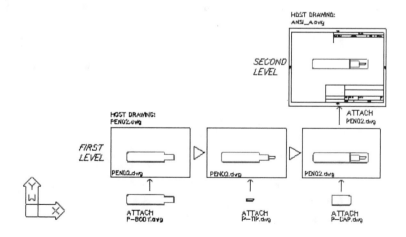

The Overlay option of the XREF command introduces an alternative to continually attaching Xrefs to a host drawing. If the primary purpose of externally referencing a file is for review or to see how one drawing relates to the other, use the Overlay option. At the first level of hierarchy, the result of overlaying an Xref is identical to attaching the Xref. Overlaid Xrefs, however, are not displayed if that host drawing is attached or overlaid into a host at the second level, as illustrated in figure 11.7. In the following exercise, you use the Overlay option to create the PEN02 drawing.

Figure 11.7

Result of overlaying an Xref.

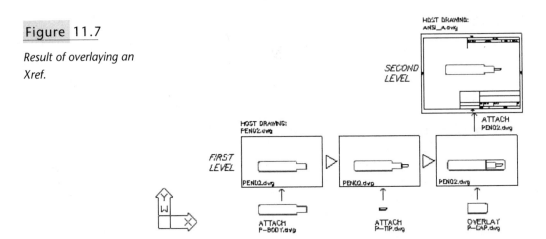

OVERLAYING THE PEN CAP ON THE DRAWING

1. Begin a new drawing from scratch and save it as **PEN02**, then choose Zoom All from the Standard toolbar.

2. Choose Edit, External Reference, Attach; then choose P-BODY from the sample directory.

3. Enter **0,0** for the Insertion point and press Enter to accept the defaults for X scale factor, Y scale factor, and Rotation.

4. Press the spacebar to reissue the XREF command, then press Enter for the Attach option and choose the drawing P-TIP.

5. Enter **0,0** for the Insertion point and press Enter to accept the remaining defaults as shown in figure 11.8.

Figure 11.8

Attaching Xrefs to the PEN02 drawing.

6. Open the External Reference toolbar (see fig. 11.9) by choosing View, Toolbars. Choose External Reference from the Toolbars listing, then OK.

Figure 11.9

The External Reference toolbar.

7. Choose P-CAP from the sample directory and insert it at 0,0.

8. Choose Edit, External Reference, List, then press Enter to accept the default of all Xrefs to see how an overlaid Xref is noted:

```
Xref name                     Path              Xref type
---------------------         ----              ----------
    P-BODY                    P-BODY.DWG          Attach
    P-TIP                     P-TIP.DWG           Attach
    P-CAP                     P-CAP.DWG           Overlay

    Total Xref(s): 3
```

9. Begin a new drawing using ANSI_A.DWT as the template, then choose Zoom Extents from the Standard toolbar.

10. Choose Edit, External Reference, Attach, then choose PEN02 from the sample directory and enter **0,0** for the Insertion point.

11. Figure 11.10 displays the drawing without a cap because the file P-CAP was overlaid in the drawing PEN02.

12. Choose Save and save the drawing as **PEN02-OL**.

Figure 11.10

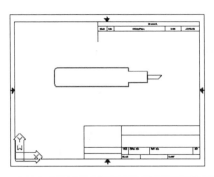

*Second-level result of
overlaying an Xref.*

Utility Features of the XREF Command

After a project is completed, drawings are frequently archived to other drives or
directories or backed up onto floppies. Because LT saves the path name for any
attached or overlaid Xrefs with the host drawing, if a host drawing is opened and
AutoCAD LT is *unable* to locate the Xref based upon the original path, you get a
message box as shown in figure 11.11.

Figure 11.11

*AutoCAD LT's Message
box regarding opening
an Xref.*

Upon choosing OK from the message box, LT continues with the loading of the
drawing and adds a notation similar to the following:

```
xref p-cap.DWG
```

For those of you on a network and using the AutoCAD LT feature of file locking, if the
unresolved Xref file is currently being used by another user, LT cannot open a locked
file and will be unable to resolve the Xref. In either case, this notation will be in the
current text style and is placed at the insertion point of the unresolved Xref. You also
will be alerted to the absence of the Xref when listing all the blocks of the drawing
(BLOCK/?) with a notation in the table similar to the following:

```
Defined blocks.
P-BODY
P-CAP            Xref: unresolved
P-TIP            Xref: resolved
REVDATE
TITLEBLOCK
```

User Blocks	External References	Dependent Blocks	Unnamed Blocks
3	2	0	2

Reloading an Xref or Specifying a New Path

To correct the situation resulting in an unresolved Xref, you can use the Path and/ or Reload option of the XREF command. The simplest method of correction is to copy or move the unresolved file (which may currently be archived on a floppy or on a network drive) to the same path as the host drawing. Then use the Reload option (Edit, External Reference, Reload) and enter the name of the Xref to be resolved. This is also the method to be used when the file previously locked by another user on the network becomes available.

NOTE

> The Reload option does not allow for a path to be entered when specifying the Xref file to be reloaded. Reload reloads the file only from the original path location.

The Path option of the XREF command enables you to enter a new path for the specified unresolved file at the prompt line (you can't choose it from a dialog box). When using this option, you must not only enter the path but also the name of the Xref file that is unresolved:

```
Edit path for which xref(s): P-CAP

Scanning...
```

At this point, AutoCAD LT scans to see whether you entered a valid Xref name. If it recognizes your entry as valid, it moves to the next prompt after it displays what it sees as the old path name:

```
Xref name: P-CAP
Old path: p-cap.DWG
New path: \ACLTWIN\INSIDE\P-CAP
Regenerating drawing.
Reload Xref P-CAP: \ACLTWIN\INSIDE\P-CAP
P-CAP loaded. Regenerating drawing.
```

After this message, LT regenerates the drawing with the resolved Xref if the path and file name entered result in a fruitful search.

Summary

The concept of externally referencing files is simplistic but frequently misunderstood. As you have seen in this chapter, the XREF command contains a subtle power that enables an edited drawing to externally update the host drawing(s) into which it has been referenced. A feature similar to this will be seen in Chapter 23, "Using OLE and the Windows 95 Editing Features," in which these concepts are applied to files from other applications.

RELATED COMMANDS

XREFCTL
XBIND

ADVANCED TEXT CONCEPTS

As you work with AutoCAD LT, you frequently create and manipulate graphical drawing objects. However, there are instances when graphic elements alone are insufficient to convey the scope or intent of the project. For example, the construction of a new mechanical part might require the inclusion of a set of design and build notes for its completion. In AutoCAD LT, textual data can include notes, specifications, schedules, leader callouts, or any "character-string" –based elements.

Historically, hand lettering a drawing was time-consuming and error-prone. Correcting a misspelled or omitted word was difficult. Today, by using AutoCAD LT for Windows 95's powerful text entry and editing commands, the resultant lettering is carried out faster, is more accurate, and follows a more uniform style than manual techniques do.

This chapter covers the following procedures related to drawing annotation:

- *Creating single-line and paragraph text*
- *Using text styles and fonts*
- *Formatting text*

- *Using special characters*
- *Using quick text*
- *Importing text*
- *Editing text*
- *Using the spell checker*

Creating Single-Line and Paragraph Text

AutoCAD LT provides the TEXT, DTEXT, and MTEXT commands to place text in your drawing. You use TEXT to create a single line of text. DTEXT enables you to generate multiple lines of text dynamically by displaying the characters as you type them. With TEXT and DTEXT, each character string is a separate object. With MTEXT (a new paragraph-style text feature), you type or import bulk text to fit within points you specify, which AutoCAD LT then treats as one object.

NOTE

AutoCAD LT has had a TEXT command since its initial release; however, the DTEXT and MTEXT commands provide greater flexibility. The TEXT command is retained for menu macro usage and its compatibility with older software versions.

Figure 12.1 shows an example of the two types of text.

Figure 12.1

Single-line and paragraph text.

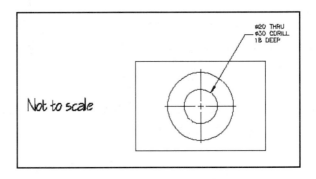

Plotted versus Drawn Text Height

Because AutoCAD LT draws all objects at full size, you need to determine the corresponding text height so that geometry and text descriptions are properly proportioned. What text height should you use so that the plotted height meets industry standards?

Suppose you want to plot your drawing at a scale of $1/4$"=1', and you want the text height to appear $1/8$" high on the final plot. What should the drawn text height be? At this plot scale, every $1/4$" plotted represents 1' drawn; therefore, a $1/8$" plot height calculates to a 6" drawn height. In the next exercise, you specify a text height of 6" to place a single label at a specified location.

Tip

Use snap for consistent, orderly text spacing and placement.

Placing a Single Text Label

Begin a new drawing named CHAP12 using the HOSPROOM drawing from the PROJECTS directory on the companion CD. Zoom to the view shown in figure 12.2, then set snap to 3" and grid to 6". Set the FURNITURE layer current.

1. Choose Draw, Text, Line Text, and you see the following prompt:

   `Justify/Style/<Start point>:`

2. Enter 12',11'6" at 1, and you are prompted for the text height.

3. Specify 6 and press Enter to indicate a 6" text height. You are prompted for the rotation angle.

4. Press Enter to accept the default horizontal angle, and you are prompted for the actual text. Type **CHAIR** and press Enter twice to terminate the entry. Your drawing should appear as shown in figure 12.2.

5. Choose Real-Time Pan on the Standard toolbar to move to the view shown in figure 12.3. To label the remaining pieces of furniture in the hospital room, turn on the snap and grid modes, and type **DTEXT** and press Enter at the `Command:` prompt.

Figure 12.2

The chair annotated with a label.

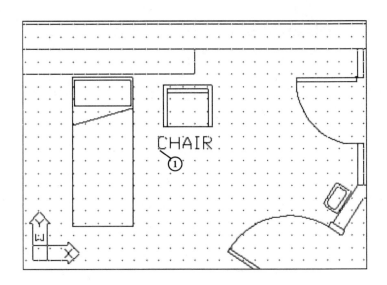

Figure 12.3

Bedroom furniture labeled with DTEXT.

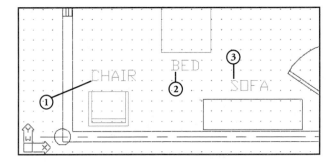

6. Pick the point 5',7' at ① (see fig. 12.3) to write the label **CHAIR**, accepting the default 6" height and 0" rotation angle. At the next **Text:** prompt, pick the insertion point at 9',7'6" at ② to write the label **BED**. At the next Text: prompt, pick the insertion point at 12',6'6" at ③ to write the label **SOFA**.

7. At the next Text: prompt, press Enter to end the sequence.

8. Save the drawing.

In the preceding exercise, you picked alternate text insertion points by reading the coordinate display in the status line. A single DTEXT command enables you to enter all three text labels.

TIP

You can also use object snap modes to help place text. To add a line below existing text, use DTEXT with object snap mode Insertion, pick the existing text, and enter only a space on the first line. Then press Enter to space down for the next line.

As shown in the preceding exercise, the DTEXT command enables you to place multiple lines of text at various locations in the drawing. Often, however, grouping several lines of text to be treated as a single block becomes desirable. Some examples are door schedules, design and build specifications, and mechanical tolerance notes. Rather than using the BLOCK or BMAKE commands to "glue" the text lines together (see Chapter 9, "Drawing with Basic Blocks"), you can utilize a powerful, new feature called MTEXT—text treated as paragraphs.

Using MTEXT to Place Text

Because MTEXT enables you to create paragraph-style text that is treated as a single object, you can enter the text quickly and reposition its boundary frame to a new, uncluttered location in the drawing.

In the next exercise, you create a paragraph of text. You need not press Enter to format the text lines—MTEXT word-wraps like a word processor. Then, you see how to reposition the paragraph location.

PLACING PARAGRAPH TEXT WITH MTEXT

Continue in the CHAP12 drawing from the previous exercise and use real-time pan to move to the view shown in figure 12.4. The text will be added in this exercise.

1. From the Draw toolbar, pick Paragraph Text, and you see the following prompt:

```
Justify/Style/Height/<Insertion point>:
```

2. Pick the point at ① (see fig. 12.4), and you see the following prompt:

```
Justify/Style/Height/Width/2Points/<Other corner>:
```

Figure 12.4

*The completed approval
note.*

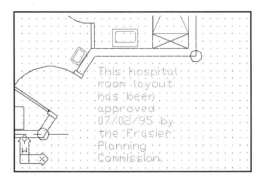

Pick the point at ② , then enter the text in the Edit MText dialog box (see fig.
12.5), then choose OK.

Figure 12.5

*The approval note in the
Edit MText dialog box.*

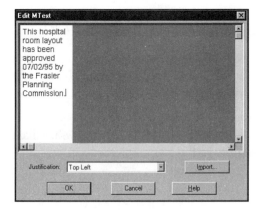

3. At the Command: prompt, pick the text to display the grips at the corner points.
   Pick any grip, then press Enter. AutoCAD LT enters autoediting move mode
   and drags the text box with the cursor.

4. Move the cursor around, then press Esc three times to cancel.

5. Save the drawing.

Refer to figure 12.4 for the results of this exercise.

NOTE

Entering -MTEXT at the Command: prompt displays all prompts at the command line instead of providing a dialog box.

Using Text Styles and Fonts

All AutoCAD LT text is drawn by using a text style. AutoCAD LT enables you to control the appearance of text in many ways, such as the base font, character width, slant, and baseline format. Because you have all these parameters with which you can control the appearance of your text, drawing management can become an important issue.

By defining text styles in a drawing, you create, name, and recall different text formats for various applications. For example, you can use a bold style for section markers, a slanted style for specification change requests, an easy-to-read style for dimensions, and a more ornate style for corporate logos.

You define a *text style* to alter the basic shape of a character set typeface, or *font*. AutoCAD LT provides a default text style called STANDARD, which uses a basic stick-lettering font called TXT. The previous exercises used TXT. Because only one text style needs to be defined to enable text to be entered, some users find the default style sufficient. However, most users customize the STANDARD style by linking it to another font or make the effort to define additional styles.

NOTE

AutoCAD LT for Windows 95 supports a variety of fonts from third-party vendors. Besides its native source (SHP) and compiled (SHX) shape file font formats, AutoCAD LT also handles Type 1 PostScript source (PFB) and compiled (PFA) fonts, as well as Windows TrueType (TTF) fonts. You can use these additional font types in virtually all Windows 95 applications.

Figure 12.6 shows a selected sample of text fonts (in alphabetical order) included with AutoCAD LT.

Figure 12.6

The AutoCAD LT font
sampler.

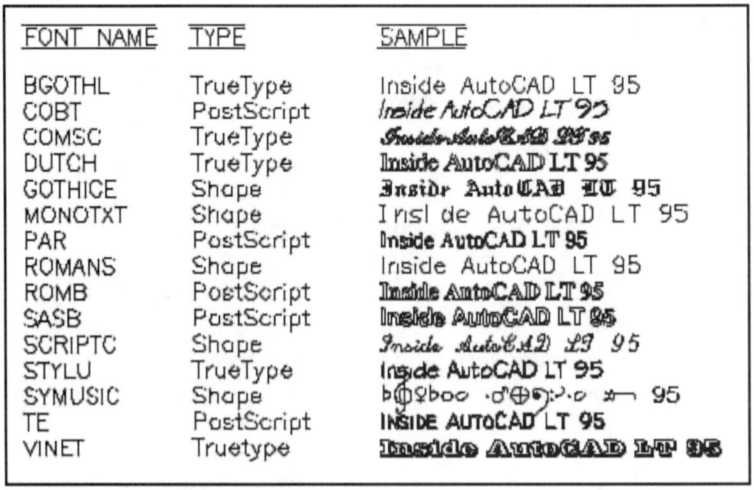

FONT NAME	TYPE	SAMPLE
BGOTHL	TrueType	Inside AutoCAD LT 95
COBT	PostScript	Inside AutoCAD LT 95
COMSC	TrueType	Inside AutoCAD LT 95
DUTCH	TrueType	Inside AutoCAD LT 95
GOTHICE	Shape	Inside AutoCAD LT 95
MONOTXT	Shape	I nsl de AutoCAD LT 95
PAR	PostScript	Inside AutoCAD LT 95
ROMANS	Shape	Inside AutoCAD LT 95
ROMB	PostScript	Inside AutoCAD LT 95
SASB	PostScript	Inside AutoCAD LT 95
SCRIPTC	Shape	Inside AutoCAD LT 95
STYLU	TrueType	Inside AutoCAD LT 95
SYMUSIC	Shape	b⚬♪b♡♡ ·♂⊕♂♪·♡ ♯♫ 95
TE	PostScript	INSIDE AUTOCAD LT 95
VINET	Truetype	Inside AutoCAD LT 95

TIP

Figure 12.6 is not all-inclusive, but the new DDSTYLE command (covered in the next exercise) enables you to preview a particular font style. You also can open the sample drawing called TRUETYPE.DWG to see an example of each of the included TrueType (TTF) fonts.

In the following exercise, you assign another font to the default STANDARD style to enhance its appearance.

REVISING A TEXT STYLE

Continue to use the CHAP12 drawing from the previous exercise.

1. Choose Format, Text Style to open the Text Style dialog box (see fig. 12.7).

2. In the Font group, choose Browse to open the Select Font File dialog box that lists all possible fonts (see fig. 12.8). Scroll the list, choose Romans, then choose Open. The Text Style dialog box reflects the style change in the Character Preview window.

3. In the Effects group, change the Width factor to 0.8 and the Obliquing angle to 10 (measured from the vertical), which again updates the Character Preview window.

4. Choose Apply, then Close.

5. At the `Command:` prompt type **REGEN**.

6. Save the drawing.

Figure 12.7

The Text Style dialog box.

Figure 12.8

*The Select Font File
dialog box.*

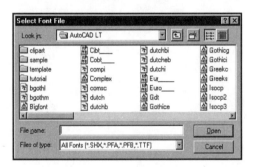

After you complete the exercise, your STANDARD style uses the smoother ROMANS font and is slanted (italicized) and slightly narrower than normal, as shown in figure 12.9.

Figure 12.9

The modified STANDARD style.

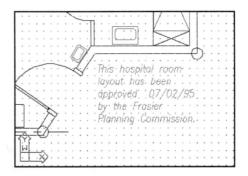

T IP

You can use the RENAME command to change the name of an existing text style. By adopting a suitable naming convention for table entries (layers, blocks, and so on), you can assist in the maintenance of company-wide standards. You can remove unused styles with the PURGE command.

Figure 12.10 shows examples of several text style effects.

Figure 12.10

Examples of text styles.

PARAMETER	VALUE	RESULT
Width factor	0.50	ABC 123
Width factor	0.75	ABC 123
Width factor	1.00	ABC 123
Width factor	1.25	ABC 123
Obliquing angle	−20	ABC 123
Obliquing angle	0	ABC 123
Obliquing angle	20	*ABC 123*
Obliquing angle	45	*ABC 123*
Upside down	Y	ABC 123
Backwards	Y	ABC 123

Font Mapping and Substitution

AutoCAD LT accesses a variety of support files when you open a drawing for its initial screen display. In particular, AutoCAD LT checks to ensure that all referenced font files can be found in its search path. If a font file cannot be found, AutoCAD LT either uses an alternate font or displays an error message and prompt for an alternative font file.

This situation can occur if you fail to load all the fonts during AutoCAD LT installation (see Appendix E for details). Another problem involving "missing" font files can occur when you send a drawing to another user. The drawing can contain styles linked to third-party font files. If the font files are not included on the disk, the second user cannot access the referenced styles.

NOTE

AutoCAD LT substitutes the default TXT font for any missing font file when opening a drawing. Use the FONTALT system variable (see Appendix A) to change this selection.

WARNING

Including third-party font files with your drawing for use by others may be an infringement of your third-party license. Check with the font supplier.

Formatting Text

When you use any text-entry command (TEXT, DTEXT, or MTEXT) to enter text in a drawing, AutoCAD LT needs to know how you want to place and format the text. The following four options apply to the initial Justify/Style/<Start point>: prompt:

- **Justify** issues the prompt for text justification. You also can enter justification directly at the Justify/Style/<Start point>: prompt or let it default to left justification.

- **Style** specifies a new text style default. The style must have already been created with the DDSTYLE command.

- **<Start point>** specifies the bottom left justification point.

- **Press Enter** highlights the last text entered and prompts for a new text string when you press Enter at the prompt. AutoCAD LT places the new text directly below the highlighted text, using the same style, height, and rotation. When you use DTEXT, you also can specify a new pick point before you enter the text.

After you specify this information, you are prompted for each of the following options:

- **Height** specifies the text height (the default is 0.2). The height prompt is omitted if you use Align justification or any text style that has a predefined nonzero height.

- **Rotation angle** specifies the baseline angle for text placement (the default is 0).

- **Text** specifies the text string.

The default height shown in the TEXT command is rounded off to your unit's precision setting and might not accurately display its true value.

When you use AutoCAD LT text, you need to consider two angles. The obliquing angle is the slant of each character, and you use the DDSTYLE command to control it. The rotation angle is the slope of the text baseline, and you control it by using the TEXT and DTEXT commands.

Whenever AutoCAD LT prompts for a text-related height or angle, it displays a rubber-band line from the start point to the cursor. To indicate the desired measurement, you can pick a point rather than type a value. When you do so, use snap for precision.

Text Justification

Justification (or alignment) specifies the positioning of the text, relative to the start and optional endpoint(s) you specify.

The following list describes each option for TEXT and DTEXT justification (MTEXT justification is discussed in the next section):

- **Align** specifies the beginning and ending points of the text baseline. The text height is scaled so that the text between these points is not distorted.

- **Fit** specifies the beginning and ending points of the text baseline. The text width is distorted to fit the text between these points without changing the height.

- **Center** specifies a point for the horizontal center and the vertical baseline of the text string.

- **Middle** specifies a point for the horizontal and vertical midpoint of the text string. The Middle justification method centers text both horizontally and vertically; use it to place text labels in the center of bubble tags and for other similar applications.

- **Right** specifies a point for the right baseline of the text string.

Figure 12.11 shows an example of each option. Once you become familiar with these options, you can enter them directly at the `Justify/Style/<Start point>:` prompt, without first specifying the Justify option.

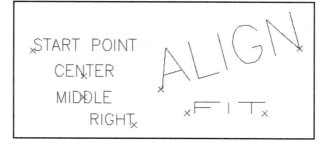

Figure 12.11

TEXT and DTEXT justification options.

WARNING

If you use a justification other than the default left justification, DTEXT entry is still shown as left-justified during entry. Completing the command adjusts the alignment to the format you specify.

TIP

If you respond to the TEXT or DTEXT start point prompt by pressing Enter, the new text starts one line below the last text you entered in the drawing. The new text assumes the height, style, and justification of the previous text, even if you used other AutoCAD LT commands since the last text entry.

Formatting Paragraph-Style Text

When you use the MTEXT command to place paragraph-style text in a drawing, AutoCAD LT asks for other information before it places the text. The initial prompt appears as follows:

```
Justify/Style/Height/<Insertion point>:
```

Several options are available:

- **Justify** controls the alignment of the text boundary to the insertion point. The Justify option issues the TL/TC/TR/ML/MC/MR/BL/BC/BR: prompt; TL (top left) is the default. You also can enter any of these attachment options directly at the <insertion point>: prompt without first using the Justify option. The list is as follows:

    - **TL** specifies a point for the left of the text string, aligned with the top of the tallest character.

    - **TC** specifies a point for the center of the text string, aligned with the top of an uppercase character.

    - **TR** specifies a point for the right side of the text string, aligned with the top of an uppercase character.

    - **ML** specifies a point for the left side of the text string, aligned halfway between the top of an uppercase character and the text baseline.

    - **MC** specifies a point for the center of the text string, aligned halfway between an uppercase character and the bottom of the text baseline.

    - **MR** specifies a point for the right side, between the top of an uppercase character and the text baseline.

    - **BL** specifies a point for the left side of the text string, aligned at the bottom of a descender.

    - **BC** specifies a point for the center of the text string, aligned at the bottom of a descender.

    - **BR** specifies a point for the right side of the text string, aligned at the bottom of a descender.

    Figure 12.12 shows an example of each option.

- **Style** specifies the default style used by the MText paragraph. The style must already exist (DDSTYLE command) in the current drawing; its name, however, can later be changed (using the DDMODIFY command) within the Modify MText dialog box.

- **Height** specifies the default height of uppercase text for the MText paragraph. This value can be changed within the Modify MText dialog box.

- **Insertion point** (the default) specifies the text boundary corner at its insertion point. This is the upper-left corner of the paragraph, unless you first specify a different attachment. The insertion point is a grip point and can be snapped with the Insertion object snap.

If you respond to the insertion point prompt, AutoCAD LT presents three additional options:

- **Width** specifies the horizontal width of the text boundary. You can pick a point to indicate the width or enter a width value.

- **2Points** specifies the width of the text boundary by specifying any two points.

- **Other corner** (the default) specifies the diagonally opposite corner of the text boundary that the prompt implies.

Figure 12.12

MTEXT justification options.

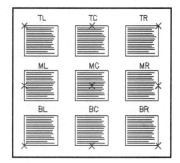

The AutoCAD LT system variables TEXTSTYLE and TEXTSIZE store the current text style and text height, respectively.

In the next exercise, you use several options to place an MTEXT paragraph.

USING MTEXT PARAGRAPH INSERTION OPTIONS

Continue in the CHAP12 drawing from the preceding exercise. Zoom to the view shown in figure 12.14.

1. Choose Paragraph Text from the Draw toolbar.

2. Enter **J**, then enter **BL** for bottom-left justification.

3. At the next prompt, enter **H** and specify 4".

4. For the insertion point, pick ① (see fig. 12.14). For the other corner, pick ②.

5. Enter the text shown in figure 12.13, then choose OK.

6. Save the drawing.

Figure 12.14 shows the results of this exercise.

Figure 12.13

Completing the paragraph text.

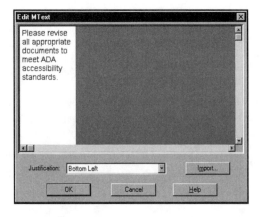

Figure 12.14

Inserted paragraph text.

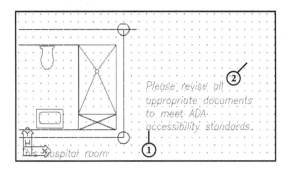

Using Special Characters with TEXT or DTEXT

Some symbols used in engineering drawings are not found on standard keyboards. These symbols include underscores, overscores, plus/minus, and so on. The coding methods that are used by TEXT and DTEXT differ from those used by MTEXT. To generate these symbols, you type special code entries that AutoCAD LT will translate, as shown in table 12.1.

Table 12.1

Special Characters with TEXT or DTEXT

Code Entry	Unicode Entry	Symbol Translation
%%O		Overscore
%%U		Underline
%%D	%\U+00B0	Degree
%%C	%\U+2205	Circle diameter
%%P	%\U+00B1	Plus/minus

The %%*x* codes can be used only with TEXT or DTEXT. The Unicode codes can be used with TEXT, DTEXT, or MTEXT. Unicode codes provide better international compatibility.

For example, to generate this character string:

"AutoCAD LT text entry has a <u>plethora</u> of options."

enter the following TEXT or DTEXT input:

```
Text: AutoCAD LT text entry has a %%uplethora%%u of options.
```

You can enter the special character that follows the two percentage signs in upper- or lowercase.

In the following exercise, use DTEXT dynamically to enter multiple lines of text that include special symbols.

USING DTEXT SPECIAL CHARACTERS

Continue from the previous exercise, in the CHAP12 drawing, and use real-time pan to move to the area shown in figure 12.16.

1. Choose Line Text from the Draw toolbar. For the start point, pick ① (see fig. 12.15). Specify a 4" text height and a 0 rotation angle.

2. In the following text entry, you deliberately misspell a word:

```
Text: Due to the nature of convalesince, ↵
Text: do %%Unot%%U use 68%%D ↵
Text: thermostat setback. ↵
Text: ↵
Command:
```

3. Save the drawing.

Figure 12.15

*DTEXT during text entry
with special character
codes.*

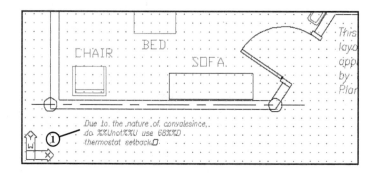

Figure 12.16

*Completed DTEXT with
formatted characters.*

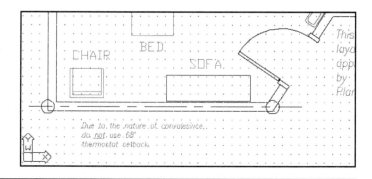

As you type DTEXT entries, AutoCAD LT displays the characters without modification or justification. When you type the final Enter on a separate line, AutoCAD LT translates any special character %% sequences and rejustifies the text if required.

Don't worry about the misspelled word; you use AutoCAD LT's new spelling checker to fix it later.

Controlling Text Display Quality and Speed

Adding many objects to your drawing slows the performance of zooms, redraws, and regens. Filled PostScript or TrueType fonts and multistroke fonts such as COMPLEX are particularly slow to redraw and regenerate. To decrease regeneration time, AutoCAD LT offers two options for accelerating text display. The first alternative is to enter all text with styles using a simple font, such as TXT, for initial drawing development or for test plotting. For the final plot, you can define the styles to a more elegant font, such as ROMANC. The second alternative is to use the QTEXT command.

The QTEXT (Quick TEXT) command enables you to control the screen and plotted appearance of text and attributes. When QTEXT is on, AutoCAD LT replaces text, dimensions, and attributes by approximating rectangles.

The Options, Text pull-down menu contains four selections that affect text display quality and speed. Filled Text turns QTEXT off and sets the TEXTFILL system variable to 1—PostScript or TrueType fonts display as solid-filled. Outline Text also turns QTEXT off but sets TEXTFILL to 0—these font types then display in outline form. Text Frame Only turns on QTEXT. Finally, Text Quality sets the TEXTQLTY system variable to adjust the font display resolution. A higher value yields a smoother appearance.

As shown in figure 12.17, turning on quick text mode reduces the regeneration time for drawings that contain many text objects.

Figure 12.17

QTEXT turned on.

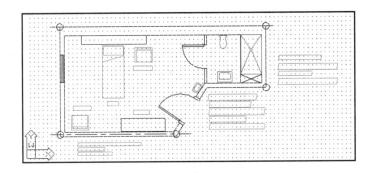

 NOTE

The effect of turning QTEXT on or off is not seen until the next regeneration.

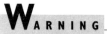

If you plot with QTEXT on you get the outline boxes and not text.

In the exercises to this point, you entered text by typing the information line by line from the keyboard. For large blocks of text, this method can become quite tedious and error-prone.

A faster method is to *import* text—that is, read the text from a separate file into the current drawing. The next section shows some ways to do this.

Importing Text

Occasionally, you may want to import text from an external file. For example, a secretary could type job specifications into a word processing document, save it as a plain ASCII file, then hand you the disk or, in a networked environment, load the file into a shared folder.

In the Windows 95 operating environment, you can open and run several applications at once. To bring a text file into a drawing, open Windows 95 Explorer and LT so that you can drag icons into the AutoCAD LT graphics window. Then, press and drag the file icon from the Explorer folder tree to the AutoCAD LT drawing. The resulting text appears as an MTEXT object using the current default MTEXT properties. Dragging and dropping a text file to create an MTEXT object uses the same process as dragging and dropping a drawing file to insert it as a block. This process is shown in an exercise in Chapter 23, "Using OLE and the Windows 95 Editing Features."

Figure 12.18 shows a text file in Explorer being dragged into the AutoCAD LT graphics window. Releasing the pointing device in the AutoCAD LT window inserts the MTEXT object. Then, you can use AutoCAD LT editing techniques to modify the text.

TIP

When you use the drag-and-drop feature, make sure that the imported text file has a TXT suffix.

Figure 12.18

Using drag-and-drop to import text.

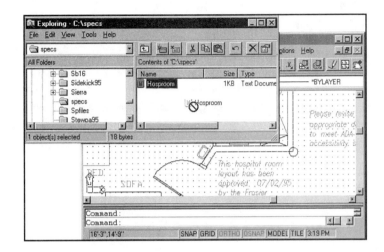

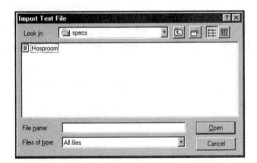

WARNING

In AutoCAD LT, you may be tempted to use the Import option in the File pull-down menu to accomplish this task. However, this method works only with Windows metafiles (WMF) and drawing interchange files (DXF), not text.

The Edit MText dialog box also contains a direct text file import feature. The Import button opens the Import Text File dialog box (see fig. 12.19), which you use to select any ASCII text file. When you specify a file and choose OK, the file contents appear in the Edit MText dialog box just prior to insertion.

Figure 12.19

The Import Text File dialog box.

Editing Text

You should verify an AutoCAD LT drawing that contains both graphic objects and supporting text for technical accuracy. For example, an architect might issue design changes to an initial proposed layout and place revision marks on the plot sheet. Then, the CAD operator incorporates these modifications to update the drawing. The process could then proceed through several revision phases until a final proposal is approved. Therefore, checking and rechecking the design must be thorough, yet efficient. This section covers the various methods you can use to update existing textual information.

Using DDEDIT to Change Text

Issuing the DDEDIT command presents selected text in a dialog box that corresponds to the type of text. When you use the DDEDIT command with an object created by TEXT or DTEXT, you can change the characters of a single line of text. Using DDEDIT with an attdef object (see Chapter 10, "Drawing with Advanced Blocks") enables you to change the tag, prompt, and default values of the attribute definition. If you use DDEDIT with an MTEXT object, DDEDIT opens the same Edit MText dialog box as does the MTEXT command. The only difference between accessing this dialog box with DDEDIT and with MTEXT is that DDEDIT presents the selected text.

Selecting a text object opens the Edit Text dialog box. AutoCAD LT then highlights the entire string for replacement. Clicking in the box positions the cursor. Any new text is inserted at the cursor's location and replaces all highlighted text. Choosing OK closes the dialog box and applies the changes. The command again prompts for an annotation object to edit until you press Enter at the next selection prompt or cancel the command. You also can enter U to undo the previous change.

Changing TEXT or DTEXT Characters

In the next exercise, you use DDEDIT to make a simple change to a line of text. You modify one of the furniture text labels.

CHANGING A SINGLE TEXT LABEL

Continue the CHAP12 drawing from the preceding exercise. If you did not perform or save the results of the earlier DTEXT exercise, use DTEXT to label the chair, as shown in figure 12.21, then continue.

1. Choose Edit Text from the Modify toolbar (see fig. 12.20).

2. At the prompt to select an annotation object, pick the text CHAIR next to the bed.

3. Type **RECLINER** (see fig. 12.21) and press Enter.

4. Click on the Enter button on the pointing device to exit the command.

5. Save the drawing.

Figure 12.20

The Edit Text (DDEDIT) toolbar icon.

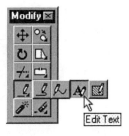

Figure 12.21

Modifying single-line text using the Edit Text dialog box.

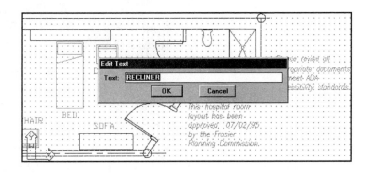

Changing MTEXT Formatting

In the next exercise, you use DDMODIFY to change the format and content of a text paragraph. You alter the text style and change the wording.

EDITING PARAGRAPH TEXT

Continue from the previous exercise in the CHAP12 drawing.

1. Choose Properties from the Object Properties toolbar (see fig.12.22), which issues a variation of the DDMODIFY command.

2. Pick the paragraph containing Frasier Planning Commission, then click on the Enter button on the pointing device.

3. In the Modify MText dialog box (see fig. 12.22), choose the Style drop-down list at ①, then pick CB (city blueprint).

4. Choose the Edit Contents button, and the Edit MText dialog box appears. Press and drag over the text hospital room and type **preliminary**. Choose OK twice to exit the DDMODIFY operation. AutoCAD LT updates the paragraph.

5. Save the drawing.

Figure 12.22

The Modify MText dialog box.

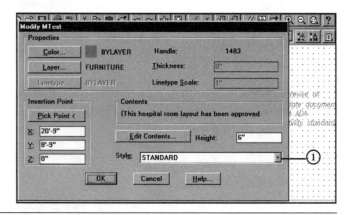

For a long time, AutoCAD LT users bemoaned the lack of a built-in spell checker. However, the latest release of AutoCAD LT makes this wish-list item a reality. The next section shows you how to use the built-in SPELL command.

Using the Spell Checker

The SPELL command enables you to verify the spelling of any selected text in your drawing. Sometimes AutoCAD LT flags a word that you know is spelled correctly. By creating and maintaining custom dictionaries, you can store words that AutoCAD LT never again flags as an error. For example, you can add employee names, product model names, or any industry-specific nomenclature to a custom dictionary.

In the following exercise, you verify the spelling of the text in the hospital room layout drawing.

USING THE SPELL CHECKER

Continue in the CHAP12 drawing.

1. Choose Spelling from the Standard toolbar.

2. At the `Select objects:` prompt, type **ALL** and press Enter twice.

3. AutoCAD LT opens the Check Spelling dialog box (see fig. 12.23) and displays the misspelled convalesince in the Current Word section, convalesce in the Suggestions box, and the correct convalescence in the Suggestions list box.

4. Select convalescence, then choose Change.

5. If there are no further mistakes, choose OK and AutoCAD LT makes the necessary corrections.

6. Save the drawing.

Figure 12.23

The Check Spelling dialog box.

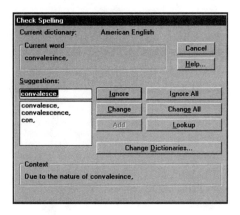

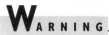

The spell check verifies TEXT, DTEXT, and MTEXT objects. AutoCAD LT does not correct misspelled dimension text or block attributes.

Summary

In this chapter, you learned about entering text elements into your LT drawing. In addition, you explored various methods of formatting and editing the text. Finally, you ensured that all text was spelled correctly.

CHAPTER 13

DIMENSIONING STYLES

There are many different kinds of dimensions, any of which can have dozens of different settings that define how they look. Because of the numerous dimensioning variables, or settings, that govern the look of a dimension (text height, location on the dimension line, angle, and so forth), AutoCAD LT enables you to save your settings in a named dimension style. A dimension style is simply a collection of dimensioning variable settings, and the default dimension style name is STANDARD. This chapter discusses the following:

- *Anatomy of a Dimension*
- *Annotated Glossary of the Dimensioning Dialog Boxes*
- *Viewing the Settings for Various Dimension Styles*
- *Modifying the Settings of an Existing Style*
- *Updating an Existing Dimension with a Different Style*
- *Creating a New Dimension Style*

Anatomy of a Dimension

Before dimension styles can be discussed, the elements of a dimension must first be presented to establish a point of reference. Once again, LT for Windows 95 significantly benefits from the development of the dimensioning features in Release 13 for Windows. This section begins with the general anatomy of a dimension, including terms and dimensioning variables. Each of the dimensions shown in figure 13.1 are single objects. When you place a dimension, AutoCAD LT combines several objects to make a single dimension object. The default dimension style named STANDARD was used in creating each of the dimensions.

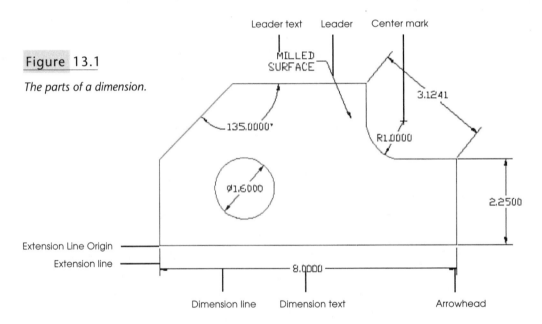

Figure 13.1

The parts of a dimension.

Understanding the Power of a Dimension Style

Borrowing once again from the significant dimensioning improvements found in Release 13, AutoCAD LT enables you to easily create and modify a dimension style using the Dimension Style dialog box. The Dimension Style dialog box shown in figure 13.2 enables you to set values for the various dimensioning elements.

Save button to save
any changes

Figure 13.2

*The default Dimension
Styles dialog box.*

Dimension Style families

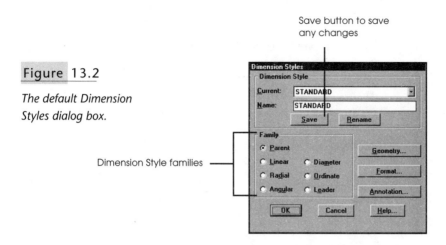

The following list gives you the settings for the dimension elements shown in figure 13.1, followed by the [*dimension variable*] name and the button to select from the Dimension Style dialog box to change the setting:

Arrowhead size: 0.1800 [DIMASZ] Annotation

Center mark size: 0.0900 [DIMCEN] Annotation

Decimal places for all dimensions in this style: 4 [DIMDEC] Annotation

Dimension line extension past the extension line: 0.0000 [DIMDLE] Geometry

Extension of the extension line above the dimension line: 0.1800 [DIMEXE] Geometry

Extension line origin offset: 0.0625 [DIMEXO] Geometry

Gap from dimension line to the dimension text: 0.0900 [DIMGAP] Geometry

Current dimension style: STANDARD [DIMSTYLE] Main dialog box

Place text above the dimension line; 0=Off (in-line), 1=On: 0 [DIMTAD] Format

Text inside extensions is horizontal: On [DIMTIH] Format

Text outside horizontal: On [DIMTOH] Format

Current text style: STANDARD [DIMTXSTY] Annotation

Dimension text height: 0.1800 [DIMTXT] Annotation

NOTE

Thanks to the various dimensioning dialog boxes, you rarely use individual dimension variables. It is a good idea, however, to become familiar with the more commonly modified variables. This will enable you to edit them individually at the keyboard.

Annotated Glossary of the Dimensioning Dialog Boxes

This section presents the three primary dialog boxes available from the Dimension Styles dialog box and the Primary Units dialog box. A brief definition of each dialog box item is followed by its related dimension variable(s) in brackets ([]).

The Geometry Dialog Box

Figure 13.3 shows the Geometry dialog box items. Figure 13.5 shows dimensioning results of settings from the Geometry dialog box.

Figure 13.3

The Geometry dialog box.

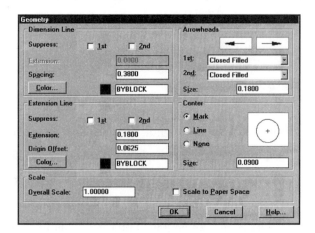

The features of the Geometry dialog box are described in the following list:

■ **Suppress:** This option, found in the Dimension Line section of the dialog box, enables suppression of 1st and 2nd half of the dimension line of a dimension with centered dimension text. [DIMSD1, DIMSD2, DIMSOXD]

■ **Extension:** This option in the Dimension Line section of the dialog box sets the extension distance of the dimension line beyond the extension line when using the oblique arrowhead or tick mark. [DIMDLE]

- **Spacing:** This option sets the distance between dimension lines in baseline dimensions. [DIMDLI]

- **Color:** This button, in the Dimension Line section of the dialog box, opens the Select Color dialog box from which you can choose the desired color for the dimension line and leader. [DIMCLRD]

- **Suppress:** This option, found in the Extension Line section of the dialog box, enables suppression of the 1st and 2nd extension line. [DIMSE1, DIMSE2]

- **Extension:** This option in the Extension Line section of the dialog box sets the distance that the extension lines extend beyond the dimension line. [DIMEXE]

- **Origin Offset:** This option sets the distance between the object to dimension and the beginning of the extension line. [DIMEXO]

- **Color:** This button, in the Extension Line section of the dialog box, opens the Select Color dialog box from which you can choose the desired color for the extension lines. [DIMCLRE]

- **Arrowheads:** (Left and Right Arrows) These image tiles cycle the predefined arrowheads with each pick (see fig. 13.4).

- **1st:** A selection from the 1st arrowhead drop-down list sets the first and second arrowhead type. [DIMBLK, DIMBLK1, DIMSAH]

- **2nd:** A selection from the 2nd arrowhead drop-down list sets the 2nd arrowhead only. [DIMBLK2]

- **Mark:** This radio button, when activated, places a cross (+) at the center of a circle or arc when adding radial or diameter dimension. [positive DIMCEN value]

- **Line:** This radio button, when activated, places center lines through the center of a circle or arc when adding radial or diameter dimension. [negative DIMCEN value]

- **None:** This radio button, when selected, does not place a center mark on the circle or arc when adding radial or diameter dimension. [DIMCEN]

- **Size:** This option sets the size of the center mark type. [DIMCEN]

- **Overall Scale:** This option indicates the factor by which all size-related dimensioning elements are multiplied. [DIMLFAC, DIMSCALE]

- **Scale to Paper Space:** This option adjusts the dimensioning scale factor to that of the floating model space viewport. [DIMSCALE]

- **Help:** This button opens context-sensitive help for the Geometry dialog box.

Figure 13.4

The predefined arrowheads.

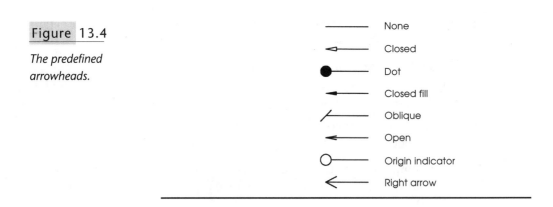

Figure 13.5

Examples of geometry settings.

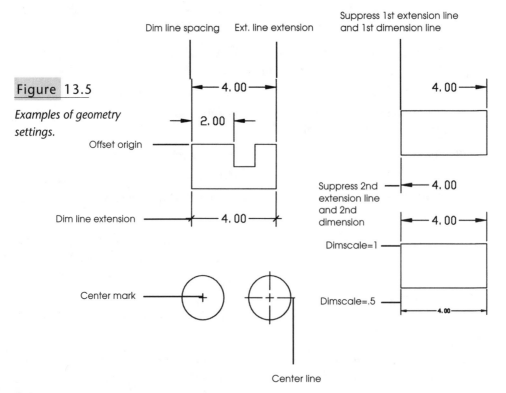

> **N**OTE
>
> The width—or "weight"—of a plotted line in AutoCAD LT is based upon the color of the object. Depending upon your output device, you may customize the width of the lines by modifying the pen width values for each color. The Color option for the dimensioning elements of dimension line, extension lines, and text can be configured to allow for more control over the "boldness" of the specific dimension elements.

The Format Dialog Box

Figure 13.6 shows the Format dialog box items. Figure 13.8 shows dimensioning results of settings from the Geometry dialog box.

Figure 13.6

The Format dialog box.

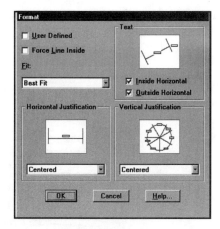

The features of the Format dialog box are described in the following list:

- **User Defined:** This option, when checked, prompts you to position the dimension text. This is off by default. [DIMUPT]

- **Force Line Inside:** This option forces the dimension line to be drawn between the extension lines if the dimension text is outside. [DIMTOFL]

- **Fit:** This option provides a drop-down list of options to control the placement of dimension text and arrows, as shown in figure 13.7. [DIMFIT, DIMSOXD, DIMTIX]

- **Horizontal Justification:** (Image tile) This option cycles through the horizontal justification of the dimension text with each pick (see fig. 13.8).

- **Horizontal Justification:** (Drop-down list) This option presents a list of horizontal justification options for the dimension text. [DIMJUST]

- **Vertical Justification:** (Image tile) This option cycles through the vertical justification of the dimension text with each pick (see fig. 13.8).

- **Vertical Justification:** (Drop-down list) This option provides a list of vertical justification options for the dimension text. [DIMTAD]

- **Text:** (Image tile) This option cycles through the position options for the dimension text with each pick (see fig. 13.8).

- **Inside Horizontal:** This check box indicates whether to set the dimension text position inside the extension lines. [DIMTIH]

- **Outside Horizontal:** This check box indicates whether to set the dimension text position outside the extension lines. [DIMTOH]

- **Help:** This button opens context-sensitive help for the Format dialog box.

Figure 13.7

The Fit options from the Format dialog box.

Text (orientation)

Figure 13.8

Some common ways to format dimensions and text.

The Annotation Dialog Box

Figure 13.9 shows the Annotation dialog box items.

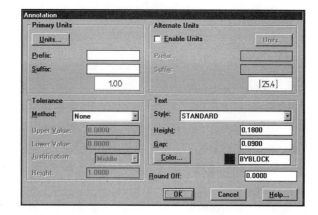

The features of the Annotation dialog box are described in the following list:

- **Units:** This button opens the Primary Units dialog box.

- **Prefix:** Enter a prefix to dimension text in this edit box in the Primary Units section of the dialog box. [DIMPOST]

- **Suffix:** Use this edit box in the Primary Units section of the dialog box for a dimension text suffix. [DIMPOST]

- **Primary Units:** (Image tile) This option cycles through the five methods of displaying tolerance dimensions (see fig. 13.10). [DIMLIM, DIMGAP, DIMTOL]

- **Method:** This drop-down list provides the five tolerance methods shown in figure 13.10.

- **Upper Value:** This option sets the upper value for symmetrical, deviation, or limits tolerance dimensions. [DIMTP]

- **Lower Value:** This option sets the lower value for deviation or limits tolerance dimensions. [DIMTM]

■ **Justification:** Use this drop-down list for symmetrical or deviation tolerance dimensions. [DIMTOLJ]

■ **Height:** Use this edit box in the Tolerance section of the dialog box for the scale factor to be applied to the height of tolerance dimension text. [DIMTFAC]

■ **Enable Units:** This option enables or disables use of alternate units for metric dimensioning. [DIMALT, DIMALTU]

■ **Units:** This button opens Alternate Units dialog box, similar to figure 13.11, showing the Primary Units dialog box. [DIMALTD, DIMALTF, DIMALTTD, DIMALTTZ]

■ **Prefix:** Use this edit box for a prefix to alternate units dimension text. [DIMAPOST]

■ **Suffix:** Use this edit box for an alternate units dimension text suffix. [DIMAPOST]

■ **Alternate Units:** (Image tile) This cycles through the five methods of displaying alternate units tolerance dimensions (see fig. 13.10). [DIMLIM, DIMGAP, DIMTOL]

■ **Style:** This drop-down list displays existing text styles. [DIMTXSTY]

■ **Height:** Use this edit box to set height of dimension text. [DIMTXT]

■ **Gap:** Use this edit box to set distance of the dimension text above the dimension line, the gap from the dimension line to the dimension text for centered dimension or to enable a basic dimension. [DIMGAP, DIMTVP]

■ **Color:** This button opens the Select Color dialog box from which you can choose the desired color for the dimension text. [DIMCLRT]

■ **Round Off:** Use this edit box to set the round-off increment for decimal dimensions. [DIMRND]

■ **Help:** This button opens context-sensitive help for the Annotation dialog box.

The Primary Units Dialog Box for Dimensioning

Figure 13.11 shows the Format dialog box items. Figure 13.8 shows dimensioning results of settings from the Geometry dialog box.

Figure 13.10

The tolerance display methods.

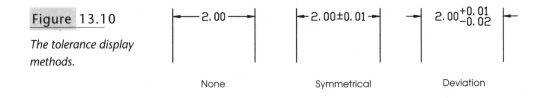

None   Symmetrical   Deviation

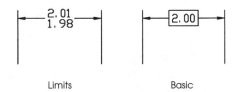

Limits   Basic

Figure 13.11

The Primary Units dialog box.

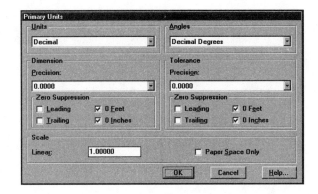

The features of the Primary Units dialog box are described in the following list:

■ **Units:** This drop-down list enables you to set the dimension unit type. [DIMDEC, DIMUNIT]

■ **Precision:** Use this drop-down list in the Dimension section of the dialog box to set dimension unit precision. [DIMDEC, DIMUNIT]

■ **Leading:** This check box enables you to suppress leading zeros in the dimension text in the Dimension section of the dialog box. [DIMZIN]

■ **Trailing:** This check box enables you to suppress trailing zeros in the dimension text in the Dimension section of the dialog box. [DIMZIN]

■ **0 Feet:** This check box enables you to suppress the display of 0' (0 feet) in dimension text in the Dimension section of the dialog box. [DIMZIN]

- **0 Inches:** This check box enables you to suppress the display of 0" (0 inches) in dimension text in the Dimension section of the dialog box. [DIMZIN]

- **Linear:** Use this edit box for scale factor to apply to dimensions placed in paper space. [DIMLFAC]

- **Angles:** Use this drop-down list to set the angular unit type. [DIMAUNIT]

- **Precision:** Use this drop-down list to set angular unit precision in the Tolerance section of the dialog box. [DIMUNIT]

- **Leading:** This check box enables you to suppress leading zeros in angular dimensions in the Tolerance section of the dialog box. [DIMZIN]

- **Trailing:** This check box enables you to suppress trailing zeros in angular dimensions in the Tolerance section of the dialog box. [DIMZIN]

- **0 Feet:** This check box enables you to suppress the display of 0' (0 feet) in angular dimensions in the Tolerance section of the dialog box. [DIMZIN]

- **0 Inches:** This check box enables you to suppress the display of 0" (0 inches) in angular dimensions in the Tolerance section of the dialog box. [DIMZIN]

- **Paper Space Only:** This check box enables you to apply dimension settings to dimensions in paper space. [DIMLFAC]

- **Help:** This button opens context-sensitive help for the Primary Units dialog box.

NOTE

A short definition of dimension variables can be gotten by typing STATUS at the `Dim:` prompt.

Viewing the Settings for Multiple Dimension Styles

You may have a dimension style for an architectural application using ticks rather than arrowheads and another style to be used for leaders with a right angle arrowhead. Another style may use tolerances. In the following exercise, you open a drawing with several dimension styles and use the Dimension Style dialog box to review the existing styles.

REVIEWING THE EXISTING DIMENSION STYLES

1. Open the drawing DIMSTYL1.DWG located in the PROJECTS/CH13 directory of the CD-ROM and notice the different configurations of the dimensions.

2. Choose List from the Standard toolbar, then select the tolerance dimension at ① (as shown in fig. 13.12) and the minus dimension at ②. Press Enter to see the following:

```
DIMENSION  Layer: DIM
Space: Model space
Handle = 47
type: vertical
1st extension  defining point: X=    0.158  Y=    1.439  Z=    0.000
2nd extension  defining point: X=   -0.142  Y=    2.679  Z=    0.000
dimension line defining point: X=    0.716  Y=    2.679  Z=    0.000
default text position: X=    0.716  Y=    2.059  Z=    0.000
default text
dimension style: TOLERANCE

DIMENSION  Layer: DIM
Space: Model space
Handle = 56
type: horizontal
1st extension  defining point: X=   -0.642  Y=    1.439  Z=    0.000
2nd extension  defining point: X=    0.158  Y=    1.439  Z=    0.000
dimension line defining point: X=    0.158  Y=    0.985  Z=    0.000
default text position: X=   -0.242  Y=    0.985  Z=    0.000
default text
dimension style: MINUS
```

Figure 13.12

*The DIMSTYL1 drawing
with various dimension
styles.*

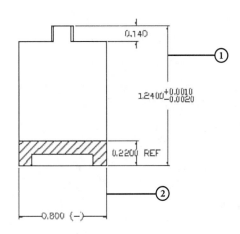

3. Choose Format, Dimension Style to open the Dimension Style dialog box shown.

4. Choose TOLERANCE from the Current style drop-down list, then choose Annotation and notice the tolerance settings in the Primary Units and Tolerance areas of the dialog box. Choose OK.

5. Set MINUS to be the Current style, then choose Annotation again and notice the Suffix of (-) in the Primary Units area.

6. Choose OK to close the Annotation dialog box, then OK again to close the Dimension Style dialog box.

Changing the Dimension Style

Occasionally, you need to change an existing dimension's setting. This section presents some exercises in which you change the dimension style settings, update an existing dimension, and create a new dimension style in the current drawing.

Modifying the Settings of an Existing Style

In the following exercise, you modify some settings of an existing dimension style and see how dimensions originally created in that style are automatically updated.

MODIFYING THE DIMENSION STYLE SETTINGS

1. Choose Dimension Styles from the Dimensioning toolbar to open the Dimensioning Style dialog box.

2. From the Current style drop-down list, choose TOLERANCE.

3. Choose Annotation to open the Annotation dialog box, then choose Units to open the Primary Units dialog box.

4. From Dimension Precision drop-down list, choose 0.000, then choose OK.

5. Click once in the tolerance method image tile located in the Primary Units area to change the tolerance method to Limits (shown in the Tolerance Method drop-down list). Choose OK.

6. In the Text area, open the Style drop-down list and scroll up to select NOTES, then choose OK.

7. Choose Save to save the new settings to the TOLERANCE dimension style, then choose OK.

8. Your drawing will automatically update the vertical tolerance dimension and the text style, as shown in figure 13.13.

9. Choose Save to save the drawing.

Figure 13.13

The tolerance dimension updated.

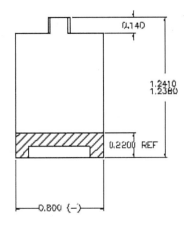

NOTE

If you change a setting for a dimension style, then choose OK to close the dialog box and fail to choose Save to save the changes, when you return to the Dimension Style dialog box next time you will see a plus sign (+) beside the current dimension style. This is to remind you that changes have been made to the style and will not be applied to dimensions in that style until you choose Save. You learn more about dimension overrides later in this chapter.

Updating an Existing Dimension with a Different Style

As you have seen in this chapter, a drawing can have many dimension styles. Similar to the concept of layers and text styles, only one dimension style can be current at any given time. Sometimes, you need to switch a dimension from one style to another. For instance, a dimension may have been created in the MECH dimension style and you need to have it in the TOLERANCE style. In the following exercise, you learn how to apply the current dimension style to an existing dimension.

UPDATING AN EXISTING DIMENSION WITH A DIFFERENT STYLE

1. Choose Dimension Styles from the Dimensioning toolbar to open the Dimensioning Style dialog box.

2. Choose REF-INSIDE from the Current drop-down list, then choose OK.

3. At the `Command:` line enter **DIM**, and you see the following prompt:

    Dim:

4. Enter **UPDATE** and select the horizontal 0.800 (-) dimension, then press Enter.

5. The dimension will be updated with the REF-INSIDE dimension style settings as shown in figure 13.14.

6. Save the drawing.

Figure 13.14

The suffix dimension updated.

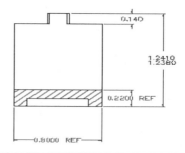

NOTE

Another way to update a dimension with an existing dimension style is to use the DIMSTYLE command with the Apply option. The current dimension style will then be applied to the selected dimension(s).

Creating a New Dimension Style

Now that you have an idea of the concepts involved with dimension styles, it's time to create a new one. A new dimension style is easily created from an existing style. After the settings are changed, a new style is created by saving the changes. The following exercise takes you through the process of creating a new dimension style.

CREATING THE DOT DIMENSION STYLE

1. Choose Dimension Styles from the Dimensioning toolbar, then choose MECHANICAL from the Current drop-down list.

2. Double-click in the Name edit box and type DOT for the new dimension style name. Press Enter to create the new style.

3. Choose Geometry, then open the 1st drop-down list located in the Arrowhead area and choose Dot, as shown in figure 13.15.

Figure 13.15

The Dot selection in the Arrowheads area.

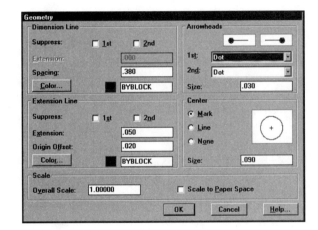

4. In the Extension Line area, change the Extension value to **.050**, then choose OK.

5. Choose Format and change the Vertical Justification to Above by clicking once in the graphic display, then choose OK.

6. Choose Annotation, then choose Units to open the Primary Units dialog box.

7. Set the Primary Units Precision to **0.000**, then click in the Leading box in the Units Zero Suppression area to suppress the leading zeros in a dimension. Choose OK.

8. In the Annotation dialog box, change the Gap value to **.050**, then choose OK.

9. Choose Save to save the changes to the DOT dimension style, then choose OK.

10. Enter **DIM** to change to the Dim: prompt, then enter **UPDATE**.

11. Choose the 0.800 REF dimension and press Enter, after which the drawing will update the selected dimension, as shown in figure 13.16.

*The dimension in the new
DOT dimension style.*

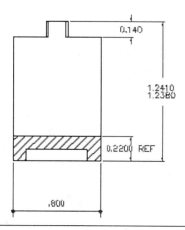

Dimension styles can be very useful and are real time-savers when you consider the various dimension settings you need in the drawings you typically create. Make sure the dimension styles are in your prototype. Therefore, each drawing you begin will have them available.

RELATED COMMANDS

DIMSTYLE

DDIM

14

DIMENSIONING THE DRAWING

From day one, Autodesk has been improving the dimensioning features of its products. Historically, the dimensioning of a drawing was a job that few people wanted. With each release of AutoCAD, however, the task got easier. As with the dimensioning styles seen in Chapter 13, "Dimensioning Styles," a majority of the dimensioning tools available in AutoCAD Release 13 are now available in AutoCAD LT for Windows 95.

■ *The Dimensioning toolbar overview*

■ *Placing Horizontal, Vertical (Linear), and Aligned dimensions*

■ *Adding a Continued dimension*

■ *Creating Angular Baseline*

■ *The circular dimensions of Radius and Diameter*

■ *Adding linear or spline Leaders as annotation*

■ *Working with Ordinate dimensions*

■ *The geometric tolerance feature control frame*

■ *Applying alternative metric dimensions*

The Annotated Dimensioning Toolbar

The most efficient means of adding dimensions to the drawing is by using the Dimensioning toolbar. The available dimension types are shown in figure 14.1, which displays the five dimension toolbars, four of which are flyouts from the primary toolbar.

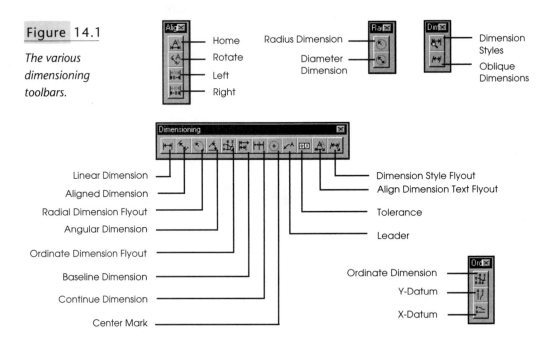

Figure 14.1

The various dimensioning toolbars.

Figure 14.2 displays several dimension types that can be generated using the tools from the Dimensioning toolbar.

Figure 14.2

An illustration of several dimensioning types.

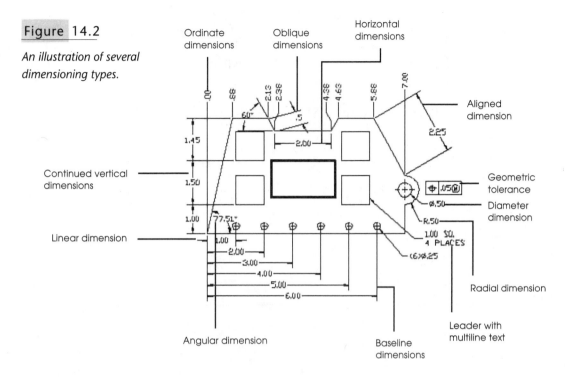

Adding the Dimensions

Now that you have an idea of the types of dimensioning available, this section takes you through several exercises that give you an opportunity to add dimensions. Dimension styles (see Chapter 13, "Dimensioning Styles") also play a role in the exercises in this chapter.

Linear and Aligned Dimensions

The linear dimension is probably the most commonly placed dimension. Releases 1 and 2 of AutoCAD LT had separate commands for placing a horizontal or vertical dimension. Although those commands can still be entered from the Dim: prompt line, the new DIMLINEAR command invoked from the Dimensioning toolbar can create either.

Prior to adding a dimension, of course, you need to create a dimensioning layer and set a running object snap. In this first series of exercises, you create a new dimension style for the dimensions on an architectural plan.

ADDING A LINEAR DIMENSION TO THE FLOOR PLAN

1. Open the drawing DIM-ARCH.DWG located in the PROJECTS/CH14 directory of the CD-ROM, then create a layer named **DIMS** and set it to be current.

2. Double-click on OSNAP on the status bar and set the running object snap to Endpoint.

3. Choose View, Toolbars to open the Toolbars dialog box, then scroll down and choose Dimensioning. Choose OK.

4. Dock the Dimensioning toolbar vertically along the right side of the drawing window, then choose Dimension Styles from the toolbar.

5. Double-click on STANDARD in the Name edit box, then type **ARCH** and choose Save to create a new style.

6. Choose Geometry and change the arrowheads to Oblique (tick marks) and their Size to **3"** as shown in figure 14.3.

7. Set the Dimension Line Extension value to **3"**, the Extension Line Extension to **3"**, and the Origin Offset to **3"**. Choose OK.

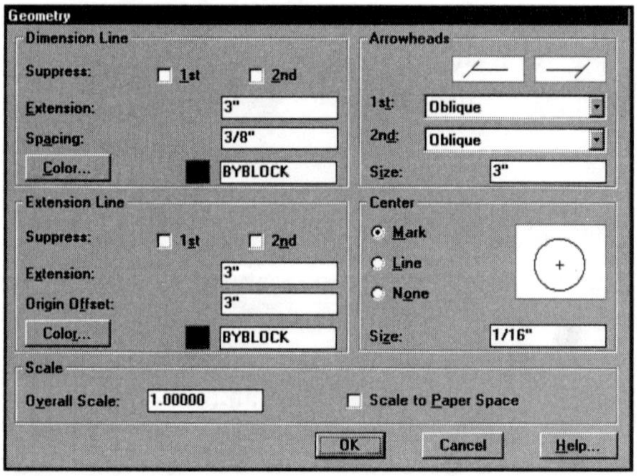

Figure 14.3

The Geometry dialog box for the ARCH dimension style.

8. Choose Format, then click once in the Vertical Justification image tile to set the justification to Above. Choose OK.

9. Choose Annotation, then choose Units to open the Primary Units dialog box.

10. Set the Units to Architectural (stacked) and turn off the suppression of 0 Inches. Choose OK to close the Primary Units dialog box.

11. Set the Text Height to **6"** and the Gap to **3"** and choose OK. Then choose Save to save these settings to the ARCH dimension style.

12. Choose OK to close the Dimension Styles dialog box. Now that you have the dimension style set, the next series of steps takes you through the placement of a linear dimension:

13. Choose Linear Dimension from the toolbar, and you see the following prompt:

```
First extension line origin or RETURN to select:
```

14. Pick ① as shown in figure 14.4, and you see the next prompt:

```
Second extension line origin:
```

15. Pick ② as the second point, and the next prompt appears:

```
Dimension line location (Text/Angle/Horizontal/Vertical/Rotated):
```

16. Move your cursor left and right to see the (vertical) dimension, then move the cursor vertically and pick ③ to place the horizontal dimension.

17. Choose Save to save the DIM-ARCH drawing.

Figure 14.4

Pick points for the linear dimension.

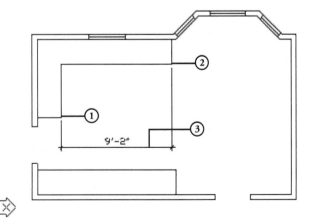

NOTE

The default setting for the DIMSCALE variable is 1 and is displayed in the Geometry dialog box. When using this default value, the plot scale factor is applied to the dimensioning values given. For example, an arrowhead size setting of .5000" would result in plotted arrowheads .2500" long when plotted at half scale.

An alternative would be to set the DIMSCALE setting to the inverse of the desired plot scale factor for the drawing, then set the geometric and annotation dimensioning values to their desired size when plotted. This enables you to retain the plotted sizes should the plot scale factor be changed. For example, if the plot scale required changing from half scale to quarter scale, simply change the DIMSCALE setting to 4, the inverse of the plot scale factor. This eliminates the need to individually change each geometry or annotation dimension value.

The phrasing in the first dimension prompt—or RETURN to select—gives you an alternative to picking two points individually for the dimension. If you press Enter (or Return on some keyboards), AutoCAD LT automatically finds the endpoints of the line selected and pulls the dimension from those endpoints. In the next exercise, you place another linear dimension after pressing Enter to select the line.

ADDING A VERTICAL DIMENSION

1. Continue from the previous exercise and choose Linear Dimension from the Dimensioning toolbar. Press Enter in response to the first prompt, and you see the following:

   ```
   Select object to dimension:
   ```

2. Pick ① as shown in figure 14.5, after which you are prompted for the position of the dimension line. Then pick ② to place the vertical dimension.

3. Choose the Dimension Styles tools to open the Dimensioning Styles dialog box, then choose Format.

4. Click once in the Text image tile to turn off the Inside and Outside Horizontal options, then choose OK.

5. Choose Save to save this setting change to the ARCH dimension style. Choose OK and you see the vertical dimension change format. Your drawing should look similar to figure 14.6, which shows the updated dimension.

Figure 14.5

Pick points for the vertical dimension.

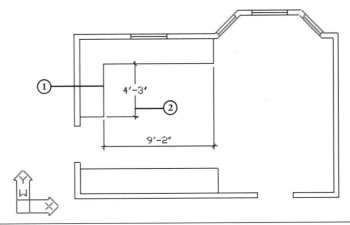

NOTE

When you press Enter to select an object in response to the first dimension prompt, AutoCAD LT places the first extension line at the endpoint closest to the point you selected.

The continued dimension may be placed consecutively during the initial dimensioning sequence or added later to an existing dimension. In the following exercise, you add a continued dimension to the 4'-3" dimension placed in the previous exercise and two others to the original 9'-2" horizontal dimension.

ADDING CONTINUED DIMENSIONS

1. Continue from the previous exercise and choose Continued Dimension from the Dimensioning toolbar. You see the following prompt:

   `Second extension line origin or RETURN to select:`

2. If a dimension sequence has ended, it's usually a good idea to establish the dimension from which the next dimension is to be placed. Press Enter, and you see the following prompt:

   `Select continued dimension:`

3. Pick ① as shown in figure 14.6, and pick ② as the second extension line origin. Press Esc to complete the sequence.

Figure 14.6

Placing continued dimensions on the floor plan.

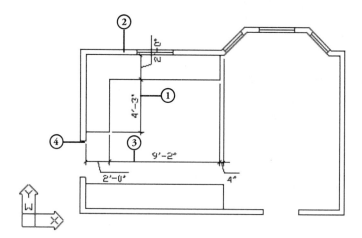

4. Choose Continued Dimension again, then press Enter and pick ③ as the continued dimension (and the side of the dimension line). Pick ④ as the second extension-line origin.

5. Press Enter again, then pick the horizontal dimension at ⑤ as the continued dimension. Pick ⑥ as the location of the second extension-line origin.

6. Press Esc to cancel the continued dimension sequence, then choose Save to save the drawing.

Another type of dimension frequently used is the aligned dimension. As shown in figure 14.2 at the beginning of this chapter, the aligned dimension line is parallel to the object being dimensioned. In the next exercise, you add aligned dimensions to the bay window.

ADDING SOME ALIGNED DIMENSIONS

1. Continue from the previous exercise and zoom into the floor plan as shown in figure 14.7. Choose Aligned Dimension from the Dimensioning toolbar, and you see the following prompt:

   `First extension line origin or RETURN to select:`

2. Press Enter, then pick ① as shown in figure 14.7, and you see the following prompt:

   `Dimension line location (Text/Angle):`

3. Pick ② as the dimension-line location to complete the aligned dimension sequence.

4. Choose Aligned Dimension again, then press Enter and pick ③ as the object to dimension.

5. Pick ④ to place the dimension line and complete the aligned dimension.

6. Place the third aligned dimension on the drawing, then choose Save.

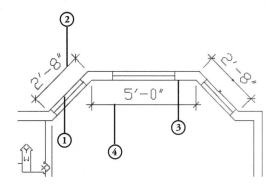

Figure 14.7

Pick points for the aligned dimensions.

Angular, Baseline, and Circular Dimensions

Mechanical applications frequently require circular dimensioning, such as radial or diameter dimensions, as well as the angular dimensions required on non-orthogonal line work, such as plates or piping. Baseline dimensioning is another common application that creates a series of dimensions, all pulling from a single point. In the following sequence of exercises, you add several dimensions to an angle bracket by using the default dimension style STANDARD.

ADDING AN ANGULAR DIMENSION TO THE BRACKET

1. Open the drawing DIM-BRKT.DWG located in the PROJECTS/CH14 directory of the CD-ROM, then choose Angular Dimension from the Dimensioning toolbar, and you see the following prompt:

```
dimangular
Select arc, circle, line, or RETURN:
```

2. Pick ① as shown in figure 14.8, then ②, and you see the following prompt:

```
Dimension arc line location (Text/Angle):
```

3. Move your cursor around the chamfered corner to see the changes in the angular dimension value, then pick ③ to place the angular dimension and end the command.

14.8

An angular dimension.

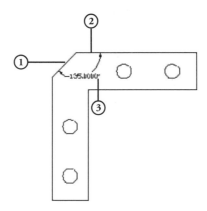

4. Choose Dimension Styles from the toolbar and double-click on STANDARD in the Name edit box. Enter **ANGULAR**, then choose Save.

5. Choose Annotation, then choose Units from the Primary Units area.

6. Set the Dimension Precision to **0.0**, then choose OK back to the Dimension Styles dialog box, then choose Save.

7. Enter **DIMSTYLE** at the Command: line, and you see the following prompt:

```
Dimension Style Edit (Save/Restore/STatus/Variables/Apply/?)
<Restore>:
```

8. Enter **A** for the Apply option and select the angular dimension, then press Enter to apply the settings of the current ANGULAR dimension style to the selected dimension.

9. Choose Save to save the drawing.

In the next exercise, you add baseline dimensions to specify the placement of the holes. Similar in application to that of the continued dimension, a baseline dimension is added to an existing linear dimension. First, you change the setting in the Geometry dialog box, which specifies the distance between the dimension lines of baseline dimensions.

ADDING SOME BASELINE DIMENSIONS

1. Continue from the previous exercise and choose Dimension Styles from the toolbar. Set the STANDARD style to be current, then choose Geometry.

2. Set the Dimension Line Spacing to **0.5000** and choose OK, then save the change and choose OK to close the Dimension Styles dialog box.

3. Double-click on OSNAP on the status bar, and set Endpoint and Center as the running object snaps.

4. Choose Linear Dimension and pick ①, then ②, as shown in figure 14.9. Then pick ③ to place the vertical dimension.

Figure 14.9

The baseline dimensions.

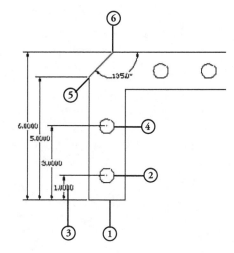

5. Choose Baseline Dimension, and you see the following prompt:

   `Second extension line origin or RETURN to select:`

6. Pick the next circle at ④, and the baseline dimension will be automatically placed .5" from the vertical dimension.

7. Pick the bottom corner of the chamfer at ⑤, then the top corner of the chamfer at ⑥.

8. Press Esc to cancel the baseline dimensioning sequence, then save the drawing.

Dimensioning of radii and diameters has been improved over earlier releases of LT, because now you can dynamically rotate the position of the circular dimension, much like you did with the angular dimension. In the next exercise, you apply some fillets to the bracket, then create a new style and add radial and diameter dimensions.

ADDING THE CIRCULAR DIMENSIONS

1. Continue from the previous exercise and choose Fillet from the Modify toolbar. Set the Radius to **.2**.

2. Press the spacebar to reissue the FILLET command, then enter **P** for the Polygon option and pick anywhere on the bracket to apply the fillets to all the corners.

3. Press the spacebar again and change the Radius to **1.25**, then reissue the FILLET command and pick ① and ② (as shown in figure 14.10) to apply to the fillet.

4. Choose Dimension Styles and create a new dimension style named RADIAL from STANDARD, then choose Annotation.

5. From the Primary Units dialog box, set the Dimension Precision to **0.00**, then save the new setting and close the Dimension Styles dialog box by choosing OK.

6. Choose Radius Dimension and pick ③, move the cursor to see the dynamic placement feature within the confines of the arc of the fillet, then pick ④ to place the dimension.

Figure 14.10

Applying the fillets and adding the radius dimension.

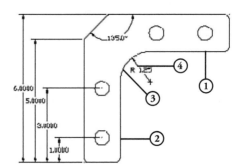

The Radius Dimension routine automatically places an R immediately in front of the radial dimension text. To separate the R from the dimension, follow the next few steps to add a Prefix in the Annotation dialog box:

7. Choose Dimension Styles, then choose Annotation.

8. In the Prefix edit box, enter **R** and press the spacebar to add a space. Choose OK.

9. Choose Save, then choose OK and the radius dimension will automatically change.

10. To add a center mark, choose Center Mark and pick ③ as shown in figure 14.10.

To add the diameter dimensions, it helps to zoom into the drawing more closely:

11. Use Zoom Window and change your display to that shown in figure 14.11. Choose Dimension Styles.

12. Choose STANDARD from the Current drop-down list, then create a new dimension style named DIAMETER.

13. Choose Annotation and pick the Suffix edit box, press the spacebar, and enter the text **TYP. 4x**. Choose OK.

14. Choose Save to save the suffix setting to the CIRCULAR dimension style, then choose OK.

15. Choose Diameter Dimension from the Radial Dimension flyout, and you see the following prompt:

```
Select arc or circle:
```

16. Choose the circle at ① (as shown in figure 14.11) and you see the next prompt:

```
Dimension text <0.6000>:
Dimension line location (Text/Angle):
```

17. Pick ② to accept the default dimension text value, and place the diameter dimension.

18. Choose Save to save the drawing.

Figure 14.11

*Adding the diameter
dimension with the suffix.*

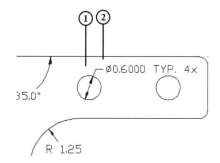

Creating Leaders

When notation needs to be added to a drawing with leader line and an arrowhead, AutoCAD LT provides the DIMLEADER command, which is invoked by using the Leader tool in the Dimensioning toolbar. This section presents several of the primary features available with this routine.

Adding a Leader to the Drawing

When placing a leader, the first point picked is the placement of the arrowhead, after which you may pick additional points for the leader line. After the leader line has been started, the Annotation option provides additional options with which to annotate the object. You may choose to place a geometric tolerance symbol, copy an existing object, insert a block, or add multiple lines of text. By default, you simply enter the desired annotation when finished picking points for the leader line.

When adding a leader, you may want to have the leader text in a different style. In the following exercise, you create a new style and change the text style for the dimension (leader) text.

ADDING A LEADER IN THE LEADER STYLE

1. Continue from the previous exercise and choose Dimension Styles, then choose STANDARD from the Current drop-down list and create a new dimension style named LEADER.

2. Choose Annotation, then choose LEADER-TEXT from the the Style drop-down list in the Text area. Choose OK and save the new setting to the LEADER dimension style.

3. Choose Zoom All to return to a display similar to that shown in figure 14.12. Then choose Leader from the Dimensioning toolbar, and you see the following prompt:

   ```
   From point:
   ```

4. Double-click on OSNAP on the status bar, then pick ① (as shown in figure 14.12). You see the next prompt:

   ```
   To point:
   ```

5. Pick ② to place the next point of the leader, and you see a new prompt:

   ```
   To point (Format/Annotation/Undo)<Annotation>:
   ```

6. Press Enter to accept the default option for Annotation, and you see the next prompt:

   ```
   Annotation (or RETURN for options):
   ```

7. Type **R .2** (TYP.) and press Enter, and you get the following prompt referring to multiline text:

   ```
   Mtext:
   ```

8. Press Enter again to add the leader text and complete the command, then save the drawing.

Figure 14.12

*Placing the
leader with text.*

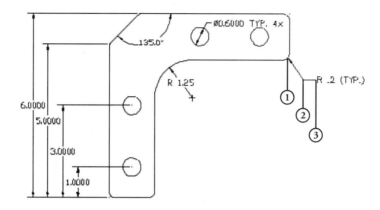

NOTE

> The position of the leader text in relation to the end of the last segment of the leader line
> is determined by the current setting of the Vertical Justification in the Format dialog box.

Creating the Curved Leader Line

For purposes of clarity, leader lines are frequently created by using curved lines. The
Spline feature available from the Format options enables you to pick the spline
points for the leader line. In the following exercise, you add a spline leader line.

ADDING A LEADER IN THE LEADER STYLE

1. Continue from the previous exercise and choose Leader, then pick ①, and
   pick ② as shown in figure 14.13.

2. Enter **F** for the Format option, and you see the following prompt:

   `Spline/STraight/Arrow/None/<Exit>:`

3. Enter **S** for Spline, then pick ③ and ④. Press Enter to begin the annotation.

4. Enter **POLISH SMOOTH**, then press Enter twice to complete the command.

Figure 14.13

*Placing a spline
leader line.*

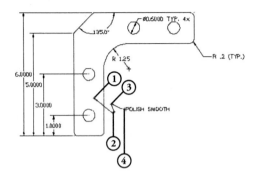

Multiline Text in the Leader

In earlier versions of AutoCAD LT, you could have only a single line of text associated automatically with the leader line. With the introduction of multiline text, you may enter more than one line. In the following exercise, you add a couple lines of text at the end of the leader.

ADDING MULTILINE TEXT FOR THE LEADER

1. Continue from the previous exercise and choose Leader, then pick ① and ② as shown in figure 14.14.

2. Turn on Ortho and pick ③, then press Enter to accept the default option for annotation. Type **ROUND BOTH CORNERS**, then press Enter. You see the following prompt:

    `Mtext:`

3. Type **ON 1"x1" CHAMFER** and press Enter twice to add the multiline text and end the command.

4. Choose Save to save the drawing.

Figure 14.14

Adding a multiline text leader.

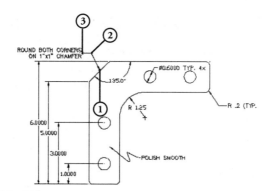

You noticed on the last exercise that multiline text for leaders is justified to the side of the leader line. As multiline text, it is also editable by using the DDEDIT command.

N O T E

Entering LEADER at the Command: line invokes the same command as choosing the Leader tool from the Dimensioning toolbar. Entering LEADER at the Dim: prompt, however, is the leader routine from Release 2 and does not give you the options available using the toolbar.

Ordinate Dimensioning and Geometric Tolerances

Ordinate dimensioning involves specifying the X or Y location of a feature relative to the origin of the current UCS, which is the *datum* point for the dimension value. Ordinate dimensioning is used primarily in mechanical engineering environments, often for specifying the locations of holes or features to be drilled, punched, or machined in sheet metal or plate steel. Geometric tolerances are also frequently associated with engineering applications. Adding tolerances is a method by which conditions and parameters relating to the fabrication of the object are annotated on the drawing.

Applying Ordinate Dimensions

The default datum point for ordinate dimensions is the origin of the current UCS (User Coordinate System), or the absolute coordinate 0,0. AutoCAD LT calculates the distance from the datum point, then adds the dimension text in either the X or Y ordinate. In the following exercise, you open a plate drawing and add several ordinate dimensions.

TI P

It is easier to align the leader endpoints for a neater appearance if you use construction lines to align the extension line endpoints.

ADDING SOME ORDINATE DIMENSIONS

1. Open the drawing DIM-ORD.DWG located in the PROJECTS/CH14 directory and double-click on OSNAP on the status bar. Set Center as the running object snap.

2. Choose Ordinate Dimension from the Dimensioning toolbar, and you see the following prompt:

    Select feature:

3. Enter **0,0**, and you see the following prompt:

    Leader endpoint (Xdatum/Ydatum/Text):

4. Choose Snap to Perpendicular and pick ① on the horizontal construction line (as shown in figure 14.15) to place the ordinate dimension and end the command.

Figure 14.15

The X and Y ordinate dimensions.

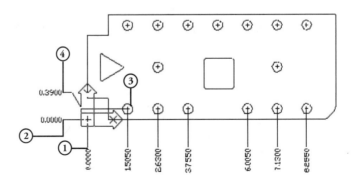

5. Press the spacebar to reissue the DIMORDINATE command. Then enter **0,0**, choose Snap to Perpendicular, and pick ② on the vertical construction line.

6. Choose Ordinate Dimension and pick ③, then use Perpendicular object snap and pick the horizontal construction line.

7. Press the spacebar and pick the circle at ③ again, then press F8 to turn off Ortho.

8. Enter **NEA** at the prompt line for the leader endpoint and pick the vertical construction line at ④.

9. Place the remaining X datum ordinate dimensions as shown in figure 14.15, then erase the construction lines.

10. Choose Dimension Styles to open the Dimension Styles dialog box, then choose Geometry.

11. In the Extension line dialog box, set the Origin Offset value to **.25**, then choose OK.

12. Choose Save to save the change to the current style, then choose OK to close the Dimension Styles dialog box, after which the extension lines of the ordinate dimensions will be updated.

13. Choose Save to save the drawing.

Geometric Tolerance Symbology and Applications

Geometric tolerance dimensioning is simply the application of symbology that graphically specifies the manner in which a part is to be machined or fabricated. Figure 14.16 presents the geometric tolerance symbols available from the Tolerance tool of the Dimensioning toolbar, and figure 14.17 displays a table of the various GDT (Geometric Dimensioning and Tolerancing) symbols and their meanings.

Figure 14.16

The Symbol dialog box for geometric tolerancing.

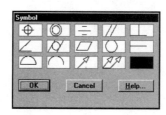

Figure 14.17

Geometric dimension and tolerance symbols and their meanings.

—	STRAIGHTNESS	Ⓜ	AT MAXIMUM MATERIAL CONDITION
⬭	FLATNESS	Ⓛ	AT LEAST MATERIAL CONDITION
○	CIRCULARITY	Ⓢ	REGARDLESS OF FEATURE SIZE
⌯	CYLINDRICITY	Ⓟ	PROJECTED TOLERANCE ZONE
⌒	PROFILE OF A LINE	∅	DIAMETER
△	PROFILE OF A SURFACE	⟾	CONICAL TAPER
∠	ANGULARITY	⟍	SLOPE
⊥	PERPENDICULARITY	⊔	COUNTEBORE/SPOTFACE
//	PARALLELISM	∨	COUNTERSINK
⊕	POSITION	⊽	DEPTH
◎	CONCENTRICITY	□	SQUARE
⩲	SYMMETRY	⌒	ARC LENGTH
⌁	CIRCULAR RUNOUT		
⌁⌁	TOTAL RUNOUT		

After you specify the geometry and symbols in the dialog box, LT places the notation, or "feature control frame," on the drawing. In the following exercise, you add a tolerance notation to the plate drawing.

ADDING THE GEOMETRIC TOLERANCE

1. Continue from the previous exercise and choose Tolerance from the Dimensioning toolbar to display the Symbol dialog box shown in figure 14.16.

2. Choose the upper left symbol (for position), then choose OK to open the Geometric Tolerance dialog box.

3. Set the Value for Tolerance 1 to **.05**, then click in the MC field for Tolerance 1 to display the Material Condition dialog box shown in figure 14.18.

Figure 14.18

The Material Condition dialog box.

4. Choose the circle M for Maximum, then choose OK to assign that symbol to Tolerance 1.

5. Set the Datum for Datum 1 to **A**, Datum 2 to **B**, and Datum 3 to **C**. Then choose OK, and you see the following prompt:

   `Enter tolerance location:`

6. Pick the point at ① (as shown in figure 14.19) to place the feature control frame.

7. Choose Save to save the drawing.

Figure 14.19

The feature control frame for the geometric tolerance.

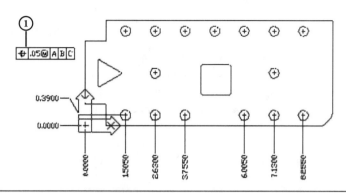

In the next exercise, you place the GDT feature control frame at the end of a leader line by using the Format option of the LEADER command.

ADDING THE CONTROL FRAME ON A LEADER

1. Continue from the previous exercise and use the vertical scroll bar to pan up to a display similar to that shown in figure 14.20.

2. Choose Leader, pick the circle at ①, pick ② and ③, then press Enter for the default Annotation option. You see the following prompt:

```
Annotation (or RETURN for options):
```

3. Press Enter, and you see the next prompt:

```
Tolerance/Copy/Block/None/<Mtext>:
```

4. Enter **T** to open the Symbol dialog box, then create a feature control frame similar to that created in the previous exercise.

Figure 14.20

Adding the feature control frame to a leader.

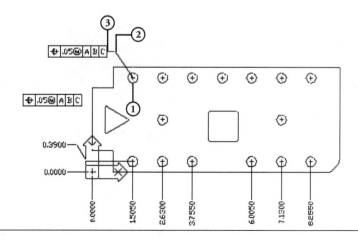

A Word about Alternative Metric Dimensioning

AutoCAD LT provides the Alternate Units area in the Annotation dialog box for dimension settings for objects that are created in inches but which also need to have metric equivalents. By default, the multiplier for alternate units is 25.4 (1"=25.4mm). This section presents the process of adding the alternative metric dimensions.

Including the Metric Dimension

In addition to enabling the Alternate Units feature of LT, you may also want to add an alternative units suffix. In the following exercise, you add alternative metric dimensions to the plate drawing.

ADDING METRIC DIMENSIONS

1. Continue from the previous exercise and choose Dimension Styles, then create a new style named METRIC from the STANDARD style.

2. Choose Annotation and click in the Enable Units box in the Alternate Units area to enable metric dimensioning. Choose Units in the same area; notice the default value of 25.4000 for the Linear Scale.

3. Choose OK to close the Alternate Units dialog box, then choose Units from the Primary Units area.

4. Set the Dimension Precision to **0.000**, then choose OK.

5. Choose Save to save the settings to the METRIC style, then choose OK.

6. Set Endpoint to be the running object snap, then choose Linear Dimension from the Dimensioning toolbar.

7. Press Enter to select the object, pick ① as shown in figure 14.21, then pick ② to place the dimension.

8. Press Enter to reissue the DIMLINEAR command, pick ③, then ④, and place the dimension line at ⑤.

9. Choose Save to save the drawing.

Figure 14.21

Some alternative metric dimensions.

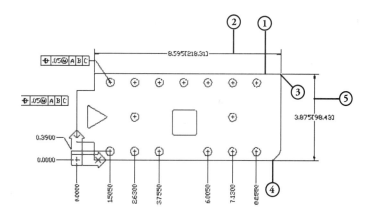

> **N**OTE
>
> When creating a metric drawing, set the desired units (such as DECIMAL) and create the drawing as you normally would create a drawing in inches. When you dimension the drawing, however, create a new dimension style and set the Overall Scale factor in the Geometry dialog box to 12.7 to accommodate the default scaled settings, such as heights, offset distances, and the like.
>
> If alternate units in inches is required, enable alternate units and set the Linear Scale factor in the Alternate Units dialog box to the reciprocal of 25.4 (0.03937).

Summary

The possibilities for dimensions are endless. As you have seen in this chapter, AutoCAD LT has extensive capabilities in creating dimensions for nearly all applications. It is clear from what you have seen in this chapter and in Chapter 13, "Dimensioning Styles," that having a dimension style that contains your commonly used settings is very helpful in adding and editing dimensions.

15

EDITING DIMENSIONS

In the CAD continuum of life, few drawings escape without editing. In most drawings, any changes to the objects result in a change in the dimension.

This chapter presents some timely features you will find helpful when faced with editing dimensions in a drawing.

■ *Associative dimension definition*

■ *Overriding the settings of a dimension style*

■ *Editing the linear dimension placement using grips*

■ *Repositioning the dimension text*

■ *Using grips to reposition angular and circular dimensions*

■ *Changing and restoring the dimension text manually*

■ *Editing the ordinate dimension with grips*

Editing Associative Dimensions

Dimensions are not cast in stone. Nor are they that difficult to modify. In Chapter 13, "Dimensioning Styles," and Chapter 14, "Dimensioning the Drawing," you saw the power of dimension styles and the global manner in which they are applied. In this chapter, you learn how to override dimension styles, as well as how to edit the dimension position and the dimension content.

A word should also be mentioned here regarding the dimension block itself. By default, a dimension in AutoCAD LT is a single object recognized as an unnamed block. This is due to its block-like characteristics of having several objects (the extension lines, dimension line, and dimension text); all considered to be one object.

Dimensions in LT also are associative by default. As you will learn in this chapter, when stretching a dimensioned object or repositioning the extension line origin of a dimension, the dimension(s) automatically update per the change in the object or location. The dimension value is *associated* with the object it dimensions, specifically the location of the dimension definition points, or def points.

As with blocks, dimensions can be exploded but they lose their associativity and become nothing more than lines and text. The creators of Autodesk have made great strides in their effort to accommodate dimensioning applications, although you might find it necessary to edit the dimension linework individually. This chapter will hopefully be an encouragement to you with respect to the many ways in which you can manipulate associative dimensions.

Overrides and Dimension Styles

To override dimension style settings, you can elect to either change the dimension variable from the DIM: prompt or change the setting using the Dimension Style dialog box. In Chapter 13, "Dimensioning Styles," you learned that if you change a setting and then choose Save to save the changes to the current style, all dimensions created in that style are updated. If you choose OK rather than Save, however, only the new dimensions will reflect the change.

In the following exercise, you change a dimension variable as well as change a setting in the dialog box. You also learn how to view the current overrides for a specified dimension style.

NOTE

The Clear option of the DIMOVERRIDE command enables you to select dimensions from which you want to clear overrides.

OVERRIDING THE DIMENSION SETTINGS

1. Open the drawing DIMARCH2, then open the Dimensioning toolbar and dock it along the right side of the drawing window.

2. Choose Geometry and set the 1st Arrowhead to **Dot**. Choose OK to close the Geometry dialog box and then choose OK to close the Dimension Styles dialog box (don't save this change to the ARCH style).

3. Enter **DIM** at the Command: prompt and then enter **DIMCLRT** at the Dim: prompt. You see the following prompt:

   ```
   Current value <BYBLOCK> New value:
   ```

4. Type **BLUE** and press Enter, and then choose Linear Dimension from the Dimensioning toolbar.

5. Press Enter and pick the exterior wall line at ① when prompted to select the object (see fig. 15.1). Pick ② to place the dimension.

Figure 15.1

Placing the dimension with overrides.

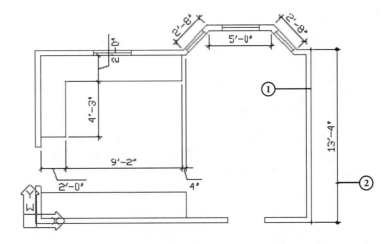

6. Choose the List tool on the Standard toolbar and then choose the dimension. You see the following dimension style override information:

```
dimension style: ARCH
dimension style overrides:
      DIMBLK1    DOT
      DIMBLK2    DOT
      DIMCLRT  5 (blue)
```

7. To see the existing overrides for a particular dimension style, invoke the DIMSTYLE command and inquire about the overrides by prefacing the dimension style name with the tilde (~) character.

8. Enter **DIMSTYLE** at the `Command:` prompt and you see the following prompt:

```
dimension style: ARCH
dimension style overrides:
      DIMBLK1    DOT
      DIMBLK2    DOT
      DIMCLRT  5 (blue)
Dimension Style Edit (Save/Restore/STatus/Variables/Apply/?) <Restore>:
```

9. Enter **R** for the Restore option and you see the following prompt:

```
?/Enter dimension style name or RETURN to select dimension:
```

10. Enter **~ARCH** and you see the following override information for the ARCH dimension style:

```
Differences between ARCH and current settings:
ARCH                    Current Setting
DIMBLK1    OBLIQUE            DOT
DIMBLK2    OBLIQUE            DOT
DIMCLRT  BYBLOCK           5 (blue)


?/Enter dimension style name or RETURN to select dimension:
```

11. Enter **ARCH** to restore the original settings of the dimension style, essentially removing the overrides.

12. To confirm the removal of the dimension overrides, issue the DIMSTYLE command again, then enter **R** for the Restore option.

13. Enter **~ARCH** to see any differences between ARCH and the current settings and you see the following:

```
Differences between ARCH and current settings:
ARCH                    Current Setting
No Differences.
```

14. Choose Save to save the drawing.

TIP

If you enter a variable such as DIMCLRT at the Command: line rather than the Dim: prompt, you must enter the numeric equivalent of your selection, such as five for the color blue used in the previous exercise.

When the current dimension style displayed in the Dimension Styles dialog box is prefaced by +, settings that have been modified without being saved to the current style exist. If you choose to Save, and then choose OK, you effectively will save the settings and apply those settings to all dimensions created in that style.

Editing Associative Dimensions with Grips

The dimensional element that enables associative dimensions to automatically update when the dimensioned object is edited is the definition point or, *defpoint*. For example, when you use the STRETCH command to edit an object and you include a defpoint in the selection set window, the dimension is updated per the change in distance. Later in this chapter you use the STRETCH command to edit the bracket and the dimension.

With the introduction of grips in an earlier release of AutoCAD LT, associative dimensions became much easier to edit because all associative dimensions have grip positions. For linear or aligned dimensions, there is a grip at each defpoint, each arrowhead, and one on the dimension text. Figure 15.2 illustrates a horizontal dimension with and without the grips displayed.

Figure 15.2

Associative dimension grips.

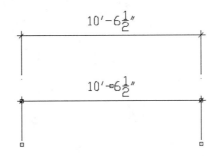

In the following exercise, you experiment with each of the associative dimension grips using the grip's STRETCH autoediting mode.

EDITING THE LINEAR DIMENSION USING GRIPS

1. Continue from the previous exercise and zoom into the bay window as shown in figure 15.3. Then turn off osnap on the status bar.

2. Click on the 5'-0" dimension at ① to display the grips, and then pick the left arrowhead grip at ②.

3. Enter **C** to invoke the Copy option of the STRETCH autoedit mode, and then pick ③ to place a copy of the dimension.

4. Press Esc three times to clear the selection set and the grips.

5. Pick the new dimension at ④ to display the grips, and then pick the left defpoint grip at ⑤ to display the hot grip.

6. Use Endpoint object snap to pick ⑥ to reposition the dimension extension line (keep in mind this was originally an aligned dimension).

7. Pick the defpoint at ① as shown in figure 15.4 to display the hot grip. Use Endpoint object snap to pick ② to align the dimension horizontally.

8. Press Esc three times to clear the grips and then save the drawing.

Figure 15.3

Copying and repositioning the dimension using grips.

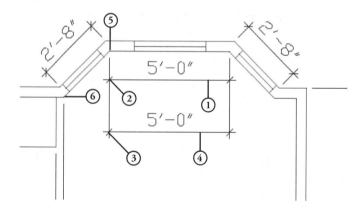

Figure 15.4

Creating a new dimension
with the defpoint grips.

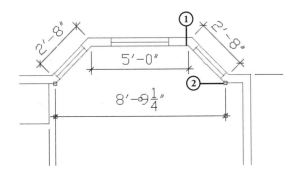

As you can see, the grips on associative dimensions provide useful methods by which to modify not only the position of the dimension line, but also the dimension itself.

Editing the Linear Dimension Text Orientation

For reasons of clarity, it may become necessary not only to reposition the dimension line, but also to edit the position of the text on the dimension line. The DIMTEDIT command enables you to position the dimension text to the left or right of the dimension line. You also have an option to rotate the dimension text.

AutoCAD LT provides a dimension editing function that enables you to oblique, or slant, the extension lines of linear dimensions. This obliquing function is a result of the Oblique option of the DIMEDIT command. In the following exercise, you use the tools found on the Align Dimension Text flyout and the Oblique Dimensions tool located on the Dimension Style flyout to edit the dimensions (see fig. 15.5).

Figure 15.5

The Align Dimension
Text flyout from the
Dimensioning toolbar.

TIP

Turn on the User Defined setting in the Format dialog box to position your dimension text anywhere along the dimension line. When User Defined is not selected, AutoCAD LT uses the Horizontal Justification specified in the Format dialog box.

Also, you must turn on the User Defined setting if you want to dynamically reposition the dimension line leaders on Radial and Diameter dimensions.

ALIGNING TEXT ON THE DIMENSION LINE

1. Open the drawing DIMBRK-T.DWG located in the sample directory, and then choose Left from the Align Dimension Text flyout. You see the following prompt:

   ```
   dimtedit
   Select dimension:
   ```

2. Pick the 6.0000 dimension at ① as shown in figure 15.6 and you see the following prompt, after which LT automatically positions the dimension text at the bottom of the dimension line:

   ```
   Enter text location (Left/Right/Home/Angle): _|
   ```

3. Choose Right from the flyout and then pick the 5.0000 dimension at ② when prompted to select the dimension. LT automatically repositions the text to the top of the drawing.

Figure 15.6

Repositioning the dimension text.

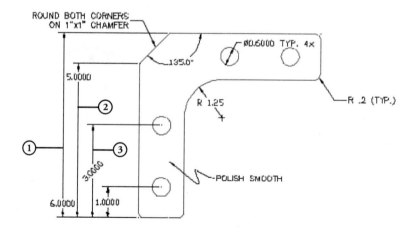

4. Choose Rotate from the flyout, then choose the 3.0000 dimension at ③ and you see the following prompt:

```
Enter text location (Left/Right/Home/Angle): _a
Enter text angle:
```

5. Enter **45** as the text angle to rotate the dimension text 45 degrees.

6. Choose Linear Dimension, and then use Center object snap and pick the circles at ① and ② (see fig. 15.7). Position the dimension line at ③.

7. Choose Oblique Dimensions from the Dimension Style flyout; you see the following prompt:

```
dimedit Dimension Edit (Home/New/Rotate/Oblique) <Home>: _o
Select objects:
```

8. Choose the horizontal dimension you just created and then press Enter to display the following prompt:

```
Enter obliquing angle (RETURN for none):
```

9. Enter **–75** for the obliquing angle to angle the extension lines **–75** degrees from a horizontal beginning at the defpoint of the dimension (see fig. 15.7).

10. Choose Save to save the drawing.

Figure 15.7

The obliqued horizontal dimension.

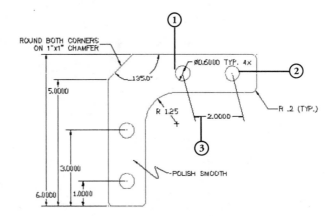

NOTE

By default, the angle entered for the obliquing of extension lines is taken from a horizontal line emanating from the dimension defpoint, a positive angle entry being counterclockwise.

Editing Angular and Circular Dimensions

The dynamic placement of the angular and circular dimensions gives you an indication of the flexibility that is possible in positioning dimensions. In the following exercise, you edit the angular and circular dimensions of the bracket drawing using dimension grips.

REPOSITIONING THE ANGULAR AND CIRCULAR DIMENSIONS WITH GRIPS

1. Continue from the previous exercise and choose View, Zoom, Center, and you see the following prompt:

```
All/Center/Extents/Previous/Window/<Scale(X/XP)>: _C
Center point:
```

2. Pick the circle with the 0.6000 diameter dimension and you see the following prompt:

```
Magnification or Height <7.5000>:
```

3. Enter **1.5X** after which LT magnifies the drawing by 50 percent and centers the new display on the selected circle.

4. Turn off OSNAP and ORTHO on the status bar, and then pick the angular dimension at ① to display the grips. See figure 15.8.

5. Pick the dimension text grip at ②, and then pick ③ to position the 45-degree angular dimension. Press Esc twice to clear the grips.

Figure 15.8

The pick points to reposition the dimension text.

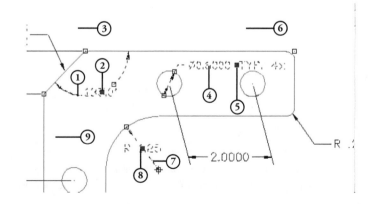

6. Pick the 6.0000 diameter dimension at ④ to display the dimension grips.

7. Pick the dimension text grip at ⑤, and then pick ⑥ to reposition the dimension text.

8. Press Esc twice to clear the grips, and then pick the 1.25 radial dimension at ⑦ to display the dimension grips.

9. Pick the dimension text grip at ⑧, and then pick ⑨ to reposition the radial dimension text.

10. Choose Save to save the drawing. Your drawing should look similar to that shown in figure 15.9.

Figure 15.9

New positions for the angular, diameter, and radial dimensions.

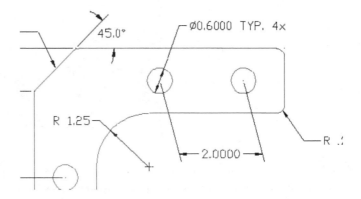

NOTE

Leader lines and the associated annotation are separate objects. Multiline and single line leader annotation each have a single grip by which they can be repositioned. A leader and its arrowhead are treated as a single object, with separate grips for the leader line endpoints and the arrowhead.

Modifying the Dimension Text Value

You can change at any time the text, or value, of any associative dimension or leader annotation. When adding a new dimension, the Text option enables you to replace the default value with user-specified text. To edit the dimension text value of existing dimensions, use the DDEDIT command from the Special Edit flyout on the Modify toolbar.

When editing dimension text or leader annotation, you are presented with the Edit MText dialog box. Associative dimensions that have not been edited display < > to indicate that the current dimension value has been calculated by AutoCAD LT (see fig. 15.10). The leader annotation is displayed in the dialog box and also can be edited here. In the following exercise, you use the DDEDIT command to edit different dimension types.

Figure 15.10

The Edit MText dialog box for an unedited associative dimension.

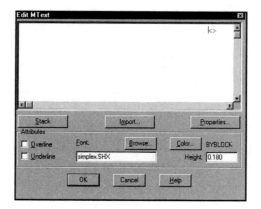

> **N**ote
>
> The New option of the DIMEDIT command and the NEWTEXT command issued at the Dim: prompt also prompts you to select a dimension. This also displays the Edit MText dialog box for the editing of dimension text.

EDITING THE DIMENSION TEXT VALUE

1. Continue from the previous exercise and choose Zoom Previous, then choose Edit Text from the Special Edit flyout of the Modify toolbar.

2. Pick the 5.0000 dimension at ① to open the Edit MText dialog box (see fig. 15.11).

3. Press the End key to place the cursor at the end of the brackets. Then press Enter.

4. Type **VIF** on the line below the brackets, and then choose OK to add the notation to the dimension.

5. While at the prompt to select annotation, choose the 2.0000 horizontal dimension, and then delete the < > brackets.

6. Enter **2.1250** and then choose OK to change the dimension. Press Enter to end the DDEDIT command.

NOTE

If you edit the dimension to display something other than the dimension calculated by AutoCAD LT, any editing of the dimension's defpoints will not change the dimension. By editing the dimension text, you have, in essence, overridden the correct dimension and LT will ignore any further edits. In the next series of steps, you see how you can correct this for future edits of the object and dimensions.

7. Type **S** to invoke the STRETCH command and pick ① and ② to create the crossing window (see fig. 15.12). Press Enter.

8. Type **.5,0** and press Enter twice to stretch the bracket and the horizontal dimension (which doesn't change per the edit).

9. Choose Modify, Objects, Edit Text, and pick the 2.1250 dimension to display the Edit MText dialog box.

10. Highlight the text and then type **< >**. Choose OK to cause LT to recognize the true distance between the defpoints.

11. Choose Save to save the drawing.

Figure 15.11

Editing the dimensions with DDEDIT.

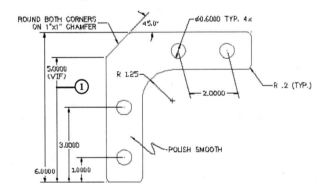

Figure 15.12

*Creating the crossing
window to stretch
the bracket.*

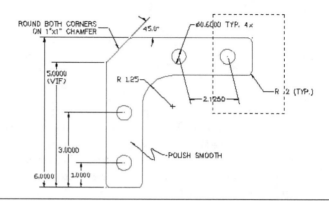

N O T E

When using DDEDIT to select an existing geometric tolerance control frame for editing,
the Geometric Tolerance dialog box opens, from which you can make the desired edits.

Editing Ordinate Dimension Positions

When editing, ordinate dimensions present a unique situation in that they have a
single extension line. Because associative ordinate dimensions are directly related
to the origin of the coordinate system active when they were created, moving the
origin or the extension line defpoint automatically updates the ordinate dimension
text. In the following exercise, you reposition the user coordinate system and some
ordinate dimensions using grips.

EDITING ORDINATE DIMENSIONS

1. Open the drawing DIMORDED.DWG, located in the sample directory. Pick the
    ordinate dimension at ① to display the dimension grips (see fig. 15.13).

2. Pick the dimension text grip at ② and then pick ③ as the new position.
    Notice how AutoCAD LT automatically breaks the extension line.

3. Pick the origin defpoint grip at ④ and then use ENDPoint object snap. Pick ⑤
    as the new point from which the ordinate dimension is calculated.

4. Press Esc twice to see the change in the dimension text. Pick the .3900
    ordinate dimension at ① (see fig. 15.14).

5. Pick the defpoint grip at ② and then use Center snap. Pick the circle at ③ to change the ordinate dimension definition point.

6. Press Esc twice to see the new dimension value.

7. Save the drawing.

Figure 15.13

Editing the ordinate dimension.

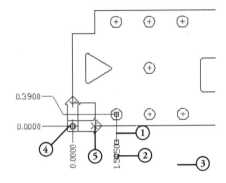

Figure 15.14

Repositioning the extension line defpoint of the ordinate dimension.

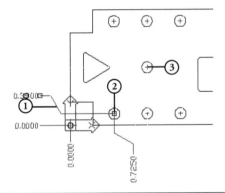

NOTE

Every associative ordinate dimension has a defpoint at the 0,0 origin point of the coordinate system. Editing the grip at the 0,0 defpoint is only for the dimension(s) in the current selection set.

You easily can edit associative dimensions using dimension styles or grips. You also can easily edit the value of the dimension text or leader annotation using the DDEDIT command. There might be occasions where an extension line needs to be broken, in which case the dimension must be exploded. For the most part, the dimension editing capability of AutoCAD LT remains quite powerful.

RELATED COMMANDS

NEWTEXT

DIMTEDIT

DIMEDIT

DDEDIT

PART **IV**

COMPOSITIONS & PLOTTING

16

WORKING WITH MODEL AND PAPER SPACE

In AutoCAD LT, you can use either one of two environments, the model space environment (also referred to as "tiled model space") or the paper space environment, to create and edit a drawing. The paper space environment is designed to enable you to model the layout of the final paper plot—hence the term "paper space." Paper space is especially useful for composing complex drawing layouts consisting of multiple details at different scales.

Switching back and forth between the two environments as a drawing is developed is easy. More often than not, tiled model space is where most of the development of the drawing occurs, and paper space is used primarily for the composition of the final drawing sheet. Composing and plotting a sheet layout is covered in detail in Chapter 17, "Sheet Composition and Plotting." This chapter covers the tools used to enable and control the paper space environment. In this chapter, you learn how to do the following:

- *Set up paper space for existing and new drawings.*
- *Switch back and forth between tiled model space and paper space.*
- *Set up and control floating viewports in paper space.*
- *Switch between paper space and floating model space.*
- *Work with layers in paper space.*

Switching to Paper Space with Tilemode

So far, all your drawing work has been done in the tiled model space environment. Switching to the paper space environment for an existing drawing is simply a matter of changing the setting of one system variable, Tilemode. A quick way to set Tilemode is select the TILE button on the status bar. When the TILE button is bold, Tilemode is on (value of 1), and you are in tiled model space. When the Tile button is faded or grayed-out, Tilemode is off (value of 0) and you are in the paper space environment. Alternatively, paper space can be enabled by choosing View, Paper Space; Model space can be enabled by choosing View, Model Space (Tiled). You can also set Tilemode from the Standard toolbar by choosing Standard Toolbar, Space, Model Space (Tiled) and choosing Standard Toolbar, Space, Paper Space.

In addition to the TILE button, the shape of the UCS icon displayed gives another visual clue that the paper space environment is active. In paper space, the displayed UCS icon is different from the icon displayed while in tiled model space (see fig. 16.1).

Figure 16.1

*The UCS icon
in paper space.*

Another visual clue that indicates that the paper space environment is current is that the menu item Paper Space in the View pull-down menu has a checkmark next to it. If the tiled model space environment is active, the menu item Model Space (Tiled) has a checkmark next to it.

In the following exercise, you switch back and forth between tiled model space and paper space.

SWITCHING BETWEEN PAPER AND MODEL SPACE

1. Open the drawing NRP_OFF, a floor plan for an office. Notice how the UCS icon appears. If the UCS icon is not displayed, choose Options, UCS icon, On.

2. Choose the TILE button from the status bar. The system variable Tilemode is now off, and the paper space environment is now current. Notice that the Tile button is now faded and that the UCS icon is different.

3. Choose the TILE button from the status bar. Tilemode is now on, and the tiled model space environment is now current.

4. Choose View, Paper Space. This is another method for switching to the paper space environment.

In the next exercise, you set up viewports.

Setting Up Floating Viewports

When paper space is enabled for the first time in a drawing, the drawing environment is normally empty, a situation similar to having a blank piece of paper on the drawing board in front of you. Although it is impossible to view the contents of the paper space environment from the tiled model space environment, it is possible to view the contents of tiled model space from paper space. Using the MVIEW command, one or more viewports is created in paper space, enabling you to view and edit the contents of tiled model space. The various options of the MVIEW command are accessible by choosing View, Floating Viewports. The MVIEW command displays the following prompt:

```
ON/OFF/Hideplot/Fit/2/3/4/Restore/<First Point>:
```

■   Use ON to turn on a viewport. The contents of a viewport are displayed only when the viewport is on (choose View, Floating Viewports, Viewports On).

■   Use OFF to turn off a viewport, which causes the contents of the viewport to not be displayed (choose View, Floating Viewports, Viewports Off).

■   The Hideplot option is used to tag a viewport so that the hidden lines are removed during plotting (choose View, Floating Viewports, Hideplot).

■   Fit is used to create a single viewport to fit the drawing window (choose View, Floating Viewports, 1 Viewport, and then specify the Fit option).

■   2 divides a user-specified rectangular area vertically or horizontally into two viewports (choose View, Floating Viewports, 2 Viewports).

- 3 divides a user-specified rectangular area vertically or horizontally into three equal viewports, or into three viewports with the major viewport placed above, below, to the left, or to the right of the other two viewports (choose View, Floating Viewports, 3 Viewports).

- 4 divides a user-specified rectangular area into four equal viewports (choose View, Floating Viewports, 4 Viewports).

- Restore restores a saved viewport configuration (VPORTS) into its equivalent in paper space, using floating viewports rather than tiled viewports (choose View, Floating Viewports, Restore).

- The default option, First point, enables you to create a new floating viewport by picking two points to define its size and location (choose View, Floating Viewports, 1 Viewport).

NOTE

> The Floating Viewports menu is active only while paper space is enabled. Conversely, the Tiled Viewports menu (the VPORTS command) is inactive while in paper space.

The viewports created with MVIEW are similar to the viewports created with the VPORTS command used in tiled model space. The paper space viewports have several advantages:

- You can choose the locations of the viewports.

- You can specify the size of each individual viewport.

- You can edit the viewport objects directly.

- Layer visibility can be controlled on an individual viewport basis.

Because of their mobility and flexibility, paper space viewports are referred to as *floating* viewports.

In the following exercise, you set up several floating viewports in paper space.

CREATING SOME FLOATING VIEWPORTS

1. Continue to use the drawing NRP_OFF. The paper space environment should be current.

2. Make a new layer named **VIEWPORTS**, assign the color red to it, and make it current.

3. Choose View, Floating Viewports, 1 Viewport, and enter the following points, pressing Enter after each step:

```
ON/OFF/Hideplot/Fit/2/3/4/Restore/<First Point>: 1,1
Other corner: @5,5
```

Notice that a regeneration occurs when a new viewport is opened. The viewport border is red because it resides on layer VIEWPORTS.

4. Choose View, Floating Viewports, Restore, and enter the following data, pressing Enter after each step:

```
?/Name of window configuration to insert <TRI-VIEW>: TRI-VIEW
Fit/<First Point>: 7,1
Second point: @8,8
```

The tiled viewport configuration named TRI-VIEW is restored as a group of floating viewports within the windowed area.

5. Save the drawing.

Editing Floating Viewports

Each floating viewport is a drawing object (much like a line or circle object) and is delineated by its border. As an object, it resides on the layer it was drawn on and takes on the current layer color but not the linetype (the border is always drawn with the continuous linetype). Because a floating viewport is a drawing object, it is edited like any other object. It can be moved, stretched, rotated, and copied. A floating viewport even has grip points and can be arranged to overlap another viewport.

If you do not want the viewport borders visible on the final plot, use the following procedure:

■ Make a new layer on which the viewport objects are to be drawn and make it current.

■ Create the required viewport objects with MVIEW.

■ Turn off or freeze the layer on which the viewports are drawn.

Turning off or freezing the layer the viewports are on makes the viewport borders invisible. The contents of each viewport, however, are not affected.

In the following exercise, you edit the viewports created in the previous exercise.

MODIFYING THE FLOATING VIEWPORTS

1. Continue to use the drawing NRP_OFF and stay in the paper space environment.

2. Choose Object Properties, Layers and change the color assigned to the layer VIEWPORTS to green. Exit the Layer Control dialog box.

   Notice that the viewport borders change color because the objects were drawn with a BYLAYER color setting.

3. Using the following sequence, edit the viewports using grips:

   Command: **Pick ① (see fig. 16.2)**
   Command: **Pick ②**
   ** STRETCH **
   <Stretch to point>/Base point/Copy/Undo/eXit: ↵
   ** MOVE **
   <Move to point>/Base point/Copy/Undo/eXit: **@-0.5,-0.5** ↵
   Command: **Depress the Esc key**
   Command: **Depress the Esc key**
   Command: **Pick ③**
   Command: **Pick ④**
   ** STRETCH **
   <Stretch to point>/Base point/Copy/Undo/eXit: ↵
   ** MOVE **
   <Move to point>/Base point/Copy/Undo/eXit: **@-0.5,0** ↵
   Command: **Depress the Esc key**
   Command: **Depress the Esc key**
   Command: **Pick ⑤**
   Command: **Pick ⑥**
   ** STRETCH **
   <Stretch to point>/Base point/Copy/Undo/eXit: **@2,0** ↵

   Notice that LT maintains the rectangular shape of the viewport even though you are only stretching a single corner point.

4. Save the drawing.

Figure 16.2

Moving and stretching the viewports.

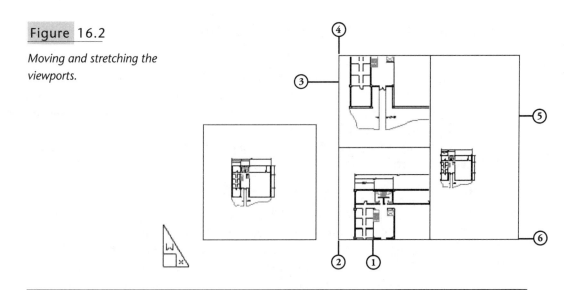

Adjusting the Display

In the paper space environment, display commands such as ZOOM and PAN affect the display differently depending on whether paper space or floating model space is active.

Adjusting the Paper Space Display

When TILEMODE is turned off, you are placed in the paper space drawing environment. You can verify that paper space is current with the following visual hints:

- The UCS icon is changed (refer to figure 16.1).

- The crosshairs extend across the entire width and height of the drawing window.

- There is a button labeled PAPER on the status bar.

While in paper space, display commands such as ZOOM and PAN do not affect the contents of the individual floating viewports; rather, the commands affect the entire paper space area. In effect, you are zooming in or panning around the entire sheet of paper. There is, however, a performance penalty when changing the display in paper space. Every time a zoom or pan operation is carried out, the drawing is regenerated and, depending on the complexity of the drawing, this might take some time.

Changing the Viewport's Display

To adjust the view in a particular viewport, the model space of that viewport (referred to as floating model space) must be accessed. To access model space, choose the button on the status bar labeled PAPER (which issues the MSPACE command), and you are placed into the floating model space of one of the viewports. To go back to paper space, choose the button on the status bar labeled MODEL (which issues the PSPACE command). There are several visual clues that indicate that floating model space is current:

■ The label on the button on the status bar is changed from PAPER to MODEL.

■ Because tiled model space and floating model space are the same, the UCS icon, if its display is turned on, is displayed in the current viewport and is the same as the icon displayed in tiled model space. The only difference is that the term "floating model space" refers to the fact that the model space is being accessed through a floating viewport in the paper space environment.

■ The crosshairs are displayed only up to the border of the current viewport.

As an alternate to using the PAPER or MODEL button, choose View, Model Space (floating) to access floating model space and choose View, Paper Space to make paper space current. From the Standard toolbar, choose Standard Toolbar, Space, Model Space (floating) to issue the MSPACE command and choose Standard Toolbar, Space, Paper Space to issue the PSPACE command.

When you access floating model space and have several floating viewports, the correct viewport might not be made current. To make a specific floating viewport current (also known as making the viewport active), simply move the cursor to a point within the desired viewport and pick a point. (This procedure is identical to selecting the current viewport back in tiled model space.) Alternatively, use a Ctrl+R sequence to toggle to the next viewport.

After gaining access to the floating model space of the desired viewport, the view displayed in that viewport is modified by issuing the appropriate ZOOM, PAN, DDVIEW, VPOINT (for a 3D view of the drawing), or DDLMODES command. Unlike paper space, performing a zoom or pan operation in floating model space does not automatically cause a regeneration.

As with tiled viewports, the view in each floating viewport can be adjusted to show a different portion of the same drawing. The settings for the SNAP, GRID, and UCSICON commands can also be set for each viewport.

The view in each viewport can be adjusted so that the view reflects a specific drawing scale. Setting a viewport's scale, and other sheet composition considerations, are covered in Chapter 17, "Sheet Composition and Plotting."

Performing Redraws and Regens

Issuing a REDRAW or a REGEN while in paper space affects only the objects drawn in paper space and not the displays of the floating viewports. Issuing a REDRAW or a REGEN while in floating model space affects the objects in the current viewport only. There is no way to redraw or regenerate all viewports simultaneously.

Using the Aerial View Window

In paper space, the aerial view window is disabled. However, the aerial view window is available when floating model space is current. When the Auto Viewport mode of the aerial view window is enabled, the contents of the window reflect the view of the current floating viewport, and any operations carried out in the aerial view window affect the current viewport. As different viewports are made current, the contents of the aerial view window are changed to reflect the new current viewport.

When the Auto Viewport mode is disabled, the contents of the aerial view window reflect the view of the floating viewport current at the time the window was opened or when the Auto Viewport mode was disabled. Any operations carried out in the window affect the display of that viewport, which may no longer be the current viewport.

Operating the aerial view window in the paper space environment is identical to operating the window in the tiled model space environment.

Exceeding the Maximum Number of Viewports

You can create as many floating viewports as you want; however, by default, LT updates the views in only 16 viewports. The 16-viewport limit is set in the MAXACTVP (MAXimum ACTive ViewPorts) system variable. This limit can be raised or lowered as needed. If a new viewport is created that causes the total number of viewports to exceed the limit set in MAXACTVP, LT automatically turns off one of the older viewports. At no time does LT maintain (update) more floating viewports than the number set in MAXACTVP. The ON and OFF options of the MVIEW command can be used to turn the display on and off explicitly for the various viewports should the MAXACTVP limit be exceeded.

The overall paper space display is considered a viewport in itself and is also referred to as the *paper space viewport*. The paper space viewport counts as one of the viewports affected by the MAXACTVP setting.

In the following exercise, you change the area being viewed in paper space and then adjust the views in the viewports.

CHANGING THE DISPLAY

1. Continue to use the drawing NRP_OFF.

2. Choose Standard Toolbar, Zoom Out.

   Notice that this operation caused a regeneration.

3. Choose Standard Toolbar, Zoom In, which also causes a regeneration.

4. Choose the PAPER button from the status bar, which switches you to floating model space. Pick ① (see fig. 16.3) to make the left viewport current. Choose Standard Toolbar, Zoom Out.

   Notice that zooming out in floating model space, unlike zooming out in paper space, does not automatically cause a regeneration.

5. Choose Standard Toolbar, Aerial View, and make sure the Auto Viewport option of the aerial view window is enabled. Pick ②, pick ③, and pick ④, and notice how the aerial view window is updated to reflect the current viewport.

6. Save the drawing.

Figure 16.3

Changing the display of the viewports.

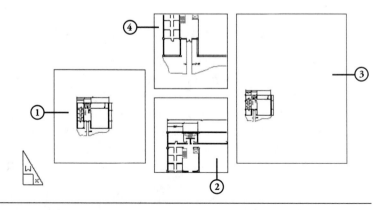

Controlling the Layer Display

Layer states such as on/off, freeze/thaw, lock/unlock, color, and linetype are controlled through the Layer Control drop-down list and DDLMODES command, just as in tiled model space. One other option is available in the paper space environment that is not available in the tiled model space environment. The display of layers can be controlled on a per viewport basis. In contrast, layers in tiled viewports can be affected only on a global basis.

The layer operations of turning on/off, freezing/thawing, locking/unlocking, and changing colors or linetypes always operate on a global basis. When a layer's color is changed, it affects the display of objects in both paper space and floating model space. In both the Layer Control drop-down list (see fig. 16.4) and the Layer Control dialog box (see fig. 16.5), there are variations of the standard freeze/thaw icon and buttons that enable you to freeze or thaw a layer for just the current viewport.

Figure 16.4

The Layer Control drop-down list.

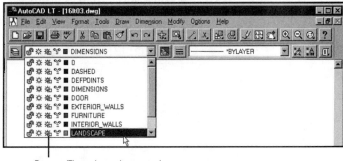

Freeze/Thaw layer in current viewport only

Figure 16.5

The Layer Control dialog box.

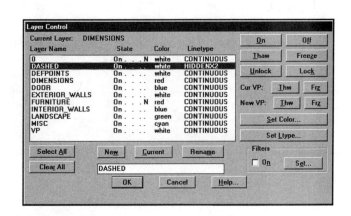

Selecting these buttons or icons results in the layer being frozen or thawed in the current viewport only, whether it is a floating viewport or the paper space viewport. When a layer is frozen in the current viewport, the letter "C" appears in the states column.

Another option available in the Layer Control dialog box, but not in the Layer Control drop-down list, is the option to freeze and thaw layers in new viewports. This option does not affect the current viewport, but only viewports that are created after the option is set. A letter "N" appears in the state column for a layer that has this freeze option enabled.

Tip

Freezing and thawing layers for new viewports is useful when you decide in advance that you want certain layers not to be visible in the viewports you are about to create.

In the following exercise, you adjust the views in the floating viewports you created.

CONTROLLING LAYER VISIBILITY

1. Continue to use the drawing NRP_OFF. Choose the MODEL button on the status bar, and you are placed back into paper space.

2. Choose Object Properties, Layers and turn off the layer FURNITURE.

    Notice that the furniture symbols disappear from all viewports.

3. Choose Object Properties Layers and turn on the layer FURNITURE.

4. Choose the PAPER button on the status bar. Make the top middle floating viewport current.

5. Choose Object Properties, Layers, and select the layer FURNITURE. Choose the FRZ button to the right of the label CUR VP. Notice the letter "C" in the states column.

6. Choose OK and note that the furniture symbol is visible in all viewports other than the current viewport.

7. Save the drawing.

Closing Floating Viewports

Unlike tiled viewports, there are no options that can be used to merge or close multiple floating viewports. Closing a floating viewport is just a matter of erasing the viewport object itself from paper space. Deleting a viewport object does not delete the objects displayed in it.

Using the Expert Wizard for New Drawings

When beginning a new drawing, you have the option of starting the drawing session in the paper space environment rather than the tiled model space environment. If you choose to use a template drawing and the template drawing is set up for the paper space environment (and left that way), the new drawing session is started in the paper space environment. Another method for beginning a new drawing session in the paper space environment is to use the Advanced Setup wizard (see fig. 16.6) rather than the Quick Setup wizard.

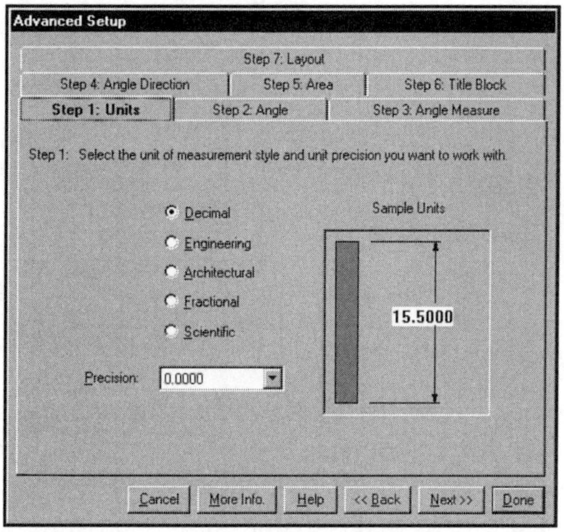

Figure 16.6

The Advanced Setup dialog box.

Setting the following causes LT to set up the paper space environment and draw the title block in paper space rather than in tiled model:

- Space length units

- Angle units

- Direction of zero degrees

- Direction of measurement of positive angles

- Area

- Title block

- Choose step 7

- Layout

- Enabling the Yes option (default setting—see fig. 16.7)

Additionally, a single floating viewport is created within the boundaries of the title block.

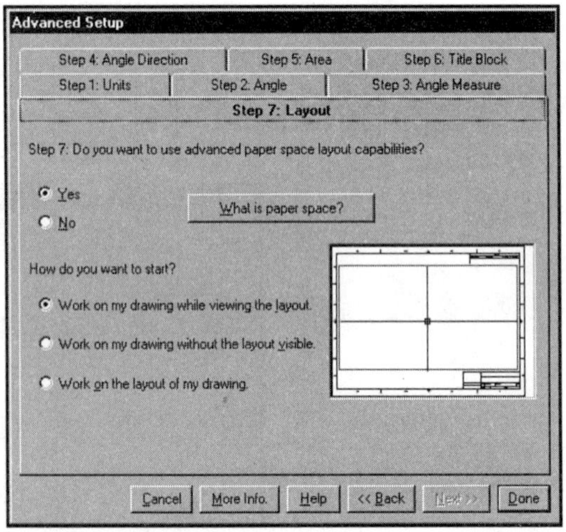

Figure 16.7

The layout portion of the Advanced Setup dialog box.

You then have to choose whether the drawing session is to begin in floating model space, tiled model space, or in paper space. If you enable the Work on my drawing while viewing the layout option (which is the default setting), the floating viewport is made active and your drawing session starts in floating model space. If you enable the Work on my drawing without the layout visible option, Tilemode is turned on and your drawing session starts in the tiled model space environment. You have to turn off Tilemode in order to view the title block already drawn. If you enable the Work on the layout of my drawing option, your drawing session starts in paper space.

> ### NOTE
>
> LT keeps track of two drawing limits, one for tiled model space and one for paper space. The drawing limits set in the Area portion of the Advanced Setup are the model space limits. The paper space limits are automatically set to the edges of the title block. This wizard sets up only one floating viewport. You can, however, modify the layout and add additional viewports after the initial viewport is drawn.

In the following exercise, you set up a new drawing by using the Advanced Setup wizard.

USING THE ADVANCED SETUP WIZARD

1. Choose Standard Toolbar, New and choose the Advanced Setup wizard.

2. Set the length units to architectural units.

3. Choose Step 6, the Title Block tab, and select the ANSI E title block.

4. Choose the Done button, and the wizard proceeds to turn off Tilemode, draw the title block in paper space, create a single floating viewport, and make the viewport current.

   You can now draw in floating model space or turn Tilemode on and revert back to tiled model space.

   This exercise is now complete.

Summary

In this chapter, you have learned which tools to use to enable paper space and to work in it. In the next chapter, you learn when to use paper space.

SEE ALSO

VPLAYER

RELATED SYSTEM VARIABLE

CVPORT

CHAPTER 17

SHEET COMPOSITION AND PLOTTING

Thus far, you have set up new drawings using a single scale factor for the entire sheet. There are, however, times when you will be required to create a drawing having a complex layout, composed of multiple details at varying scales. In this chapter, you learn how to:

■ *Compose drawings having complex layouts in model space*

■ *Compose drawings having complex layouts in paper space*

■ *Use the PLOT command from both model and paper space*

Sheet Composition in Model Space

You know how to set up a drawing with a single drawing scale but how would you set up a drawing as shown in figure 17.1?

Figure 17.1

A complex layout with three details at three different scales.

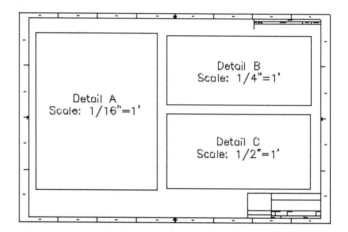

Detail A
Scale: 1/16"=1'

Detail B
Scale: 1/4"=1'

Detail C
Scale: 1/2"=1'

The drawing shown in figure 17.1 is to consist of three details. Detail A is to be drawn at a $^1/_{16}$"=1' scale, detail B at a $^1/_4$"=1' scale, and detail C at a $^1/_2$"=1' scale. If model space is to be used to compose the example layout, use the following procedure:

1. Draw each of the details in separate drawing files. Draw detail A in drawing A and set up drawing A for a $^1/_{16}$"=1' scale. Draw detail B in drawing B and set up drawing B for a $^1/_4$"=1' scale. Draw detail C in drawing C and set up drawing C for a $^1/_2$"=1' scale.

2. Create a fourth drawing, drawing D. Set up drawing D for a 1=1 scale and treat drawing D as the model of the actual final plot. Draw the border and title block. Then insert drawing A (using DDINSERT) using a scale factor of $^1/_{192}$ (the equivalent of $^1/_{16}$"=1'). Insert drawing B using a scale factor of $^1/_{48}$ (the equivalent of $^1/_4$"=1'). Insert drawing C using a scale factor of $^1/_{24}$ (the equivalent of $^1/_2$"=1').

3. Plot drawing D at a 1=1 scale.

In the preceding procedure, drawing D is a model of the actual drawing sheet. The procedure works quite well but there are several drawbacks.

- Instead of keeping track of one drawing, there are four drawing files to keep track of.

■ Making revisions to one of the details involves changing the associated drawing and then reinserting the drawing into drawing D.

■ If some of the details are just blowups of the same model (such as details of a plan drawing of the same machine), the above procedure requires that the same information be drawn multiple times. Making revisions would also have to be repeated multiple times if the changes are visible in various details.

Some of the difficulties of using model space to compose a complex layout can be alleviated by attaching the detail drawings (drawings A, B, and C) to drawing D as external references rather than inserting the drawings as blocks. That way, when changes are made to the detail drawings, the changes are automatically transmitted to the host drawing, drawing D, the next time drawing D is opened.

The only way to eliminate the listed difficulties completely is to utilize paper space.

In the following exercise, you compose a layout similar to that shown in figure 17.1 using model space.

COMPOSING A LAYOUT IN MODEL SPACE

1. Choose Standard Toolbar, New. Use a wizard and choose the Advanced Setup wizard. Specify decimal units and an ANSI D title block. Choose Step 7: Layout and enable the No option. Choose Done.

A D-size title block is inserted onto layer TITLE_BLOCK, in tiled model space.

2. Make a new layer named **DETAILS** and make it current. You are going to create the drawing shown in figure 17.2.

The detail on the left is to be at a $1/8"=1'$ scale. The detail in the upper right corner is to be at a $1/4"=1'$ scale. The detail in the lower right corner is to be at a $1/2"=1'$ scale.

3. Choose Draw, Block flyout, Insert Block. Specify the file NRP_OFF from the PROJECTS/CH17 directory and choose OK. Enter the following data:

```
Insertion point: 0.5,6.5 ↵
X scale factor <1> / Corner / XYZ: 1/96 ↵
Y scale factor (default=X): ↵
Rotation angle <0>: ↵
```

NRP_OFF is a full-size drawing of an office layout and is set up for a $1/8"=1'$ scale. You have just inserted NRP_OFF and reduced it by a factor of 96 (the reciprocal of $1/8"=1'$).

Figure 17.2

The layout you are composing.

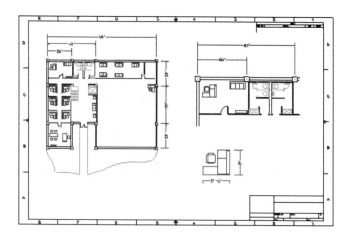

4. Choose Draw, Block flyout, Insert Block. Specify the file NRP_OFF2 from the PROJECTS/CH17 directory and choose OK. Enter the following data:

```
Insertion point: 18.5,10 ↵
X scale factor <1> / Corner / XYZ: 1/48 ↵
Y scale factor (default=X): ↵
Rotation angle <0>: ↵
```

NRP_OFF2 is a full-size drawing of a portion of the NRP_OFF office layout and is set up for a $1/4$"=1' scale. You have just inserted NRP_OFF2 and reduced it by a factor of 48 (the reciprocal of $1/4$"=1').

5. Choose Draw, Block flyout, Insert Block. Specify the file NRP_OFF3 from the PROJECTS/CH17 directory and choose OK. Enter the following data:

```
Insertion point: 19,5 ↵
X scale factor <1> / Corner / XYZ: 1/24 ↵
Y scale factor (default=X): ↵
Rotation angle <0>: ↵
```

NRP_OFF3 is a full-size drawing of a portion of the NRP_OFF2 office layout and is set up for a $1/2$"=1' scale. You have just inserted NRP_OFF3 and reduced it by a factor of 24 (the reciprocal of $1/2$"=1').

All that is left is to finish annotating the drawing and plotting it, and the drawing is complete.

TIP

As an alternative, rather than using the DDINSERT command, you could have used the XREF command to attach overlay drawings NRP_OFF, NRP_OFF2, and NRP_OFF3 as external references.

6. Save the drawing with the name **MODEL**.

Sheet Composition in Paper Space

In Chapter 16, "Working with Model and Paper Space," you learned how to switch to the paper space environment and how to create viewports with which to view model space. Here, you learn how to use paper space to compose a complex layout. Using the same example shown in figure 17.1, the following procedure could be utilized to compose the layout in paper space:

1. In tiled model space, draw details A, B, and C at full size but leave out any drawing elements such as text and dimensions that are dependent on the drawing scale.

2. Using the TILE button on the status bar, change over to the paper space environment.

3. Draw the border and title block at a 1=1 scale.

4. Use the MVIEW command to position three viewports corresponding to the desired locations of details A, B, and C.

5. Use the MSPACE command to access the floating model space in each viewport and adjust the view to correspond to the desired detail.

Now, there are only four major problem areas to deal with:

1. Setting the view in each viewport to correspond to the desired drawing scale.

2. Drawing any needed dimensions such that all dimensions in all three views appear consistent. For example, the arrowheads on a dimension line should appear to be the same size in all three details.

3. Drawing any linetypes other than the continuous linetype, such that the linetypes are consistent. For example, the lengths of the dashes and spaces for the dashed linetype should appear to be the same in all three details.

4. Drawing any other annotation such that the annotation appears consistent in size in all three details.

Setting the Viewport Scale

To set the scale of a viewport, use the XP option of the ZOOM command while accessing the floating model space of the specific viewport. XP stands for "relative to paper space" and is specifically designed to be used to set the scale of the view in a floating viewport and has no other function. To set the scale of detail A as shown in figure 17.1, first use MSPACE to access the floating model space of the viewport displaying that detail. Then, issue the ZOOM command and enter $^1/_{196}$XP as the scale factor and the resulting view will correspond to a $^1/_{16}$"=1' scale. Fine-tune the position of the view within the viewport with the PAN command. If necessary, adjust the size of the viewport itself.

To set the scale of detail B, access the floating model space of the corresponding viewport. Issue the ZOOM command and enter $^1/_{48}$XP as the scale factor. The resulting view will correspond to a $^1/_4$"=1' scale.

To set the scale of detail C, access the floating model space of the corresponding viewport. Issue the ZOOM command and enter $^1/_2$XP as the scale factor. The resulting view will correspond to a $^1/_2$"=1' scale.

If you forgot what scale a viewport is set for, use the LIST command on the viewport. The scale of a viewport is recorded with the viewport.

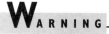

WARNING

It is very easy to accidentally change the scale of the view in a viewport by using the ZOOM command inadvertently.

In the following exercise, you compose the same layout you used in the previous exercise, except that paper space is used instead of model space.

COMPOSING A LAYOUT IN PAPER SPACE

1. Choose Standard Toolbar, New and choose the Advanced Setup wizard. Specify decimal units and an ANSI D title block. Choose Done.

The ANSI D title block is inserted in paper space and a single viewport is automatically created. The floating model space of the viewport is made current.

2. Choose MODEL from the status bar, making paper space current.

3. Choose Options, UCS Icon, On. This turns on the display of the UCS icon in the current viewport.

4. Choose Modify, Erase flyout, Erase and erase the single viewport.

5. Choose TILE from the status bar, making tiled model space current.

6. Choose Draw, Block flyout, Insert Block. Specify the file NRP_OFF from the PROJECTS/CH17 directory. Enable the Explode option and choose OK. Enter the following data:

```
Insertion point: 0,0 ↵
Scale factor <1>: ↵
Rotation angle <0>: ↵
```

The block NRP_OFF is exploded as it is inserted.

7. Choose Standard Toolbar, Zoom flyout, Zoom All.

Now you can see the entire drawing that was just inserted.

8. Choose Options, UCS Icon, On. This turns on the display of the UCS icon in the current viewport.

9. Choose TILE from the status bar. This switches you back to paper space. Make a new layer named **VPORTS**, assign the color red to it, and make it current.

10. Choose View, Floating Viewports, 1 Viewport and enter the following points:

```
ON/OFF/Hideplot/Fit/2/3/4/Restore/<First Point>: 2,2.5 ↵
Other corner: 16,20 ↵
```

11. Choose View, Floating Viewports, 1 Viewport and enter the following points:

```
ON/OFF/Hideplot/Fit/2/3/4/Restore/<First Point>: 17,10.5 ↵
Other corner: 29.5,19.6 ↵
```

12. Choose View, Floating Viewports, 1 Viewport and enter the following points:

```
ON/OFF/Hideplot/Fit/2/3/4/Restore/<First Point>: 17,3 ↵
Other corner: 29.5,9 ↵
```

You have just opened three viewports. Next, you have to adjust the views in the viewports.

13. Choose PAPER from the status bar and make the left viewport current.

14. Choose Standard Toolbar, Zoom flyout, Zoom Scale and enter the following:

```
All/Center/Extents/Previous/Window/<Scale(X/XP)>: 1/96XP↵
```

15. Use either the PAN or RTPAN command to position the model in the viewport so that all of the model is visible.

16. Make the upper right viewport current. Choose Standard Toolbar, Zoom flyout, Zoom Window and enter the following points:

```
All/Center/Extents/Previous/Window/<Scale(X/XP)>: 193,764 ↵
Other corner: 760,1010 ↵
```

You now have the correct portion of the floor plan visible but it is not at the correct scale.

17. Choose Standard Toolbar, Zoom flyout, Zoom Scale and enter the following:

```
All/Center/Extents/Previous/Window/<Scale(X/XP)>: 1/48XP ↵
```

18. Make the lower right viewport current. Choose Standard Toolbar, Zoom flyout, Zoom Window and enter the following points:

```
First corner: 250,850 ↵
Other corner: 340,940 ↵
```

The correct portion of the drawing is now displayed, but the scale is not yet correct.

19. Choose Standard Toolbar, Zoom flyout, Zoom Scale and enter **¹/₂₄XP**. The scale for the lower right viewport is now correct.

20. Choose MODEL from the status bar. Using grips, size the lower right viewport to isolate the desk and chair and exclude the other objects in the floor plan.

You now have the three views at the required scales, but the dimensions are still sized incorrectly (see fig. 17.3). In the next exercise, the dimensions are corrected.

Save the drawing as PAPER.

Figure 17.3

A layout in paper space.

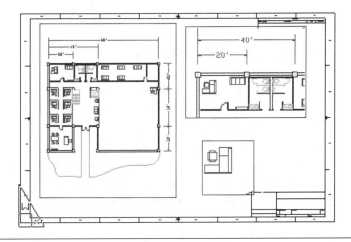

Drawing Dimensions in Viewports

To draw the dimensions in viewports that are at varying scales is really not that much different from drawing them in tiled model space for drawings set up for a single scale factor. The only difference is that the overall scale for the dimension style has to be changed to a different value for each detail. The problem can be approached using one of three methods.

Dimensioning with Method A

With method A, set up three dimensions styles, STYLE-A, STYLE-B, and STYLE-C, that are identical in all settings except one, the overall scale that be found at the bottom of the Geometry dialog box (DDIM command). For STYLE-A (to be used with detail A), set the overall scale factor to 196; for STYLE-B, set the overall scale factor to 48; for STYLE-C, set the overall scale factor to 24. Now it is just a matter of switching to the appropriate dimension style as each detail is dimensioned.

Dimensioning with Method B

Method B requires using only one dimension style and the enabling of the Scale to Paper Space option (which is found at the bottom of the Geometry dialog box). With method B, dimensioning should be performed in the floating model space of the viewports. When the Scale to Paper Space option is enabled, LT automatically sets the overall scale to the reciprocal of the scale of the current floating viewport. For example, if the scale of the current viewport is $^1/_{48}$XP, then the overall scale factor for the current dimension style is automatically set to 48. Method B enables you to switch viewports as you dimension and have LT automatically change the overall scale factor to the appropriate value for the current viewport. If method B is used while in tiled model space or when paper space is current, LT sets the overall scale factor to 1. In tiled model space, an overall scale factor of 1 would probably make dimension features such as arrowheads and text appear quite small compared to the model being dimensioned.

If method B is employed and the scale of the viewport is to be changed after the dimensions are drawn, use the Apply option of the DIMSTYLE command to force LT to adjust the overall dimension scale of the dimensions to the new viewport scale. The Apply option can also be used with method A to change the style of existing dimensions, should it be necessary.

If a dimension is to appear in multiple viewports at different scales, then the dimension must be drawn once in each viewport on a separate layer, thawed only in that viewport. For example, if a dimension is to be visible in two viewports at differing scales, draw the dimension in viewport A on layer DIM-A and draw the same dimension in viewport B on layer DIM-B. Then, freeze layer DIM-A in viewport B and freeze layer DIM-B in viewport A resulting in each of the viewports displaying a correctly scaled version of the dimension.

Dimensioning with Method C

The third method, method C, involves drawing all the dimensions in paper space. Method C would require multiple dimension styles with the overall scale factor set to 1. For the example shown in figure 17.1, three styles would be required, identical in all settings except one, the linear scale factor (found at the bottom of the Primary Units dialog box). The linear scale factor would be set to the reciprocal of the scale factor of the viewport to be dimensioned. For example, if detail C in figure 17.1 is to be dimensioned in paper space, a dimension style with a linear scale factor of 24 (reciprocal of $1/2$"=1') would be required. You are able to select points to dimension from within the floating model space of a viewport while paper space is current, as long as object snap is used to select the points.

The drawback to using method C is that the dimensions would reside in a different space from the model and this could lead to problems when the model is subsequently changed. For example, if the model is stretched in model space, the associated dimensions would not be correspondingly stretched because the dimensions reside in paper space. To correct the problem, the dimensions in paper space would have to be stretched separately from the model.

Tᵢₚ

Of the three methods, method C is the most cumbersome because of the difficulties encountered when changing the model. Method A is more appropriate when paper space is used only to compose the drawing layout and tiled model space is used to do all drawing work. Method B is more appropriate when you feel comfortable drawing the dimensions in floating model space.

In the next exercise, the existing dimensions are corrected for the various viewport scales and new dimensions are drawn.

DRAWING DIMENSIONS IN THE VIEWPORTS

1. Continue to use the drawing PAPER. Make sure you are in floating model space (the MODEL button should be visible on the status bar). Make the left viewport current.

2. Choose Format, Dimension Style and specify the style MODEL. Choose Geometry and enable the Scale to Paper Space option. Choose OK, choose SAVE and then OK again. Choose View, Toolbar and display the dimensioning toolbar. Dock the toolbar if you want. The dimensions are automatically updated to reflect the new dimension setting. The Scale to Paper Space setting results in an overall scale factor of 96 being applied to all dimensions drawn with the dimension style MODEL. The overall scale of 96 is perfect for the left viewport but not for the upper right viewport. Note that the dimensions in the upper right viewport appear twice as big as the ones in the left viewport.

The dimensions in the upper right viewport are corrected next.

3. Keep the left viewport current. Choose Modify, Duplicate Flyout, Duplicate Objects and enter the following data:

```
Select objects: Pick ① (see fig. 17.4)
Select objects: Pick ②
Select objects: ↵
<Base point or displacement>/Multiple: 0,0 ↵
Second point of displacement: ↵
```

The copies are placed on top of the original dimensions.

4. Choose Object Properties toolbar, Layers. Make the new layer **DIMENSIONS2** and assign the color blue to it. Make DIMENSIONS2 the current layer.

5. Choose Object Properties, Properties. Enter **P** to select the previously selected objects and change the layer of the objects to DIMENSIONS2.

Now one version of the two dimensions resides on layer DIMENSIONS while the other version resides on layer DIMENSIONS2.

6. Choose Object Properties, Layers. Select layer DIMENSIONS. Choose the FRZ button next to the label CUR VP. Choose OK.

The layer DIMENSIONS2 has just been frozen in the current viewport only. Now only one version of the dimensions is visible in the left viewpad.

7. Make the upper right viewpad current. Choose Standard Toolbar, Layers. Make Layer DIMENSIONS2 current. Select layer dimensions (make sure DIMENSIONS2 is not selected) and choose the FRZ button next to the label CUR VP.

8. Choose Dimension toolbar, Update Dimension and select the two dimensions visible in the upper right viewport.

The overall scale factor of the dimensions is corrected for the scale of the current viewport, $^1/_{48}$XP.

The problem now is that the blue dimension is visible in both the left and current viewports and now has to be made invisible in the left viewport.

9. Make the lower right viewport current. Make the new layer **DIMENSIONS3** and assign the color green to it. Make DIMENSIONS3 the current layer.

10. Draw a vertical and horizontal dimension as shown in figure 17.4. Use ③, ④, and ⑤ which are the corners of the desk. If you need to, switch to paper space, zoom into the lower left viewport, and then switch back to floating model space to draw the dimensions.

The green dimensions are visible in the left and upper right viewports and displayed at the wrong scale. In the next step, this problem is corrected.

11. Make the left viewport current. Choose the layer drop-down list. Find the layer DIMENSIONS3 on the list. Choose the Freeze layer in current viewport icon (3rd icon from the left) for layer DIMENSIONS3 and exit the drop-down list.

Repeat this procedure for the upper right viewport.

The dimensions are now appropriately sized for all viewports. Save the drawing.

Figure 17.4

Drawing dimensions in the viewports.

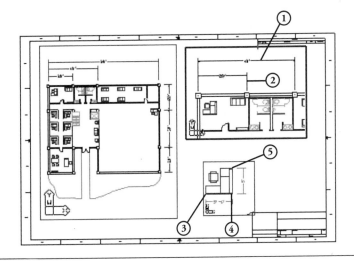

Drawing Linetypes in Viewports

In using linetypes (other than the continuous linetype) with floating viewports, the goal is to make the appearance of the linetypes consistent in all viewports. For example, the lengths of the dashes and spaces for a centerline linetype should appear to be the same in all viewports regardless of the viewport's scale. To accomplish this goal, simply make sure that the system variable PSLTSCALE is on (its default value). PSLTSCALE has no effect in tiled model space, but in paper space, its effect is to make the display of all linetypes consistent in all viewports. Choose Options, Linetypes, Paper Space Linetype Scale to access PSLTSCALE. By default, PSLTSCALE is turned on.

The results produced by PSLTSCALE are affected by the other linetype scale factors, LTSCALE and CELTSCALE (the object's own linetype scale). When using paper space, LTSCALE (global linetype scale) and CELTSCALE should both be set to 1 (or thereabouts). Do not set LTSCALE to the reciprocal of the drawing scale as is the custom when setting up a drawing for a single scale.

T_{IP}

If you find yourself switching back and forth between paper and tiled model space, set LTSCALE to an appropriate value that enables you to see the linetypes properly in tiled model space. Worry about setting LTSCALE to 1 for paper space only when you are ready to plot.

In the next exercise, you verify that PSLTSCALE does indeed work as advertised.

WORKING WITH LINETYPES IN PAPER SPACE

1. Continue to use the drawing PAPER.

2. Choose Options, Linetypes, Paper Space Linetype Scale. This disables the system variable PSLTSCALE.

3. Choose Standard Toolbar, Layers. Select the layer EXTERIOR_WALLS. Assign the linetype DASHED to the layer. Load the linetype if it is not already loaded.

4. Choose Options, Linetypes, Global Linetype Scale and set it to 96.

   The dashed linetypes are visible in the left and upper right viewports. Notice that the lengths of the dashes and spaces are different between the two viewports.

5. Choose Options, Linetypes, Paper Space Linetype Scale. This enables PSLTSCALE. There should now be a check mark next to the menu item Paper Space Linetype Scale.

6. Choose Options, Linetypes, Global Linetype Scale and set it to 1.

7. Make the left viewport current. Type the command **REGEN**.

8. Make the upper right viewport current. Type the command **REGEN**.

   Notice that the lengths of the dashes and spaces are now consistent between the two viewports.

   Save the drawing.

Drawing Text in Viewports

Unlike dimensions and linetypes, when it comes to drawing text in viewports, LT has no mechanism that automatically adjusts the height of text objects for a viewport's scale. If you draw the text in model space, then the height of the text must be set appropriately to correspond to the scale of the viewport in which the text appears. Setting up several fixed height text styles and switching between them as needed can make the drawing of text in model space easier.

Some text should be drawn in paper space rather than in model space. General labels for the details, drawing notes, title block information, and so on, should be drawn in paper space. Other text could be drawn in either space; however, remember that if the model in model space is edited, any associated text drawn in paper space will have to be edited separately.

TIP

It is quite all right to draw text and other objects in paper space such that the objects overlap the views displayed in the viewports, making the objects appear to be an integral part of the views.

In the following exercise, you complete the layout by adding some text to the drawing.

Adding Some Text to the Layout

1. Continue to use the drawing PAPER.

2. Make paper space current (the button PAPER on the status bar should be visible).

3. Turn off the layer VPORTS. This makes the viewport borders invisible. Make a new layer named TEXT and make it current.

4. Choose Draw, Text flyout, Line Text and enter the following:

```
Justify/Style/<Start point>: C ↵
Center point: 8.5,2.9 ↵
Height <0.2000>: 0.5 ↵
Rotation angle <0>: ↵
Text: Scale: 1/8"=1'
Text: ↵
```

5. Choose Draw, Text, Line Text and enter the following:

```
Justify/Style/<Start point>: C ↵
Center point: 23.5,9.5 ↵
Height <0.5000>: 0.5 ↵
Rotation angle <0>: ↵
Text: Scale: 1/4"=1'
Text: Press Enter
```

6. Choose Draw, Line Text and enter the following:

```
Justify/Style/<Start point>: C Press Enter
Center point: 19.3,2.8 ↵
Height <0.5000>: 0.5 ↵
Rotation angle <0>: ↵
Text: Scale: 1/2"=1'
Text: ↵
```

7. The drawing is now complete. Save the drawing.

Figure 17.5

Adding text to the drawing layout.

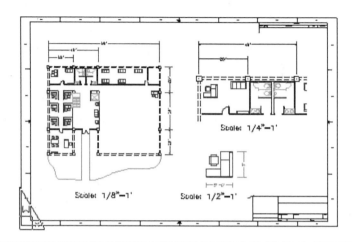

Drawing Other Drafting Details

Other drafting details, such as callout bubbles, revision symbols, and so on, should be drawn in paper space when possible. Drawing such details in paper space does away with the need to adjust the size of the symbol for the scales of the different viewports. The downside of drawing the details in paper space is that when changes are made in model space, the associated drafting details residing in paper space have to be changed separately.

The alternative to drawing drafting details in paper space is to draw the details in model space with the models. You will, however, have to make the scale adjustments for the various viewports, yourself.

Printing the Drawing

Eventually, you have to make a plot of your layout. The command you use is PLOT, and it is issued by choosing File, Print or by choosing Standard Toolbar, Print. The Plot Configuration dialog box (see fig. 17.6) is the mechanism by which you choose the printer/plotter to be used, the portion of the drawing to be plotted, and the scale of the plot.

Figure 17.6

*The Plot Configuration
dialog box.*

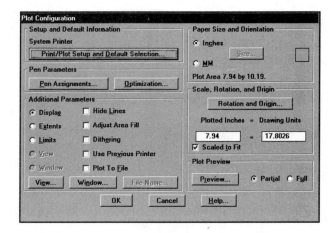

Figure 17.6

*The Plot Configuration
dialog box.*

The basic procedure for producing a plot is as follows:

1. Make sure that the printer or plotter to be used is ready to plot.

2. Issue the PLOT command.

3. Select the plotter to be used from the list of available devices.

4. Set the pen table.

5. Select a sheet size

6. Set a plot scale.

7. Preview the plot settings and either plot the drawing or adjust the settings some more.

In the sections that follow, the specifics for carrying out the preceding procedure and setting the options of the Plot Configuration dialog box are discussed in detail.

Checking the Plotter Configuration

LT can plot to a variety of devices and file formats. To choose the device or file format to plot to, choose the Print/Plot Setup and Default Selection buttons and the following dialog box will appear (see fig. 17.7).

Figure 17.7

The Print/Plot Setup and
Default Selection dialog
box.

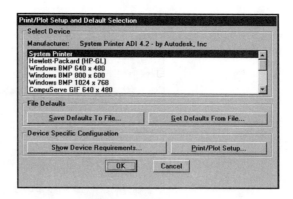

By default, LT is configured to plot to the Windows 95 system printer. You can also
choose to plot to an HP-GL–compliant device, such as an HP 7475 plotter, or even
one of several file formats.

To ensure a smooth plot, it is best to install your particular plotter as a system printer
using Windows 95's Control Panel. To do so, you will need a Windows 95 driver from
the manufacturer of your plotter and to follow the installation instructions of the
manufacturer.

If more than one system printer is configured in Windows 95, a specific printer can
be chosen by pressing the Print/Plot Setup button. A list of available system printers
is then displayed via the Print Setup dialog box (see fig. 17.8).

Figure 17.8

The Print Setup dialog
box.

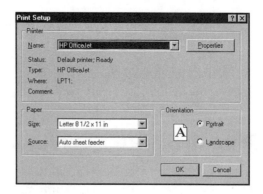

The rest of the options available in the Print Setup dialog box are dependent on the
driver of the particular system printer chosen.

Previewing the Plot

As you decide on the exact settings for the plot, a preview of the results can be displayed via the Preview button located in the lower right corner of the Plot Configuration dialog box. The preview can be either a partial (the default setting) or a full preview. In a partial preview, a dialog box similar to that shown in figure 17.9 is displayed.

Figure 17.9

The Preview Effective
Plotting Area dialog box.

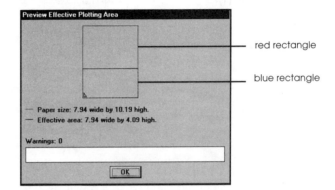

red rectangle

blue rectangle

The specified paper size is represented by the red rectangle and the portion of the paper that will actually be used (the effective area) is represented by the blue rectangle. Below the rectangles, the actual dimensions of the two areas are given. If the preview function detects any possible errors, you will be warned of them. One common error is specifying a scale that requires more paper area than you indicated was available.

With a full preview, an image of the actual plot itself is displayed. The option of zooming into an area of the preview is also available by choosing the Zoom and Pan button. A rectangle replaces the normal cursor. Position the rectangle in the area to be magnified. Click the pick button to size the rectangle. Click the pick button again to reposition the resized rectangle. Clicking the pick button switches between the resizing and positioning modes. Once the desired size and location of the rectangle is obtained, press Enter or the spacebar, and the specified area is displayed. After the magnified view is displayed, choose to either view the previous view or end the plot preview.

If the preview does not look right, go back and change the plot settings and preview the results once again. Continue this process until the desired results are achieved and then choose OK to proceed with the plot.

Setting Pen Parameters

After selecting the device to use, set up the pen table to be used for the plot. Access the pen table by choosing the Pen Assignments button located in the upper left portion of the Plot Configuration dialog box. The following dialog box is then displayed (see fig. 17.10).

Figure 17.10

The Pen Assignments dialog box.

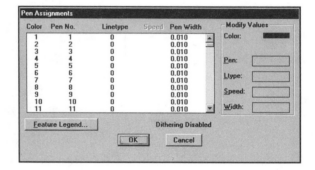

The Pen Assignments dialog box is used to assign a pen, linetype, speed, and pen width to a particular drawing color. The term "pen" may be confusing to you especially if your output device does not even use pens (a LaserJet or an inkjet, for example).

In the early days of CAD, the basic output device was a pen plotter. The simplest ones were single pen plotters, which meant that the plotter could only be loaded with one pen at a time. The more sophisticated ones were multi-pen plotters that employed pen carousels. The carousel was a storage unit for the pens. Each pen was stored in a numbered position in the carousel. The pen in position #1 was referred to as pen #1, the pen in position #2 was referred to as pen #2, and so on. Multiple-pen plotters facilitated the generation of plots with varying colors and/or line weights. For example, if a pen with red ink was stored in position #3 and red lines were to be drawn on the plot, the CAD software would have to be instructed to pick up pen #3.

To produce a color plot, specific pens are assigned to specific drawing colors. By setting the pen table, PLOT is instructed to use a particular pen for a particular drawing color. Then, if pens with color ink are actually inserted into the carousel, a multicolor plot can be produced.

To produce a plot with varying line weights, elements in the drawing are drawn in different colors. Then specific pens are assigned to those colors via the pen assignments table and the pens with the appropriate sized pen tips are installed in the plotter's pen carousel.

What if the device is not a pen plotter, such as a laser or LED or inkjet plotter? Plotting technology has moved away from using physical pens but still employs the concept of "logical" pens. Logical pens are basically imaginary pens to which properties such as line weight, color, and darkness (or shading) can be assigned. With logical pens, a laser plotter can be programmed to draw a line of a certain width or color whenever it gets instructions to use a certain logical pen.

The linetype parameter is another holdover from the old plotting technology. The earliest CAD software could only draw continuous lines. To draw noncontinuous linetypes, the software had to rely on linetypes that were defined in the plotter itself. These linetypes were referred to by number. For example, linetype 1 might have been a hidden linetype. Linetype 2 might have been a dotted linetype. Just as with pens, linetypes are assigned by color. Plotter linetypes became obsolete when the CAD software enabled the user to draw noncontinuous lines in the drawing itself. Now, the linetype setting is no longer used and should be left at 0 unless otherwise instructed by the manufacturer of the plotting device.

The speed parameter is also a holdover from pen plotters. Depending on the media the plot was being produced on and the type of pen being used, the speed of the pens would have to be adjusted to allow the ink to flow properly onto the media. Even today, if a pen plotter is to be used, the pen speeds may have to be set. With technology that does not employ pens, such as lasers or inkjets, the pen speed setting is not relevant and should be left at the default setting unless otherwise instructed by the manufacturer of the device.

The pen width setting is used to set the pen width of a particular pen. AutoCAD uses this information when it draws solid-filled areas and for the Adjust Area Fill option of PLOT. To fill in a solid area, AutoCAD draws one stroke and then moves the pen over $1/2$ of the pen width to draw the next stroke. If the pen width setting is smaller than the actual pen width, then there is a lot of redundant overlapping of strokes. If the pen whereas setting is larger than the actual pen width, there are gaps (blank spaces) between the strokes. For some plotters, you are allowed to set a pen width for each pen, whereas for others you can only set a global pen width for all pens. Pen widths are defined in inches, not in mm, when you elect to define the paper size in inches (which is the default setting). So, if you are using a 0.35mm pen, enter a pen width of 0.014 inches. Usually, leaving this setting at its default value of 0.01 (equivalent to 0.254mm) is satisfactory.

Tip

> If you are accustomed to working with line widths defined in millimeters, set the paper size units to mm, then assign the pen widths. After which, you can change the paper size units back to inches.

To set the values for a particular pen, select the pen to be set. The pen's current values are then placed into the edit boxes to the right where they can be changed.

To set several pens simultaneously, select several pens first and then change the values in the edit boxes to the right.

Setting the Pen Motion Optimization

In processing the drawing data for plotting, AutoCAD can be instructed to try to optimize the order in which the information is sent to the plotter. The goal of the process is to minimize any wasted motion (moving pens, for example) that the plotter would physically have to undertake for the plot. For example, it is more efficient for a pen plotter to draw all the lines requiring one pen before drawing the lines requiring another pen, rather than switching pens all through the plot. Consequently, PLOT can be instructed to perform "pen sorting." When this option is activated, AutoCAD will process the entire drawing and send out all plotting instructions for one pen first, and then repeat the process for the next pen and so on.

To set the level of optimization, click on the Optimization button which brings up the Optimizing Pen Motion dialog box (see fig. 17.11).

Figure 17.11

The Optimizing Pen Motion dialog box.

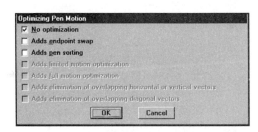

As you see, there are various levels of optimization that you can utilize. The levels are arranged in order of complexity and are cumulative. If you select the 3rd level of optimization, the 1st and 2nd levels will be automatically selected.

With modern plotters employing faster technologies such as laser or inkjet, the optimization level is meaningless and should be set to No optimization.

Defining the Area to Be Plotted

The Additional Parameters section of the PLOT dialog box is where the portion of the drawing to be processed is specified.

The available choices are:

- **Display:** The portion of the drawing area that is displayed in the current viewport is processed. If a tiled or floating viewport is current, then it is the drawing area displayed in that viewport that is processed for plotting.

- **Extents:** The rectangular portion of the drawing area that actually has objects drawn in it is processed.

- **Limits:** The drawing area defined by the drawing limits is processed.

- **View:** If named views have been defined with the DDVIEW or VIEW commands, one of those views can be specified. Choosing the View button brings up a list of defined views from which one can be chosen. The View button and option are only active if named views have already been defined in the drawing. Otherwise, the button and option are disabled.

- **Window:** Choose this button to window a rectangular area to be processed. A dialog box listing the points defining the current window is displayed (see fig. 17.12). To window a different area, choose the Pick button.

Figure 17.12

The Window Selection dialog box.

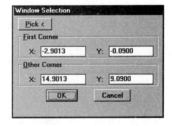

Setting the Paper Size

The Size button is located in the upper right corner of the Plot Configuration dialog box. Choose this button to set the size of the paper that is in the plotter. The size can be defined in either inches (the default) or mm. Choosing the Size button displays the Paper Size dialog box (see fig. 17.13).

Figure 17.13

The Paper Size dialog box.

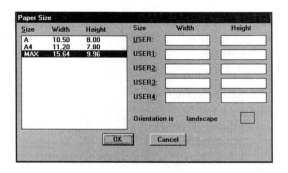

The term "paper size" is misleading because the area specified is actually the net usable area available on the sheet (also referred to as the plot area). The physical sheet size is the actual physical size of the paper in the plotter. A plotter cannot plot right up to the edges of a sheet of paper. There will always be some margin around the edges that the plotter cannot access (see fig. 17.14).

Figure 17.14

Physical area versus maximum available plot area.

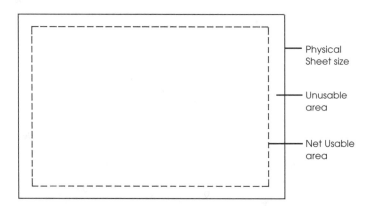

The actual margin varies from plotter to plotter, so look up that information in your plotter's manuals. When the margins are subtracted from the physical sheet size, you are left with the maximum available plot area, which is what should be entered in the Paper Size dialog box. For example, suppose that the instruction manual of your plotter states that the plotter leaves a $1/2$" margin all the way around the edge of the paper. Then on a 24"×36" piece of paper, the maximum usable area (or plot area) is 23"×35".

On the left of the dialog box is a list of standard sheet sizes with their associated plot areas. Either select a plot area from the list or enter your own dimensions via the edit boxes on the right labeled USER, USER1, and so on. A sheet size defined with these edit boxes is referred to as a user defined sheet.

TıP

The list of predefined plot areas is not optimized for specific plotters. You can usually get more plot area for a specific sheet size than what is stated on the list. In which case, use the edit boxes to define your own user defined sheet size.

The specified paper size is used to calculate the scale if the Scaled to Fit option is enabled. The Scaled to Fit option is discussed in more detail in a following section. If a specific scale (such as $\frac{1}{8}$"=1') is used, then the sheet size is not as critical. If a sheet size larger than what is actually available (like the MAX sheet size) is specified, then the plotter still only plots to the limits of the plotter. If a sheet size less than the maximum available plot area is specified, then you lose the usage of the area that is the difference between the two, and the plot could be cut off.

In the bottom right corner of the Paper Size dialog box is a message indicating the orientation of the paper. This is the assumed orientation of the loaded media. This is just a message and is not a choice. The message will vary for different plotters. For some it will indicate landscape; for others, it will indicate portrait.

If the Size button is not available, it means that the selected printer does not allow the option of using different sizes of paper.

Setting the Rotation and Origin

Choosing the Rotation and Origin button displays the following dialog box (see fig. 17.15).

Figure 17.15

The Plot Rotation and Origin dialog box.

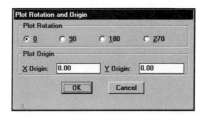

Use the settings in the Plot Rotation and Origin dialog box to shift the position or rotate the plot on the sheet of paper. Some plotters have a smaller margin on one edge of the paper than the opposing side. In such cases, the plot appears off balance with more blank space on one side than the other. To even the margins out, set the origin to center the plot. The values of the X and Y origins are in inches (or mm) and describe the desired shift in position on the sheet of paper.

The Origin option can also be used to fit several small plots onto a single large sheet of paper, when the plotter is capable of accepting a sheet of paper rather than a roll of paper. After the first plot is generated, insert the sheet of paper back into the plotter. Then set the origin such that the next plot does not overlap the area occupied by the first plot, and plot the next drawing.

The Rotation option is typically used to align the long edge of the drawing with the width of the roll of paper, thereby minimizing wasted media.

Setting the Plot Scale

The plot scale is found in the Scale, Rotation, and Origin portion of the Plot Configuration dialog box. The scale is the relationship you set between a distance on the plot (plotted in inches or mm) to the equivalent distance in the drawing (drawing units).

If the units for the drawing are set for architectural or engineering units, foot and inch marks can be used in the scale specification. Regardless of the units set, the scale can always be specified in decimal units. For example, if the drawing to be plotted is set up for $1/8"=1'$ scale, then any of the following scale specifications would be valid:

Plotted Inch=Drawing Units

$1"=8'$

$1/8"=1'$

$1"=96"$

$1=96$

When plotting to scale is not important and the goal is to get as large a plot as can fit on the sheet of paper, then enable the Scaled to Fit option. Enabling the Scaled to Fit option forces LT to calculate and use the scale that results in the largest plot possible on the specified paper size. The resulting scale does not conform to any standard drafting scales and LT does not inform the user of the value of the calculated scale.

Hiding Lines for 3D Drawings

The Hide Lines option, found in the Additional Parameters section of the Plot Configuration dialog box, should only be used with 3D drawings. Enabling this option forces LT to remove any hidden lines in the drawing. Hidden lines are lines that lie behind opaque surfaces and are therefore hidden from the viewer. Enabling this option for 2D drawings just forces LT to perform additional, unnecessary calculations.

Enabling the Adjust Area Fill Option

If the Adjust Area Fill option is enabled, LT adjusts for the pen width when drawing solid-filled areas. This adjustment causes LT to adjust the location of the plotter pen inward, by $1/2$ of the pen width (set in Pen Assignments) when drawing the edges of a filled area. The result is that the edges of filled areas better match the coordinates of the filled area boundaries as measured in the drawing. Objects that are affected by this setting include solids and polylines with width.

Unless an extreme degree of accuracy in the placement of lines on the plots is required (such as for printed circuit board artwork), do not enable this option.

Using the Dithering Option

The Dithering option, found in the Additional Parameters section of the Plot Configuration dialog box, is only available when the device you are plotting to can support this option. Enabling Dithering forces LT to simulate more colors on the plot than the plotter is actually capable of supporting, by mixing colors and white space to create the effect of a new color. It is most commonly used when the drawing has large areas filled solid with color (such as solid objects or closely spaced hatch objects or wide polylines).

For most line drawings, this option has no visible effect and should just be ignored.

Using the Previous Printer

The Use Previous Printer option, found in the Additional Parameters section of the Plot Configuration dialog box, is only available when the system printer is the chosen plot device. If there is more than one system printer configured, LT normally uses the default system printer. By using the Print/Plot Setup option found in the Print Plot Setup and Default Selection dialog box, a specific printer other than the default can be chosen as the device to be used for the current plot. The next time the PLOT command is issued, the previously chosen device can be selected simply by enabling the Use Previous Printer option.

Plotting to a File

The Plot To File option, found in the Additional Parameters section of the Plot Configuration dialog box, is only available if the chosen output device supports it. If the Plot To File option is enabled, the generated plot information is sent to a file rather than to the device itself. Choose the File Name button to specify the specific filename to which the plot information is to be written.

Saving Your Plot Parameters

In the Print/Plot Setup and Default Selection dialog box, choosing the Save Defaults To File button saves the current plot parameters to a file. You supply the filename and a file is created with a file-name extension of .PCP (Plot Configuration Parameters). Use the Get Defaults From File button to restore a saved set of plot settings. This option is especially handy for saving and restoring pen settings when switching from one set of pen settings to another.

Plotting Hints and Tips

Invariably, at one time or another, you will have problems plotting. To minimize the chances of problems, check on the following items before you issue the PLOT command:

- Be sure the plotter is turned on and is online.

- Check to be sure the necessary paper and pens are loaded. If the plotter is a penless device, make sure that the ink cartridges have sufficient ink, especially if multiple plots are to be made.

- Make sure you know what scale you should be using.

- Decide what area (extents, window, and so on) of the drawing is to be processed.

- Check to be sure that the appropriate layers are turned on or off.

Some other steps that can be taken to ensure fewer plotting problems are the following:

■ Read the instructions that come with the plotter and the driver being used.

  Different models of plotters have different capabilities. Read the instructions to get the most out of the plotter.

■ Create standards for the pen settings.

  If you have standard pen settings for your plots, then you can save them in .PCP files and restore them when needed.

■ Create standards for the drawing creation.

  Everyone in your organization should be setting up drawings the same way. A standard setup makes it easier to standardize the settings used for plotting.

■ Always verify drawings from other sources.

  If you get drawings from a client or a subcontractor, do not assume that the drawings are set up the same way as your drawings. Check the units and colors used. Ask whoever supplied the drawings how the drawings were intended to be plotted.

Some of the more common problems encountered when plotting are as follows:

■ **Part of the plot gets chopped off:** Check to be sure that the correct scale and sheet size were specified. A scale requiring more paper than is available might have been specified. Alternatively, a plot area smaller than what is available might have been specified; PLOT will not plot beyond the specified plot area even if there is plenty of space available.

■ **Solid-filled areas aren't getting filled:** Is FILL turned off in the drawing? Also check on the pen widths. If the pen width is too large, then PLOT may be moving the pen over too far when overlapping the previous pen stroke. A common mistake is to specify the pen widths in mm when the units are still set for inches.

■ **Text characters are being connected together or are missing parts:** Again, check the pen widths. When the width is too large, text characters can be chopped off or connected together.

■ **The plot comes out the size of a postage stamp:** Check the scale. If Scaled to Fit is enabled with the plot area set to Extents, check the drawing extents. Sometimes the drawing extents are not reset correctly prior to plotting so PLOT thinks the drawing occupies more room than it actually does. The easiest way to check the extents is to issue the ZOOM command with the Extents option specified.

■ **The PLOT command completes, but the plotter doesn't respond:** This problem is most commonly encountered on networks. Usually, the problem is that the plot data gets sent to the wrong device. Check to be sure the correct LPT ports are being captured correctly by the network.

■ **PLOT command says plotter is not responding:** Check to see if the plotter is online. Check to be sure the cable is correctly connected. Check to be sure the plotter configuration is set to the correct parallel or serial port.

■ **Pen seems to be skipping on the plot:** The pen is moving too fast. Lower the pen speeds. Also, check the type of pens you are using. There are different types of pens that work best with different types of media.

Summary

In this chapter, you learned how to compose and plot a complex drawing layout using paper space and model space. Although you can model a layout in model space, paper space has inherent advantages, especially when it comes to 3D drawings and drawings consisting of multiple views of the same model.

RELATED COMMANDS

PLOTID

PLOTROT MODE

PLOTTER

V

ISOMETRIC & 3D DRAWINGS

DRAWING 2D ISOMETRIC VIEWS

In this chapter, you learn to do the following:

- *How to invoke isometric mode*

- *How to control the isometric environment*

- *How to specify points, lengths, and angles in isometric mode*

- *How to draw in isometric mode*

- *How to plot an isometric drawing*

Invoking Isometric Mode

To ease the drawing of isometric views, LT has a special isometric mode that is invoked through the Drawing Aids dialog box (see fig. 18.1).

Figure 18.1

Invoking isometric mode with the Drawing Aids dialog box.

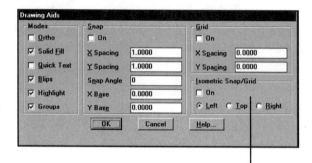

Isometric mode settings

To invoke isometric mode, simply enable the On option located in the lower right corner of the dialog box. To turn isometric mode off, disable the On option. With isometric mode turned on, the drawing environment is adjusted to give the user the illusion of drawing in 3D space when, in fact, everything is drawn as a 2D object.

Isoplanes Explained

By definition, an isometric view is one in which the viewer's line of sight is colinear with one of the diagonals of a cube. The line of sight is at a 45-degree angle relative to the base and elevated at a 35.26-degree angle from the base (see fig. 18.2).

Figure 18.2

The definition of an isometric view.

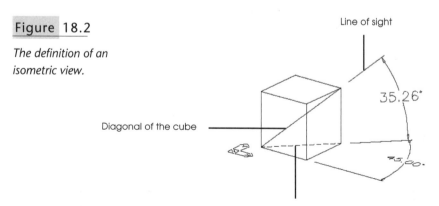

Line of sight

35.26°

Diagonal of the cube

Projection of diagonal on XY plane

In an isometric view, only three faces of a cube are visible. In isometric drafting, these three faces are used as aids in constructing the isometric view. While isometric mode is enabled, LT creates the illusion that you are drawing in one of these three distinct surfaces, or *planes*. These three planes are referred to as *isometric planes*, or *isoplanes*, and are referenced as the left, right, and top isoplanes (see fig. 18.3).

Figure 18.3

An isometric view of a cube.

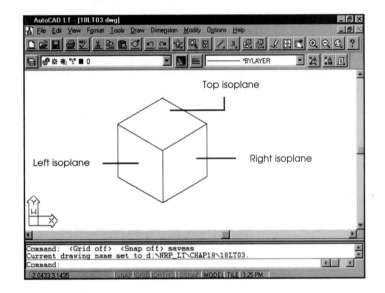

As you switch between isoplanes, LT automatically changes the appearance of the crosshairs and grid to make it look as if they lie in the current isoplane.

To switch between isoplanes, use either the Left, Top, or Right options in the Drawing Aids dialog box, use the F5 function key, press the Ctrl+E accelerator key, or button #8 of a digitizer puck.

In the following exercise, you begin a new drawing and enable isometric mode.

STARTING AN ISOMETRIC DRAWING

1.   Begin a new drawing. Use the Quick Setup wizard. Choose decimal units and a 12x9 drawing area.

2. Choose Options, Drawing Aids and enable the On option located in the Isometric Snap/Grid section of the dialog box.

Also enable the Top option and choose OK.

3. Make a new layer named PART and make it current. Save the drawing under the name **BRACKET**.

Points, Distances, and Angles in Isometric Mode

Isometricmode is a 2D simulation of 3D space. The 2D XY coordinate system is not affected by isometric mode. This requires a little adjustment in how points and angles are specified. In an isometric view of a cube, the cube's visible edges are aligned at 30, 90, and 150 degrees relative to a horizontal line (see fig. 18.4).

Figure 18.4

Angles of isometric lines.

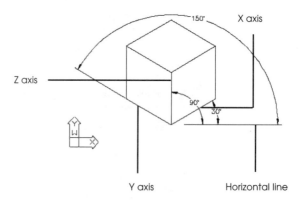

The visible edges are referred to as *isometric lines,* and any lines parallel to them are also isometric lines. The 90-degree line represents the Z axis. With the Z axis orientation established, the right-hand rule dictates that the X axis is represented by the 30-degree line, and the Y axis is represented by the 150-degree line.

In isometric views, only distances measured along isometric lines are true measurements. Any measurements along a nonisometric line are distorted. For example, the measured length of one of the diagonals of one of the faces of a cube (isoplane) is distorted, whereas the measured lengths of the face's edges (isometric lines) are correct.

To further the illusion of working in 3D, the crosshairs and the SNAP and GRID points are adjusted to be aligned with the isometric lines of the current isoplane (see fig. 18.5).

Figure 18.5

Figure 18.5

*Isometric drawing
environment.*

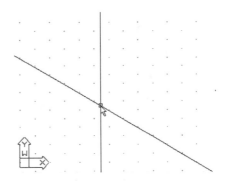

Because the 2D XY coordinate system remains unaffected by isometric mode, the coordinates of a snap point in normal nonisometric space end up being rotated either 30 or 150 degrees about the origin. The result is that the X coordinate value of the snap grid points is never a multiple of the X snap spacing, as would normally be expected.

Ortho mode can be used as drawing lines in the current isoplane that are supposed to be at right angles to each other. As with the crosshair, snap, and grid points, ortho mode is adjusted for the current isoplane.

Points and distances along nonisometric lines have to be located utilizing appropriate construction techniques developed for drawing isometric views.

Drawing in Isometric Mode

Lines, circles, circular and elliptical arcs, text, spirals, and dimensions are easily drawn in isometric mode. Other geometric features, such as spirals or ellipses, are drawn with the aid of standard drafting construction techniques.

Drawing Lines

The easiest way to draw lines in isometric mode is to utilize snap points, object snap modes, ortho mode, and relative coordinates whenever possible. To use relative coordinates to draw a line appearing to be parallel to the X axis, specify an angle of 30 or 210 degrees. If the line is to appear to be parallel to the Y axis, use an angle of 150 or -30 degrees, and if the line is to appear to be parallel to the Z axis, use an angle of 90 or -90 degrees.

To draw a line not parallel to any of the three isometric axes, use object snap modes, snap points, or standard drafting construction techniques.

In the following exercise, you draw the basic outline of a bracket.

DRAWING THE OUTLINE OF THE BRACKET

1. Continue to use the drawing BRACKET. Choose Draw, Line flyout, Line. With your snap, grid, and ortho modes on, pick the following points:

   From point: **Pick ① at 0.8660,3.500 (see fig. 18.6)**
   To point: **Pick ② at 5.1962,6.0000**
   To point: **Pick ③ at 8.6603,4.0000**
   To point: **Pick ④ at 4.3301,1.5000**
   To point: **C** ↵

Figure 18.6

The basic outline of the bracket.

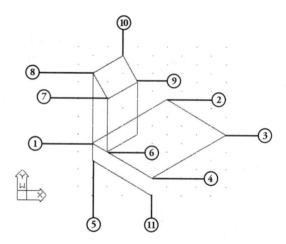

2. Repeat the LINE command and enter the following points:

   From point: **Pick ⑤ at .8660,2.5000**
   To point: **Pick ⑪ at 4.3301,0.500**
   To point: ↵

3. Choose Options, Drawing Aids and enable the Left option. This sets the left isoplane current.

4. Repeat the LINE command and enter the following points:

```
From point: Pick ⑤
To point: @5<90 ↵
To point: @2<30 ↵
To point: ↵
```

5. Repeat the LINE command and enter the following points:

```
From point: Pick ⑥ at 1.7321, 3.0000
To point: @0,3 ↵
To point: @2<30 ↵
To point: ↵
```

6. Repeat the LINE command and enter the following points:

```
From point: Pick ⑥
To point: @2<30 ↵
To point: @0,3 ↵
To point: ↵
```

In the next steps, a couple of nonisometric lines are drawn.

7. Repeat the LINE command and enter the following points:

```
From point: Pick ⑦
To point: Pick ⑧
To point: ↵
```

8. Repeat the LINE command and enter the following points:

```
From point: Pick ⑨
To point: Pick ⑩
To point: ↵
```

The basic outline of the bracket is now complete. Save the drawing.

Drawing Circles and Arcs

Circles in orthogonal views (plan and elevation views) appear as ellipses in isometric views. To represent a circle in an isoplane, draw an ellipse with its axes aligned in such a way as to make it appear that the ellipse lies in that isoplane. To help draw such ellipses, use the Isocircle option of the ELLIPSE command. The Isocircle option appears only in the list of ELLIPSE options when isometric mode is enabled:

```
Arc/Center/Isocircle/<Axis endpoint 1>:
```

After selecting the Isocircle option, the prompt for the location of the circle's center point and its radius or diameter appears. The appearance of the ellipse is automatically adjusted for the current isoplane.

Circular arcs appear as portions of ellipses in isometric views. There are two approaches to drawing these elliptical arcs. You can draw a full isocircle (ELLIPSE), then trim or break the unneeded portion. Alternatively, select the Arc option of the ELLIPSE command and the following prompt appears:

```
<Axis endpoint 1>/Center/Isocircle:
```

The Isocircle option is available only when isometric mode is enabled. After selecting the Isocircle option, the following prompt for the center of the isocircle appears:

```
Center of circle:
```

Then, the next prompt for the circle's radius (default option) or its diameter appears:

```
<Circle radius>/Diameter:
```

Next, the prompt for a starting angle or parameter for the elliptical arc appears:

```
Parameter/<start angle>:
```

Finally, an ending angle (default option), or the included angle or a parameter, must be supplied:

```
Parameter/Included/<end angle>:
```

As with the arc option when isometric mode is not enabled, the orientation of zero degrees is temporarily changed to align zero degrees with the first axis endpoint when the prompts for a start and end angle appear. Unfortunately, in isometric mode, this behavior makes it difficult to specify the angles with typed values. To overcome this difficulty, use the distance and angle display on the status bar, snap points, or object snap modes to specify the start and end angles.

Drawing any other type of curve, such as a spiral curve, requires the usage of standard isometric drafting construction techniques.

In the following exercise, you add some holes and fillets to the view by drawing some ellipses.

ADDING SOME CURVES TO THE BRACKET

1. Continue to use the drawing BRACKET. Choose Options, Drawing Aids and enable the Right option.

2. Choose Draw, Ellipse, Axis, End and enter the following data:

```
Arc/Center/Isocircle/<Axis endpoint 1>: I ↵
Center of circle: Pick ① at 2.5981,5.500 (see fig. 18.7)
<Circle radius>/Diameter: O ↵
```

This circle represents a hole in the bracket. You can embellish the hole by hatching the ellipse.

Figure 18.7

Adding a hole and fillets to the bracket.

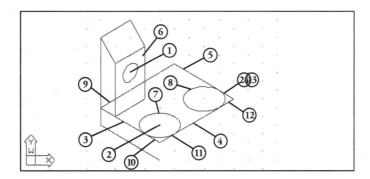

3. Choose Options, Drawing Aids and enable the Top option. In the next few steps, the corners are filleted.

4. Repeat the ELLIPSE command and enter the following data:

```
Arc/Center/Isocircle/<Axis endpoint 1>: I ↵
Center of circle: Pick ② at 4.3301,2.5
<Circle radius>/Diameter: 1 ↵
```

5. Choose Modify, Duplicate flyout, Duplicate Object and select the ellipse just drawn. Enter the following data:

```
<Base point or displacement>/Multiple: 3<30 ↵
Second point of displacement: ↵
```

Turn snap mode off. Choose Modify, Trim flyout, Trim and select points ③ through ⑧ as prompted. Press Enter after you have selected these points. Then at the `<Select object to trim>/Project/Edge/Undo:` prompt, pick ⑨, ⑦, ⑧, ⑩, ⑪, ⑫, ⑬. Press Enter again.

As an alternative for the corners, you can use the Arc option of FILLET to draw the elliptical arcs. In the next step, a copy of the filleted top edge is made.

6. At the `Command:` prompt, select the following objects:

①, ②, ③ (see fig. 18.8).

Figure 18.8

Finishing the rounded corners.

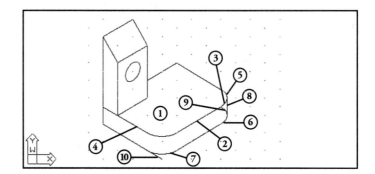

You should now see the grip points for the selected objects.

7. Select the grip point ④. This activates grips. Depress the space bar until you see the MOVE grip command and enter the following data:

```
** MOVE **
<Move to point>/Base point/Copy/Undo/eXit: C ↵
** MOVE (multiple) **
<Move to point>/Base point/Copy/Undo/eXit: @1<-90 ↵
** MOVE (multiple) **
<Move to point>/Base point/Copy/Undo/eXit: ↵
```

In the next step, you draw a line to represent the right silhouette edge of the bracket.

8. Zoom into the area where ⑤ and ⑥ are located.

9. Issue a REGEN to view the curves better prior to trying to draw the next line. Now, using Nearest object snap mode, draw a vertical line so that it appears to be tangent to the two elliptical arcs at ⑤ and ⑥.

Unfortunately, the Tangent object snap does not work with ellipses, which is why this tangent line is being approximated.

10. Zoom out to view the overall bracket. Choose Modify, Trim flyout, Trim and select the following objects:

```
Select cutting edges: (Projmode = UCS, Edgemode = No extend)
Select objects: Pick ⑦
Select objects: Pick ⑧
Select objects: ↵
<Select object to trim>/Project/Edge/Undo: Pick ⑨
<Select object to trim>/Project/Edge/Undo: Pick ⑩
<Select object to trim>/Project/Edge/Undp: ↵
```

11. The bracket is now complete so save the drawing.

Drawing Text

To draw text that appears to lie in the current isoplane, use multiples of 30 degrees for the oblique and rotation angles. The baseline of the text and the spine of the letters must appear to be parallel to the appropriate isometric lines. To make text appear to lie upright in the XZ plane (right isoplane), for example, use an oblique angle of 30 degrees and a rotation angle of 30 degrees (see fig. 18.9).

Figure 18.9

Text in isoplanes.

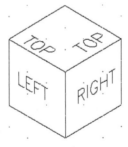

To make text appear to lie upright in the YZ plane (left isoplane), use an oblique angle of -30 degrees and a rotation angle of -30 degrees. To make text appear to lie in the XY plane (top isoplane) and running parallel to the Y axis, use a 30-degree oblique angle and a -30-degree rotation angle. To make text appear as if it is running parallel to the X axis, use the same oblique angle but a rotation angle of 30 degrees.

TIP

Make two text styles, one with an oblique angle of 30 degrees and one with an oblique angle of -30 degrees. Then set the style to the appropriate one prior to drawing text in an isoplane. If you happen to choose the wrong style, use DDMODIFY to reassign the style, rather than erasing and redrawing the text.

In the following exercise, you create some text styles and use them to add some text to the isometric view of the bracket.

ADDING TEXT

1. Continue to use the drawing BRACKET. Make a new layer named **TEXT** and make it the current layer. In the next step, you create the needed text styles.

2. Choose Format, Text Styles. Enter **LEAN_RIGHT** as the style name and choose New. Enter **ROMANS** for the font file and 30 degrees for the oblique angle and choose Apply.

   Enter **LEAN_LEFT** as the style name and choose New. Enter **-30 degrees** for the oblique angle and choose Apply. Choose Close to end the dialog box.

   Select LEAN RIGHT to set it as the current style and then choose Close.

3. Choose Options, Drawing Aids, set the Y snap spacing to 0.5, enable snap mode, and choose OK. Press the F5 function key until the top isoplane is current.

4. Choose Draw, Text, Dynamic Text and enter the following data:

   ```
   Justify/Style/<Start point>: S ↵
   Style name (or ?) <LEAN_LEFT>: LEAN_RIGHT ↵
   Justify/Style/<Start point>: C ↵
   Center point: Pick ① at 3.4641,2.5 (see fig. 18.10)
   Height <0.2000>: 0.5 ↵
   Rotation angle <330>: -30 ↵
   Text: TOP ↵
   Text: ↵
   ```

Figure 18.10

Adding some text to the
bracket.

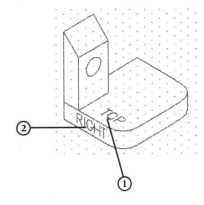

5. Press Ctrl+E until the left isoplane is current. Repeat the DTEXT command and enter the following data:

```
Style name (or ?) <LEAN_RIGHT>: LEAN_LEFT ↵
Justify/Style/<Start point>: M ↵
Middle point: Pick ② at 2.5981,2.0000
Height <0.5000>: 0.5 ↵
Rotation angle <330>: ↵
Text: RIGHT ↵
Text: ↵
```

6. Save the drawing.

Drawing Dimensions

Unfortunately, dimensions are not automatically adjusted by LT for the current isoplane. To draw dimensions so that the dimensions appear to lie in the current isoplane, certain dimension settings must be adjusted. The extension lines and dimension lines should be drawn parallel to the appropriate isometric lines. Just as with text, increments of 30 degrees are used to create the illusion.

The general procedure is as follows:

1. Make two text styles, one with an oblique angle of 30 degrees (name it **LEAN_RIGHT** because the letters lean right) and the other having an oblique angle of -30 degrees (name it **LEAN_LEFT** because the letters lean left).

2. Make two dimension styles, one using the LEAN_RIGHT text style (name it **DIM_RIGHT**) and the other using the LEAN_LEFT text style (name it **DIM_LEFT**). It is possible to use just one dimension style and switch

between the two styles, but then some or all of the dimensions would be drawn with dimension overrides, and there are certain consequences in using overrides (see Chapter 14, "Dimensioning the Drawing," for discussion of overrides).

3. Use the DIMALIGNED command to draw the initial dimension. Use the Angle option to rotate the text parallel to the dimension line. Alternatively, adjust the angle of the text after the dimension is drawn, with the Rotate option of the DIMEDIT command. When drawing a dimension along the Z axis, an alternative to DIMALIGNED is DIMLINEAR.

4. Use the Oblique option of the DIMEDIT command to change the angle of the extension lines to be parallel to the appropriate isometric lines.

For dimensions lying in the left isoplane, oblique the extension lines 150 degrees or -30 degrees. For dimensions lying in the right isoplane, angle the extension lines 30 degrees or 210 degrees. For dimensions lying in the top isoplane, oblique the extension lines 30, -30, 150, or 210 degrees.

Defining text styles with the appropriate oblique angles must be done because there is no way to modify the oblique angle of the text after an associative dimension is drawn other than by using text styles.

In dimensioning isometric views, remember that only measurements along isometric lines are correct. Measurements along nonisometric lines are distorted.

TI P

> If you find that you have used the wrong text style to draw a dimension, use DDMODIFY to change the dimension style. You could just change the text style, but that would be recorded as a dimension override.

In the following exercise, you add dimensions to the part bracket.

DIMENSIONING THE BRACKET

1. Continue to use the drawing BRACKET. Display the Dimensioning toolbar if it is not already visible. Choose Dimensioning, Dimension Style flyout, Dimension Styles.

   Enter **DIM_L** as the style name and choose Save. Choose Annotation and set the text style to LEAN_LEFT. Choose Units and set the dimension precision to **0.0** and choose OK. Choose OK. Choose Geometry and enter **3.0** as the overall scale. Choose OK and Save.

Enter **DIM_R** as the style name and choose Save. Choose Annotation and set the text style to LEAN_RIGHT. Choose OK and Save.

Choose OK to end the dialog box. DIM_R is now the current dimension style. The two dimension styles are identical except for the text style setting.

2. Choose Dimensioning, Aligned Dimension and enter the following data:

```
First extension line origin or RETURN to select: Pick ① (see fig. 18.11)
Second extension line origin: Pick ② at 3.8971,0.2500
Dimension line location (Text/Angle): A ↵
Enter text angle: -30 ↵
Dimension line location (Text/Angle): Pick ③ at 2.1651,0.2500
Dimension text <4.0>: ↵
```

Figure 18.11

Dimensioning the bracket.

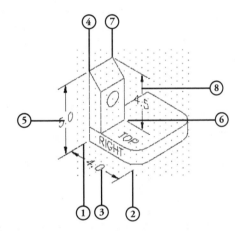

3. Choose Dimensioning, Dimension Style flyout, Oblique Dimensions and select the dimension just drawn:

```
Enter obliquing angle (RETURN for none): -150 ↵
```

4. Choose Dimensioning, Linear Dimension and enter the following data:

```
First extension line origin or RETURN to select: Pick ①
Second extension line origin: Pick ④
Dimension line location (Text/Angle/Horizontal/Vertical/Rotated): A↵
Enter text angle: 30 ↵
Dimension line location (Text/Angle/Horizontal/Vertical/Rotated): Pick ⑤ at
-0.8660,3.500
Dimension text <5.0>: ↵
```

5. Choose Dimensioning, Dimension Style Flyout, Oblique Dimensions and select the dimension just drawn:

```
Enter obliquing angle (RETURN for none): -150 ↵
```

6. Choose Format, Dimension Style and set the current style to DIM_L and choose OK.

7. Choose Dimensioning, Linear Dimension and enter the following data:

```
First extension line origin or RETURN to select: Pick ⑥
Second extension line origin: Pick ⑦
Dimension line location (Text/Angle/Horizontal/Vertical/Rotated): A ↵
Enter text angle: -30 ↵
Dimension line location (Text/Angle/Horizontal/Vertical/Rotated): Pick ⑧ at
4.7631,5.2500
Dimension text <4.5>: ↵
```

8. Choose Dimensioning, Dimension Style flyout, Oblique Dimensions and select the dimension just drawn:

```
Enter obliquing angle (RETURN for none): ↵
```

9. The dimensions are finished. Save the drawing.

Plotting and Composing an Isometric Drawing

To plot an isometric drawing, remember that it is just another 2D drawing. Everything you learned about plotting 2D drawings applies to plotting isometric views. If the plot is to be just a pictorial (which is true more often than not), use the FIT scale. If, however, you plan to scale distances from the plot along isometric lines, you can set a scale for the PLOT command.

Because you can switch isometric mode on and off at will, you can mix isometric elements and nonisometric elements within a drawing layout. For example, the title block, some labels, orthogonal views and so on, would be drawn in nonisometric mode. One interesting point to note is that isometric mode can be enabled in the paper space viewport (TILEMODE=0).

RELATED COMMANDS

SNAP

ISOPLANE

SNAPSTYL

SNAPISOPAIR

19

DRAWING IN 3D

LT is primarily a 2D program; however, it does have limited 3D modeling capabilities that can be used to generate wireframe and surface models. In order to understand how to use 3D in LT, you should be familiar with a few terms (see fig. 19.1).

- **XY plane:** *An XY plane is a flat, 2D surface that contains the X and Y axes. There are an infinite number of parallel XY planes, but every 2D drawing you have created up to this point has utilized the XY plane with the Z coordinate of 0.*

- **Z axis:** *The Z axis is the third axis of a 3D coordinate system, the other two being the X and Y axes. The Z axis is always perpendicular to the XY plane (see fig.19.1).*

- **Plan View:** *A plan view is a view of the XY plane in which the line of sight is parallel to the Z axis.*

- **Elevation:** *An object's elevation is its position as measured along the Z axis, from the XY plane having a Z value of 0. An object's elevation is also referred to as its Z coordinate.*

■ **Thickness:** *An object's thickness is its length as measured along the Z axis. This term is used to describe an object's height when the object is an extruded 2D object. The terms height and thickness are used interchangeably.*

■ **Wireframe Model:** *A 3D wireframe model consists of lines and curves that have no assigned thickness. In effect, a wireframe model is akin to a skeleton without any surfaces covering it.*

■ **Surface Model:** *A 3D surface model consists of opaque surfaces that can obscure objects lying behind the surfaces.*

Figure 19.1

Defining some 3D terms.

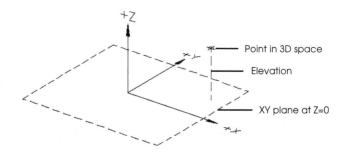

In this chapter, you learn to do the following:

■ Generate simple surface models by extruding 2D objects

■ View 3D models from various viewing angles

■ Compose and plot a 3D model from paper and model spaces

■ Pick points in 3D space, using XYZ point format, object snap modes, point filters, cylindrical coordinates, and spherical coordinates

■ Carry out basic editing and construction commands on 3D models

■ Apply UCSs in a 3D environment

Extruding 2D Objects

A basic 3D surface model is created by taking an ordinary 2D object and extruding it along the Z axis. The extrusion is accomplished by assigning a base elevation and thickness to the 2D object.

Setting the Current Elevation

Up to this point, you had to deal only with X and Y coordinates when specifying points. In fact, LT's coordinate system is 3D, and a point in this system actually has X, Y, and Z values. When LT is given only X and Y values, it automatically assigns a default Z value for the point. The default Z value, normally 0, is referred to as the current elevation. Did you notice that, so far, the coordinates displayed by ID, LIST, or DDMODIFY have a Z component that always seems to be zero? Now you know where the zero came from and why.

The current elevation is set via the Current Properties dialog box (DDEMODES) and can be changed anytime. DDEMODES is accessed by choosing Current Properties off the Format menu or off the Standard Toolbar.

The current elevation may be either a positive or negative value. Unless overridden, all objects drawn are drawn at the current elevation. The current elevation can be overridden by explicitly supplying a Z coordinate when typing point specifications or by using object snap to select existing points. In a 3D model, you position an object above or below another object by using different Z coordinates.

An existing object's elevation can be changed with either the MOVE command (by supplying a Z component) or with the DDMODIFY command.

Setting the Current Thickness

In addition to having an assigned elevation, a 3D object also has to have thickness or height. A 2D object can be given a thickness that results in the object being extruded along the Z axis, resulting in a 3D object.

Every object drawn is automatically assigned the current thickness. By default, the current thickness is normally zero, which is why all the objects you have drawn thus far have been 2D. Just as with the current elevation, the current thickness is set via the Current Properties dialog box.

When a 2D object is assigned a non-zero thickness, it is extruded along the Z axis and becomes 3D. If the thickness is a positive value, the 2D object is extruded in the positive Z direction, and the original 2D object becomes the base of the new 3D object (see fig. 19.2). If the thickness is a negative value, the 2D object is extruded in the negative Z direction, and the original 2D object becomes the top of the new 3D object.

Figure 19.2

Extruding 2D objects.

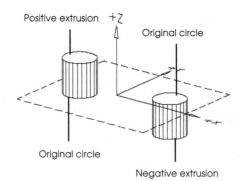

When an inquiry (such as LIST or DDMODIFY) is performed on an extruded 2D object, the Z value of the object's defining points is always the Z value of the original 2D object. For example, if a LIST is performed on a 3D cylinder formed by extruding a circle in the positive Z direction, the coordinates displayed are those of the original 2D circle (the base of the cylinder).

All the objects you have learned to draw, with several exceptions, are affected by the current thickness. Text, mtext, spline, ellipse, and dimension objects are always drawn with zero thickness, regardless of the current thickness setting. Text objects can, however, be given a thickness after being drawn.

To change an object's assigned thickness, use the DDMODIFY or DDCHPROP commands.

In the following exercise, you draw a simple 3D model of a house with extruded lines.

CREATING A SIMPLE 3D HOUSE

1. Begin a new drawing. Use the Quick Setup wizard. Specify architectural units and use a 60' width and 50' height. Make a new layer named **WALLS** and make it current. Save the drawing as **HOUSE**.

2. Choose Object Properties, Current Properties. Set the elevation to 0' and the thickness to 10'.

3. Choose Draw, Line Flyout, Line and enter the following data:

    ```
    From point: 10',10' ↵
    To point: @30'<0 ↵
    To point: ↵
    ```

4. Repeat the LINE command and enter the following data:

   ```
   From point: @3'<0 ↵
   To point: @7'<0 ↵
   To point: @15'<90 ↵
   To point: ↵
   ```

5. Repeat the LINE command and enter the following data:

   ```
   From point: @5'<90 ↵
   To point: @10'<90 ↵
   To point: @40'<180 ↵
   To point: @30'<-90 ↵
   To point: ↵
   ```

   The outer walls are drawn with two openings, one for a door and one for a picture window. In the following steps, the openings are finished.

6. Choose Format, Current Properties and set the thickness to 6'. Leave the elevation at 0'.

7. Repeat the LINE command and enter the following data:

   ```
   From point: 40',10' ↵
   To point: @3'<60 ↵
   To point: ↵
   ```

   The door is now in. Next, draw the header for the door opening.

8. Choose Check Properties, Current Properties and set the thickness to 4' and the elevation to 6'.

9. Repeat the LINE command and enter the following data:

   ```
   From point: 40',10' ↵
   To point: @3'<0 ↵
   To point: ↵
   ```

   The door opening is now complete. Next, complete the window opening.

10. Choose Object Properties, Current Properties and set the thickness to 3' and the elevation to 0'.

11. Repeat the LINE command and enter the following data:

    ```
    From point: 50',25' ↵
    To point: @5'<90 ↵
    To point: ↵
    ```

    The sill for the window opening is now in. Next, draw the header.

12. Choose Object Properties, Current Properties and set the elevation to 8' and the thickness to 2'.

13. Repeat the LINE command and enter the following data:

```
From point: 50',25' ↵
To point: @5'<90 ↵
To point: ↵
```

14. The basic floorplan is now complete (see fig. 19.3). Save the drawing.

Figure 19.3

*Floorplan of a simple
house.*

Generating Different Viewpoints of a 3D Model

Your current viewing point is positioned directly above the XY plan (see fig. 19.4). Your line of sight is parallel to the Z axis, perpendicular to the XY plane. The resulting view is a plan view of the model, whether it is a 2D or 3D model.

Figure 19.4

*Your current viewing
angle.*

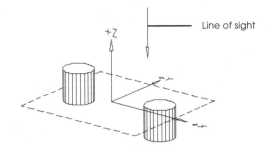

As a consequence of this viewing angle, you cannot see an object's height or discern its elevation relative to other 3D objects.

Before proceeding with the new commands that are used to view the 3rd dimension, a few terms need to be defined:

■ **Camera position:** If you use the analogy of a camera, you, the observer, are the camera through which the 3D model is being viewed. This term may be used interchangeably with the term "observer's position."

■ **Target point:** When you point a camera or look at something with your eyes, you are focusing on a distinct point, the target point.

■ **Line of sight:** This is the imaginary line that connects the camera's position with the target point.

The commands that are described in the following sections are issued by choosing View, 3D Viewpoint or by choosing Standard Toolbar, Named Views.

Generating Nonplanar Views

The VPOINT command is used to control the camera position from which the model is viewed. To issue the VPOINT command, choose either Tripod or Vector from the 3D Viewpoint submenu of the View pull-down menu.

VPOINT displays the following prompt:

    Rotate/<View point> <0.0000,0.0000,1.0000>:

Specify the TRIPOD option by pressing Enter at the VPOINT command prompt or by choosing View, 3D Viewpoint, Tripod. The compass and axes tripod are then displayed (see fig. 19.5), enabling you to set your camera position dynamically.

Figure 19.5

*VPOINT's compass
and axes tripod.*

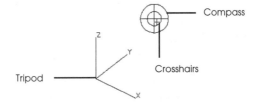

The compass is the icon in the upper right corner of the screen. The normal crosshair is replaced with a shorter crosshair and represents the camera position. The tripod is the XYZ icon on the left side of the display. The tripod indicates the positive direction of the X, Y, and Z axes. As the crosshair is moved about the compass, the tripod display is adjusted to show the corresponding orientation of the X, Y, Z axes.

The compass is a 2D representation of 3D space. Set the viewing point by picking a point within the compass. Picking a point in the compass sets the angle in the XY plane and the angle from that same XY plane simultaneously.

The center point of the compass and the two circles represent different angles from the XY plane. Picking the exact middle of the compass places the observer directly above the XY plane (90 degrees), resulting in a plan view of the model (see fig. 19.6). Picking a point within the inner circle sets the angle of the line of sight from the XY plane at a value between 0 and 90 degrees. Picking a point on the inner circle sets the angle from the XY plane at 0 degrees and results in an elevation view of the model.

Figure 19.6

The VPOINT compass.

Picking a point between the inner and outer circles sets the angle from the XY plane at a value between 0 and -90 degrees and places the camera below the model. Picking a point on the outer circle sets the angle from the XY plane at -90 degrees, which places the camera directly below the model. Picking a point beyond the outer circle is ineffective and should not be done.

The vertical and horizontal lines of the compass represent 0, 90, 180, and 270 degrees in the XY plane. The pick point's position relative to the vertical and horizontal compass lines determines the camera's angle in the XY plane.

The default option is to set the camera position by specifying a vector. Specify this option by choosing View, 3D Viewpoints, Vector. The vector is simply a set of XYZ coordinates defining the camera's position relative to the target, which is assigned the coordinates 0,0,0. See table 19.1 for some commonly used vector values.

The third option is accessed by choosing View, -3D Viewpoints, Vector and then specifying the Rotate option at the command prompt. The Rotate option enables you to set the viewing point by specifying the angle in the XY plane and an angle from the XY plane of the line of sight (see fig. 19.7).

Figure 19.7

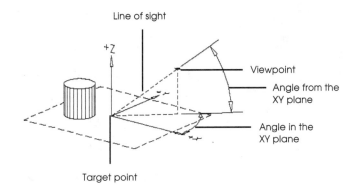

Figure 19.7

Defining the angles for VPOINT.

Generating Plan Views

The PLAN command is used to specify a plan view of the model. To issue the PLAN command, choose View, 3D Viewpoint, Plan View and then choose Current, World, or Named. PLAN displays the following prompt:

```
<Current UCS>/Ucs/World:
```

The default option <Current UCS> is used to generate a plan view of the current UCS. The UCS option enables you to generate a plan view of a named UCS. The World option is used to generate a plan view of the world UCS regardless of the current UCS.

3D Viewpoint Presets

On the 3D Viewpoint submenu (Choose View, 3D Viewpoint) are several menu items that issue the VPOINT command with a specific vector. Choosing one of these menu items results in a specific view of the model as detailed in table 19.1.

Table 19.1

Presets and Their Equivalent Vectors and Angles

Menu Item Label	Equivalent Vector	Equivalent Angles (in degrees)	
Top	0,0,1	In XY: 270	From XY: 90
Bottom	0,0,-1	In XY: 270	From XY: -90
Left	-1,0,0	In XY: 180	From XY: 0

continues

Menu Item Label	Equivalent Vector	Equivalent Angles (in degrees)	
Right	1,0,0	In XY: 0	From XY: 0
Front	0,-1,0	In XY: 270	From XY: 0
Back	0,1,0	In XY: 90	From XY: 0
SW Isometric	-1,-1,1	In XY: 225	From XY: 45
SE Isometric	1,-1,1	In XY: 315	From XY: 45
NE Isometric	1,1,1	In XY: 45	From XY: 45
NW Isometric	-1,1,1	In XY: 135	From XY: 45

The preceding preset viewpoints can also be set through the View Flyout of the Standard Toolbar.

TI P

After using VPOINT or PLAN to generate the desired view, name the view so that the view can be restored at will. Use DDVIEW to name and restore views.

In the following exercise, you generate various views of the 3D house just drawn.

GENERATING VIEWS

1. Continue to use the drawing HOUSE.

2. Choose View, 3D Viewpoint, SW Isometric.

   You can now see the heights and elevations assigned to the various lines you drew.

3. Choose View, Named View and New. Enter the name **SW-ISO** and choose Save View. Choose OK to end the dialog box. You have just assigned the name SW-ISO to the current view.

4. Choose View, 3D Viewpoint, Vector and enter the following data:

    ```
    Rotate/<View point> <-0'-1",-0'-1",0'-1">: R ↵
    Enter angle in XY plane from X axis <225>: 45 ↵
    Enter angle from XY plane <35>: 20 ↵
    ```

5. Choose Standard Toolbar, View Flyout, Named Views and choose New. Enter the name **SE-VIEW** and choose Save View. Choose OK to end the dialog box.

6. Choose View, 3D Viewpoint, Plan View, World. Choose Standard Toolbar, View Flyout, Named Views and name this view **PLAN**.

7. Choose Standard Toolbar, View Flyout, Named Views, select SW-ISO, and choose Restore. This restores the view named SW-ISO.

8. Save the drawing.

Using Multiple Viewports

At times, displaying several views of your model simultaneously on your monitor can be useful as the model is drawn and edited. You can configure the drawing window for multiple viewports using the VPORTS command and have each viewport display a different view of your mode. For example, with three viewports configured, one viewport can display a plan view, another an elevation view, and the third an isometric view. Then, simply make the viewport holding the view you want to work with the current viewport.

In the following exercise, you set up multiple viewports and restore a different view in each one.

CONFIGURING MULTIPLE VIEWPORTS

1. Continue to use the drawing HOUSE.

2. Choose View, Tiled Viewports, 2 Viewports and specify the Vertical option. This splits your single viewport into two viewports. Both viewports should have the identical view of the model.

3. Make the left viewport current by moving the crosshairs over to it and depressing the pick button. Choose View, Named Views and restore the view SE-VIEW.

You can draw and edit in either viewport and change the view in the viewports at will.

4. Save the drawing.

Removing Hidden Lines

Extruded 2D objects are normally displayed as wireframe models even though they are actually surface models. The surfaces, however, do not play a role in the model display until either the HIDE or SHADE command is issued. HIDE is issued by choosing View, Hide, and it removes the hidden lines from the current view. Hidden lines are the edges of the model that are obscured by other surfaces and are therefore hidden from view.

To restore the wireframe display of the model, issue the REGEN command.

TIP

> Although it is possible to edit the model by using a view with hidden lines removed, it gets tricky because some of the objects are not displayed completely or are not displayed at all. As a general rule, do not edit the model by using a hidden line removed view.

If multiple viewports are used, HIDE affects only the view in the current viewport. REGEN also affects only the current viewport.

Using HIDE, you can see which surfaces are generated with extruded 2D objects. Any extruded 2D object that encloses an area, such as a circle, solid, or a polyline with width, has top and bottom surfaces. For example, a circle that is extruded into a cylinder has a top and bottom surface.

Other extruded 2D objects that do not enclose an area, such as a line, arc, or polyline with zero width, do not have top or bottom surfaces. If a rectangle is drawn with four lines and the lines are subsequently extruded, the resulting model will have four sides but no top or bottom surfaces.

TIP

> The SOLID command is a quick and easy way to generate triangular and quadrilateral 3D shapes that have top and bottom surfaces. In plan view, a solid is normally filled, but in a nonplanar view, a solid is not filled. If you prefer not to have the solids filled in plan view, turn FILLMODE off. To affect existing solids after changing FILLMODE, issue the REGEN command.

Text and mtext, as you might recall, are always drawn with zero thickness. Unfortunately, HIDE will not recognize zero-thickness text and mtext objects properly. Consequently, text objects are not hidden correctly until the objects are assigned at least some nominal thickness (such as 0.01 units) using DDMODIFY or DDCHPROP. Mtext objects cannot be assigned a thickness and consequently are never hidden correctly by the HIDE command.

The other objects that are never given a thickness are dimensions, splines, and ellipses. Unlike text or mtext objects, HIDE recognizes these objects correctly.

> A wireframe model can play tricks with your vision. You might think you are viewing the model one way when, in fact, you are viewing the model from a completely different viewing point. Issuing the HIDE command can clarify the situation. When you finish with the view, issue the REGEN command to restore the wireframe display of the model.

Generating Shaded Views

In addition to having the hidden lines removed, the model can be rendered with the SHADE command (choose View, Shade). SHADE has no options and simply generates a shaded view in the current viewport. SHADE affects only objects that are on visible layers and the current viewport. The image produced by SHADE remains on the viewport until a REGEN is issued (restores the wireframe model). You cannot edit or select objects with a shaded image, so regenerate the display prior to performing any further work on the model.

Even though SHADE itself has no options, its actions are affected by two system variables, SHADEDGE and SHADEDIF.

SHADEDGE

SHADEDGE is set to one of four values:

- **0:** Causes surfaces to be shaded but with none of the edges highlighted. Choose View, Shade, 256 color to specify this setting and issue the SHADE command.

- **1:** Causes surfaces to be shaded with the edges highlighted in the background color. Choose View, Shade, 256 Color Edge Highlight to specify this setting and issue the SHADE command.

- **2:** Causes surfaces to be shaded in the background color with the edges drawn in the object's color. Choose View, Shade, 16 Color Hidden Line to specify this setting and issue the SHADE command.

- **3:** Causes the surfaces to be drawn in the object's color with no shading and the edges drawn in the background color. Choose View, Shade, 16 Color Filled to specify this setting and issue the SHADE command.

Options 0 and 1 force SHADE to account for various portions of the surface reflecting varying amounts of light. The amount of light a surface reflects is dependent on its angle to the light source. A surface reflects the most light if it is at a right angle to the light rays. A surface at any other angle to the light reflects less light and will appear darker. This effect is most readily seen with curved surfaces, such as those of a cylinder.

SHADE utilizes a single light source for the shading calculations, which is located behind the observer's location and shines directly on the model. You cannot affect the location of this light source in any way.

The curious effect of setting SHADEDGE to a value of 0 or 1 is that you might actually get a surface drawn with colors other than the object's assigned color. For example, you might have drawn a cylinder in red, but after issuing a SHADE command, you might see portions of the cylinder in magenta, purple, and so forth. This is especially true if your graphics card is capable of only 16 colors. SHADE is not capable of more realistic renderings because it is designed for cards that display 256 or fewer colors; more realistic renderings require many more colors and different algorithms.

If SHADEDGE is set to 2, the resulting effect is similar to the HIDE command; however, a different algorithm is utilized.

TIP

> If the results of the HIDE command are not satisfactory, (that is, lines that should be hidden are not being hidden), try the SHADE command with SHADEDGE set to 2 and see whether the result is any better.

Regardless of the setting of SHADEDGE, SHADE cannot generate shadows or take into account the affect of shadows on the rendered image.

SHADEDIF

SHADEDIF controls the amount of reflection from the model's surface due to diffuse reflection of light versus ambient light. *Ambient light* is light that appears to come from all around the model with the same intensity. *Diffuse reflection* is reflection that bounces off a surface in various directions, such as uneven reflection off a surface. The value of SHADEDIF is, by default, 70, which indicates that 70 percent of the light from the model is diffuse reflective light from SHADE's single light source. The remaining 30 percent is from ambient light. The more light that comes from ambient light, the less contrast you get with the rendered model (the effect is similar to a "white-out" that you experience with snowstorms).

SHADEDIF only affects the results of SHADE when SHADEDGE is set to 0 or 1. To set the value of SHADEDIF, choose View, Shade, Diffuse.

In the following exercise, you generate a hidden line removed view and a shaded view of the house.

USING HIDE AND SHADE

1. Continue to use the drawing HOUSE. Make the right viewport current.

2. Choose View, Hide. The hidden lines are removed from the view in the current viewport.

3. Make the left viewport current. Choose View, Shade, 16 color filled. The view in the current viewport is shaded.

4. Type the command **REGEN**, and the view in the current viewport is regenerated.

5. Save the drawing.

The DVIEW Command

Although VPOINT is a very useful command for generating 3D views, it has several major shortcomings:

- VPOINT can generate only views with the viewing point positioned beyond the model extents. The practical effect of this is that the camera position can be positioned only outside the model and never within the model.

■ The camera position cannot be set a specific distance from the target point, making it impossible to simulate the real-world view from a particular camera position with any accuracy.

■ VPOINT can produce only parallel projection views, not perspective views.

DVIEW is a more powerful command for generating views of 3D models and addresses the shortcomings of VPOINT and more. Choose View, 3D Dynamic View to issue the DVIEW command.

DVIEW initially prompts you to select objects, and then the following prompt is displayed:

```
CAmera/TArget/Distance/POints/PAn/Zoom/TWist/CLip/Hide/Off/Undo/
➥<eXit>:
```

The DVIEW options are explained in detail in the sections that follow.

The Initial Selection of Objects

Initially, DVIEW prompts you to select objects. The selected objects are then displayed in the current viewport for the duration of the DVIEW command. Several of the options enable you to set a value for a setting *dynamically*, which means that the display changes as you decide on a value for the setting. The result is similar to the dragging that occurs during the MOVE or COPY commands. For complicated models, a dynamic display can be very slow. Because you can select the objects to be displayed in DVIEW, you can select just the prominent parts of a model to use as a frame of reference for setting the options, thereby speeding up the dynamic display of DVIEW.

If no objects are selected, DVIEW automatically displays a block named DVIEWBLOCK. DVIEWBLOCK is a simple wireframe 3D model of a house (see fig. 19.8).

The intent behind DVIEWBLOCK is to provide a simple frame of reference while in DVIEW, even when you choose not to select any portion of your model. You can even define your own block named DVIEWBLOCK (draw it as a 1×1×1 block) and use it with DVIEW.

Figure 19.8

The DVIEWBLOCK block used by DVIEW.

TIP

> For large models, the trick is to select just enough of the model to provide an accurate frame of reference with which you can set the various parameters. If the model is very complicated and is a single object, use DVIEWBLOCK (by not selecting anything) as a reference picture within DVIEW.

Positioning the Camera and Target

Keep the analogy of a camera in mind as you fine-tune the DVIEW settings. You control the camera, and the view displayed is the view through the lens of the camera. The first task is establishing the location of the camera and the target point.

The initial view displayed by DVIEW is that of the current view in the current viewport. DVIEW has three options that are used to set the positions of the camera and target:

■ Points

■ Camera

■ Target

Points enables you to set the position of the target and camera by specifying points. The target point is initially positioned in the center of the current view with a rubber band extending from it. If you want to leave the target point at its current position, press the Enter key; otherwise, specify another location.

After selecting the new target point, a rubber band is extended from the new target point. Use the rubber band to help you visualize the line of sight as you specify a new camera point.

Camera enables you to set a new camera position by rotating the camera about the target point. The camera may be rotated in the XY plane or from the XY plane (similar to VPOINT).

You choose the angles dynamically by moving the crosshairs. When the crosshairs are moved horizontally across the screen, the camera is rotated in the XY plane. If the crosshairs are moved vertically, the camera's angle, relative to the XY plane is affected.

Controlling both angles can be confusing or unwanted, so there is an option to "lock" one of the angles as you dynamically set the other angle. In the command window, the following prompt is displayed:

```
Toggle angle in/Enter angle from XY plane <-8.8035>:
```

To lock the angle from the XY plane, type an angle or accept the default (the current angle), after which the crosshair affects only the angle in the XY plane. The effect of setting the angle from the XY plane is to limit the motion of the camera to that of circling about the target point.

Choosing the Toggle option displays the following prompt and enables you to unlock the angle and, at the same time, gives you the option of locking the other angle, the angle in the XY plane:

```
Toggle angle from/Enter angle in XY plane from X axis <-3.96373>:
```

To lock the angle in the XY plane, type an angle or accept the default (the current angle), after which your crosshair affects only the angle from the XY plane. The effect of locking the angle in the XY plane is to limit the motion of the camera going up and down relative to the target point. To unlock the angle after locking it, choose the Toggle option and the previous prompt is displayed. Toggle switches you back and forth between the two angles.

As an alternative to setting the angles dynamically, type in both angles and forgo using the crosshair.

The *Target* option is similar to the Camera option except that it controls the angle of the target point in the XY plane and from the XY plane. The angles are measured relative to the camera position.

The net effect is similar to the effect you get when you swivel a camera about its fixed tripod, pointing the camera at different points.

Of the three options, only Points enables you to set a distance between the target and camera points while defining their positions. The other two options, Camera and Target, enable you to set only angles, not distances. Distance is crucial for generating perspective views.

Even when you use the Points option to set the actual locations of the target and camera points, the view that is generated is not the view you would get if you were actually standing at the camera point. The points establish only the line of sight. To generate the actual view you would get by standing at the camera point, you have to enable DVIEW's perspective viewing mode.

TIP

Before you begin DVIEW, think about possible positions for placing the camera and target points. If these positions are not already on objects (which you can then select with object snap), draw some points at those locations, making it easier to select the positions with object snap.

Zooming, Panning, and Twisting

While in DVIEW, the ZOOM and PAN commands do not work. Instead, DVIEW has its own ZOOM and PAN options. The ZOOM option enables you to zoom in and out. You set the zoom scale factor by positioning the slider bar, enabling you to set a zoom scale factor ranging from 0x to 16x.

As an alternative to the slider bar, type in a scale factor. The scale factor is always applied relative to the current view (similar to the X option of ZOOM).

The Pan option enables you to pan your view and is similar to the PAN command. You must define the distance to pan by picking a base point and a point to pan to; there is no displacement option.

The Twist option enables you to twist the view around the line of sight. A rubber band will extend from the center of your view and to your crosshairs. The angle of the rubber band sets the twist angle. The standard 2D angle orientation applies where 0 degrees is horizontal and pointing to the right. The effect is similar to what you get when you rotate the camera in your hands.

Clipping the View

A clipping plane is an opaque plane that is positioned somewhere along and perpendicular to the line of sight (see fig. 19.9). A clipping plane's function is to obscure objects or portions of objects from the camera's view. Two clipping planes are available to you, the front and back clipping planes.

Figure 19.9

DVIEW and clipping planes.

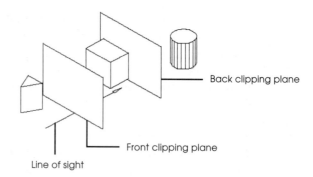

Back clipping plane

Front clipping plane

Line of sight

By using the two clipping planes, views can be produced where portions of the model are blocked out of the camera's view, resulting in a view of a "slice" of the model.

The front clipping plane obscures any objects in front of it, and the back clipping plane obscures any objects behind it. When the Clip option is specified, the following prompt is displayed:

```
Back/Front/<Off>:
```

The default option <Off> is to turn off all clipping planes. *Back* enables you to position the back clipping plane and turn it off or on. *Front* enables you to position the front clipping plane and turn it off or on.

When the Front option is specified, the following prompt is displayed:

```
Eye/ON/OFF/<Distance from target> <11.1394>:
```

Specifying the Eye option positions the front clipping plane at the camera point. ON turns on the clipping plane at its present location. OFF turns off the clipping plane.

The distance of the front clipping plane from the target point is set via the slider bar at the top of the screen. The distance corresponding to the position of the slider bar is displayed in the status bar. In place of the slider bar, a specific distance can be typed. Once the clipping plane is positioned, clipping is automatically turned on. A positive distance places the clipping plane in front of the target point, and a negative distance places the plane behind the target.

If the Back option is specified, the following prompt is displayed:

```
ON/OFF/<Distance from target> <-6.9630>:
```

The options are identical to the ones for the front clipping plane.

TIP

> There is no point in placing the front clipping plane behind the camera. Keep the plane in front of the camera.
>
> Do not place the back clipping plane too close to the camera or you will not have much left of the model to see.

Once the clipping planes are turned on, they stay on when you leave DVIEW. To turn off the clipping planes, specify the DVIEW's Clip option and specify the OFF option.

TIP

> Although you can edit a drawing with clipping planes on, it is not recommended. For example, it is possible to move a model so that a different portion of the model gets completely obscured by one of the clipping planes.

Hiding the View

You can perform a hidden line removal operation on the view with the Hide option. The full wireframe view is restored when another option is selected or when DVIEW is terminated. The Hide option enables you to preview the results of the HIDE command while in the DVIEW command.

Generating Perspective Views

By default, DVIEW generates parallel projection views, just like VPOINT. To generate a perspective view, the Distance option must be specified. The Distance option enables you to set the camera a specific distance away from the target. The default distance is the current 3D distance between the camera and target points.

Using the Distance option automatically causes the generation of a perspective view and also turns on the front clipping plane and positions it at the camera (if clipping isn't already turned on). The resulting view is what would actually be seen through the camera lens at the specified distance away from the target along the line of sight established between the target and camera points.

When perspective mode is on, an icon appears in the lower left corner of your screen (see fig. 19.10).

Figure 19.10

The perspective mode
icon.

This icon (which resembles a box in a perspective view) serves as a reminder that the view on the screen is a perspective view. Points cannot be selected from the screen while in perspective view, making it very difficult to perform general drawing and editing work. The best thing to do is not to attempt to draw or edit in a perspective view.

To turn off perspective viewing, use the Off option of DVIEW. When perspective mode is on, the field of vision is adjusted with the Zoom option. The prompt displayed by Zoom is different when perspective mode is on. Instead of being prompted for a zoom factor, you are prompted for a lens length. The default is a 50mm lens. If a wider angle shot is desired, specify a shorter lens length, such as 35mm. If a tighter shot is desired, use a larger, longer lens length, such as 75mm. The lens length is set via the slider bar or by typing a value. Zoom does not change the distance between the camera and target points.

In the next exercise, you use DVIEW to generate several new views of the house.

USING DVIEW TO GENERATE VIEWS

1. Continue to use the drawing HOUSE. Choose View, Tiled Viewports, 1 Viewport to restore a single viewport.

2. Choose View, Named Views and restore the PLAN view.

3. Choose View, 3D Dynamic View and select all objects in the drawing. Now enter the following data:

```
CAmera/TArget/Distance/POints/PAn/Zoom/TWist/CLip/Hide
/Off/Undo/<eXit>: PO ↵
Enter target point <42'-8 13/16", 25'-0", 5'-8 5/8">: 30',25' ↵
Enter camera point <42'-8 13/16", 25'-0", 5'-9 5/8">: 100',-25',30' ↵
```

You have just established the initial locations of the camera and target points. The target point is at the center of the house at the floor level, and the camera point is 30' above the ground. Continue to enter the following data:

```
CAmera/TArget/Distance/POints/PAn/Zoom/TWist/CLip/Hide
/Off/Undo/<eXit>: CA ↵
Toggle angle in/Enter angle from XY plane <14.3456>: 20 ↵
Toggle angle from/Enter angle in XY plane from X axis <-35.53768>: -30 ↵
```

Using the CAmera option, you have just adjusted the position of the line of sight higher (by raising the angle from the XY plane) and swinging the line of sight toward zero degrees in the XY plane (by entering -30). Continue to enter the following data:

```
CAmera/TArget/Distance/POints/PAn/Zoom/TWist/CLip/Hide
/Off/Undo/<eXit>: Z ↵
Adjust zoom scale factor <1>: 0.5 ↵
```

The Zoom option enables you to zoom in and out. Continue to enter the following data:

```
CAmera/TArget/Distance/POints/PAn/Zoom/TWist/CLip/Hide
/Off/Undo/<eXit>: D ↵
New camera/target distance <88'-9 1/2">: ↵
CAmera/TArget/Distance/POints/PAn/Zoom/TWist/CLip/Hide
/Off/Undo/<eXit>: ↵
```

The Distance option turns on perspective mode and requires that the distance between the target and camera points be specified. The default is the current distance between the two points.

4. Choose View, Named Views and name the current view **PERSP**.

5. Choose View, 3D Dynamic View. Do not select any objects and DVIEWBLOCK is displayed on the screen. Specify the Off option.

6. Specify the Clip option and enter the following data:

```
Back/Front/<Off>: B ↵
ON/OFF/<Distance from target> <0'-0 3/8">: -6' ↵
CAmera/TArget/Distance/POints/PAn/Zoom/TWist/CLip/Hide/Off/Undo
/<eXit>: CL ↵
Back/Front/<Off>: F ↵
Eye/ON/OFF/<Distance from target> <88'-9 1/2">: 8' ↵
CAmera/TArget/Distance/POints/PAn/Zoom/TWist/CLip/Hide
/Off/Undo/<eXit>: ↵
```

7. Choose View, Named Views and name the current view **CLIPPED**.

8. Repeat the DVIEW command and specify the Clip option. Then specify the Off option and exit DVIEW. Save the drawing.

Picking Points in 3D

In addition to assigning the elevation of objects by using the current elevation, there are several other methods that can prove more useful in different situations.

Typing Z Coordinates

All points are recorded in the drawing file as XYZ. When a point is picked without using object snap or is typed with X and Y values, LT automatically assigns the current elevation as the Z value for the point. Of course, if you type the X, Y, and Z values for a point, the typed Z value overrides the current elevation setting.

Using Object Snap

If object snap is used to pick a point, LT always uses the Z coordinate of the selected point, regardless of the current elevation setting. So what object snap modes work with extruded 2D objects?

Any object snap mode that worked with the original 2D object works with the extruded version. Furthermore, the object snap modes work with both the top and bottom edges of the extruded object. For example, an extruded circle becomes a cylinder. Using center object snap mode, the center point of the top circular face or the bottom circular face can be picked.

The only edges on an extruded object that object snap does not work with are the vertical lines that appear on curved surfaces, such as the side of a cylinder. The purpose of the vertical lines, also referred to as *tesselation lines,* is to help you better visualize the curved surface. The lines cannot be selected in any way. The exceptions are the tesselation lines that appear at the endpoints of a line or line segment of a polyline or edge of a solid; these tesselation lines can be selected with object snap modes.

Tɪᴘ

As a rule, never try to select an object snap point on an extruded 3D object by using a plan view of the object. The problem is that in plan view, every point you can select on the top surface has a corresponding point immediately below it on the bottom surface. The pick is ambiguous; did you mean to select the point on the top or bottom surface? To avoid any ambiguity in selecting points, use a view that clearly shows the desired point.

Using Grips

When editing objects with grip points, LT always uses the elevation of the grip points rather than the current elevation setting. On an extruded 2D object, the same grip points that were on the original 2D object appear on the top and bottom surfaces of the extruded 3D object. Tesselation lines do not have any grip points.

Just as with object snap, never try to select a grip point on an extruded 2D object by using a plan view of the object. The pick is ambiguous because every point selectable on the top surface has a corresponding point immediately below it on the bottom surface. To avoid any ambiguity in selecting points, use a view that clearly isolates the desired grip point.

Using Filters

You can override the Z coordinate that would normally be assigned to a point by using the .XY filter. Specifying the .XY filter prior to picking the point instructs LT to accept only the X and Y values of the selected point. LT then prompts you for the missing Z value, which can be supplied by typing the value or picking another point (the Z value of the second point is used).

Cylindrical and Spherical Coordinates

Besides specifying points in the XYZ cartesian format, LT also enables the entry of points using cylindrical or spherical coordinates. The format for cylindrical coordinates is as follows:

XY distance<angle,Z distance (for absolute coordinates)

or

@XY distance<angle,Z distance (for relative coordinates)

The point is defined by specifying the point's projected distance and angle in the XY plane from the origin and the Z distance from the XY plane (see fig. 19.11). The term "cylindrical" comes from the fact that if the angle and Z distance values were varied while the XY value was kept constant, the resulting points would form a cylinder.

Figure 19.11

Definition of terms for cylindrical coordinates.

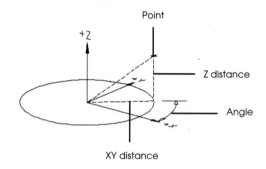

TIP

Think of cylindrical coordinates as a polar coordinate, distance<angle, but with a Z component added to it. It can be especially useful when specifying relative 3D coordinates.

Spherical coordinates use a different format:

XYZ distance<Angle in XY plane<Angle from XY plane (for absolute coordinates)

or

@XYZ distance<Angle in XY plane<Angle from XY plane (for relative coordinates)

Spherical coordinates require that you specify the XYZ distance (3D distance) from the origin to the point, an angle in the XY plane, and an angle from the XY plane to the point (see fig. 19.12).

Figure 19.12

Definition of terms for spherical coordinates.

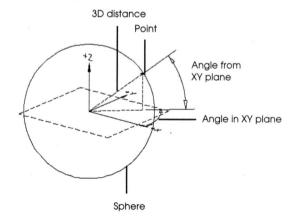

This format is called *spherical* because, for a given distance, all the possible combinations of angle values produces a group of points that form a sphere. Describing a point in spherical coordinate format is very similar to what is done to set a viewing point using the Rotate option of VPOINT. In both cases, two angles must be specified—an angle in the XY plane and an angle from the XY plane. With spherical coordinates, there is just the one additional piece of information—the actual distance to the point.

Editing in 3D

In the following sections, you learn what editing operations can be carried out on extruded 3D objects.

Modifying Thickness and Elevation

There are several approaches that can be taken to edit the elevation and thickness of existing objects. To change the elevation or thickness of one or a few select objects, use DDMODIFY. Figure 19.13 shows the dialog box that is displayed when DDMODIFY is used on a circle.

Figure 19.13

The Modify Circle dialog box.

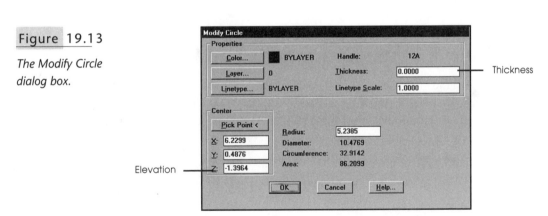

In the top portion of the dialog box, there is a separate edit box for the object's thickness but not for the object's elevation. An object's elevation is synonymous with the Z coordinate of the points that define the object, so a circle's elevation is defined by its center point. Therefore, to change the elevation of the circle, change the Z coordinate of the center point.

To change the thickness of a number of objects, use DDCHPROP. Remember that both DDMODIFY and DDCHPROP are triggered by the Properties item on the Edit menu and the Properties tool on the standard toolbar. If a single object is selected, DDMODIFY is issued, but if several objects are selected, DDCHROP is issued. Unfortunately, DDCHPROP cannot be used to change the elevation of objects.

To change the elevation of a group of objects, use the CHANGE command, which does have an option for changing the elevation of selected objects, or use the MOVE command (or the move mode of grips) to move the objects to the new Z coordinate.

TIP

A good way to use the MOVE command to change an object's elevation is to use relative coordinates to describe the desired change in elevation. For example, to move an object 2 units in only the positive Z direction, type 0,0,2 for the displacement. To move an object a certain distance and direction in the XY plane and also change its elevation, use cylindrical coordinates. For example, to move an object 2 units in a 45 degree direction in the XY plane and 3 units in the Z direction, type 2<45,3 for the displacement.

When changing the thickness of an extruded 2D object, the surface that was the original 2D object remains stationary. The other surface, the extruded surface, moves.

Using Z in the Commands You Know

For the most part, all the editing commands that you are already familiar with accept XYZ points. Remember, Z can be specified by typing XYZ coordinates and using filters, grip points, and object snap modes. What the various editing commands do with the Z value varies.

The MOVE command enables you to move an object from one elevation to another, while at the same time moving the object in the XY plane.

In general, the STRETCH command cannot be used to stretch a portion of an object from one elevation to another. Attempting to do so simply results in the object moving in the Z direction. The exceptions to the rule are lines, splines, and 3D polylines; STRETCH can be used to move the endpoint of a line, spline, or 3D polyline from one elevation to another. Under no circumstances can STRETCH be used to change the thickness of any object.

COPY can be used to create copies at elevations different from the original object's elevation.

SCALE can be used to scale up or down an extruded 2D object in a uniform manner about the specified base point. If the base point specified has a Z coordinate different from the object's, the scaling operation also changes the object's Z coordinate.

ROTATE accepts XYZ points but treats the angle of rotation as the rotation angle in the XY plane. The net effect is that ROTATE rotates only objects in the XY plane.

MIRROR accepts only a 2D mirror line. Trying to specify the mirror line with coordinates with Z values results in an error message. MIRROR can only be used to mirror objects in the XY plane.

ARRAY accepts only 2D points. Trying to specify any XYZ points results in an error message. ARRAY only creates new objects in the XY plane.

Using UCS in 3D

With the exception of lines, splines, and 3D polylines, the points defining the object must lie in the same XY plane. You can, however, draw on any desired surface simply by using the UCS command to define the orientation of the current XY plane.

Previously, you learned how to define UCS's in a 2D environment. Changing the current UCS enabled you to change the origin point and even to rotate the XY axes. In a 3D environment, UCSs can be used to define the orientation of the XY plane so that 2D objects (such as circles) can be drawn on any plane.

In the following sections, you learn how to use the UCS and control the UCS icon in a 3D environment.

Controlling the Icon

With the UCSICON command, the UCS icon can be turned off or on at will. While working in 3D, leave the icon on and turn on the origin option. Without the icon, you can get lost in 3D space very easily.

T_{I P}

When the Origin option is enabled, LT displays the UCS icon at the origin point only if the icon can be displayed in its entirety; otherwise, the icon is displayed in the lower left corner of the viewport. If this problem occurs, remedy it by zooming out a little bit (a 0.9X magnification factor, for example) to allow the icon to be displayed in its entirety at the UCS origin.

When working in 3D, it is quite possible to generate a view in which the current UCS is viewed edge on. For example, in an elevation view, the world UCS would be viewed edge on, with the XY plane appearing as a line. In this orientation, picking points in the XY plane is impossible, and any 2D objects drawn would appear as dots or lines. To warn you that the current UCS is not properly visible, LT substitutes the "broken pencil" icon for the standard UCS icon (see fig. 19.14).

Figure 19.14

The broken pencil icon.

Whenever this icon appears, it means that, in that view, you are viewing the current UCS edge on.

T_{I P}

Avoid picking points in a view displaying the broken pencil icon. If you have to pick points, use object snap modes to select existing points.

Changing the Origin

In 3D, the Origin option of the UCS command is a very good way to relocate the current XY plane to any Z coordinate you want, thereby establishing the current UCS parallel to the old UCS (see fig. 19.15). The orientation of the XYZ axes remains unchanged. This option enables you to work at any elevation without having to change the current elevation setting constantly.

Figure 19.15

*Setting the origin of
the current UCS.*

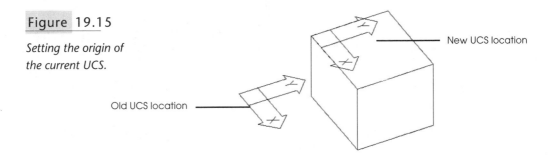

New UCS location

Old UCS location

TıP

> The current elevation is applied relative to the current XY plane. Using a non-zero value for the current elevation setting while setting a new UCS can be confusing. Objects might end up being drawn at some distance away from the current XY plane instead of in the current XY plane. Consider keeping the current elevation set to zero and then just setting the UCS at the desired elevation.

Establishing the Z

The ZAxis option of the UCS command can be used to establish the current XY plane by defining the positive direction of the Z axis. The ZAxis option requires the selection of two points. Referring to figure 19.16, the first point picked (①) is the new location of the 0,0,0 point, and the second point (②) determines the positive direction of the Z axis. The XY plane is then established perpendicular to the new Z axis.

Figure 19.16

Using the ZAxis option.

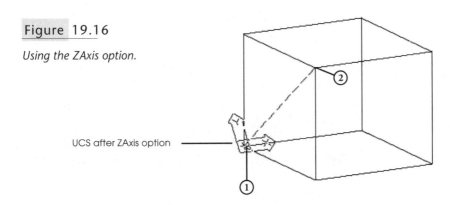

UCS after ZAxis option

This option is a quick way to establish the current UCS when the Z axis can be clearly identified. The downside of this option is that the actual orientation of the X and Y axes is established by LT using an algorithm that does so rather arbitrarily. This is a good option to use when the primary goal is to establish positive direction of the Z axis.

The 3point Option

The 3point option of the UCS command is a very accurate and easy method for establishing the current XY plane at any orientation in 3D space. The 3point option is used to establish the new UCS by selecting three points. In figure 19.17, the first point (①) establishes the new location of the 0,0,0 point. The second point (②) establishes the positive direction of the X axis, and the third point (③) establishes the direction of the Y axis. This option is very handy because you get to explicitly set the location of the origin and the orientation of the X and Y axes.

Figure 19.17

Using the 3point option.

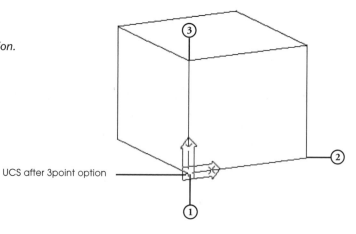

UCS after 3point option

Using Objects

The Object option of the UCS command is a quick and easy way to establish the current UCS so that the selected object ends up lying in the new XY plane. This option requires the selection of the object. LT then establishes the orientation of the X and Y axes so that the object lies in the XY plane. The downside of the option is that the rule used to establish the orientation of the XY axes is dependent on the type of object selected (see table 19.2).

Table 19.2

The Method Used to Determine the New UCS for Various Objects

Object Type	Method of UCS Determination
Arc	The arc's center point becomes the new origin. The X axis is aligned to pass through the endpoint nearest the pick point.
Circle	The circle's center point becomes the new origin. The X axis is aligned to pass through the pick point.
Dimension	The middle point of the dimension text becomes the new origin. The X axis is aligned to be parallel to the X axis in effect at the time the dimension was drawn.
Line	The endpoint nearest the pick point becomes the origin. The line becomes the X axis.
Point	The point becomes the origin. The orientation of the X axis is determined arbitrarily with an algorithm.
2D Polyline	The start point of the polyline becomes the new origin. The X axis is aligned to go through the next vertex point.
Solid	The first point of the solid becomes the origin. The X axis is aligned to go through the second point.
Shape	
Text	
Insert	
Attribute	
Definition	The insertion point becomes the new origin. The X axis is aligned with the object's rotation about its extrusion direction.

Not all objects can be selected; only the objects listed in the preceding table are recognized by this option.

Using the Current View

The View option of the UCS command is used to set the current UCS parallel to the current view (see fig. 19.18). In effect, it makes the new UCS parallel to the monitor screen. The origin is arbitrarily set.

Figure 19.18

Using the View option.

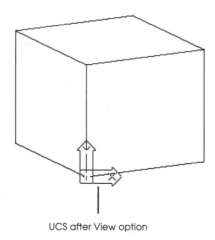

UCS after View option

Rotating about the Axes

The X, Y, and Z options of the UCS command are very handy when you can establish the new UCS by rotating about one of the axes of the existing UCS. The hardest part of using this option is figuring out which direction corresponds to a positive rotation angle. You can easily establish this direction via the right-hand rule, which states that if you stick the thumb of your right hand in the positive direction of the axis you are rotating about, and curl your fingers about the axis, the curl of your fingers is the direction of a positive rotation angle.

Restoring the World UCS

Working in 3D space can be very disorienting, but remember that to return to the World Coordinate System (WCS), simply use the World option of the UCS command, which is the default option.

Using the Presets

You may also select a UCS orientation from a set of preset orientations via the DDUCSP command. DDUCSP is issued by choosing View, UCS, Preset UCS or by choosing Standard toolbar, UCS, Preset UCS.

In effect, each of the options of the DDUCSP command issues the UCS command with the X, Y, or Z axis options specified. The location of the origin point of the new UCS is the same as the old UCS.

Getting a Plan View

The PLAN command can be used to easily generate a plan view of the current UCS. The default option is to display the plan view of the current UCS. You also have the option of displaying the plan view of a named UCS and of the WCS.

Making a Viewport Follow

When configuring multiple viewports, a viewport can be set to always display the plan view of the current UCS. You do so by making the desired viewport the current viewport and then turning on the UCSFOLLOW system variable. UCSFOLLOW can be set independently for each viewport.

TI P

> If you use multiple viewports, be sure to have the UCSFOLLOW system variable turned off in the viewport you want to use when setting the current UCS; otherwise, as soon as you finish with the UCS command, the view in the current viewport is replaced with a plan view of the current UCS.

In the following exercise, you use the UCS command to draw a roof on the house.

ADDING THE ROOF

1. Continue to use the drawing HOUSE. Restore the view SW-ISO. Make a new layer named **SKELETON** and make it current.

2. Choose Format, Current Properties and set the elevation and thickness to 0.

3. Choose Draw, Line and enter the following points:

From point: **Using endpoint object snap, pick ① (see fig. 19.19)**
To point: **@0,15',10'** ↵
To point: **Using endpoint object snap, pick ②**
To point: ↵

Figure 19.19

Picking points for the roof.

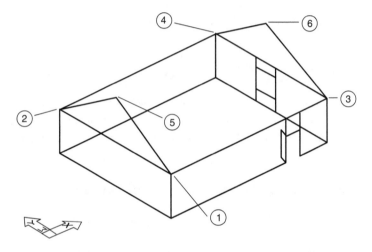

4. Repeat the LINE command and enter the following points:

From point: **Using endpoint object snap, pick ③**
To point: **@0,15',10'** ↵
To point: **Using endpoint object snap, pick ④**
To point: ↵

5. Make a new layer named **ROOF**, assign the color red to it and make it current.

6. Choose Options, UCS Icon, Origin. This forces the UCS icon to be displayed at the origin of the current UCS.

7. Turn on the running object snap mode of endpoint (choose OSNAP from the status bar).

8. Choose View, Set UCS Icon, 3 point and enter the following data:

Origin point <0,0,0>: **Pick ①**
Point on positive portion of the X-axis <10'-1",40'-0",10'-0">: **Pick ②**

```
Point on positive-Y portion of the UCS XY plane
<10'-1",40'-0",10'-0">: Pick ⑤
```

This sets the UCS in the plane of the side of the roof.

9. Choose Draw, 2D Solid and enter the following points:

```
First point: Pick ①
Second point: Pick ②
Third point: Pick ⑤
Fourth point: ↵
Third point: ↵
```

The left side of the roof structure is now done.

10. Repeat the SOLID command and enter the following points:

```
First point: Pick ③
Second point: Pick ④
Third point: Pick ⑥
Fourth point: ↵
Third point: ↵
```

The right side of the roof structure is now done.

11. Choose View, Set UCS, 3 point and enter the following points:

```
Origin point <0,0,0>: Pick ①
Point on positive portion of the X-axis <30'-1",0'-0",0'-0">: Pick ③
Point on positive-Y portion of the UCS XY plane
<30'-0",0'-1",0'-0">: Pick ⑤
```

This sets the UCS on the plane of the front surface of the roof structure.

12. Choose Draw, 2D Solid and enter the following points:

```
First point: Pick ①
Second point: Pick ③
Third point: Pick ⑤
Fourth point: Pick ⑥
Third point: ↵
```

13. Choose View, Set UCS, 3 point and enter the following points:

```
Origin point <0,0,0>: Pick ④
Point on positive portion of the X-axis <30'-1",0'-0",0'-0">: Pick ②
Point on positive-Y portion of the UCS XY plane
<30'-0",0'-1",0'-0">: Pick ⑥
```

This sets the UCS on the plane of the front surface of the roof structure.

14. Choose Draw, 2D Solid and enter the following points:

```
First point: Pick ④
Second point: Pick ②
Third point: Pick ⑥
Fourth point: Pick ⑤
Third point: ↵
```

This completes the roof. Turn off the layer SKELETON.

15. Choose View, Hide.

16. Choose View, Shade, 16 color Filled.

17. Save the Drawing.

Drawing 3D Objects

In 3D work, there are extruded 2D objects and there are true 3D objects. The difference between the two classes is that the points defining extruded 2D objects must all lie in the same XY plane, whereas the points defining a true 3D object do not have to lie in the same XY plane. Lines and splines are 3D objects because the points defining them may have varying Z values. Drawing 3D objects is much easier because you do not have to worry about the orientation of the current UCS as much.

There is a third 3D object that can be drawn in LT, the 3D polyline object. It is drawn with the undocumented command 3DPOLY, which does not appear in any of the pull-down menus or toolbars. It functions similarly to the PLINE command but lacks the options to draw arcs and assign thickness. Unlike the vertices of a polyline, the vertices of a 3D polyline can have varying Z values.

Composing and Plotting a 3D Model

The layout of a 3D drawing can be composed in either paper space or in model space. For simple layouts, tiled model space (TILEMODE=1) may suffice; however, paper space definitely has several advantages for more complicated layouts, especially for a layout that consists of multiple views of the same 3D model:

■ In paper space, each floating viewport can display a different view of the same model (something impossible with tiled model space). One floating viewport can display a plan view while another displays an elevation view.

■ Layers can be frozen in selected viewports. For example, a layer could be frozen in one floating viewport yet be displayed in all the others.

Composing a layout for a 3D model is similar to composing a layout of a 2D model. The only difference is the additional usage of the VPOINT or PLAN commands in setting the views in the individual floating viewports.

As with 2D drawings, the PLOT command is used to plot 3D drawings. There are, however, a couple of differences when it comes to hiding lines and scaling. When plotting from model space or floating model space, the Hide option in the PLOT command has to be enabled in order to have the hidden lines removed from a plot. It is not necessary to issue the HIDE command prior to plotting; the HIDE command affects only the display, not the results, of PLOT.

WARNING

Unfortunately, the extra lines that are drawn for curved surfaces (tesselation lines) are plotted. There is no way to suppress the display or plotting of the tesselation lines.

If paper space is used to compose the layout and the hidden lines are to be removed from the viewports when plotting, the Hideplot option of the MVIEW command must be used to tag the viewports that are to have the hidden lines removed when plotting. The Hide option of the PLOT command does not work when plotting from the paper space viewport but does work when plotting from floating model space.

Remember that for 3D views, the only views that can be scaled directly are orthogonal views, such as elevations, and isometric views. For such views, a scale factor can be set when plotting or when using the ZOOM command's XP option. For all other types of views, scaling to fit is sufficient.

RELATED COMMANDS

ELEV

RELATED SYSTEM VARIABLES

ELEVATION THICKNESS	UCSORIG
UCSICON	UCSXDIR
UCSNAME	UCSXYDIR

CUSTOMIZING

20

CREATING AND IMPLEMENTING SCRIPTS

By now, you have gained a healthy exposure to most of the more common AutoCAD LT drawing and editing commands. With practice, you will become very familiar with the command sequences and option responses.

However, over time, you may find that you perform many tasks repetitively. Two examples are layer management and plotting session administration. These procedures can easily become mundane chores if you continue to specify the same individual commands repeatedly. To expedite the processing of tedious tasks such as these, AutoCAD LT provides scripting capability.

Virtually any sequence of LT commands and responses can be "stacked up" in an ASCII text file (the script), and "played" by summoning the name of this file. In this chapter, you explore the usage of scripts and their time-saving benefits, including these basics:

- *Creating a script file*
- *Executing a script file*
- *Manually pausing and continuing a script file*
- *Automatically delaying and repeating a script file*
- *Making and viewing slides*
- *Creating a slide show*
- *Applications*

Creating a Script File

Any sequence of LT commands and responses to prompts that can be entered interactively at the Command: prompt can also be stored in a text file. Each line of the file must contain a command, option response, or a single blank. A blank line in a script file is significant; AutoCAD LT interprets blanks and spaces as pressing the Enter key.

You can also place each command with its responses on a single line, by using spaces to simulate the Enter key. Therefore, the following two script commands are equivalent:

```
LINE
1,1
@1<0
@1<90
@1<180
CLOSE
```

and

```
LINE 1,1 @1<0 @1<90 @1<180 CLOSE
```

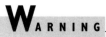

Don't use blank lines (by using the Enter key) or spaces to assume default values when specifying a command response in a script file. The expected values might have been changed during the drawing session, and results will be unpredictable.

To provide script compatibility with earlier versions of AutoCAD LT, don't abbreviate commands and options.

Figure 20.1 shows an example of a script file that performs several tasks: thaw all layers, set the current layer to 0, zoom to the extents, and finally save the current drawing. Notice that the blank line in the script is required; it represents the Return required to end the Layer command.

Running this script file is a great way to "tidy up" your drawing before taking a well-deserved break! This script is included on the companion CD as filename LUNCH.SCR.

Figure 20.1

A script with several AutoCAD LT commands.

LUNCH.SCR

```
LAYER
THAW
*

SET
0

ZOOM
EXTENTS
QSAVE
```

As you discovered in Chapter 17, "Sheet Composition and Plotting," there are many options with the PLOT command. Many AutoCAD LT users find their plotting requirements are met by using just a few of these options. In the exercise that follows, you create a script file to expedite the plotting procedure.

CREATING AND USING A SCRIPT FILE FOR PLOTTING

Suppose most of your prints or plots are configured to the drawing extents on an A-size sheet at full plot scale (1=1), using the default system printer. It would certainly be convenient to have a script file that automatically sets up and uses these parameters!

1. Enter **CMDDIA 0** at the Command: prompt to turn off the dialog box for the PLOT command. With this setting in effect, all PLOT questions are interactive.

2. On the Windows 95 Taskbar, choose Start, Programs, Accessories, Notepad.

3. Click AutoCAD LT on the Windows 95 Taskbar. Arrange your desktop to resemble that shown in figure 20.2. Then, enter the PLOT command and respond to all the prompts. Make sure you retype all answers, rather than accepting any default values.

Figure 20.2

AutoCAD LT and Notepad on the desktop.

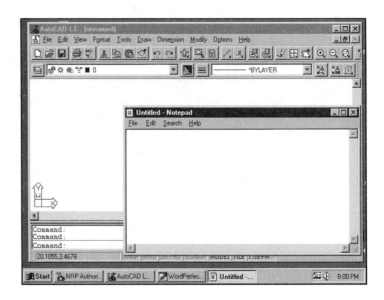

4. Press F2 to open the AutoCAD LT Text Window. Click and drag the mouse over all the responses and use the Windows Clipboard to copy (Ctrl+C) and paste (Ctrl+V) the text to the Notepad file (see fig. 20.3).

Figure 20.3

PLOT responses copied and pasted to Notepad.

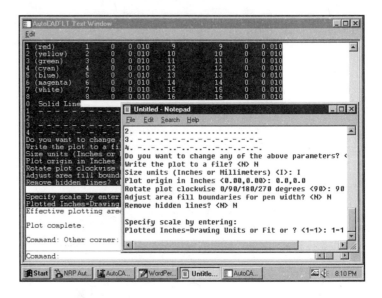

5. Edit the Notepad text so that only the prompt responses appear, one per line. Figure 20.4 shows the edited plotting script, saved as filename AFULL.SCR.

6. Reactivate dialog boxes by entering **CMDDIA 1**.

Figure 20.4

Edited PLOT responses saved as AFULL.SCR.

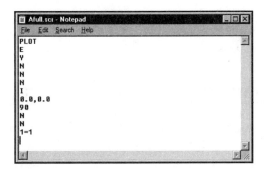

Executing a Script File

To execute an existing script file, type **SCRIPT**. Figure 20.5 shows the Select Script File dialog box.

Figure 20.5

The Select Script File dialog box.

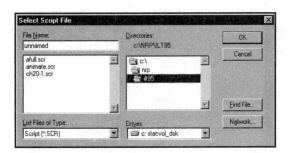

Type or select the script filename, and click on OK. The indicated script file then executes. To view the processing results, press F2 to activate the Text Window and scroll as necessary.

TIP

The script file AFULL.SCR can easily be modified to accommodate other plotting needs. Just open the file, make the changes, and save the file as a new name. For example, you could create another script file D14.SCR to plot a D-size drawing at $1/4$"=1' scale.

As you develop a variety of script files for different tasks, you may find it helpful to suspend the execution of a particular script at a specific command. Perhaps you want to study the results of prior commands or view a particular screen image before proceeding further.

AutoCAD LT provides two methods of pausing and continuing an executing script: manual and automatic. The next sections explain the differences in these two methods.

Manually Pausing and Continuing a Script File

A script file can be suspended *manually* by entering keystrokes during its execution. AutoCAD LT monitors the keyboard buffer and checks for incoming characters. Table 20.1 shows the valid keystrokes to pause and continue a script manually.

Table 20.1

Keystrokes to Interrupt a Script Manually

Character or Command	Description
Backspace key	Suspends the script
Esc key	Cancels the script
RESUME	Continues the paused script

WARNING

> When a script is paused manually, the currently executing command finishes processing. Depending on the timing of the interrupt keystrokes received by the system, one additional command may "slip through" and process.

Automatically Delaying and Repeating a Script File

A script file can be suspended automatically for a specified length of time. After this time interval elapses, the script file continues to the next command.

Use the DELAY command inside the script file, where appropriate. The delay value is given in milliseconds; therefore, a three-second delay is specified as DELAY 3000.

To cycle and repeat a script automatically, include the command RSCRIPT as the last line in the file.

A script file can execute only in a top-down fashion; each command processes one after the other. However, script files can be "chained" together. In this case, the last line of the first script can itself be a SCRIPT command that invokes a second script, and so on.

Tip

You can also do the trick of "automatically" manually halting a script by issuing a bogus command—such as FOO —to halt the script at a certain point. You can then start the script again by typing RESUME. This is good for demo-type scripts.

Figure 20.6 shows script file INFORM.SCR, which writes a text string on the screen, pauses one second, erases the string, pauses one more second, and then automatically repeats the entire sequence.

With some imagination, you can alter this script to let your coworkers know exactly where you are!

Figure 20.6

INFORM.SCR: a blinking message script.

```
INFORM.SCR

TEXT
0.5,4.5
0.75
0
STAFF MEETING AT 10 AM!
DELAY 1000
ERASE SINGLE LAST
DELAY 1000
RSCRIPT
```

Making and Viewing Slides

One of the most common applications of script files is to control a slide show. Slide shows consist of a series of AutoCAD LT slides shown in sequence controlled by a script. Slide shows are effective in demonstrations and are frequently seen at trade shows and the like.

A slide file is a drawing without its associated vector database; hence, it is an "image only" format. For example, if a line is drawn on-screen, AutoCAD LT stores its endpoints, length, and angle. Without this attached information, a line becomes merely a graphical series of pixels. Consequently, a slide file uses much less disk space than the corresponding drawing file.

The MSLIDE command creates a slide. The VSLIDE command displays an existing slide.

> **N**ote
>
> When you create a slide, make sure you center the objects on the display. Graphical drawing aids, such as the UCSICON and GRID, are not included in the slide.

> **T**ip
>
> You can always turn a drawing into a slide; however, without special utility software, you cannot turn a slide back into a drawing. Make sure you have the original drawing format available as a backup, in case you need to edit and remake the corresponding slide.

In the next exercise, you create several slide files and view them individually.

CREATING SLIDE FILES

1. In a new drawing session, choose File, Open, click on the Read Only check box in the Select File dialog box, and open drawing COLORWH.DWG from the default folder (Program Files\AutoCAD LT\Sample in a standard installation). Then, choose File, Slide, Create. Figure 20.7 shows the Create Slide File dialog box. Type the name **S1.SLD**.

2. Repeat step 1, open drawing TABLET.DWG, and create slide file **S2.SLD**. Then, open drawing TRUETYPE.DWG and create slide file **S3.SLD**.

3. Whereas the MSLIDE command creates a slide file, the VSLIDE command displays an existing slide file. To inspect a slide already created, choose File, Slide, View. Then, click or enter a slide filename. Check the integrity of slides S1 through S3.

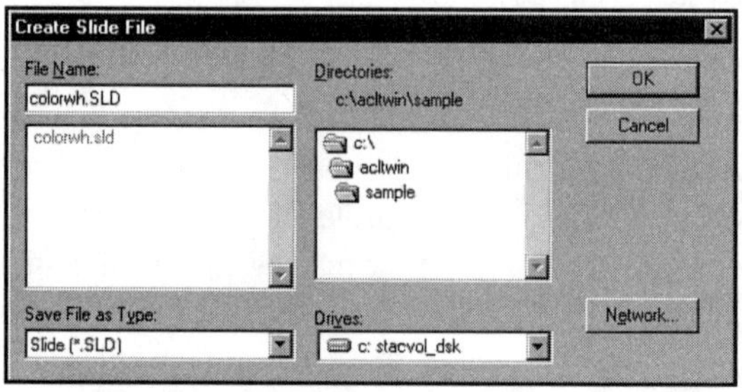

Figure 20.7

The Create Slide File dialog box.

NOTE

Use the R (REDRAW) command to clear a displayed slide. The current drawing, if any, reappears.

You just created three individual slide files. In the next exercise, you tie them together into a slide show script.

CREATING A SLIDE SHOW SCRIPT

1. Using Windows Notepad, create the script shown in figure 20.8, and save it as filename **S1-3.SCR**.

2. Run and test the script.

Figure 20.8

S1-3.SCR: a slide show script.

```
S1-3.SCR

VSLIDE  S1
DELAY  5000
VSLIDE  S2
DELAY  5000
VSLIDE  S3
DELAY  5000
```

An Animation Script

As you have seen, script files can be used for a variety of processing tasks. As a final example, you develop a script that will make an object appear to move automatically.

This "animation" technique is based on a simple fact. If you can relocate an object once using the MOVE command, you can repeat the move as many times as you'd like.

In this exercise, you develop a script (ANIMATE.SCR) that performs the following tasks:

■ Set an UNDO mark at the start of the script, so all operations (including variable reassignments) can be undone at its completion. See Chapter 6, "Editing Drawings," for details on the UNDO command.

- Turn off blips, highlighting, and the UCS icon for a cleaner look.

- Draw a red circle in the lower left corner of the screen.

- Move the circle in a rectangular path around the screen. The MOVE command moves the circle 0.5 units to the right and repeats this operation 10 times. Using the same iteration scheme, the script moves the circle up, to the left, and then down.

- Erase the circle, write an informative message on the screen, pause for two seconds, and then "undo" everything (UNDO Back).

TIP

To save typing time when creating and editing your script files, use Windows 95 cut (Ctrl+X), copy (Ctrl+C), and paste (Ctrl+V) methods.

CREATING ANIMATION SCRIPTS

1. Using Windows Notepad, create the script shown in figure 20.9 and save the file as **ANIMATE.SCR**. To minimize the typing, use copy and paste techniques for the repeated lines.

2. Run and test the script.

Figure 20.9

ANIMATE.SCR: an animation script.

```
ANIMATE.SCR

UNDO MARK
BLIPMODE OFF
HIGHLIGHT 0
UCSICON OFF
ZOOM ALL
COLOR RED
CIRCLE
0.5,0.5
0.5
MOVE SINGLE LAST ⊕ @0.5<0      }10 times
...
MOVE SINGLE LAST ⊕ @0.5<90     }10 times
...
MOVE SINGLE LAST ⊕ @0.5<180    }10 times
...
MOVE SINGLE LAST ⊕ @0.5<270    }10 times
...
ERASE SINGLE LAST
TEXT
0.5,0.5
0.75
0
+++ END OF ANIMATION +++
DELAY 2000
UNDO BACK
```

TIP

Use your creativity to modify the animation script to generate an AutoCAD LT screen saver!

Summary

As you've seen in this chapter, the details on creating and using script files need not remain a mystery. Practice the individual AutoCAD LT commands at the Command: prompt to become familiar with the various options and responses. Then, begin to link the command sequences together into a script file, in much the same way you thread beads together to form a bracelet.

In the next chapter, you'll continue further with AutoCAD LT customization techniques and learn how to create and modify the toolbars.

21

CREATING YOUR OWN TOOLBAR

AutoCAD LT Releases 1 and 2 had a customizable toolbox as well as several customizable buttons on the toolbar located below the pull-down menus. In those previous releases, you could customize the content, button image, tool assignment, and shape of the toolbox or the buttons by way of dialog boxes.

AutoCAD LT for Windows 95 benefits extensively from the environmental refinements made for AutoCAD Release 13 for Windows. One of these major refinements is the manner in which the product makes use of tools and toolbars. In AutoCAD LT for Windows 95, there is no longer an element called a toolbox, rather, several toolbars, nearly all of which are identical to those in AutoCAD Release 13.

This chapter covers the following information about customizing tools and toolbars:

■ *Comparison between current and previous tool customization*

■ *Toolbar safety measures*

■ *Creating your own toolbar*

■ *The Customize Toolbar dialog box feature map*

■ *Adding tools to the toolbar*

■ *Moving and removing tools*

- *Creating a custom tool*
- *Creating the button graphics*
- *Adding and modifying a customized flyout*

Customizing Tools and Toolbars

In Chapter 2, "Setting Up Your Drawing Environment," you learned to open and close toolbars as well as how to position them within the drawing window (floating or docked). This chapter illustrates the manner in which you create your own toolbar and add existing tools or tools and icons that you create.

Toolbar Failsafe Precautions

When working with the content of toolbars and the commands issued by the tool selections, it is important to know where AutoCAD LT is storing the files associated with these issues and with having a backup. The critical files involved with AutoCAD LT's menu structure can be found in the C:\Program Files\AutoCAD LT folder. The following list explains the role of each file:

- **ACLT.MNC:** This is the compiled menu file used by LT. It is a binary file (essentially unreadable by the user) and contains the contents of the commands and menus structure.

- **ACLT.MNR:** This is another binary file and is the menu resource file containing the bitmaps used by menu items such as toolbars.

- **ACLT.MNS:** The source menu is automatically generated by AutoCAD LT when it is initially loaded or a menu element has been modified.

- **ACLT.MNU:** The .MNU file is a template file and serves as the menu file upon which the final menu structure is built.

Your toolbar settings (sizing, position, and so forth) are stored in the ACLT.INI file. When a new toolbar is created or modified, the ACLT.MNR and MNS files are immediately updated. This means that any mistaken selections or choices are also saved. For this reason, it is very important to back up the ACLT.INI file and all MN*x* files before you do any customizing.

TIP

> You can restore the factory defaults by deleting the .MNS, .MNR, and .MNC files. AutoCAD LT will re-create them by using the original .MNU file with the "factory" defaults.

Creating a New Toolbar

Creating your own toolbar is easy, and a customized toolbar can save you time. A command alias, such as Z for the ZOOM command, can invoke only the top-level command. Tools, on the other hand, can incorporate the command and a response to all the prompts of an option. This inclusion of a command's option and the prompt response is commonly referred to as a menu macro; it is a series of responses strung together. The menu macros are used in pull-down menu items as well as in several of the tools in AutoCAD LT.

A customized toolbar is particularly useful when it contains tools normally found on a standard menu pull-down flyout or on a toolbar with flyouts that are frequently accessed, such as the Object Snap toolbar or the Zoom toolbar.

Your new toolbar can contain a collection of tools from other toolbars as well as tools you create. During the course of this chapter, you create the Inside toolbar, during which you collect existing tools and make one of your own.

The Customize Toolbars Dialog Box

The Customize Toolbars dialog box (Tools, Customize Toolbars) enables you to create new tools and toolbars and to modify any existing tool. Figure 21.1 shows the Customize Toolbars dialog box along with an explanation of each of the options available.

Figure 21.1

The Customize Toolbars dialog box.

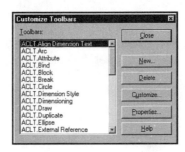

Note

The Properties option of the Customize Toolbars dialog box provides a text field for a description of your toolbar. This is useful when more than one user has access to an AutoCAD LT station.

Creating and Naming a New Toolbar

Any new toolbar starts empty. For this reason, you hardly notice the small toolbar that LT creates and places at the top of the drawing window, frequently over the top of the Object Properties toolbar. In the first exercise, you create and name the new Inside toolbar. Watch closely for the little empty toolbar.

CREATING THE *INSIDE* TOOLBAR

1. Begin a New drawing from Scratch and choose Tools, Customize Toolbars to display the Customize Toolbars dialog box.

2. Choose New to open the New Toolbar dialog box shown in figure 21.2.

Figure 21.2

The New Toolbar dialog box.

3. In the Toolbar Name edit box, enter **Inside**, then choose OK. The ACLT.Inside toolbar is added to the listing, and a small, empty toolbar appears above the Customize Toolbars dialog box.

4. Drag the Inside toolbar onto the drawing area of your screen, as shown in figure 21.3.

5. Choose Close from the Customize Toolbars dialog box. LT compiles the menu file (.MNR) and saves the source file (.MNS).

Figure 21.3

The new Inside toolbar.

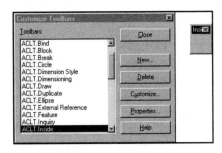

Figure 21.3

The new Inside toolbar.

Adding Tools to the Toolbar

Adding tools to the toolbars simply requires finding the tool you want to add and dragging it into the new toolbar and releasing. All AutoCAD LT tools can be chosen from the Modify Toolbars dialog box in the following list of categories:

Object Properties

Standard

Draw

Modify

Attribute

External Reference

Dimensioning

Custom

The tools collection of each category are either single or contain a flyout. The Custom category provides a blank tool for your future customizing of content and icon. In the following exercise, you add some tools to the Inside toolbar.

TIP

Because tools displayed in the Modify Toolbars dialog box don't display tooltips, simply rest your cursor on any tool in an LT toolbar to display their tooltip. If a tool is buried in a flyout in an LT toolbar, click once on the flyout to open the toolbar associated with it, from which you can display the tooltips. Any toolbars left open after your search will automatically close when you close the Customize Toolbars dialog box.

ADDING A FEW TOOLS TO THE *INSIDE* TOOLBAR

1. Choose Tools, Customize Toolbars, then scroll down the Toolbars listing and choose ACLT.Inside.

2. Choose Modify to open the Customize Toolbars dialog box shown in figure 21.4, which displays the collection of tools found in the Object Properties category by default.

Figure 21.4

*The Customize Toolbars
dialog box.*

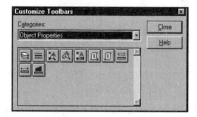

3. Click on the Categories drop-down list and choose Standard to display the Standard Toolbar collection of tools and their flyouts.

4. Use the scroll bar to review the available tools, then click and drag the Snap to Endpoint tool into the Inside toolbar, as shown in figure 21.5.

Figure 21.5

*Adding the Snap to
Endpoint tool to the Inside
toolbar.*

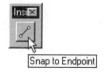

5. Scroll to the bottom of the Standard category, then click and drag the Real-Time Zoom tool to the right of the Snap to Endpoint tool in the Inside toolbar.

6. From the Categories drop-down list, open the Draw collection of tools, then click and drag the Rectangle tool into the Inside toolbar.

7. For future customization, open the Custom category, then click and drag the blank tool into the Inside toolbox. Depending on where you released the tools in your toolbar, it should resemble the one shown in figure 21.6. The tooltip for the blank tool will be No Name once the menu structure is compiled.

8. Close both customization dialog boxes; LT saves and compiles the appropriate menu files.

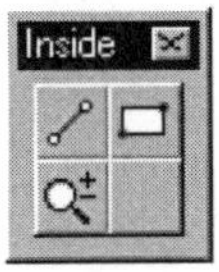

Figure 21.6

The four tools of the Inside toolbar.

Floating toolbars can be sized into a horizontal or vertical toolbar or into a matrix similar to that shown in figure 21.6 by dragging the edge of the toolbar frame into the desired configuration. When sizing a horizontal floating toolbar, however, only the horizontal edges of the toolbar can be used to drag and size the toolbar. Similarly, on vertical toolbars, only the vertical edges of the toolbar can be used to drag and size the toolbar. For those toolbars that are not linear, any edge can be used to resize the toolbar configuration.

Modifying Toolbars and Tools

Every floating toolbar can be sized, of course, by dragging the frame of the toolbar and releasing it at the desired configuration. The power of customizing becomes most evident, however, when you create your own icon with a customized command sequence. This section presents these features and several others relating to toolbars and their tools.

Moving and Removing Tools

Once created, you might want to modify the collection of tools in a specific toolbar. In the following exercise, you change the position of tools and see the ease with which tools are removed from the Inside toolbar. You also learn another method of hiding and showing toolbars.

MOVING AND REMOVING TOOLS TO THE *INSIDE* TOOLBAR

1. To open the Customize Toolbars dialog box, click on any tool in the Inside toolbar with the Enter button of the mouse or pointing device.

2. Choose Modify to open the Modify Toolbars dialog box.

3. To remove the Rectangle tool from the Inside toolbar, drag it away from the toolbar, then release it.

4. Add another tool of your choice to the Inside toolbar.

5. To create a space between tools of the Inside toolbar, drag one of the tools half the width of a tool, then release it.

6. Create a space between all tools, then resize the toolbar by dragging the toolbar frame to display 2 rows of 2 tools each as shown in figure 21.7.

Figure 21.7

The new configuration of spaced tools.

7. Close the Modify Toolbars dialog box, then choose Properties to open the Toolbar Properties dialog box.

8. Change the name of the toolbar to **Inside LT** and choose Apply, then choose Close from the Customize Toolbars dialog box.

9. To hide the Inside LT toolbar, choose View, Toolbars, then turn off Inside LT (they're listed alphabetically) and choose OK.

10. Enter **TL** at the Command: line and you see the following prompt:

    OOLBAR Toolbar name (or ALL):

11. Enter **Inside_LT** and you see the next prompt:

```
Show/Hide/Left/Right/Top/Bottom/Float:  <Show>:
```

12. Press Enter to accept the default and show the Inside LT toolbar.

To copy a tool from one toolbar to another, open the Customize Toolbars dialog box, then choose Modify. Press the Ctrl key while dragging the desired tool from one toolbar to another.

Creating Your Own Custom Tool

The command sequence, or menu macro, invoked by choosing a tool may contain command aliases, command options, AutoLISP functions, or a combination of those. In the following exercise, you assign a command with its options to the No Name tool of the Inside LT toolbar.

Note

Use the semicolon (;) to assign an Enter key to the command sequence, preface transparent commands with an apostrophe ('), and begin most macros with ^C^C (no spaces) to cancel current commands when the tool is chosen.

ADDING CONTENT TO THE BLANK TOOL

1. Double-click the Enter button of the pointing device on the No Name tool in the Inside LT toolbar to open the Button Properties dialog box shown in figure 21.7.

2. In the Name edit box, enter **View ALL**, then press the Tab key.

3. Enter restores the named view ALL in the Help edit box. Press the Tab key.

4. In the Macro edit box, enter **'VIEW;R;ALL**, as shown in figure 21.8, then choose Apply.

Figure 21.8

*The Button Properties
dialog box.*

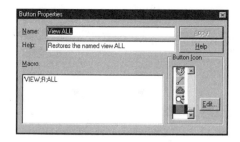

5. Choose Close from the Customize Toolbars dialog box. AutoCAD LT compiles and saves the menu files.

6. Open the drawing COLORWH located in the C:\Program Files \AutoCAD LT\Sample folder.

7. Enter **VIEW**, then enter **S** for the Save option.

8. Enter **ALL** for the view name to save.

9. Use any Zoom tool or option to zoom into an area on the color wheel.

10. Choose View ALL from the Inside LT toolbar to restore the view named ALL.

Creating the Button Graphics

One of the most interesting customizing activities is that of creating the graphics for the button. The Button Editor dialog box, shown in figure 21.9, provides the means by which you draw the picture you want for the icon of the tool.

Figure 21.9

*The Button Editor
dialog box.*

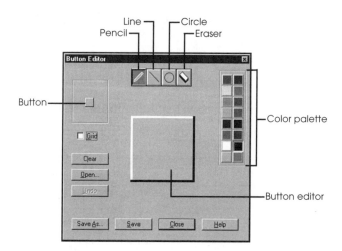

The following list describes the features of the dialog box in detail:

- **Button:** This shows the actual size of the button you are creating in the toolbar.

- **Pencil:** This option allows you to fill one pixel at a time in the current color by using click or drag.

- **Line:** This options enables you to click and drag to draw a line in the current color.

- **Circle:** This option enables you to click and drag to draw a circle in the current color.

- **Eraser:** This option erases one pixel at a time in the current color by using click or drag.

- **Color Palette:** Use the color palette to select the current color.

- **Button Editor:** Use the button editor to create icon graphics.

- **Grid:** This option turns on or off the grid line on the button editor.

- **Clear:** This option clears the current graphics from the button editor.

- **Open:** This option opens an existing .BMP from the dialog box.

- **Undo:** This option undoes the last draw or erase sequence.

- **Save As:** This option opens a dialog box to save the current graphics as a new .BMP.

- **Save:** This option saves the current graphics under same name.

- **Close:** This option closes the Button Editor dialog box but does *not* save the current changes.

- **Help:** This option opens context-sensitive help on the Button Editor dialog box.

Use the pencil, line, circle, or eraser tools to create the graphics on the large button area, either with or without a grid. In the following exercise, you create an eye for the View ALL tool.

NOTE

The circle tool is the only one that requires the click-and-drag movement to create the circle. The pencil, line, and eraser support single-click or click-and-drag.

CREATING AN EYE-CON FOR THE VIEW ALL TOOL

1. Double-click the Enter button of the pointing device on the View ALL tool in the Inside LT toolbar to open the Button Properties dialog box.

2. Choose Edit from the Button Icon section of the Button Properties dialog box to open the Button Editor dialog box.

3. Click in the Grid check box to turn on the grid for the button.

4. Using the default color of black, choose the circle tool to begin the shape of the eye.

5. Click in the center of the button grid, drag the mouse up to the right to create a circle, then release.

6. Experiment with the tools to create a button icon similar to that shown in figure 21.10.

Figure 21.10

The completed Eye icon for the View ALL tool.

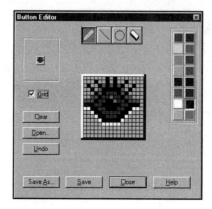

7. When finished with your button, choose Save As to open the Save As dialog box shown in figure 21.11.

8. Enter **eye** as the name of the new file, then choose Save.

9. Choose Close from the Button Editor dialog box to return to the Button Properties dialog box, which now displays your button icon.

10. Choose Apply to apply the button icon to the View ALL tool.

11. Choose Close from the Customize Toolbars dialog box to update the menus.

Figure 21.11

The Save As dialog box.

Creating and Modifying a Flyout

As you may have noticed, the Custom category contains a blank flyout tool. In this section, you add a flyout tool to the Inside LT toolbar and edit an existing button to use as the graphics. When customizing flyouts, you must first associate an existing toolbar, then add or remove tools from it. From that point, you may edit the buttons. In the following exercise, you configure a flyout for the Inside LT toolbar.

ADDING AND CUSTOMIZING THE FLYOUT TOOL

1. Click on the Enter button once on any button of the Inside LT toolbar, then choose Modify.

2. From the Modify Toolbars dialog box, choose Custom from the Categories drop-down list.

3. Drag and drop the blank (No Name) flyout tool into the Inside LT toolbar, then click on the Enter button once on the flyout to open the Flyout Properties dialog box shown in figure 21.12.

Figure 21.12

The Flyout Properties dialog box.

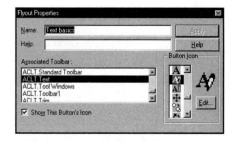

4. Enter **Text basics** in the Name edit box, then select ACLT.Text from the Associated Toolbar listing.

5. Choose the icon associated with the DDEDIT command, as shown in figure 21.12, then click in the Show This Button's Icon box.

6. Choose Apply to apply the graphics and associated toolbar to the flyout, then Close the Customize Toolbars dialog box to update the menus.

7. Click on the Enter button once on the flyout to open the Customize Toolbars dialog box, then choose Modify.

8. Click on the Text basics flyout to display the toolbar, then drag the Text tool away from the Inside LT toolbar and drop it anywhere.

9. Click on the Polygon tool in the AutoCAD LT Draw toolbar to display the Polygon toolbar.

10. Press the Ctrl key and drag a copy of the Rectangle tool from the Polygon toolbar and drop it into the Inside LT toolbar.

11. Close the Polygon toolbar, and your Inside LT toolbar should contain the tools shown in figure 21.13.

12. Close the Customize Toolbars dialog box to update the menu files, then try your flyout.

Figure 21.13

The Inside LT toolbar and new flyout.

TIP

Turn off the Show This Button's Icon to implement the flyout's "float to the top" feature of the current tool.

After you add a customized tool, whether single or from a flyout, you can edit the button graphics as necessary. Remember that you can always restore the factory defaults by deleting the MNS, MNR, and MNC files, and AutoCAD LT will re-create them with the defaults.

22

CREATING YOUR OWN LINETYPES

A customized linetype is one that contains something other than the normal patterns of dashes and dots. It can contain text objects, angled or orthogonal lines, or other shapes you can create. This chapter shows you how to use custom linetypes provided with AutoCAD LT and gives you the skills you need to create your own custom linetypes by building on those that already exist. Specifically, this chapter covers the following:

■ *Customized linetype applications*

■ *Adding a sample customized linetype to a drawing*

■ *Examples of simple and complex linetypes*

■ *Anatomy of the simple linetype code*

■ *Creating a simple linetype from scratch*

■ *Anatomy of the complex linetype code*

■ *Creating a complex linetype from scratch*

■ *Adding a complex linetype to the drawing*

■ *Modifying an existing customized linetype*

Creating and Using Customized Linetypes

AutoCAD LT for Windows 95 not only benefits from the many toolbars found in AutoCAD Release 13, LT also is able to implement the flexibility of Release 13's customized linetypes. Applications such as civil and mechanical engineering, as well as architectural applications, benefit from the capability of creating a linetype pattern specific to a particular need.

Using the Sample Linetypes

Customized linetypes are contained in editable definition files that define the look of the linetype. These files have the extension .LIN and are stored in the root directory of AutoCAD LT. Figure 22.1 illustrates the seven sample customized linetypes found in the LTYPESHP.LIN file.

Figure 22.1

Sample linetypes from the LTYPESHP.LIN file.

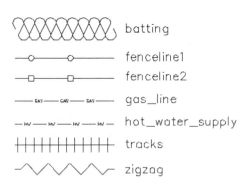

To use the linetype definitions found in the LTYPESHP.LIN file in a drawing, open the Select Linetype dialog box, from which you may load the file containing the linetype definition you want to use. In the following exercise, load the linetype definition file, then use some sample linetypes in a drawing.

NOTE

> The LINETYPE command provides you with options to create a new linetype, load an existing linetype from a .LIN file, or set a linetype to be current. The LINETYPE command and its options is the command-line equivalent of the dialog box selections covered in this chapter.

DRAWING LINES WITH A CUSTOMIZED LINETYPE

1. Open the drawing LTSITE.DWG located in the sample folder, then choose the Linetype tool on the Object Properties toolbar to open the Select Linetype dialog box.

2. Choose the Load button to open the Load or Reload Linetypes dialog box, then choose the File button at the top to open the Select Linetype File dialog box.

3. Choose LTYPESHP.LIN from the File Name listing, then choose OK to close the Select Linetype dialog box and display the Load or Reload Linetypes dialog box shown in figure 22.2.

Figure 22.2

The linetype definitions from the LTYPESHP.LIN file.

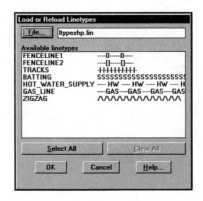

4. Choose Select All to select all seven linetypes, then choose OK.

5. Choose OK to close the Select Linetype dialog box; then from the Linetype Control drop-down list, choose TRACKS.

6. Choose Line from the Draw toolbar and pick ①, then ②, as shown in figure 22.3, then press Enter.

7. Set the layer FENCE1 to be current, then choose Format, Linetype to open the Select Linetype dialog box.

8. Choose FENCELINE1 from the Loaded Linetypes listing, then change the Linetype Scale value to ¹/₂ and choose OK.

9. Use the LINE command to draw the fence line by picking ③ through ⑥.

Figure 22.3

*Creating the railroad
and fence lines.*

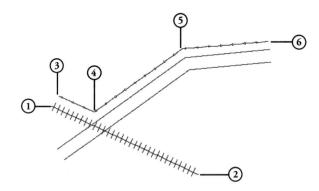

In the next sequence of steps you create a new line, then modify the linetype property of the line to one of the customized linetypes.

10. Type **OF** to issue the OFFSET command, enter **10'** as the offset distance, then pick the edge of the roadway at ① as shown in figure 22.4.

11. Pick ② when prompted for the side to offset, then press Enter to end the command.

12. Choose Properties from the Object Properties toolbar, pick the new line at ③, then press Enter to open the Modify Polyline dialog box.

13. Choose Layer to open the Select Layer dialog box, choose UTILITY, then choose OK.

14. Choose Linetype to open the Select Linetype dialog box, choose GAS_LINE from the list, then choose OK.

15. Change the value in the Linetype Scale edit box to **1.5**, then choose OK to apply the changes.

16. Choose Save to save the drawing.

Figure 22.4

*Modifying the linetype of
the offset polyline.*

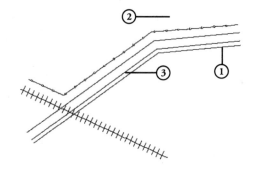

> **N**OTE
>
> The sample ISO linetypes found in the ACLT.LIN file are designed for metric use with a pen width of 1 mm. To use them with the ISO-predefined pen widths, the line has to be scaled with the appropriate value (for example, pen width 0.5 mm, ltscale 0.5).

Creating Customized Linetypes

Now that you have seen how to load and use the sample linetypes and what they can do for a drawing, this section shows you how to create new linetype definitions. There are two types of linetype definitions: simple and complex. *Simple linetypes* are those containing dots, dashes, and spaces much like the typical noncontinuous linetypes available in the Select Linetype dialog box. *Complex linetypes* are those that combine the dots and dashes with other text objects and shapes.

Table 22.1 lists the complex linetypes used in the previous exercise as well as some of the simple linetypes you have become familiar with when using AutoCAD LT. These linetype definitions are found in the LTYPESHP.LIN and ACLT.LIN files.

Table 22.1

Complex Linetypes

Linetype	Appearance	Definition
*FENCELINE1	——0——0——	A,.25,[CIRC1,l typeshp.shx,s=.1], -.2,1
*FENCELINE2	——[]——[]——	A,.25,[BOX,ltypeshp. shx,s=.1],-.2,1
*TRACKS	-|-|-|-|-|-|-|-|-|-	A,.15,[TRACK1, ltypeshp. shx, s=.25],.15
*BATTING	SSSSSSSSSSSSSSSSSSSSSSSS	A,.0001,[BAT, ltypeshp. shx,s=.1], -.4
*HOT_WATER_SUPPLY	—— HW —— HW —— HW ——	A,.5,-.2,["HW", STANDARD, S=.1,R=0.0,X=-0.1,Y= -.05],-.2

continues

Linetype	Appearance	Definition
*GAS_LINE	——GAS——GAS——GAS——GAS	A,.5,-.2,["GAS", STANDARD, S=.1,R=0.0,X=-0.1,Y= -.05],-.25
*ZIGZAG	/\/\/\/\/\/\/\/\/\/\/\	A,.0001,[ZIG, ltypeshp.shx,s=.2],-.8
*BORDER	__ __ . __ __ . __ __ . __ __	A,.5,-.25,.5,-.25,0,-.25
*BORDER2	__.__.__.__.__.__.__.__.__	A,.25,-.125,.25, -.125,0,-.125
*BORDERX2	___ ___ . ___ ___ .	A,1.0,-.5,1.0,-.5,0,-.5
*CENTER	___ _ ___ _ ___ _ ___ _	A,1.25,-.25,.25,-.25
*CENTER2	__ _ __ _ __ _ __ _	A,.75,-.125,.125,-.125
*CENTERX2	_____ __ _____ __	A,2.5,-.5,.5,-.5

In this section, you add to the LTYPESHP.LIN file from which the linetype definitions were loaded in the previous exercise.

NOTE

The LTYPESHP.SHX file used in the fencelines, tracks, and batting linetype definitions is a compiled shape file provided with AutoCAD LT. The creating of shape files cannot be done in LT, but shape files created by using AutoCAD Release 13 can be used in the definition of complex linetypes.

Inside a Simple Linetype Pattern Definition

There are several terms that are important to understand when creating your own linetype. As you have seen in table 22.1, each linetype uses two lines of code to define the look or pattern of the linetype. The first line is the name of the linetype and a graphic description. The name begins with an asterisk and is followed by a comma after which you may add an optional description to help you visualize the linetype.

Linetype nameLinetype description (optional)

*INSIDE_DD,__.__ · · __.__ · · ___.__ · · __.__

The second line of the linetype definition is the code defining the pattern for the pen motion in creating a line in this linetype. The pattern always begins with the alignment code of A (the only code allowed for now), followed immediately by a comma-delimited series of descriptors to define the first full sequence of the linetype pattern. No spaces are allowed in the linetype definition. For simple linetypes, use the following syntax in creating the pattern definition:

- **Positive number:** The length of the dash in drawing units (pen down) is stated using a positive number.

- **Negative number:** The length of the space in drawing units (pen up) is stated using a negative number.

- **0 (zero):** A dot (pen down, pen up in one location) is specified using a 0 in the pattern definition.

The following linetype pattern definition is for the INSIDE_DD linetype:

```
A,.25,-.1,0,-.1,.25,-.125,0,-.125,0,-.125
```

> The description of the linetype may be a graphic representation of the pattern or a line of text, such as use this linetype for property lines. This description is displayed in the Load or Reload Linetypes dialog box. If you elect to omit the description on the first line, do not follow the linetype name with a comma.

Creating a Simple Linetype

One of the great benefits of working in the Windows environment is the capability of switching to another application, creating or editing the desired file or document, then switching back to the original application. You may have several applications or programs open concurrently.

In the following exercise, you open the Windows 95 Notepad in which you create a new linetype definition file from LTYPESHP.LIN and add the linetype pattern definition for the INSIDE_DD linetype.

> **N**OTE
>
> You can create a linetype definition by using the Create option of the LINETYPE command, but it is much simpler to edit an existing linetype definition or add a new one to an existing linetype file by using a text editor.

CREATING AND ADDING A NEW LINETYPE

1. Continue from the previous exercise and open the Windows 95 Notepad (found in Start, Programs, Accessories by default).

2. Choose File, Open, then choose the drive to which your AutoCAD LT for Windows 95 was installed from the Look in drop-down list.

3. Change the pattern in the File name: edit box to ***.LIN**, then choose the folder for AutoCAD LT.

4. Choose LTYPESHP from the listing, then choose Open to open the file in the Notepad window.

5. Choose File, Save As, enter **INSIDE.LIN**, then choose OK to make a new linetype file and set it to be the current open file as shown in figure 22.5.

Figure 22.5

The INSIDE.LIN file in the Windows 95 Notepad.

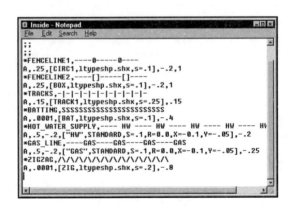

6. Begin the new linetype name and definition below the pattern definition for the ZIGZAG linetype and enter the following:

   *INSIDE_DD,__.__ .. __.__ .. __.__ .. __.__

7. On the second line, enter the following pattern definition (there are no spaces in this definition):

   A,.25,-.1,0,-.1,.25,-.125,0,-.125,0,-.125

8. Choose File, Save to save the INSIDE.LIN file, then switch back to the current session of AutoCAD LT in the LTSITE drawing.

In the next series of steps you load the INSIDE.LIN linetype file and draw a line using the INSIDE_DD linetype:

9. Choose Linetype from the Object Properties toolbar to open the Select Linetype dialog box, then choose Load.

10. Choose File and select INSIDE.LIN from your AutoCAD LT folder, then choose OK to return to the Load or Reload Linetypes dialog box.

11. Choose INSIDE_DD from the Available linetypes listing and choose OK.

12. From the Loaded Linetypes list, choose INSIDE_DD and set the Linetype Scale to **1**, then choose OK.

13. Choose Polyline from the Draw toolbar and pick the points at ① through ④ as shown in figure 22.6, then press Enter and save the drawing.

Figure 22.6

Placing the INSIDE_DD linetype.

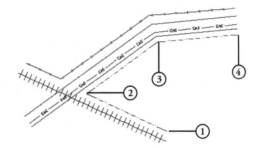

NOTE

> By default, noncontinuous linetypes begin the repetition of their patterns at each endpoint of a line or polyline. To force the continuation of the pattern placement around the corners of multisegment lines, set the PLINEGEN variable to 1. For lines already drawn, use the DDMODIFY command and toggle on the LT Gen checkbox.

Inside a Complex Linetype Pattern Definition

Linetypes containing text objects or shapes are considered complex because their pattern definition is a bit more complex than those containing dots, dashes, and spaces. Complex linetype definitions, however, may also contain the descriptors used in creating simple patterns. There are two lines of definition for the complex pattern also, and the first line containing the name and optional description are identical to that of the simple linetype.

The second line of the complex definition contains transformation elements in brackets that define the text and shapes used. The following is an example of a complex linetype using a line of text in the pattern, and figure 22.7 illustrates where some of the values are applied:

```
A,1,["DOG FENCE",instyle,S=.25,R=30,X=0,Y=-.75],-1.50
```

Figure 22.7

The DOGFENCE linetype and the applied variables.

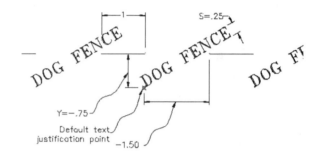

The beginning A and the pen up, pen down values are identical to the syntax used in simple linetypes. The [*bracketed transformation elements*] are defined in the following, each element being separated by a comma (no spaces):

■ **"text string":** Any text characters to be used in the complex linetype must be in quotes.

■ **textstyle:** The text style called for as the second element in the brackets *must exist* in the drawing, or the complex style will not be loaded. If no text style is specified, LT uses the current style.

■ **S=value:** The scale factor to be used for the text height is designated with S=. If the height of the specified text style is preset (>0), this factor is multiplied by the height setting. If the height of the style is 0, the S=value entered is the height of the text.

■ **R=value:** The rotation value entered is from the default justification point of the text (lower left) and is specified with the R=syntax.

■ **X=value:** This value specifies the distance the text is shifted along the X-axis of the linetype. If this value is 0 or omitted, the linetype is generated with no offset.

■ **Y=value:** Enter a negative value for this element to cause the middle of the text string to be inline with the linetype, such as "-text-". If left as 0, text will appear as "_text_".

NOTE

After the alignment character of A, the first numeric entry is for the length of the first dash. Although common in simple linetype definitions, it's not necessary to follow the dash length with a "pen up" negative value when creating complex linetypes with transformation variables in brackets, especially if the text is to be rotated.

Creating a Complex Linetype

Using the same method in which you created the simple linetype, in the following exercise, you switch back to the Windows 95 Notepad and add the new complex linetype for one of those electrical dog fences to the INSIDE.LIN linetype file. Then you add it to the current drawing.

CREATING AND ADDING THE COMPLEX LINETYPE

1. Continue from the previous exercise, switch back to the Windows 95 Notepad, and place your cursor at the bottom of the file.

2. Enter the following for the first line of the complex linetype:

   *DOGFENCE,—DOG FENCE—DOG FENCE—DOG FENCE—

3. On the second line, enter the following pattern definition:

   A,1,("DOG FENCE",instyle,S=.25,R=30,X=0,Y=-0.75),-1.50

4. Choose File, Save to save the INSIDE.LIN, then switch back to the current session of AutoCAD LT in the LTSITE drawing.

5. Choose Linetype from the Object Properties toolbar to open the Select Linetype dialog box, then choose Load.

6. Choose DOGFENCE from the Available linetypes listing and choose OK. (If DOGFENCE does not appear in the listing, choose File and select INSIDE.LIN to load the definitions found in that file.)

7. From the Loaded Linetypes list, choose DOGFENCE, then choose OK and zoom into the drawing so that your display is similar to the one shown in figure 22.9.

8. Choose Properties from the Object Properties toolbar and pick the polyline you added using the INSIDE_DD simple linetype, then press Enter to open the Modify Polyline dialog box.

9. Choose Linetype and select DOGFENCE from the listing, then choose OK.

10. Set the Linetype Scale to **.25**, then choose OK to apply the new linetype to the selected polyline, as shown in figure 22.8.

Figure 22.8

The DOGFENCE linetype applied to the existing polyline.

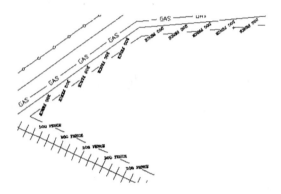

NOTE

Any shapes or text contained in complex linetypes are always drawn in their entirety. AutoCAD LT always begins and ends the complex linetype with a dash by making minor adjustments in the lengths of the segments at either end. Text and shapes in the complex linetype, therefore, will not be trimmed.

Modifying an Existing Complex Linetype

When creating new linetype definitions, especially complex ones, the result of your efforts is not always desirable. In the previous exercise, the length of the text is a little too long and the frequency could be a bit less. The rotation of 30 degrees also is probably unnecessary, but it was interesting to see the results of rotated text in the complex linetype.

In the following exercise, you switch back to the Notepad window and modify the rotation angle setting, change the text from DOG FENCE to DOG, and increase the spacing of the text along the line.

MODIFYING THE COMPLEX LINETYPE

1. Continue from the previous exercise and switch back to the Windows 95 Notepad. Change the linetype description in the first line of the linetype definition to **—DOG—DOG—DOG—**.

2. In the second line, change rotation element from **R=30** to **R=0** and change the text in quotes from "**DOG FENCE**" to "**DOG**".

3. Because the word is shorter now and is inline, change the Y=value from **Y=-0.75** to **Y=-0.1**.

4. Make the necessary dash and space changes to the beginning and ending of the definition so that your complex linetype definition for DOGFENCE looks like the following:

   ```
   A,1.5,-.25,["DOG",instyle,S=.25,R=0,X=0,Y=-0.1],-1
   ```

5. Choose File, Save to save the INSIDE.LIN, then switch back to your drawing.

6. Choose Linetype from the Object Properties toolbar to open the Select Linetype dialog box, then choose Load.

Although the INSIDE.LIN file is displayed in the File edit box, you must reload the file because it has changed:

7. Choose File and select INSIDE.LIN from the listing, then choose OK to return to the Load or Reload Linetypes dialog box. The linetype description in the Available linetypes listing should reflect the change to DOG from DOGFENCE.

8. Choose DOGFENCE from the listing, then choose OK.

9. From the Select Linetype dialog box, choose OK, then choose Properties from the Object Properties toolbar.

10. Pick the DOGFENCE polyline, then press Enter to open the Modify Polyline dialog box.

11. Choose Linetype and select DOGFENCE from the listing, then choose OK to return to the Modify Polyline dialog box.

12. Change the Linetype Scale to **.35**, choose OK to apply the new linetype to the selected polyline (as shown in figure 22.9), then save the drawing.

Figure 22.9

*The modified DOGFENCE
linetype.*

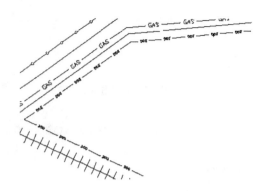

Because shape objects cannot be generated from within AutoCAD LT, adding text to a complex linetype is the most visually dynamic aspect of the operation. Figure 22.10 presents the application of the spacing variables used in the previous exercise so that you can more fully understand the results.

Figure 22.10

*The updated variables for
the DOG FENCE linetype.*

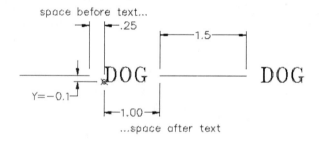

RELATED COMMANDS

LINETYPE

DDEMODES

DDLMODES

DDLTYPE

23

USING OLE AND THE WINDOWS 95 EDITING FEATURES

A seldom used but powerful tool in Windows environments (Windows 3.11, Windows 95, and Windows NT) is that of the dynamic linkage between applications. As Windows 95 continues to gain acceptance, this linkage will be utilized more and more as users understand its capabilities. This chapter defines and describes the linkage that exists between AutoCAD LT for Windows 95 and other applications by way of Object Linking and Embedding (OLE). In this chapter you will learn the following:

■ *Understanding the data exchange concepts*

■ *OLE defined*

■ *AutoCAD LT as the source application*

■ *Establishing the linkage*

■ *Updating linked objects*

■ *AutoCAD LT as the container application*

- *Linking to the source application*
- *Editing OLE objects in LT*

Data Exchange Between Applications

The Windows 95 environment, as with other Windows environments, enables the AutoCAD user to share information between applications. When making the customized linetypes in Chapter 22, you switched between the Windows 95 Notepad and AutoCAD LT. Although you didn't take data from one application to the other, it was very convenient to switch back and forth between them.

Data exchange takes place when you copy information from one Windows application into another. As an author, I frequently copy AutoCAD or LT prompts directly from the Text Window and paste them into Word for Windows. The power of this capability is most evident when there is a link established between the shared information in each application. In Chapter 11, "External References," you learned how changes made to an externally referenced drawing are seen in the "host" drawing into which the drawing referenced because of the linkage that exists.

In this section you learn about features in LT that enable you to link drawings or objects in LT with other applications. The linking and embedding exercises use the Windows 95 WordPad to illustrate and walk you through the OLE capabilities found in AutoCAD LT. Those of you with other word-processing applications such as Word, WordPerfect, or Ami Pro can apply the principles learned in the exercises in this chapter to those applications as well.

OLE Defined

A powerful feature of the Windows 95 environment is that of object linking and embedding (OLE). As the name indicates, there are two possible features: linking objects between applications and embedding objects from one application into another. For the sake of discussion, there are some commonly accepted terms used when explaining these features that need to be clarified:

- **Object application:** The "object" application is the application *from* which the graphic or textual object(s) originate, frequently referred to as the *source* or the *source file*. In this application you choose the Cut, Copy, or Copy Link items from the Edit menu, after which you are prompted to select the objects.

- **Container application:** The application *into* which the graphic or textual object(s) are embedded or linked is the "container" application. In this application you choose Paste or Paste Special to embed or link the objects from the source application.

- **Linking:** This feature is similar to the external referencing of drawings in LT. An external drawing is essentially "linked" to the host drawing. By virtue of that link, the external drawing is shared with the host, and any updates to the external drawing are reflected in the host drawing. Similarly, a document from an application such as WordPad or Word for Windows can be linked to an LT drawing. If the document is changed, it is updated in the drawing because of the linkage, or the "sharing" of information.

- **Embedding:** When an object is embedded there is no linkage, hence there is no "sharing" of information or updating when the objects are changed. This is similar to the concept of inserting a drawing into another drawing. When objects are embedded, a copy of the information is pasted into the container application and there is no linkage back to the information in the object application.

AutoCAD LT for Windows 95 can act as either the object or container application. Figures 23.1 through 23.4 illustrate the linking features possible between LT and WordPad.

Figure 23.1

The object application, AutoCAD LT for Windows 95.

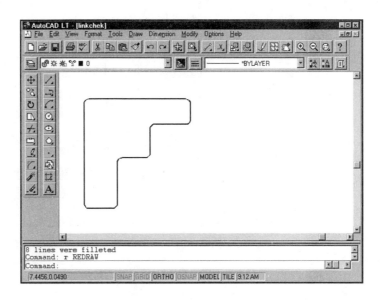

Figure 23.2

The container application, Windows 95 WordPad.

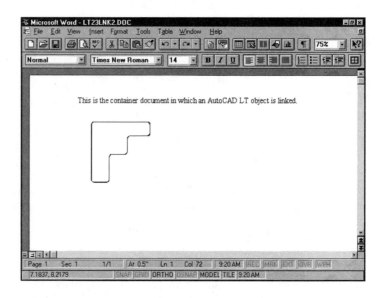

Figure 23.3

The object application in which the object has been modified.

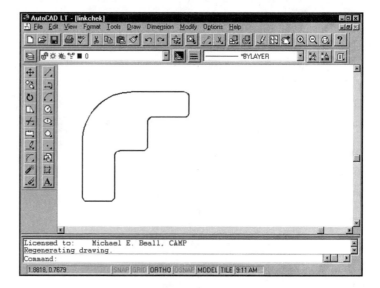

Figure 23.4

The updated container application.

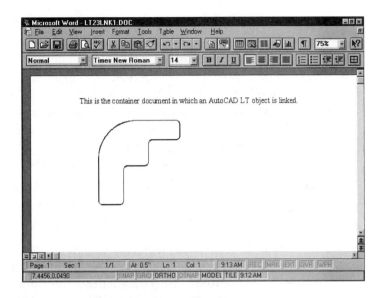

If the AutoCAD LT object had simply been embedded into the WordPad document, the document would not have been updated with the edits made to the LT drawing.

NOTE

The decision to link or embed information is made on the container side of the equation. When working in the source application, your goal is simply to select/capture the graphic or textual information.

Using AutoCAD LT for Windows 95 as the Source Application

AutoCAD LT for Windows 95 will most frequently be used as the object application, the source of the objects to be linked or embedded. As such, LT provides you with three features from the Edit pull-down menu that define the process you can use in linking or embedding objects. Each process results in the information being placed in the Windows 95 Clipboard Viewer (the CLIPBRD.EXE program can be found in the Other folder on the Windows 95 CD-ROM).

■ **Cut:** This item enables you to select objects you want to cut (erase) from the current AutoCAD LT drawing. This item invokes the CUTCLIP command, which also copies the selected objects to the Clipboard Viewer. This command can also be issued using Ctrl+X.

- **Copy:** Choosing the Copy item invokes the COPYCLIP command. This command is also invoked with Ctrl+C. Those of you familiar with earlier versions of LT will encounter this frequently because Ctrl+C was once the method by which an AutoCAD LT command was canceled. As a Windows-compliant application, Ctrl+C begins the COPYCLIP command in both Release 13 and LT for Windows 95. The Copy command functions in the same fashion as Cut by copying the selected objects to the Clipboard but it doesn't erase the selected objects from the current drawing. You can also issue this command by choosing Copy from the Standard toolbar.

- **Copy Link:** This feature invokes the COPYLINK command. You are not prompted to select objects, and the display of the current viewport, not the drawing, is copied to the Clipboard.

All three of these routines create information that can be linked or embedded into the container application. The other similarity in all three routines is that, although you are prompted to select objects when using the Cut and Copy features, the current drawing area is also captured. Figures 23.5 and 23.6 illustrate the selected objects in the drawing and the result displayed in the Clipboard Viewer. Notice the relationship of the object to the entire drawing and how it is duplicated in the Clipboard.

Figure 23.5

The object application containing the selected object.

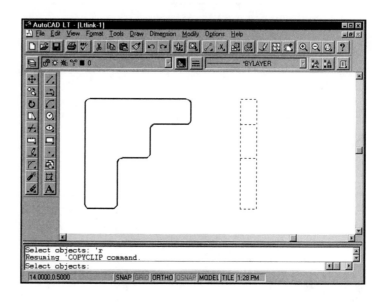

Figure 23.6

The object displayed in the Clipboard Viewer.

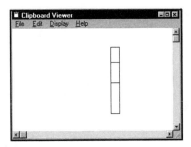

Note

The only difference between the Copy and Copy Link features found in the Edit menu of AutoCAD LT is the selection. Copy enables the user to select the objects to be copied whereas Copy Link copies the display of the current viewport.

If a floating viewport is current in paper space, the display in that viewport is copied. If paper space is current at the time of the copy, all objects and the display of viewports in paper space are copied.

Establishing a Link Between a Drawing and a Document

The first step to understanding OLE comes when using the editing features of Cut, Copy, and Copy Link from the AutoCAD LT Edit menu. The destination or container document will be served by the Windows 95 "applet" (mini-application) of WordPad, found in the Accessories folder by default. In the following exercise you open a drawing in LT as well as a new WordPad file, copy the current view in LT, then link it to the document.

Note

When a file is saved in the WordPad application, it is saved in Word 6.0 format with an extension of .DOC. This is illustrated in the last step of the following exercise.

LINKING THE AutoCAD LT DRAWING TO A DOCUMENT

1. Open the drawing LTLINK01.DWG located in the PROJECTS/CH23 directory on the accompanying CD-ROM.

2. To begin WordPad, choose Start from the Windows 95 taskbar, then Programs, Accessories, WordPad.

3. From the AutoCAD LT pull-down menu, choose Edit, Copy (or Copy from the Standard toolbar), then pick the edge of the stepped polyline and press Enter.

4. Switch to WordPad and choose Edit, Paste Special and you see the dialog box shown in figure 23.7.

Figure 23.7

The Paste Special dialog box from WordPad.

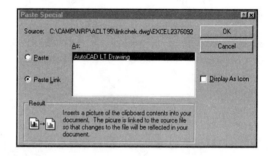

5. Choose Paste Link, then choose OK for the default selection of an AutoCAD LT Drawing Object.

6. Scroll up in the WordPad document to display the contents of the LTLINK01 drawing similar to that shown in figure 23.8.

7. Switch back to AutoCAD LT and choose File, Exit to quit the current session of LT.

Figure 23.8

The linked object in the container application (WordPad).

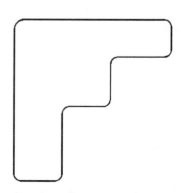

8. Switch to WordPad, then choose File, Save As and enter **LINKAPP1** in the File name edit box, then choose Save to save the document to the Program Files, Accessories folder.

N OTE

When information is *embedded* into a container application, it is physically a part of the file or document. When information is *linked* to a file or document, the linked information is only displayed in that file while the container application is open. The receiving (container) file establishes a "pointer" or "flag" that references the linked information each time the receiving file is opened; the linked information is not physically stored in the receiving file. This enables the dynamically shared information to be the most current available from the source file.

Updating Linked Objects

The process of capturing the information, specifically the current display in the previous exercise, can be done very easily from the Edit menu selections. In the container application, you can either opt to Paste, in which case the captured information is simply embedded, or you can use Paste Link to establish a link between the source and the container application.

After information has been linked, the Links dialog box (see fig. 23.9) enables the user to set the manner in which the objects from the source file (the object application) are to be handled. The Links dialog box is opened by selecting the linked object in the container application, then choosing Edit, Links. The following is a brief overview of the available options in the Links dialog box:

Figure 23.9

The Links dialog box in WordPad.

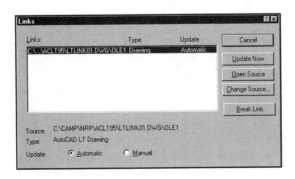

- **Update Now:** Choose Update Now if the object from the source application has been edited and the change is not reflected in the current (container) application. You should also use this feature if the Manual setting has been specified as the Update method.

NOTE

The update of the object in the container application will only update if the source application was opened using the Open Source feature of the Links dialog box.

- **Open Source:** If the source application for the linked objects is not currently open, choose Open Source to open that application. You can also open the source application by double-clicking on the linked object in the document. This method enables the updating of an edited source object in the container application.

- **Change Source:** Similar in concept to the Path option of the XREF command, this feature opens the Change Source dialog box, which enables you to specify a new drive or directory in case the originally linked file has been archived or moved to another location. You can also select a different drawing or file to be linked from this Change Source dialog box as well, although the appropriate linkages may not be established automatically.

- **Break Link:** This option severs the linkage between the source and the container. Any edits made to the source file will not be seen in the receiving (container) file. Break Link is similar in concept to the Bind option in the XREF command.

- **Automatic Update:** This default Update option automatically updates the container application file with the most current version of the linked information.

- **Manual Update:** In situations where it is not necessary to always see the linked information in a container document, use the Manual Update option. The receiving file will only reflect the current source file when Update Now is chosen.

TIP

If you need to change the source directory due to networking issues, it might be more advantageous to break the existing link then paste the desired object into the container file again. This establishes a new link to the source.

In the following exercise you modify the drawing in LT, then update the document in Microsoft Word.

MODIFYING AND UPDATING THE LINKED DRAWING

1. Continue from the previous exercise and double-click in the middle of the polyline object in the WordPad document to automatically launch AutoCAD LT and open the drawing linked to LINKAPP1.

2. Choose Fillet from the Feature flyout of the Modify toolbar and change the Radius to 1.

3. Reissue the FILLET command, then pick ①, then ② as shown in figure 23.10 to apply the fillet to the corner.

Figure 23.10

Editing the corners of the polyline.

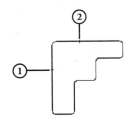

4. From the File pull-down menu in LT, choose Update LINKAPP1 in WordPad.

5. Switch to WordPad and scroll up to see the updated object in the container application.

The object in the container application (WordPad) is hatched indicating it is currently dynamically linked to the object in the source application (AutoCAD LT).

6. Return to AutoCAD LT and choose File, Exit. The object in WordPad will no longer be hatched because the linkage has been resolved and the source application closed.

NOTE

When forwarding a container application file to another person by way of diskette, it is important to include the linked information from the source file. This is because the objects from the source application are not physically placed in the container application file.

Another scenario might be a situation in which you have modified the object in the source application, such as LT and have yet to open the container application in which the objects from the drawing file were linked. In the next exercise you see how a container file is automatically updated with the current version of the linked information.

AUTOMATICALLY UPDATING THE DOCUMENT

1. Continue from the previous exercise and switch back to WordPad, then choose File, Exit to close the application, and choose Yes to save the LINKAPP1 document.

2. Start AutoCAD LT, and open the LTLINK01 drawing.

3. Choose Stretch from the Resize flyout of the Modify toolbar, then pick ①, then ② as shown in figure 23.11.

4. Confirm that SNAP is on and pick ③, then ④ to stretch the plate size down .25".

Figure 23.11

Stretching the polyline in the source file.

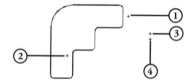

5. Choose Circle Center Radius from the Circle flyout of the Draw toolbar, then pick ① as shown in figure 23.12 to place the center of the circle and enter **.25** for the radius.

6. Press the spacebar to reissue the CIRCLE command and pick ② to add another circle with a .25 radius, then choose File, Exit and save the changes.

Figure 23.12

Adding the circles to the source file.

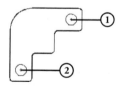

7. Reopen WordPad, then choose LINKAPP1 from the list of the four recently edited files in the File pull-down menu.

8. Click anywhere in the object frame, then choose Edit, Links to open the Links dialog box.

9. Choose Update Now to automatically launch AutoCAD LT and open the drawing file linked to the container application, LTLINK01.

10. After the drawing has finished opening, switch to WordPad and choose Close to see the updated object with the drawing edits.

11. Choose File, Exit and save the LINKAPP1 document.

12. Switch back to LT and choose File, Exit.

Using AutoCAD LT for Windows 95 as the Container Application

Although possibly a less frequent scenario, AutoCAD LT can also be the container for documents, spreadsheets, and other Windows applications. Figure 23.13 shows text from WordPad linked to AutoCAD LT.

Figure 23.13

AutoCAD LT with linked text from WordPad.

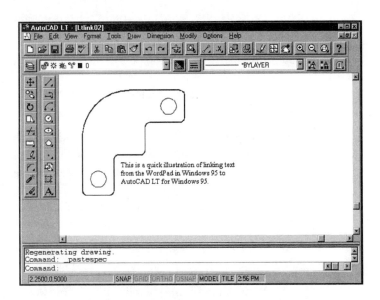

This section takes you through the process of using AutoCAD LT as the container document for WordPad text. As the receiving application, LT has two items from the Edit menu that enable you to insert incoming files from source applications. Each process results in the information being pasted from the Windows 95 Clipboard Viewer into LT.

- **Paste:** This function issues the PASTECLIP command, which pastes the objects currently in the Clipboard at the top of the current LT viewport. This feature can also be accessed by typing Ctrl+V or by choosing Paste from the Standard toolbar.

- **Paste Special:** The PASTESPEC command opens the Paste Special dialog box shown in figure 23.14, which is similar to that seen in WordPad (refer to figure 23.7).

Figure 23.14

The Paste Special dialog box in AutoCAD LT.

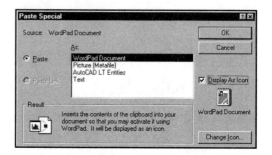

From the Paste Special dialog box, you have several options that relate to the method in which the pasted object is to be recognized.

- **Paste:** Inserts the contents of the Clipboard into the current viewport of AutoCAD LT. If the source application is not currently open, double-click on the linked object to activate the source application and open the source file.

- **Paste Link:** When this feature is used, a "picture" or graphical image of the source file is linked to AutoCAD LT. This is, of course, similar to the XREF concept of attaching a file (see Chapter 11, "External References"). If and when the source file is ever modified, LT will be updated per the current update setting in the Links dialog box for that application (refer to figure 23.9).

- **As:** From the listing, select the desired object type to import. The source application file type is listed first, if available.

- **Display as Icon:** When this box is checked, the source file is represented by an icon of the source application such as WordPad or AutoCAD LT. Check this box just to view the icon that will be used. Depending on the application, you may be given the option to change the icon if this feature is selected.

Establishing an Editable Link to the Source

When a file from a source application is pasted into LT, paste method notwithstanding, the way it is treated depends on the source application. The following are some possibilities and how AutoCAD LT recognizes the objects:

- **An AutoCAD graphic:** If the object in the Clipboard is an AutoCAD graphic (generated by AutoCAD R13 or LT), it is inserted as a block into the current viewport onto the current layer. If the graphic was created using COPYCLIP (Ctrl+C or Edit, Copy), which enables you to select the objects to be copied, the insertion point is the lower left corner of the objects. If the method used was Edit, Copy Link, which copies all objects in the current viewport, the insertion point is the lower left corner of the current viewport.

  When pasted, the prompts are for the insertion point, X and Y scale factors, and rotation angle. The inserted object is considered a User Block and given a system-generated name per the following report produced from the BLOCK command using the ? option for all <*> blocks:

  ```
  Defined blocks.
  A$C2012
  User      External     Dependent    Unnamed
  Blocks    References   Blocks       Blocks
  1         0            0            0
  ```

  As a block it can be exploded or treated as any other block reference.

- **Application Document:** When pasting text from a word processor, the Paste Special dialog box in LT (refer to figure 23.14) gives you the option of inserting it as ASCII Text or as a Document. If the contents of the Clipboard are pasted in as a document, the incoming object is inserted as an OLEFRAME object whose upper left corner is placed in the upper left corner of the current viewport. It is similar to a slide in that it is not recognized as an object (LIST will not recognize it), and the frame is placed over the top of any existing objects.

  The OLE frame has the standard eight edit points that can be used to size the object, although the commonly used Shift+Pick cropping feature is not available.

- **Text:** When using the Paste Special option of Text, the inserted object comes in as an MTEXT object whose upper left corner is placed at the upper left corner of the current viewport. As a text object, it can be edited using the DDEDIT command.

NOTE

For the dynamic linking feature to be effective, the source files must be named *before* the link is established. This is required because only a copy of the graphic is pasted into the container document and linked back to the source file. If there is no name for the source file, the link information cannot be completed for automatic updates.

When any inserted or pasted object is double-clicked, the source application is switched to or launched, and the source file opened. In the following exercise you use WordPad to create a document that you paste into LT.

LINKING A DOCUMENT TO AUTOCAD LT

1. Continue from the previous exercise or open the LINKLT01 drawing, then choose File, Save As and enter **LINKLT02** as the Filename and choose OK.

2. Open WordPad again and type the following:

   This is a quick illustration which links
   text from the WordPad in Windows 95 to
   AutoCAD LT.

3. Choose Save from the WordPad Toolbar and enter **LINK2LT** in the File name edit box, then choose Save to save the document.

4. Choose Edit, Select All to highlight the text, then type **Ctrl+C** to copy the selected text to the Clipboard.

5. Switch back to AutoCAD LT, then choose Edit, Paste Special to open the Paste Special dialog box.

6. Choose OK to paste the WordPad document (the contents of the Clipboard) into the current drawing as shown in figure 23.15.

Figure 23.15

The LINKLT02 drawing
with the pasted
document.

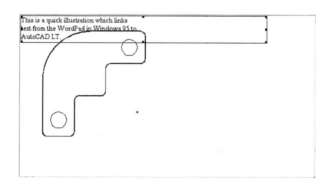

7. Place the positioning cursor inside the frame of the text, then click and drag it to a position within the step of the drawing polyline.

8. Pick anywhere in the drawing to release the frame from around the text, then choose Save to save the drawing.

9. Switch back to WordPad and choose File, Exit to close the application.

Editing OLE Objects in AutoCAD LT

When creating documents using a word-processing application you have the benefit of all the nifty tools for formatting, fonts, alignment, spacing, and the like. Therefore, when a drawing requires a large body of text for general notes or legends, it is to your advantage to link the document to LT using the OLE features. That way, if (more probably, *when*) the notes change, you can use the broad array of editing features available in the word-processing application, then save the document and the drawing is updated.

In another situation, you might have linked a schedule or spreadsheet that is maintained in the source application. As you continue to edit the spreadsheet, the drawing is also updated. In the following exercise you launch the WordPad document editor in the drawing and change the text, after which the drawing automatically updates the text.

Note

To enable you to have several linked objects in a drawing, AutoCAD LT displays diagonal lines across the linked object currently being edited in your drawing. Click anywhere outside of the OLE framed object to clear the diagonal lines.

Tip

When dynamically editing linked applications, you may enjoy watching the linkages update if you size the smaller application (WordPad, for instance), so you can see the objects in both windows as they are being edited.

LINKING A DOCUMENT TO AUTOCAD LT

1. Continue from the previous exercise and double-click anywhere on the text to open the WordPad application window as shown in figure 23.16.

Figure 23.16

The WordPad editor launched from AutoCAD LT.

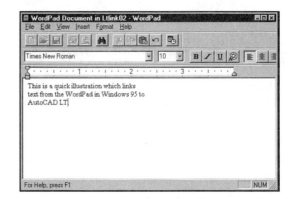

2. Add the words **for Windows 95** at the end of the sentence and change "...which links.." to "...**linking**...," then switch back to AutoCAD LT and the linked text object automatically updates with the edits.

3. Choose File, Exit & Return to LTLINK02 to close WordPad and return to the drawing.

4. Choose Save to save the drawing.

The key issue to using the OLE features to link and share objects between applications is to save both the source file and the container or receiving file. The fact that object linking and embedding is possible between more and more Windows and Windows 95 applications adds even more power to AutoCAD LT for Windows 95. Linking and embedding drawings into other documents enables LT to be a significant factor in Windows 95.

RELATED COMMANDS

COPYLINK
COPYCLIP
INSERTOBJ
PASTECLIP
PASTESPEC

VII

APPENDICES

SYSTEM VARIABLE TABLES

This appendix is a list of AutoCAD LT's system variables. You can use the following table to find the values and functions of all AutoCAD LT environment settings. The table does not include AutoCAD LT's dimensioning variables; they appear in Appendix B.

The table lists the names of the system variables and their initial values, where applicable. A brief description is given for each variable, and the meaning is given for each code. Most variables are set by various dialog boxes or commands. These variables also can be set or checked by the SETVAR command, and most can be entered directly at the Command: prompt. The italicized names, however, can only be directly accessed by the SETVAR command because AutoCAD LT has a command with the same name as the variable. All values are saved with the drawing unless noted with (CFG) for ConFiGuration file or (NS) for Not Saved. The Command Name column lists the commands that set the system variables. Variables marked (RO) are read-only, which means you cannot change them.

Note: Variable names followed by an asterisk (*) are new in Release 3.

Table A.1

System Variables Table

Variable Name	Initial Value	Command Name	Description
ACLTPREFIX	"C:\Program Files\ AutoCAD LT\"	PREFERENCES	(NS)(RO) Directory path specified in the Preferences dialog box.
ACLTVER	"3"	—	(NS)(RO)
ACIS15	0		(NS) Used for solid model translations from AutoCAD. AutoCAD LT release number.
AFLAGS	0	DDATTDEF, ATTDEF	(NS) Current state of ATTDEF modes. The value is the sum of: 0 = No attribute mode selected 1 = Invisible 2 = Constant 4 = Verify 8 = Preset
ANGBASE	0	DDUNITS, UNITS	The direction of angle 0 in the current UCS.
ANGDIR	0	DDUNITS, UNITS	Angle measure direction from 0: 0 = Counterclockwise 1 = Clockwise
APERTURE	10	DDOSNAP, APERTURE	(CFG) OSNAP target size, in pixels.
AREA	0.0000	AREA, LIST, DBLIST	(NS)(RO) Stores the last computed area.
ATTDIA	0	INSERT	Controls the attribute entry method: 0 = Attribute prompts 1 = DDATTE dialog box.

Variable Name	Initial Value	Command Name	Description
ATTMODE	1	ATTDISP	Controls attribute display: 0 = OFF 1 = Normal 2 = ON
ATTREQ	1	INSERT	Attribute values used by insert: 0 = Uses default 1 = Prompts for values
AUDITCTL	0	—	(CFG) Controls ADT (Audit Report) file: 0 = No File 1 = ADT File
AUNITS	0	DDUNITS, UNITS	Sets Angular Units mode: 0 = Decimal Degrees 1 = Deg/min/secs 2 = Grads 3 = Radians 4 = Surveyor's Units
AUPREC	0	DDUNITS, UNITS	Sets number of decimal places for angular units.
BACKZ	0.0000	DVIEW	(RO) The DVIEW back clipping plane offset in drawing units. (See VIEWMODE.)
BLIPMODE	1	—	Controls display of marker blips: 1 = Blips 0 = No Blips
CDATE	varies	TIME	(RO)(NS) Current date and time in YYYMMDD.HHMMSS format.

continues

Variable Name	Initial Value	Command Name	Description
CECOLOR	"BYLAYER"	DDEMODES, COLOR	Sets default object color.
CELTSCALE(*)	1.0000	LTSCALE, PSLTSCALE	Sets default global linetype scale. for new objects.
CELTYPE	"BYLAYER"	DDEMODES, LINETYPE	Sets default object linetype.
CHAMFERA	0.5000	CHAMFER	First chamfer distance.
CHAMFERB	0.5000	CHAMFER	Second chamfer distance.
CHAMFERC(*)	1.0000	CHAMFER	Chamfer length.
CHAMFERD(*)	0	CHAMFER	Chamfer angle.
CHAMMODE(*)	0	CHAMFER	(NS) Determines method AutoCAD LT uses to create chamfers: 0 = Two distances 1 = Length and angle
CIRCLERAD	0.0000	CIRCLE	(NS) Default radius value for new circles: 0 = None
CLAYER	"0"	DDLMODES, LAYER	Current layer.
CMDACTIVE(*)	1	CMDACTIVE	(NS)(RO) Indicates an AutoCAD LT command is active. The value is the sum of the following: 1 = Ordinary command 2 = Ordinary, transparent 4 = Script 8 = Dialog box
CMDDIA	1	—	(CFG) Controls whether PLOT uses a

Variable Name	Initial Value	Command Name	Description
			dialog box or command prompts: 0 = prompts 1 = Dialog box
CMDNAMES(*)	""	—	(NS)(RO) Names of any active commands.
COORDS	1	[^D][F6]	Controls coordinate display updates: 0 = On picks only 1 = Absolute, continuous updates 2 = Relative, prompts only
CVPORT(*)	2	VPORTS	Current viewport number.
DATE	varies	TIME	(NS)(RO) Current date and time, in Julian format.
DBMOD(*)	0	Most	(NS)(RO) Drawing modification status. Sum of the following: 1 = Object database 2 = Symbol table 4 = Database variable 8 = Window 16 = View
DCTCUST(*)	""	**SPELL**	(CFG) Current custom dictionary and path.
DCTMAIN(*)	varies	**SPELL**	(CFG) Current main dictionary type: enu = American English ena = Australian English ens = Brit. English (ise) enz = Brit. English (ize) ca = Catalan cs = Czech

continues

Variable Name	Initial Value	Command Name	Description
			da = Danish
			nl = Dutch (Primary)
			nls = Dutch (Secondary)
			fi = Finnish
			fr = French (unacc. caps)
			fra = French (acc. caps)
			de = German (Scharfes s)
			ded = German (Dopple s)
			it = Italian
			no = Norwegian (Bokmal)
			non = Norwegian (Nynorsk)
			pt = Portuguese (Iberian)
			ptb = Portug. (Brazilian)
			ru = Russian (infreq. io)
			rul = Russian (freq. io)
			es = Spanish (unacc. caps)
			esa = Spanish (acc. caps)
			sv = Swedish
DELOBJ(*)	1	—	Controls whether objects used to create other objects are deleted from the database: 0 = Deleted 1 = Retained
DIASTAT(*)	1		(NS)(RO) Last dialog box exit code: 0 = Cancel 1 = OK
DISTANCE	0.0000	DIST	(NS)(RO) Stores distance computed by DIST command.

Variable Name	Initial Value	Command Name	Description
DITHER	0	—	Controls raster output 0=Off 1=On
DONUTID	0.5000	DONUT	(NS) Sets default inner diameter for donuts.
DONUTOD	1.0000	DONUT	(NS) Sets default outer diameter for donuts.
DWGCODEPAGE	"ansi_1252"	—	(RO) The drawing code page. (See SYSCODEPAGE.)
DWGNAME	"unnamed"	—	(RO) Drawing name as entered by user.
DWGPREFIX	"C:\Program Files \AutoCAD LT\"	—	(NS)(RO) Directory path of current drawing.
DWGTITLED	0	NEW	(NS)(RO) Named status of current drawing: 0 = No 1 = Yes
DWGWRITE	1	OPEN	(NS) Read-only status of current drawing: 0 = Read-only 1 = Read/write
EDGEMODE(*)	0	TRIM, EXTEND	Controls cutting and boundary edges: 0 = No edge extension 1 = Extends edge to imaginary extension of cut/boundary object.
ELEVATION	0.0000	ELEV	Current UCS elevation.
EXEDIR(*)	"C:\PROGRAM FILES \AUTOCAD LT\"	—	(NS) Directory path of the executable file.

continues

Variable Name	Initial Value	Command Name	Description
EXPERT	0	—	(NS) Suppresses successive levels of "Are you sure?" warnings: 0 = None 1 = REGEN/LAYER 2 = BLOCK/WBLOCK/ SAVE 3 = LINETYPE 4 = UCS/VPORT 5 = DIM
EXTMAX	-1.0000E+20,-1.0000E+20,-1.0000E+20		(RO) The X,Y,Z coordinates of the drawing's upper right WCS extents.
EXTMIN	1.0000E+20,1.0000E+20,1.0000E+20		(RO) The X,Y,Z coordinates of the drawing's lower left WCS extents.
FFLIMIT(*)	0	—	(CFG) Limits number of PostScript and TrueType fonts in memory. Maximum 100, 0 is no limit.
FILEDIA(*)	1	—	(CFG) Controls display of file dialog boxes: 0 = Tilde (~) entry only 1 = On
FILLETRAD	0.5000	FILLET	Current fillet radius.
FILLMODE	1	SOLID, FILL	Turns on the display of fill traces, solids, and wide polylines: 0 = Off 1 = On
FRONTZ(*)	0.0000	DVIEW	(RO) DVIEW front clipping plane's offset, in drawing units. (See VIEWMODE.)

Variable Name	Initial Value	Command Name	Description
GRIDMODE	0	DDRMODES, GRID	Controls display of the grid in the current viewport: 0 = Off 1 = On
GRIDUNIT	0.5000,0.5000	DDRMODES, GRID	The X,Y grid spacing of the current viewport.
GRIPBLOCK	0	DDGRIPS	(CFG) Controls grip display for objects within blocks: 0 = Off 1 = On
GRIPCOLOR	5	DDGRIPS	(CFG) Current color of unselected grips, between 1 and 255.
GRIPHOT	1	DDGRIPS	(CFG) Current color of selected grips, between 1 and 255.
GRIPS	1	DDSELECT	(CFG) Controls the display of object grips and grip editing: 0 = Off 1 = On
GRIPSIZE	3	DDGRIPS	(CFG) The size of the grip box, in pixels.
HANDLES	1	HANDLES	(RO) Controls creation of object handles for the current drawing: 0 = Off 1 = On
HIGHLIGHT	1	DDRMODES	(NS) Highlights object selection control: 0 = Off 1 = On
HPANG	0	BHATCH, HATCH	(NS) Current hatch angle.

continues

Variable Name	Initial Value	Command Name	Description
HPBOUND(*)	1	BHATCH, BOUNDARY	Object type created by BHATCH and BOUNDARY: 0 = Polyline 1 = Region
HPDOUBLE	0	BHATCH, HATCH	(NS) User-defined hatch pattern doubling: 0 = Off 1 = On
HPNAME	"ANSI31"	BHATCH, HATCH	(NS) Default pattern for new hatches.
HPSCALE	1.0000	BHATCH, HATCH	(NS) Default hatch pattern scale. Must be nonzero.
HPSPACE	1.0000	BHATCH, HATCH	(NS) Default spacing for user-defined hatches.
INSBASE	0.0000,0.0000,0.0000	BASE	Insertion base point X,Y,Z coordinate, in current UCS.
INSNAME	""	DDINSERT,INSERT	(NS) Default block name for INSERT or DDINSERT.
LASTANGLE	0	ARC	(NS)(RO) The angle of the last arc, in current UCS.
LASTPOINT	0.0000,0.0000,0.0000	—	The last point, in current UCS.
LENSLENGTH(*)	50.0000	DVIEW	(RO) Lens length of the viewport perspective.
LIMCHECK	0	LIMITS	Controls object creation outside drawing limits: 0 = Enabled 1 = Disabled

Variable Name	Initial Value	Command Name	Description
LIMMAX	12.0000,9.0000	LIMITS	WCS upper right limit, in current space.
LIMMIN	0.0000,0.0000	LIMITS	WCS lower left limit, in current space.
LOCALE(*)	varies	—	(RO)(NS) The ISO language code of the AutoCAD LT version being used.
LONGFNAME(*)	1	PREFERENCES	(CFG)(RO) Support for long filenames (Win95): 0 = Disabled 1 = Enabled
LTSCALE	1.0000	LTSCALE	Global linetype scale factor.
LUNITS	2	DDUNITS, UNITS	The linear units mode: 1 = Scientific 2 = Decimal 3 = Engineering 4 = Architectural 5 = Fractional
LUPREC	4	DDUNITS, UNITS	Precision of decimal or fractional units.
MAXACTVP(*)	16	—	(NS) Maximum number of viewports to simultaneously regenerate.
MAXSORT(*)	200	—	(CFG) Maximum number of symbols and file names for sorted lists.
MENUECHO	0	—	(NS) Controls display of menu actions on the command line. Value is the sum of the following:

continues

Variable Name	Initial Value	Command Name	Description
			1 = Suppresses menu input 2 = Suppresses system prompts 4 = Disables ^P toggle of menu echo 8 = Displays DIESEL I/O strings
MIRRTEXT	1	MIRROR	Controls how MIRROR reflects text: 0 = Retains text direction 1 = Mirrors text
MODEMACRO(*)	""	—	(NS) DIESEL language expression to control status-line display.
MTEXTED(*)	"Internal"	DDEDIT	(CFG) Name of program that edits MTEXT objects.
OFFSETDIST	1.0000	OFFSET	(NS) Default distance for OFFSET; a negative value uses the THROUGH option.
ORTHOMODE	0	[^O][F8]	Sets current Ortho mode: 0 = Off 1 = On
OSMODE	0	DDOSNAP, OSNAP	Sets current object snap mode. Value is the sum of the following: 0 = NONe 1 = ENDpoint 2 = MIDpoint 4 = CENter 8 = NODe 16 = QUAdrant 32 = INTersection 64 = INSertion

Variable Name	Initial Value	Command Name	Description
			128 = PERpendicular 256 = TANgent 512 = NEArest 1024 = QUIck 2048 = APPint
PDMODE	0	POINT	Controls graphic display of POINT objects.
PDSIZE	0.0000	POINT	Controls size of POINT objects: Negative = Percentage of viewport size Positive = Absolute size 0 = 5 percent of graphics area height.
PELLIPSE(*)	0	ELLIPSE	Ellipse type created by the ELLIPSE command: 0 = True ellipse 1 = Polyline approx.
PERIMETER	0.0000	AREA, LIST, DBLIST	(NS)(RO) Last perimeter value calculated by AREA, LIST, DBLIST.
PICKADD	1	DDSELECT	(CFG) Controls whether selected objects are added to, or are replaced (added with Shift + select), the current selection set: 0 = Replace (Shift to add only) 1 = Added (Shift to remove only)
PICKAUTO	1	DDSELECT	(CFG) Controls implied auto-windowing for object selection: 0 = Off 1 = On

continues

Variable Name	Initial Value	Command Name	Description
PICKBOX	3	DDSELECT	(CFG) Object selection pick box size, in pixels.
PICKDRAG	0	DDSELECT	(CFG) Determines whether the pick button must be depressed during window corner picking in set selections: 0 = Off 1 = On
PICKFIRST	1	DDSELECT	(CFG) Enables object selection before command selection (noun/verb): 0 = Off 1 = On
PLINEGEN	0	—	Sets the linetype pattern generation around the vertices of a 2D polyline. Does not apply to polylines with tapered segments. 0 = Polylines start and end with a dash at each vertex 1 = Generates the linetype in a continuous pattern around the vertices.
PLINEWID	0.0000	PLINE	Default polyline width.
PLOTID(*)	varies	—	(CFG) Current plotter configuration description.
PLOTROTMODE(*)	1	PLOT	Controls plot orientation: 0 = Rotation icon aligns at lower left for 0, top left for 90,

Variable Name	Initial Value	Command Name	Description
			top right for 180, lower right for 270 1 = Aligns lower left corner of plot area with lower left corner of paper.
PLOTTER(*)	0	PLOT	(CFG) Current plotter configuration number.
POLYSIDES	4	POLYGON	(NS) Default number of sides for POLYGONs, between 3 and 1024.
PROJMODE(*)	1	TRIM, EXTEND	(CFG) Current projection mode for TRIM or EXTEND operations: 0 = True 3D (no projection) 1 = Project to the XY plane, current UCS 2 = Project to the current view plane
PSLTSCALE	1	PSLTSCALE	Paper space scaling of model space linetypes: 0 = Off 1 = On
PSPROLOG	""	—	(CFG) Name of the Postscript post-processing section of ACLT.PSF appended to PSOUT command output.
QTEXTMODE	0	QTEXT	State of quick text mode: 0 = Off 1 = On
RASTERPREVIEW(*)		0	SAVE, SAVEAS Controls preview image and format:

continues

Variable Name	Initial Value	Command Name	Description
			0 = BMP only 1 = BMP and WMF 2 = WMF only 3 = none
REINIT(*)	0	REINIT	(NS) Specifies the reinitialization type(s) to perform. The sum of: 0 = None 1 = Digitizer port 2 = Plotter port 4 = Digitizer device 8 = Display device 16 = Reload ACLT.PGP
SAVEFILE	"aclt.sv$"	PREFERENCES	(CFG)(RO) Default path for automatic file saves.
SAVENAME	""	SAVEAS	(RO)(NS) Stores the file name of the saved drawing.
SAVETIME	120	PREFERENCES	(CFG) Default time interval between automatic file saves, in minutes. Value 0 turns off the feature.
SCREENSIZE(*)	—	—	(RO) Size of the current viewport, in pixels.
SHADEDGE	3	SHADE	Controls edge and face display from SHADE: 0 = Faces shaded, edges not highlighted 1 = Faces shaded, edges in background color. 2 = Faces not filled, edges in object color. 3 = Faces in object color, edges in background color.

Variable Name	Initial Value	Command Name	Description
SHADEDIF	70	SHADE	Percentage of diffuse reflective light to ambient light.
SNAPANG	0	DDRMODES, SNAP	The angle of SNAP/GRID rotation in the current viewport and UCS.
SNAPBASE	0.0000,0.0000	DDRMODES, SNAP	SNAP/GRID base point in the current viewport and UCS.
SNAPISOPAIR	0	DDRMODES, SNAP	Current viewport isoplane: [^E], [F5] 0 = Left 1 = Top 2 = Right
SNAPMODE	0	DDRMODES, SNAP	Snap state of current [^B], [F9] viewport: 0 = Off 1 = On
SNAPSTYL	0	DDRMODES, SNAP	Snap style of current viewport: 0 = Standard 1 = Isometric
SNAPUNIT	0.5000,0.50000	DDRMODES, SNAP	Snap X,Y increment of current viewport.
SORTENTS(*)	96	DDSELECT	(CFG) Controls display of object sort order. Value is the sum of: 0 = Disabled 1 = Object selection 2 = Object snap 4 = Redraws 8 = MSLIDE creation 16 = REGENs 32 = Plotting 64 = PostScript output

continues

Variable Name	Initial Value	Command Name	Description
SPLFRAME	0	—	Shows control polygons for spline-fit polylines, meshes of surface-fit polygons, and invisible 3DFACE edges: 0 = Off 1 = On
SPLINESEGS	8	—	Number of line segments per spline-fit polyline.
SPLINETYPE	6	—	Controls the type of curve generated by PEDIT spline: 5 = Quadratic B-spline 6 = Cubic B-spline
SYSCODEPAGE	"ansi_1252"	—	(RO) System code page.
TABMODE(*)		—	(NS) Controls tablet use: 0 = Off 1 = On
TARGET(*)	0.0000,0.0000,0.0000	DVIEW	(RO) UCS coordinates of the target point in the current viewport.
TDCREATE	—	TIME	(RO) Creation time of the current drawing, in Julian format.
TDINDWG	varies	TIME	(RO) Total editing time elapsed on the current drawing, in Julian format.
TDUPDATE	varies	TIME	(RO) Date and time the drawing was last saved, in Julian format.
TDUSRTIMER	varies	TIME	(RO) User-controlled elapsed time, in Julian format.

Variable Name	Initial Value	Command Name	Description
TEXTFILL(*)	0	TEXT	Controls the filling of Bitstream, TrueType, and Adobe Type 1 fonts: 0 = Outline only 1 = Filled images
TEXTQLTY(*)	50	TEXT	Controls the resolution of Bitstream, TrueType, and Adobe Type 1 fonts: 0-100 (higher values yield better resolution).
TEXTSIZE	0.2000	TEXT	Default height for new text objects.
TEXTSTYLE	"STANDARD"	TEXT, STYLE	Default style for new text objects.
THICKNESS	0.0000	ELEV	Current 3D thickness.
TILEMODE	1	TILEMODE	Enables and disables paper space, viewport objects: 0 = Off 1 = On
TOOLTIPS(*)	1	—	(CFG) Controls the display of ToolTips: 0 = Off 1 = On
TRIMMODE(*)	1	FILLET, CHAMFER	(NS) Controls whether AutoCAD LT trims selected edges for fillets and chamfers: 0 = Leave edges intact 1 = Trim edges back
UCSFOLLOW(*)	0	—	Controls automatic display of plan view in the current viewport

continues

Variable Name	Initial Value	Command Name	Description
			when switching to a new UCS: 0 = Off 1 = On
UCSICON	0	UCSICON	Controls display of the UCS icon. Value is sum of the following: 0 = Off 1 = On 2 = At origin
UCSNAME(*)	""	DDUCS, UCS	(RO) Current UCS name for the current space.
UCSORG(*)	0.0000,0.0000,0.0000	DDUCS, UCS	(RO) The WCS origin of the current UCS for the current space.
UCSXDIR(*)	1.0000,0.0000,0.0000	DDUCS, UCS	(RO) The X direction of the current UCS.
UCSYDIR(*)	0.0000,1.0000,0.0000	DDUCS, UCS	(RO) The Y direction of the current UCS.
UNITMODE	0	—	Controls the display of user input of fractions, feet and inches, and surveyor's angles: 0 = per LUNITS 1 = As input
USERI1-5(*)	0	—	User integer variables. USERI1 to USERI5. Not listed by SETVAR.
USERR1-5(*)	0.0000	—	User real variables. USERR1 to USERR5. Not listed by SETVAR.
VIEWCTR(*)	—	ZOOM, PAN, VIEW	(RO) The X,Y view center point of the current viewport.

Variable Name	Initial Value	Command Name	Description
VIEWDIR(*)	0.0000,0.0000,1.0000	DVIEW	(RO) The camera point offset from the target in the WCS.
VIEWMODE(*)	0	DVIEW, UCS	(RO) Current viewport's viewing mode. Value is sum of the following: 0 = Disabled 1 = Perspective 2 = Front clipping on 4 = Back clipping on 8 = UCSFOLLOW On 16 = FRONTZ offset in use
VIEWSIZE(*)	varies	ZOOM, VIEW	(RO) Current view height, in drawing units.
VIEWTWIST(*)	0	DVIEW	(RO) Current viewport's view-twist angle.
VISRETAIN	0	VISRETAIN	Controls retention of XREF file layer setting in the current drawing: 0 = Off 1 = On
VSMAX(*)	varies	ZOOM, PAN, VIEW	(RO) The upper right X,Y coordinate of the current viewport's virtual screen for the current UCS.
VSMIN(*)	varies	ZOOM, PAN, VIEW	(RO) The lower left X,Y coordinate of the current viewport's virtual screen for the current UCS.

continues

Variable Name	Initial Value	Command Name	Description
WORLDUCS(*)	1	UCS	(NS)(RO) Indicates whether current UCS = WCS: 0 = No 1 = Yes
WORLDVIEW	1	DVIEW,UCS	Controls automatic switch of UCS to the WCS during DVIEW and VPOINT commands: 0 = No 1 = Yes
XREFCTL	0	—	(CFG) Controls creation of XREF results logfile: 0 = No XLG file 1 = Create XLG file

B

DIMENSIONING VARIABLES

This appendix contains a table of a subset of the system variables referred to as the dimensioning variables. Dimensioning variables contain the settings that affect the drawing of dimensions. It is far easier to set the dimension variables through the Dimension Styles dialog box. When dealing with dimension overrides and programming menu macros, however, you will need to know what the various dimension variables are and what they do.

The default values given in the table are the same as would be found in a drawing started from scratch. A brief description is given for each variable, and the valid values are listed and explained. All values are saved with the drawing unless noted with ConFiGuration file (CFG), or Not Saved (NS). A variable marked (RO) is read-only, which means the variable's value can be read but not changed.

Note: Variable names and features shown in bold are new in Version 3.0.

Variable Name	Default Setting	Variable Description
DIMALT	Off	Enables alternate units dimensioning. Enter Off (or 0) or On (or 1) for the value.
DIMALTD	2	The decimal precision of the alternate units if DIMALT is enabled.
DIMALTF	25.4000	The scale factor of the alternate units when DIMALT is enabled. The measured distance is multiplied by DIMALTF to produce the alternate dimension.
DIMALTTD	**2**	**The number of decimal places for tolerance values in alternate units dimension.**
DIMALTTZ	**0**	**Toggles suppression of zeros for alternate unit dimension values:** **0 = Off** **1 = On**
DIMALTU	**2**	**Unit format for alternate units of all dimension families except angular:** **1 = Scientific** **2 = Decimal** **3 = Engineering** **4 = Architectural (stacked)** **5 = Fractional (stacked)** **6 = Architectural** **7 = Fractional**
DIMALTZ	**0**	**Toggles suppression of zeroes for alternate unit dimension values:** **0 = Off** **1 = On**
DIMAPOST	""	The user-defined prefix or suffix for alternative dimension text.
DIMASO	On	Enables associative dimensioning. Enter Off (or 0) or On (or 1) for the value.

Variable Name	Default Setting	Variable Description
DIMASZ	0.1800	Controls the size of dimension and leader line arrows. Controls the length of the hook lines. Also affects the fit of dimension text inside dimension lines. Has no affect when DIMTSZ is set to a non-zero value.

DIMAUNIT	**0**	**Angle format for Angular dimensions:**
		    0 = Decimal degrees
		    1 = Degrees/minutes/seconds
		    2 = Gradians
		    3 = Radians
		    4 = Surveyor's units

DIMBLK	""	Name of block to draw in place of the standard arrows, dots, or ticks.
DIMBLK1	""	Name of the block for the first end of dimension lines when DIMSAH is enabled.
DIMBLK2	""	Name of the block for the second end of dimension lines when DIMSAH is enabled.

DIMCEN	0.0900	Controls center marks or center lines drawn by DIM commands with radii:
		    0 = No center marks or lines
		    <0 = Center lines are drawn
		    >0 = Center marks are drawn
		
		The absolute value specifies the length of the mark portion of the center line.

DIMCLRD	0	Controls the color of the dimension line, arrowhead, and leader line. Enter any valid color number, or one of the following:
		    0 = BYBLOCK
		    256 = BYLAYER

DIMCLRE	0	Controls the dimension extension lines' color (see DIMCLRD).
DIMCLRT	0	The dimension text's color (see DIMCLRD).

continues

Variable Name	Default Setting	Variable Description
DIMDEC	4	**The number of decimal places for the primary units dimension.**
DIMDLE	0.0000	Controls the dimension line's extension distance beyond extension lines when ticks are drawn (when DIMTSZ is non-zero).
DIMDLI	0.3800	The offset distance between successive baseline dimensions.
DIMEXE	0.1800	Controls the length of the extension lines beyond the dimension line.
DIMEXO	0.0625	Controls the offset distance from the point being dimensioned to the start of the extension line.
DIMFIT	3	**Controls the placement of text and arrowheads inside or outside extension lines based on the available space between the extension lines.**
		0 = Place text and arrow between extension lines if enough space; otherwise, place outside.
		1 = Place text and arrows between extension lines when space allows; otherwise, place text between extension lines and arrowheads outside. If there is no room for either text or arrowheads, place both outside.
		2 = Place text and arrows between extension lines when space allows; otherwise, place arrowheads between extension lines and text outside. If there is no room for either text or arrowheads, place both outside.

Variable Name	Default Setting	Variable Description
		3 = Place text and arrows between extension lines when space allows; otherwise, place text or arrowheads between extension lines, whichever fits. If there is no room for either text or arrowheads, place both outside.
		4 = Creates leader lines when there is not enough space for text between extension lines. Also allows the dimension text to be moved.
		5 = Allows dimension text to be moved but, unlike 4, does not automatically draw leader lines.
DIMGAP	0.0900	The space between the text and the dimension line; determines when text is placed outside a dimension. A negative gap value creates basic dimensions.
DIMJUST	**0**	**Controls the horizontal dimension text position:**
		0 = Center-justifies the text.
		1 = Positions text next to left extension line.
		2 = Positions text next to second extension line.
		3 = Positions text above and aligned with first extension line.
		4 = Positions text above and aligned with second extension line.
DIMLFAC	1.0000	The measured distance is multiplied by the DIMLFAC value to get the final primary

continues

Variable Name	Default Setting	Variable Description
		dimension text. When the value is set to a negative value and tilemode is off, the absolute value is used when dimensioning in paper space but is ignored and set to 1 when dimensioning in floating model space.
DIMLIM	Off	Generates dimension limits when enabled. Enter On (or 1) or Off (or 0). Enabling DIMLIM automatically enables DIMTOL.
DIMPOST	""	The user-defined prefix or suffix for dimension text, such as "mm". When the text is entered by itself, the text is used as a suffix. If the text is followed by "<>", then it is used as a prefix. If two text strings separated by "<>" are entered, both a prefix and suffix are created.
DIMRND	0.0000	The rounding factor used to round linear dimension text.
DIMSAH	Off	Enables the use of DIMBLK1 and DIMBLK2 instead of DIMBLK or the standard arrowheads, dots, or ticks. Enter On (or 1) or Off (or 0).
DIMSCALE	1.0000	The overall scale factor applied to numerical dimension variables that define the lengths and sizes used in drawing dimensions. When set to 0, paper space scaling is enabled.
DIMSD1	**Off**	**Suppresses the display of the dimension line and arrowhead between the first extension line and the text. Enter On (or 1) or Off (or 0).**
DIMSD2	**Off**	**Suppresses the display of the dimension line and arrowhead between the second extension line and the text. Enter On (or 1) or Off (or 0).**

Variable Name	Default Setting	Variable Description
DIMSE1	Off	Suppresses the display of the first extension line. Enter On (or 1) or Off (or 0).
DIMSE2	Off	Suppresses the display of the second extension line. Enter On (or 1) or Off (or 0).
DIMSHO	On	Determines whether associative dimension text is updated during dragging operation. Enter On (or 1) or Off (or 0).
DIMSOXD	Off	Suppresses the display of dimension lines outside the extension lines but only if DIMTIX is enabled. Enter On (or 1) or Off (or 0).
DIMSTYLE	"STANDARD"	(RO) Holds the name of the current dimension style.
DIMTAD	0	Controls vertical position of dimension text relative to the dimension line: 0 = Centers text between extension lines. 1 = Places the text above dimension line except when dimension line is not horizontal and text inside lines is forced horizontal (DIMTIH = 1); the current DIMGAP value sets the distance from dimension line to baseline of lowest line of text. 2 = Places the text on the side of the dimension line farthest away from the extension line origin points. 3 = Places the text to conform to a JIS representation.
DIMTDEC	4	Controls the number of decimal places used for tolerance values for the primary units dimension.

continues

Variable Name	Default Setting	Variable Description
DIMTFAC	1.0000	Scale factor applied to the dimension tolerance's text height relative to the dimension text size. Also applied to the fraction when stacked fractions are enabled.
DIMTIH	On	Forces dimension text inside the extension lines to be positioned horizontally rather than aligned. Enter On (or 1) or Off (or 0).
DIMTIX	Off	Forces dimension text inside extension lines. Enter On (or 1) or Off (or 0).
DIMTM	0.0000	The negative tolerance value used when DIMTOL or DIMLIM is on.
DIMTOFL	Off	Draws dimension line between extension lines even if text is placed outside the extension lines. Enter On (or 1) or Off (or 0).
DIMTOH	On	Forces dimension text to be positioned horizontally rather than aligned when it falls outside the extension lines. Enter On (or 1) or Off (or 0).
DIMTOL	Off	Enables the drawing of tolerance values. Enter On (or 1) or Off (or 0).
DIMTOLJ	**1**	**Sets vertical justification for tolerance values relative to nominal dimension text:** **0 = Bottom** **1 = Middle** **2 = Top**
DIMTP	0.0000	The positive tolerance value used when DIMTOL or DIMLIM is on.
DIMTSZ	0.0000	When assigned a non-zero value, forces tick marks (rather than arrows) to be drawn at the size specified by the value. Also affects the placement of the dimension line and text between extension lines.

Variable Name	Default Setting	Variable Description
DIMTVP	0.0000	When set to a non-zero value and when DIMTAD is disabled, the dimension text is offset from the dimension line by a distance equal to DIMTVP multiplied by the dimension text size. Setting DIMTVP equal to 1 is equivalent to enabling DIMTAD.
DIMTXSTY	**"STANDARD"**	**The text style of the dimension.**
DIMTXT	0.1800	Height of the dimension text, unless the current text style has a fixed height.
DIMTZIN	**0**	**Controls suppression of zeros for tolerance values:** **0 = Off** **1 = On**
DIMUNIT	**2**	**Sets units for all dimension style family members except angular:** **1 = Scientific** **2 = Decimal** **3 = Engineering** **4 = Architectural (stacked)** **5 = Fractional (stacked)** **6 = Architectural** **7 = Fractional**
DIMUPT	**Off**	**Controls cursor functionality for user positioned text:** **0 = Cursor controls only dimension line location.** **1 = Cursor controls text position as well as dimension line location.**
DIMZIN	0	Suppresses the display of zero inches or zero feet in dimension text, and leading or trailing zeros in decimal dimension text:

continues

Variable Name	Default Setting	Variable Description
		0 = Suppresses zero feet and zero inches.
		1 = Includes zero feet and zero inches.
		2 = Includes zero feet and suppresses zero inches.
		3 = Includes zero inches and suppresses zero feet.
		4 = Suppress Leading zeros.
		8 = Suppress Trailing zeros.
		12 = Suppress Both leading and trailing zeros.

C

COMMAND, DIALOG BOX, MENU, TOOL, AND ALIAS EQUIVALENTS

This appendix contains a table of AutoCAD LT commands with their dialog box names, and the pull-down menu items and tools that issue them (table C.1). It also contains a table of command aliases (table C.2).

In the **Command Name** column, names shown in **bold** are new in AutoCAD LT for Windows 95. Many menu items and tools issue specific options along with commands. For example, the View, Zoom, All menu item and the Zoom All tool both issue the ZOOM command with the All option. These options are indicated in the **Pull-Down Menu, Item** column for those menu items and tools. In many cases, multiple options are issued; these are shown separated by commas.

Commands preceded by an apostrophe (') can be executed *transparently*.

In the **Dialog Box** column, the names shown are those that appear in the dialog box title bar.

In the **Pull-Down Menu, Item** column, items are shown in the form *Menuname, childmenuname, menuitemname.* For example, View, Zoom, All translates to "Choose View to open the View pull-down menu, then choose Zoom to open the Zoom child menu, then choose All to issue the ZOOM command with the All option." A few commands, such as OPEN, have keyboard shortcuts, such as Ctrl+O; these are shown in their pull-down menu item labels—such as File, Open Ctrl+O—and are therefore shown in the **Pull-Down Menu, Item** column.

Tools are listed in the form *Toolname (Toolbarname, Flyoutname *)*; for example, *3 Points (Draw, Arc)* translates to "From the Arc flyout of the Draw toolbar, choose 3 Points to issue the ARC command." The tool names are those that appear in the ToolTips, and the toolbar names and flyout names are those that appear in their title bars when open as floating toolbars. Of course, if the 3 Points tool is the current default (last-used) tool from the Arc flyout, it will appear on the Draw toolbar and can be directly chosen. If the Arc flyout is currently open as an individual toolbar, you can choose 3 Points directly from it. Tool names shown in **bold** are the default tools of their flyouts. These tools are the ones that initially appear (each time you start AutoCAD LT) on the parent toolbar and in the ToolTip of the tool that opens the flyout; however, during an AutoCAD LT session after you have used another tool from the flyout, it becomes the current default tool.

*If the tool name is not part of a flyout on the indicated toolbar, the flyout name is omitted.

Table C.1

Command, Dialog Box, Menu, Tool Equivalents

Command Name	Dialog Box	Pull-Down Menu, Item	Tool Name (Toolbar, Flyout)
.X			**X** (Standard, X Coordinate)
.XY			XY (Standard, X,Y Coordinate)
.XZ			XZ (Standard, X,Z Coordinate)
.Y			Y (Standard, Y Coordinate)
.YZ			YZ (Standard, Y,Z Coordinate)
.Z			Z (Standard, Z Coordinate)
3DPOLY			
ABOUT	AUTOCAD(R) LT	Help, About AutoCAD LT	
APERTURE			

Command Name	Dialog Box	Pull-Down Menu, Item	Tool Name (Toolbar, Flyout)
ARC		Draw, Arc,	
		Start, Center, End	Arc Start Center End (Draw, Arc)
		Start, Center, Angle	Arc Start Center Angle (Draw, Arc)
		Start, End, Angle	Arc Start End Angle (Draw, Arc)
		Center, Start, End	Arc Center Start End (Draw, Arc)
		Center, Start, Angle	Arc Center Start Angle (Draw, Arc)
		3 Points	Arc 3 Points (Draw, Arc)
		Continue	Arc Continue (Draw, Arc)
AREA			Area (Object Properties, List)
ARRAY		Modify, Array,	
		Rectangular	Rectangular Array (Modify, Duplicate Object)
		Polar	Polar Array (Modify, Duplicate Object)
ATTDEF			
'ATTDISP		Options, Display, Attribute Display	
ATTEDIT		Modify, Objects, Attribute, Global	**Edit Attribute Globally** (Attribute)
ATTEXT	Select Template File		

continues

Command Name	Dialog Box	Pull-Down Menu, Item	Tool Name (Toolbar, Flyout)
AUDIT		File, Management, Audit	
BHATCH	Boundary Hatch	Draw, Hatch	**Hatch** (Draw)
BLIPMODE		Options, Drawing Aids	
BLOCK			
BMAKE	Block Definition	Draw, Make Block	Block (Draw, Make Block)
BMPOUT	Create BMP File	File, Export	
BOUNDARY	Boundary Creation	Draw, Boundary	Boundary (Draw, Polygon)
BPOLY	Boundary Creation		
BREAK		Modify, Break,	
		1 Point	**1 Point** (Modify, 1 Point)
		1 Point Select	1 Point Select (Modify, 1 Point)
		2 Points	2 Points (Modify, 1 Point)
		2 Points Select	2 Points Select (Modify, 1 Point)
CHAMFER		Modify, Chamfer	**Chamfer** (Modify)
CHANGE			
CHPROP			
CIRCLE		Draw, Circle,	
		Center, Radius	**Circle Center Radius** (Draw, Circle)
		Center, Diameter	Circle Center Diameter (Draw, Circle)
		3 Point	Circle 3 Point (Draw, Circle)
		Tan, Tan, Radius	Circle Tan Tan Radius (Draw, Circle)
COLOR			
COORDS		Options, Coordinate Display	

Command Name	Dialog Box	Pull-Down Menu, Item	Tool Name (Toolbar, Flyout)
COPY		Modify, Duplicate	**Duplicate Object** (Modify, Duplicate Object)
COPYCLIP		Edit, Copy Ctrl+C	**Copy** (Standard)
COPYEMBED			
COPYHIST			
COPYLINK		Edit, Copy Link	
CUTCLIP		Edit, Cut Ctrl+X	**Cut** (Standard)
DBTRANS			
'DDATTDEF	Attribute Definition	Draw, Define Attribute	**Define Attribute** (Attribute)
DDATTE	Edit Attributes	Modify, Objects, Attribute, Single	**Edit Attribute** (Attribute)
'DDATTEXT	Attribute Extraction		
'DDCHPROP	Change Properties		
'DDCOLOR	Select Color	Format, Color	**Color Control** (Object Properties)
DDEDIT	Edit Text	Modify, Objects, Edit Text	Edit Text (Modify, Edit Polyline)
'DDEMODES	Current Properties	Format, Current Properties	**Object Creation** (Object Properties)
'DDGRIPS	Grips	Options, Grips	
DDIM	Dimension Styles	Format, Dimension Style	**Dimension Styles** (Dimensioning, Dimension Styles)
'DDINSERT	Insert	Draw, Insert Block	**Insert Block** (Draw, Insert Block)
'DDLMODES	Layer Control	Format, Layers	**Layers** (Object Properties)

continues

Command Name	Dialog Box	Pull-Down Menu, Item	Tool Name (Toolbar, Flyout)
'DDLTYPE	Select Linetype	Format, Linetype	**Linetype** (Object Properties)
'DDMODIFY	Modify *ObjectName*	Edit, Properties	Properties (Object Properties)
'DDOSNAP	Running Object Snap	Options, Running Object Snap	Running Object Snap (Standard, Snap From)
'DDPTYPE	Point Style	Format, Point Style	
'DDRENAME	Rename	Format, Rename	
'DDRMODES	Drawing Aids	Options, Drawing Aids	
'DDSELECT	Object Selection Settings	Options, Selection	
'DDSTYLE	Text Style	Format, Text Style	
DDUCS	UCS Control	View, Set UCS, Named UCS	Named UCS (Standard, Named UCS)
'DDUCSP	UCS Orientation	View, Set UCS, Preset UCS	**Preset UCS** (Standard, Named UCS)
'DDUNITS	Units Control	Format, Units	
'DDVIEW	View Control	View, Named Views	**Named Views** (Standard, Named Views)
DELAY			
DIM			
DIM1			
DIMALIGNED		Dimension, Aligned	**Aligned Dimension** (Dimensioning)
DIMANGULAR		Dimension, Angular	**Angular Dimension** (Dimensioning)
DIMBASELINE		Dimension, Baseline	**Baseline Dimension** (Dimensioning)
DIMCENTER		Dimension, Center Mark	**Center Mark** (Dimensioning)

Command Name	Dialog Box	Pull-Down Menu, Item	Tool Name (Toolbar, Flyout)
DIMCONTINUE		Dimension, Continue	**Continue Dimension** (Dimensioning)
DIMDIAMETER		Dimension, Radial, Diameter	Diameter Dimension (Dimensioning, Radius Dimension)
DIMEDIT			
O		Dimension, Oblique	
DIMLINEAR		Dimension, Linear	**Linear Dimension** (Dimensioning)
DIMORDINATE		Dimension, Ordinate, Automatic	**Ordinate Dimension** (Dimensioning, Ordinate Dimension)
		X-Datum	X-Datum (Dimensioning, Ordinate Dimension)
		Y-Datum	Y-Datum (Dimensioning, Ordinate Dimension)
DIMOVERRIDE			
DIMRADIUS		Dimension, Radial, Radius	**Radius Dimension** (Dimensioning, Radius Dimension)
DIMSTYLE			
DIMTEDIT		Dimension, Align Text,	
		Home	**Home** (Dimensioning, Home)
		Rotate	Rotate (Dimensioning, Home)
		Left	Left (Dimensioning, Home)
		Right	Right (Dimensioning, Home)

continues

Command Name	Dialog Box	Pull-Down Menu, Item	Tool Name (Toolbar, Flyout)
'DIST			Distance (Object Properties, List)
DIVIDE		Draw, Point, Divide	Divide (Draw, Point)
DONUT		Draw, Circle, Donut	Donut (Draw, Circle)
DSVIEWER			**Aerial View** (Standard, Aerial View)
DTEXT		Draw, Text, Line Text	Dtext (Draw, Paragraph Text, Line Text)
DVIEW		View, 3D Dynamic View	
DXFIN	Select.DXF File		
DXFOUT	Create.DXF File		
ELEV			
ELLIPSE		Draw, Ellipse, Center	**Ellipse Center** (Draw, Ellipse)
		Axis, End	Ellipse Axis End (Draw, Ellipse)
		Arc	Ellipse Arc (Draw, Ellipse)
END			
ERASE		Edit, Clear	**Erase** (Modify)
EXIT		File, Exit	
EXPLODE		Modify, Explode	**Explode** (Modify)
EXPORT	Export Data	File, Export	
EXTEND		Modify, Extend	Extend (Modify, Trim)
FILEOPEN			
'FILL		Options, Drawing Aids	
FILLET		Modify, Fillet	Fillet (Modify, Chamfer)
GETENV			
'GRAPHSCR			

Command Name	Dialog Box	Pull-Down Menu, Item	Tool Name (Toolbar, Flyout)
'GRID		Options, Drawing Aids (or double-click Status Bar)	
GRIPS		Options, Grips	
HANDLES			
HATCH			
HATCHEDIT	Hatchedit	Modify, Objects, Edit Hatch	Edit Hatch (Modify, Edit Polyline)
'HELP		Help	**Help** (Standard)
HIDE			
'HIGHLIGHT		Options, Drawing Aids	
'ID			Point Location (Object Properties, List)
IMPORT	Import File	File, Import	
INSERT			
INSERTOBJ	Insert New Object	Edit, Insert Object	
'ISOPLANE		Options, Drawing Aids	
'LAYER			
LEADER		Dimension, Leader	**Leader** (Dimensioning)
LENGTHEN		Modify, Lengthen	Lengthen (Modify, Stretch)
'LIMITS		Format, Drawing Limits	
LINE		Draw, Line	**Line** (Draw, Line)
'LINETYPE			
LIST			**List** (Object Properties, List)
LOGFILEOFF			
LOGFILEON			

continues

Command Name	Dialog Box	Pull-Down Menu, Item	Tool Name (Toolbar, Flyout)
'LTSCALE		Options, Linetypes, Global Linetype Scale	
MAKEPREVIEW			
MEASURE		Draw, Point, Measure	Measure (Draw, Point)
MENULOAD	Menu Customization	Tools, Customize Menus	
MENUUNLOAD	Menu Customization	Tools, Customize Menus	
MIRROR		Modify, Mirror	Mirror (Modify, Duplicate Object)
MOVE		Modify, Move	Move (Modify)
MSLIDE	Create Slide File	File, Slide, Create	
MSPACE		View, Model Space (Floating) (or) Model Space (Tiled)	
MTEXT		Draw, Text, Paragraph Text	Paragraph **Text** (Draw, Paragraph Text)
MTPROP			
MULTIPLE			
MVIEW		View, Floating Viewports	Model Space (Floating) (Standard, Model Space)
NEW	Create New Drawing	File, New	**New** (Standard)
OFFSET		Modify, Offset	Offset (Modify, Duplicate Object)
OLELINKS		Edit, Links	
OOPS			Oops! (Modify, Erase)
OPEN	Open Drawing	File, Open Ctrl+O	**Open** (Standard)
'ORTHO		Options, Drawing Aids (or double-click Status Bar)	

Command Name	Dialog Box	Pull-Down Menu, Item	Tool Name (Toolbar, Flyout)
'OSNAP			
CEN			Snap to Center (Standard, Snap to Endpoint)
END			Snap to Endpoint (Standard, Snap to Endpoint)
FRO			Snap From (Standard, Snap to Endpoint)
INS			Snap to Insertion (Standard, Snap to Endpoint)
INT			Snap to Intersection (Standard, Snap to Endpoint)
MID			Snap to Midpoint (Standard, Snap to Endpoint)
NEA			Snap to Nearest (Standard, Snap to Endpoint)
NOD			Snap to Node (Standard, Snap to Endpoint)
NON			Snap to None (Standard, Snap to Endpoint)
PER			Snap to Perpendicular (Standard, Snap to Endpoint)
QUA			Snap to Quadrant (Standard, Snap to Endpoint)

continues

Command Name	Dialog Box	Pull-Down Menu, Item	Tool Name (Toolbar, Flyout)
TAN			Snap to Tangent (Standard, Snap to Endpoint)
TK			Tracking (Standard, Snap to Endpoint)
PAINTER			Property Painter (Standard)
'PAN		View, Pan, Real-Time Pan	Real-Time Pan (Standard, Real-Time Pan)
		Pan Point	Pan Point (Standard, Real-Time Pan)
PASTECLIP		Edit, Paste Ctrl+V	**Paste** (Standard)
PASTESPEC	Paste Special	Edit, Paste Special	
PEDIT		Modify, Objects, Edit Polyline	**Edit Polyline** (Modify, Edit Polyline)
PLAN		View, 3D Viewpoint, Plan View	
PLINE		Draw, Polyline	**Polyline** (Draw, Polyline)
'PLINEGEN		Options, Linetypes, Linetype Generation	
PLOT	Plot Configuration	File, Print Ctrl+P	**Print** (Standard)
POINT		Draw, Point, Single Point	**Point** (Draw, Point)
POLYGON		Draw, Polygon, Polygon	Polygon (Draw, Polygon)
PREFERENCES	Preferences	Tools, Preferences	
PSLTSCALE		Options, Linetypes, Paper Space Linetype Scale	
PSOUT	Create PostScript File		

Command Name	Dialog Box	Pull-Down Menu, Item	Tool Name (Toolbar, Flyout)
PSPACE		View, Paper Space	
PURGE		Format, Purge	
QSAVE		File, Save Ctrl+S	**Save** (Standard)
QTEXT		Options, Text, Text Frame Only	
QUIT		File, Exit	
RAY		Draw, Ray	Ray (Draw, Line)
RECOVER	Recover Drawing File	File, Management, Recover	
RECTANG		Draw, Polygon, Rectangle	**Rectangle** (Draw, Polygon)
REDO		Edit, Redo	**Redo** (Standard)
'REDRAW		View, Redraw	**Redraw View** (Standard)
REGEN		View, Regen	
REINIT	Re-initialization	Options, Reinitialize	
RENAME			
RESUME			
REVDATE		Tools, Date and Time Stamp	
ROTATE		Modify, Rotate	**Rotate** (Modify)
RSCRIPT			
'RTPAN		View, Pan, Real-Time Pan	Real-Time Pan (Standard, Real-Time Pan)
'RTZOOM		View, Zoom, Real-Time Zoom	Real-Time Zoom (Standard, Zoom Window)
SAVE		File, Save	
SAVEAS	Save Drawing As	File, Save As	
SCALE		Modify, Scale	Scale (Modify)

continues

Command Name	Dialog Box	Pull-Down Menu, Item	Tool Name (Toolbar, Flyout)
SCRIPT	Select Script File	Tools, Run Script	
SELECT			
W			**Select Window** (Standard, Select Objects)
C			Select Crossing (Standard, Select Objects)
P			Select Previous (Standard, Select Objects)
L			Select Last (Standard, Select Objects)
ALL		Edit, Select All	Select All (Standard, Select Objects)
WP			Select Window Polygon (Standard, Select Objects)
CP			Select Crossing Polygon (Standard, Select Objects)
F			Select Fence (Standard, Select Objects)
A			Select Add (Standard, Select Objects)
R			Select Remove (Standard, Select Objects
SENDMAIL		File, Send	
SETENV			
'SETVAR			
SHADE		View, Shade	
'SNAP		Options, Drawing Aids (or double-click Status Bar)	
SOLID		Draw, 2D Solid	2D Solid (Draw, Rectangle)
SPELL	Check Spelling	Tools, Spelling	**Spelling** (Standard)

Command Name	Dialog Box	Pull-Down Menu, Item	Tool Name (Toolbar, Flyout)
'SPLFRAME		Options, Display, Spline Frame	
SPLINE		Draw, Spline	Spline (Draw, Polyline)
SPLINEDIT		Modify, Objects, Edit Spline	Edit Spline (Modify, Edit Polyline)
STRETCH		Modify, Stretch	**Stretch** (Modify, Stretch)
STYLE			
SYSWINDOWS			
TABLET		Options, Tablet	
TBCONFIG	Customize Toolbars	Tools, Customize Toolbars	
TEXT			
'TEXTFILL		Options, Text, Filled Text	
'TEXTQLTY		Options, Text, Text Quality	
'TEXTSCR	AutoCAD Text Window	View, Text Window	
TILEMODE		View, Model Space (Tiled) (or double-click Status Bar)	**Model Space (Tiled)** (Standard, Model Space (Tiled)
(System variable) 0		View, Paper Space	Paper Space (Standard, Model Space (Tiled)
'TIME		Tools, Time	
TOLERANCE	Symbol	Dimension, Tolerance	**Tolerance** (Dimensioning, Tolerance)
TOOLBAR			
TRACKING			Tracking (Object Snap)
TRIM		Modify, Trim	**Trim** (Modify, Trim)

continues

Command Name	Dialog Box	Pull-Down Menu, Item	Tool Name (Toolbar, Flyout)
U		Edit, Undo Ctrl+Z	**Undo** (Standard)
UCS		View, Set UCS, Named UCS	Named UCS (Standard, Named UCS)
		Preset UCS	Preset UCS (Standard, Named UCS)
O		Origin	Origin UCS (Standard, UCS)
ZA		Z Axis Vector	Z Axis Vector UCS (Standard, UCS)
3		3 Point	3 Point UCS (Standard, UCS)
OB		Object	Object UCS (Standard, UCS)
V		View	View UCS (Standard, UCS)
X		X axis Rotate	X Axis Rotate UCS (Standard, UCS)
Y		Y axis Rotate	Y Axis Rotate UCS (Standard, UCS)
Z		Z axis Rotate	Z Axis Rotate UCS (Standard, UCS)
P		Previous	Previous UCS (Standard, UCS)
R		Restore	Restore UCS (Standard, UCS)
S		Save	Save UCS (Standard, UCS)
D		Delete	
W		World	World UCS (Standard, UCS)
?		List	

Command Name	Dialog Box	Pull-Down Menu, Item	Tool Name (Toolbar, Flyout)
UCSICON		Options, UCS Icon	
UNDO			
'UNITS			
UNLOCK		File, Management, Unlock Files	
'VIEW			
VIEWTOOLBAR		View, Toolbars	
'VISRETAIN		Edit, External Reference, Retain Settings	
VPLAYER			
VPOINT		View, 3D Viewpoint, Tripod	
NON,*0,0,1		Top	Top View (Standard, Named Views)
NON,*0,0,-1		Bottom	Bottom View (Standard, Named Views)
NON,*-1,0,0		Left	Left View (Standard, Named Views)
NON,*1,0,0		Right	Right View (Standard, Named Views)
NON,*0,-1,0		Front	Front View (Standard, Named Views)
NON,0,1,0		Back	Back View (Standard, Named Views)
NON,*-1,-1,1		SW Isometric	SW Isometric View (Standard, Named Views)
NON,*1,-1,1		SE Isometric	SE Isometric View (Standard, Named Views)
NON,*1,1,1		NE Isometric	NE Isometric View (Standard, Named Views)
NON,*-1,1,1		NW Isometric	NW Isometric View (Standard, Named Views)

continues

Command Name	Dialog Box	Pull-Down Menu, Item	Tool Name (Toolbar, Flyout)
VPORTS		View, Tiled Viewports	
VSLIDE	Select Slide File	Files, Slide, View	
WBLOCK			
WMFIN	Import WMF		
WMFOPTS	WMF Import Options		File, Import, Options
WMFOUT	Create WMF File		
XBIND		Edit, External Reference, Bind Symbols	
XLINE		Draw, Construction Line	Construction Line (Draw, Line)
XREF		Edit, External Reference, Attach	
A			Attach (External Reference)
B		Bind	All (External Reference)
D		Detach	Detach (External Reference)
R		Reload	Reload (External Reference)
P		Change Path	Path (External Reference)
?		List	List (External Reference)
O			Overlay (External Reference)
'ZOOM		View, Zoom,	
2X		In	Zoom In (Standard)
.5X		Out	Zoom Out (Standard)
W		Window	**Zoom Window** (Standard, Zoom Window)
All		All	Zoom All (Standard, Zoom Window)

Command Name	Dialog Box	Pull-Down Menu, Item	Tool Name (Toolbar, Flyout)
P		Previous	Zoom Previous (Standard, Zoom Window)
X		Scale	Zoom Scale (Standard, Zoom Window)
C		Center	Zoom Center (Standard, Zoom Window)
E		Extents	Zoom Extents (Standard, Zoom Window)
		Real-Time Zoom	Real-Time Zoom (Standard, Zoom Window)

Command Aliases

Aliases are abbreviations that can be entered at the Command: prompt to issue commands. The following table lists the default aliases found in the standard ACLT.PGP file in the C:\Program Files\AutoCAD LT\ folder. These abbreviations are normally available for use.

A command that begins with DD opens a dialog box.

NOTE

ACLT.PGP is a customizable text file. Prior to making changes, you should backup the original file to another name (such as ACLTPGP.SAV) in the default folder.

Table C.2

Command Aliases

Alias	Command Name
A	ARC
AA	AREA
AB	ABOUT

continues

Alias	Command Name
AD	ATTDEF
AE	ATTEDIT
AP	APERTURE
AR	ARRAY
AT	ATTDISP
AX	ATTEXT
B	BLOCK
BA	BASE
BM	BLIPMODE
BR	BREAK
C	CIRCLE
CC	COPYCLIP
CE	COPYEMBED
CF	CHAMFER
CH	CHANGE
CL	COPYLINK
CO	DDCOLOR
CP	COPY
CR	CHPROP
D	DIM
D1	DIM1
DA	DDRMODES
DAD	DDATTDEF
DAL	DIMALIGNED
DAN	DIMANGULAR
DAX	DDATTEXT
DC	DDCHPROP
DDI	DIMDIAMETER

Alias	Command Name
DE	DDATTE
DI	DIST
DLI	DIMLINEAR
DM	DDIM
DN	DXFIN
DO	DONUT
DOR	DIMORDINATE
DR	DDRENAME
DRA	DIMRADIUS
DS	DSVIEWER
DT	DTEXT
DU	DDUNITS
DUP	COPY
DUPLICATE	COPY
DV	DVIEW
DX	DXFOUT
E	ERASE
ED	DDEDIT
EL	ELLIPSE
EM	DDEMODES
EP	EXPLODE
ET	QUIT
EV	ELEV
EX	EXTEND
EXIT	QUIT
EXP	EXPORT
F	FILLET

continues

Alias	Command Name
FL	FILL
G	GRID
GR	DDGRIPS
H	BHATCH
HE	HATCHEDIT
HI	HIDE
I	DDINSERT
IM	IMPORT
IN	INSERT
IS	ISOPLANE
L	LINE
LA	LAYER
LC	LTSCALE
LD	DDLMODES
LE	LEADER
LEN	LENGTHEN
LM	LIMITS
LS	LIST
LT	DDLTYPE
M	MOVE
MI	MIRROR
MS	MSPACE
MT	MTEXT
MU	MULTIPLE
MV	MVIEW
N	NEW
O	OSNAP

Alias	Command Name
OF	OFFSET
OO	OOPS
OP	OPEN
OR	ORTHO
OS	DDOSNAP
P	PAN
PA	PAINTER
PB	PICKBOX
PC	PASTECLIP
PE	PEDIT
PF	PREFERENCES
PG	POLYGON
PL	PLINE
PN	PLINEGEN
PP	PLOT
PR	PURGE
PS	PSPACE
PT	POINT
PU	PSOUT
PV	PLAN
Q	QUIT
QT	QTEXT
R	REDRAW
RC	RECTANG
RD	REVDATE
RE	REDO
RG	REGEN

continues

Alias	Command Name
RI	REINIT
RN	RENAME
RO	ROTATE
S	STRETCH
SA	SAVE
SC	SCALE
SD	SHADEDGE
SE	SELECT
SH	SHADE
SL	DDSELECT
SN	SNAP
SO	SOLID
SP	SPLINE
SR	SCRIPT
SS	SAVEAS
ST	DDSTYLE
T	DTEXT
TA	TABLET
TE	DDEDIT
TH	THICKNESS
TI	TIME
TL	TOOLBAR
TM	TILEMODE
TO	TOLERANCE
TR	TRIM
TX	TEXT
UC	DDUCS

Alias	Command Name
UI	UCSICON
UL	UNLOCK
UN	UNDO
UP	DDUCSP
UT	UNITS
V	DDVIEW
VL	VPLAYER
VP	VPOINT
VS	VSLIDE
VW	VIEWPORTS
W	WBLOCK
WI	WMFIN
WO	WMFOUT
X	EXPLODE
XB	XBIND
XL	XLINE
XR	XREF
Z	ZOOM

MENU MAPS

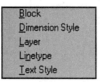

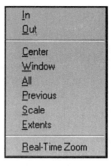

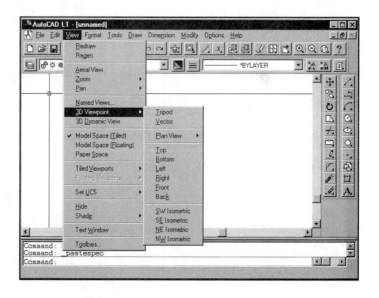

Current
World
Named

---

1 Viewport
2 Viewports
3 Viewports
4 Viewports

Restore
Save
Delete
Join

List

---

1 Viewport
2 Viewports
3 Viewports
4 Viewports

Restore

Viewports On
Viewports Off
Hideplot

Named UCS...
Preset UCS...

World
Origin
Z Axis Vector
3 Point
Object
View
X Axis Rotate
Y Axis Rotate
Z Axis Rotate
Previous

Restore
Save
Delete

List

---

256 Color
256 Color Edge Highlight
16 Color Hidden Line
16 Color Filled

Diffuse

Format

Current Properties...

Layers...
Viewport Layer Controls ▶

Color...
Linetype...
Text Style...
Dimension Style...
Point Style...

Units...
Drawing Limits

Rename...
Purge ▶

Freeze
Thaw

Reset
New Freeze
Default Visibility

List

Layers
Linetypes
Text Styles
Dimension Styles
Blocks

All

Tools

Spelling...

Time
Date and Time Stamp

Run Script...
Customize Menus...
Customize Toolbars...

Preferences...

Draw

Line
Construction Line
Ray

Polyline
Double Line

Spline
Arc   ▸
Circle   ▸
Ellipse   ▸

Polygon   ▸
2D Solid
Point   ▸

Make Block...
Insert Block...

Boundary...
Hatch...

Text   ▸
Define Attribute...

Start, Center, End
Start, Center, Angle
Start, End, Angle
Center, Start, End
Center, Start, Angle
3 Points

Continue

Center, Radius
Center, Diameter

3 Points
Tan, Tan, Radius

Donut

Center
Axis, End

Arc

Rectangle
Polygon

Single Point
Divide
Measure

Paragraph Text
Line Text

Dimension

Linear
Aligned
Radial   ▸
Angular
Ordinate   ▸
Baseline
Continue

Center Mark
Leader
Tolerance...

Oblique
Align Text   ▸
Update

Radius
Diameter

Single...
Global

Automatic
X-Datum
Y-Datum

Rectangular
Polar

Home
Rotate

Left
Right

1 Point
1 Point Select

2 Points
2 Points Select

Modify

Objects ▶

Duplicate
Offset
Mirror
Array ▶

Chamfer
Fillet

Move
Rotate
Stretch
Scale
Lengthen

Trim
Extend
Break ▶
Explode

Options

Drawing Aids...
Running Object Snap...
Coordinate Display

Selection...
Grips...

UCS Icon ▶
Display ▶

Text ▶
Linetypes ▶

Tablet ▶
Reinitialize...

On
Origin

Edit Polyline
Edit Spline
Edit Text...
Edit Hatch...
Attribute ▶

✓ Solid Fill
Spline Frame
Attribute Display ▶

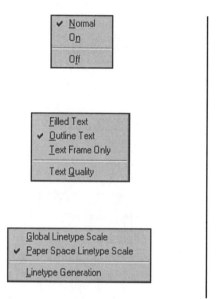

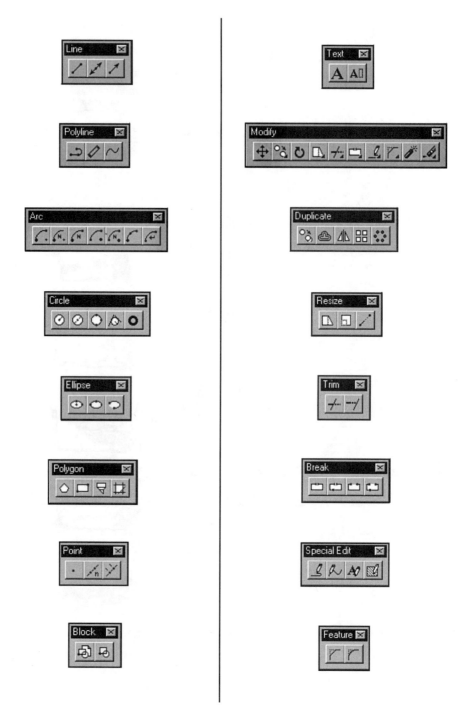

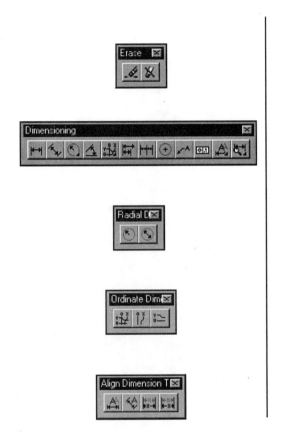

E

INSTALLATION AND SETUP OF AUTOCAD LT FOR WINDOWS 95

The installation of AutoCAD LT for Windows 95 is remarkably straightforward, primarily because of the simplicity with which programs are now designed for installation on a Windows operating system. Discussing all possible configurations and variables in detail is not practical for this appendix. The purpose of this appendix is to acquaint you with the most important setup and configuration issues. This appendix concentrates on the installation of AutoCAD LT on Windows 95, an application that takes full advantage of the multitasking, multithreaded, full 32-bit Windows 95 platform. Specifically, this appendix will cover the following:

■ *Requirements for using AutoCAD LT on Windows 95*

■ *Installing AutoCAD LT on Windows 95*

■ *Configuring the Wintab Digitizer with Windows 95*

Installation Preliminaries

Before installing any software, it is important to confirm that your computer elements (memory, disk space, and peripherals, to name a few) are sufficient for the product. This section presents the necessary minimum requirements for installation of AutoCAD LT for Windows 95.

NOTE

New Riders Publishing has two titles that would be very helpful for increasing your understanding of the Windows 95 and Windows NT platforms that support AutoCAD LT. *Inside Windows 95* and *Windows NT for the Graphics Professional* are substantial resources for optimizing and using applications such as AutoCAD LT on these platforms.

Additional installation information is available in the AutoCAD LT for Windows 95 Installation Guide and the README file that is presented at the completion of a successful installation of the product. For future reference, this README file is named README.HLP and is located in the AutoCAD LT folder.

TIP

You can find valuable information for setting up Windows 95 in the Microsoft Resource Guides for Windows 95 and Windows NT. The Microsoft Knowledge Base, available on the Internet and many online services such as CompuServe and GEnie, also is an invaluable source of information on Windows 95.

Installation Requirements

AutoCAD LT will be distributed on both CD and 3.5" disks and requires the following minimum hardware and software configuration:

- Microsoft Windows 95 or Windows NT 3.51, or later versions. Windows NT 3.51 provides significant performance improvement over earlier versions of Windows NT.

- 486 or Pentium-based system that contains a math coprocessor. 486SX systems require a math coprocessor. In 486DX systems, the math coprocessor is designed into the CPU chip.

- 16 MB of RAM minimum. The more RAM installed in your computer, the faster AutoCAD LT and Windows NT will operate. Moving into 32-bit operating systems will cause a significant increase in speed, but additional RAM is the most efficient investment to increase speed.

- 30 MB of hard disk space for all AutoCAD LT files.

- 32 MB (minimum) of space for a swap file. The swap file space must be created from available contiguous disk space. Autodesk recommends a swap file equal to four times the amount of RAM installed in the system. With the minimum recommended 16 MB RAM installed, the optimal size for the swap file is 64 MB. Additional disk space will be required for the storage of drawing (DWG) files.

- The configuration of a 32 MB paging file with Windows NT.

- A Windows-supported display adapter. A coprocessed or an accelerated graphics card is recommended on production AutoCAD LT systems.

- A pointing device. This device can be a mouse or a digitizing tablet with a stylus or puck. The digitizer must have Wintab support.

- Floppy disk drives. At least one 3.5" (1.44 MB) floppy disk drive is required.

- IBM-compatible parallel port. A parallel port is required for the network and international versions of AutoCAD LT.

Optional hardware includes the following:

- Printer/plotter. You need one or both of these to be able to produce hard-copy output of your drawings.

- Serial port. You need a serial port to use with digitizers and some plotters.

- CD-ROM drive. Software installation from CD-ROM is easier, quicker, and far less painful than installation from floppy disks. Also, large data files and software libraries often are distributed on CD-ROM.

Tɪ P

Use SCANDISK regularly to check the condition of the folders and files on your hard drive. Use DEFRAG regularly to defragment files and optimize the performance of your hard drive.

The Importance of Backup Disks

Although a hard disk crash is rare these days, it does happen. There is also the possibility of computer viruses being transmitted more easily, given the access we have to cyberspace in these times. For these obvious reasons, it is to your advantage to make backup copies of your installation disks. Those of you installing from a CD, simply make a copy of the single installation disk. Those of you not installing from a CD should make a copy of all the release disks, then install from the originals.

Installing the AutoCAD LT Software

The process of installing software over the last few years has gotten very clever. Most applications designed for use with Windows 95 incorporate what's referred to as an installation Wizard. The Wizard is essentially a series of dialog boxes that take you through the process of setting up the installation of the software and typically enable you to make selections specifying the destination folder (directory) name, setup options, and type of installation. This section takes you through the installation setup and shows you the Wizard screens and dialog boxes you will encounter as you install AutoCAD LT on Windows 95.

In the following series of exercises, you are given the options and alternatives available as you set up the installation of AutoCAD LT on Windows 95. Those of you installing AutoCAD LT on Windows NT will see notes or comments specific to your operating system when it differs from that of Windows 95.

WARNING

Prior to the release of AutoCAD LT for Windows 95, Autodesk issued a warning stating that the installation program does not execute properly when Stacker™ 4.1 is installed. Make sure Stacker™ 4.1 is not installed on the computer onto which you are loading AutoCAD LT. Refer to your Stacker manual(s) for instructions and procedures before attempting to uninstall Stacker.

SETTING UP THE INSTALLATION OF AutoCAD LT

1. Insert the AutoCAD LT for Windows 95 CD and installation disk in the appropriate drives. If you are not installing from the CD, insert the installation Disk 1 in the floppy drive.

2. If you are installing AutoCAD LT onto Windows 95, do the following:

Choose Start from the Windows 95 Taskbar, then choose Run and you will see the Run dialog box shown in figure E.1.

Figure E.1

The Run dialog box for Windows 95.

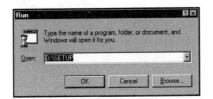

If you are installing AutoCAD LT onto Windows NT, do the following:

From the File Manager menu, choose File, then choose Run.

3. In the Run dialog box, enter the following, similar to that shown in figure E.1, then choose OK:

\<CD-ROM drive\>:\SETUP

If you are installing from floppies, replace the CD-ROM drive letter with the floppy drive letter in the previous step.

4. After the setup routine has been specified, the InstallShield Wizard will be loaded and you will see the progress indicator shown in figure E.2.

Figure E.2

The InstallShield Wizard preparation dialog box.

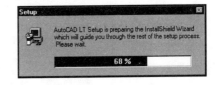

5. Once the installation Wizard has been prepared you see the Welcome dialog box displayed in figure E.3.

Figure E.3

The InstallShield Wizard
Welcome dialog box.

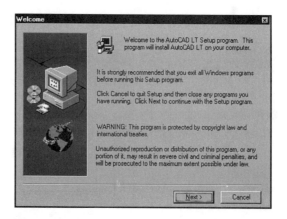

NOTE

If you have an existing version of AutoCAD LT you will be prompted to create backups of existing data files. To save the previous version of AutoCAD LT, *do not* accept the default name displayed in the dialog box. Install AutoCAD LT for Windows 95 into a new folder with an appropriate name.

Choosing Cancel from any of the setup dialog boxes will display the Exit Setup dialog box shown in figure E.4. If you mistakenly choose Cancel, choose Resume to continue with the installation. If you choose Exit Setup, you will be returned to the Windows 95 (or Windows NT) display from which you began to install AutoCAD LT.

If you install AutoCAD LT the next time, the installation process will overwrite any remaining files from the original installation attempt. If, however, you choose to install LT into a different folder, you are obligated to delete the files that remain in the folder specified during the first attempt.

Figure E.4

The Exit Setup dialog box.

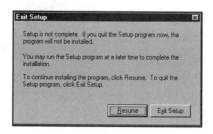

WARNING

Autodesk has also stated that minimizing the Setup window while installing AutoCAD LT will cause the setup to stop running. To restore Setup, choose the minimized icon on the Windows 95 Taskbar with the right mouse button, then choose Restore from the screen menu. Setup cannot be restored by using Alt+Tab or by choosing the icon from the Windows 95 Taskbar. After the Setup window is restored, the progress indicator disappears, dialog boxes do not appear, and the personalization information is removed from the personalization disk.

The next series of steps takes you through the installation setup dialog boxes and explains the options presented.

THE AUTOCAD LT INSTALLATION SETUP

1. From the Welcome dialog box choose Next and you see the AutoCAD LT Setup dialog box shown in figure E.5 requesting you to insert the installation diskette.

Figure E.5

The AutoCAD LT Setup dialog box.

2. Insert the installation disk into the appropriate drive (A:\ or B:\), then choose OK.

3. In the AutoCAD LT 3.0 Personalization dialog box (see fig. E.6), enter the necessary information in the two fields, then choose Next.

Figure E.6

The AutoCAD LT 3.0 Personalization dialog box.

4. In the Choose Destination Location dialog box, the default directory (folder) for the AutoCAD LT program files is displayed in the Destination Directory area at the bottom of the dialog box (see fig. E.7).

Figure E.7

The Choose Destination Location dialog box.

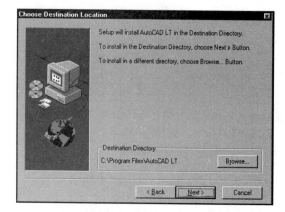

5. To change the default directory, choose Browse; otherwise, choose Next to move to the Setup type dialog box.

6. Make your selection of the setup type you want to install based on the following coverage of the different AutoCAD LT setup types.

The next series of AutoCAD LT Setup dialog boxes provides you with options for the type of LT installation. Figure E.8 shows the dialog box that displays the three types of AutoCAD LT installations.

Figure E.8

The AutoCAD LT Setup type dialog box.

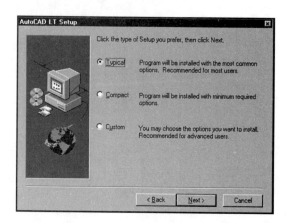

The following list explains the result and benefit of the different types of installation and the dialog box(es) that accompany each.

- **Typical:** This installation type is recommended and automatically installs the most commonly selected features and includes the following:

  - Executables and Support files

  - US Dictionary

  - TrueType©, PostScript© and default AutoCAD LT fonts

  - Sample Drawings

  - Tutorial, Orientation, and AutoCAD LT help learning tools

  Elements not included in this typical installation type are the ClipArt and Template files.

- **Compact:** The Compact installation type installs only the Executable and Support files as stated in the dialog box shown in figure E.9. If you decide you want to install other elements, you can re-install AutoCAD LT and choose the Custom installation type. The Compact type is obviously the most efficient for those systems with limited disk space, memory, or laptops with similar restrictions.

Figure E.9

The dialog box resulting from selection of the Compact installation type.

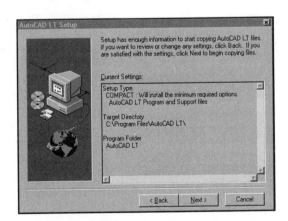

- **Custom:** When you choose the Custom installation type, you are presented with the dialog box shown in figure E.10 that displays the various components you can elect to install. Some of the components provide you with an additional dialog box by which you can change the subcomponents to be installed.

*The Custom installation
type dialog box.*

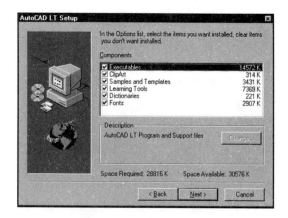

Subcomponent selections can only be changed for the Samples and Templates (see fig. E.11), Learning Tools (see fig. E.12), and Fonts (see fig. E.13)
components. To change the subcomponents installed, deselect the check
box in the Component list, then choose Change. In each Subcomponent
dialog box, check the element you want to have installed, then choose
Continue to return to the listing of Components.

Figure E.11

*The Samples and
Templates Sub-
components selection
dialog box.*

Figure E.12

The Learning Tools Sub-components selection dialog box.

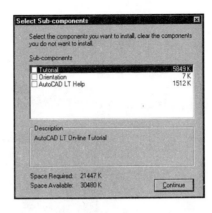

Figure E.13

The Fonts Subcomponents selection dialog box.

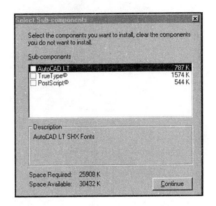

■ As you make your various selections, the component dialog boxes update
the amount of Space Required and Space Available based on your selections. When you are finished customizing your installation, choose Next from
the Component dialog box.

In the next exercise, you complete the installation of AutoCAD LT for Windows 95
based upon installation type or the components specified. The final steps involve the
setup sequence confirming the location and type of installation chosen.

COMPLETING THE AUTOCAD LT INSTALLATION SETUP

1. After choosing Next from the installation type or component selection dialog box, you see the AutoCAD LT Setup dialog box shown in figure E.14 displaying the default Program Folder for AutoCAD LT for Windows 95, as well as your existing Windows 95 folders.

Figure E.14

The folder assignment dialog box.

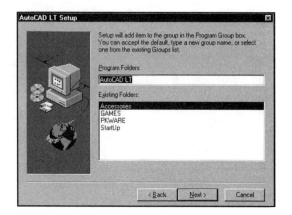

2. Choose Next to move to accept the default assignments or enter a new Program folder name for AutoCAD LT.

3. The next dialog box (see fig. E.15) displays the settings you have specified thus far in the installation setup process. This information includes the Setup Type, Target Directory, and Program Folder specified. Choose Next to accept your selections and begin the physical copying of the files onto your hard disk.

Figure E.15

The dialog box displaying your installation selections and assignments.

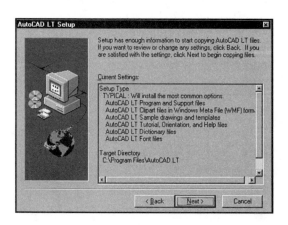

4. During the copying of the files, several screens of important information are displayed. When the installation is complete, you are prompted to view the README file as shown in figure E.16. After viewing or declining this option, choose Finish to complete the installation.

Figure E.16

The completed installation dialog box.

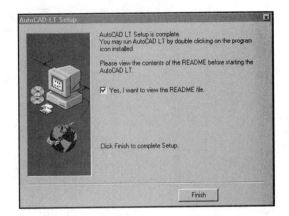

Configuring AutoCAD LT for Windows 95

When the installation is complete AutoCAD LT will be ready to use. By default AutoCAD LT is configured to use your current Windows 95 pointing device (typically a mouse). The configuration files for AutoCAD LT (*ACLTNT.CFG* and *ACLT.INI*) are placed in the folder you specified during the setup of the installation. If you accepted the default folder location, they were placed in the AutoCAD LT folder.

The *ACLTNT.CFG* file specifies the hardware configuration under which AutoCAD LT will operate when you run it for the first time. The *ACLT.INI*, like most Windows-based .INI files, contains the default settings for window sizes, default toolbar settings and sizes, and the location of AutoCAD LT support files. Chapter 1, "Opening AutoCAD LT 95" and Chapter 2, "Setting Up Your Drawing Environment" address how you can change some of these default settings within AutoCAD LT by using the Preferences dialog box and by docking the toolbars.

The default location of AutoCAD LT for Windows 95 after the installation.

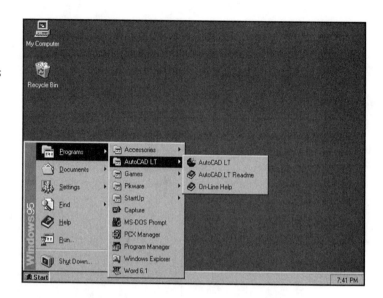

Figure E.17 illustrates the default location of the AutoCAD LT program opened from the Start Taskbar in Windows 95. Those of you with Windows NT will have an AutoCAD LT Program Group with several program items.

Configuring AutoCAD LT for a Wintab Digitizer

AutoCAD LT for Windows 95 will only work with those digitizers whose manufacturer has supplied a Wintab driver. This section presents the steps you need to take to configure AutoCAD LT for use with your Wintab digitizer. If you have yet to configure your digitizer for use with Windows 95, follow the instructions that came with your digitizer for its setup and installation. The process will probably be similar to what you encountered when installing AutoCAD LT.

NOTE

Different manufacturers of Wintab digitizers supply different versions of *WINTAB.DLL*, the driver with which AutoCAD LT for Windows 95 communicates from within its ADI driver. Make sure that all WINTAB.* files, typically found in the \WIN95 or \WIN95\SYSTEM directory, match the one supplied with the digitizer. Normally, you cannot mix *WINTAB.DLL* with the drivers from another manufacturer. The Wintab digitizer can be configured for use as a mouse only from the configuration in Windows 95.

Also, Windows 95 Wintab drivers will not necessarily work with Windows NT. You must have operating system-specific drivers.

Digitizers are frequently configured to use a tablet menu that enables you to select commands from the digitizing tablet. Normal operation of a digitizer with a tablet menu is done using a Fixed Screen pointing area.

The use of the digitizer when working with Windows 95 menus, dialog boxes, and applications can be done by turning on the floating screen feature of the digitizer. The floating screen feature refers to the capability to use the digitizer as a mouse. This feature can be toggled on and off using a toggle button designated during the time of the tablet configuration and is typically assigned to function key F12.

W ARNING

Autodesk has issued the following notices prior to the release of AutoCAD LT for Windows 95 that you should be aware of regarding the selection of tablet areas and calibration of a Wintab digitizer:

In some Wintab implementations, you might need to select the digitizer screen area points twice during configuration in order for AutoCAD LT to recognize them. This problem occurs in the Wintab drivers supplied by the tablet manufacturers.

After calibrating the tablet using the CAL option of the TABLET command, enable input from the digitizer by turning on tablet mode (Ctrl+T or F4), or setting the System Tab in Preferences to Tablet or Mouse. Turning on the tablet before it has been calibrated, or turning tablet mode off after you have calibrated the tablet disables input via a pointing device.

The following exercise steps you through the process of enabling and configuring your digitizer for use in AutoCAD LT for Windows 95. Once Windows 95 has been configured to work with your Wintab digitizer, begin AutoCAD LT by choosing the AutoCAD LT program icon from the Programs Taskbar and follow these steps:

ENABLING AND CONFIGURING THE WINTAB DIGITIZER

1. Choose Tools, Preferences to open the Preferences dialog box.

2. From the Work Space tab, choose Tablet in the Digitizer Input area, then choose OK.

3. To configure the tablet for use with the AutoCAD LT Tablet Menu, enter **TABLET** at the Command: line, and you see the following prompt:

   ```
   Option (ON/OFF/CAL/CFG):
   ```

4. Enter **CFG** and you see the following prompt:

```
Enter the number of tablet menus desired (0-4)<0>:
```

5. Enter **4** to reflect the four menu areas defined on the AutoCAD LT Tablet Menu as shown in figure E.18.

Figure E.18

The default AutoCAD LT tablet menu areas.

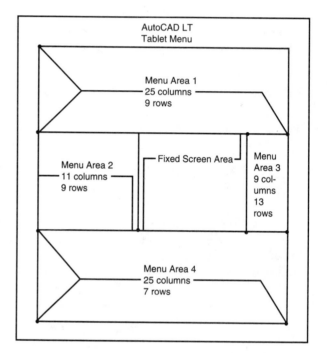

6. At the prompts, digitize the upper left, lower left, and lower right corners of menu area 1 as shown in figure E.18, after which you will receive the following prompt:

```
Enter the number of columns for menu area 1, 0 to 4991: <25>
```

7. Press Enter and you see the following:

```
Enter the number of rows for menu area 1, 0 to 1839: <9>
```

8. When prompted, digitize the upper left, lower left, and lower right corners of menu area 2.

9. For the following prompts for the number of rows and columns of menu area 2, press Enter:

```
Enter the number of columns for menu area 2, 0 to 2202: <11>
Enter the number of rows for menu area 2, 0 to 1809: <9>
```

10. At the prompts, digitize the upper left, lower left, and lower right corners of menu area 3.

11. For the following prompts for the number of rows and columns of menu area 3, press Enter:

```
Enter the number of columns for menu area 3, 0 to 539: <9>
Enter the number of rows for menu area 3, 0 to 1806: <13>
```

12. When prompted, digitize the upper left, lower left, and lower right corners of menu area 4.

13. For the following prompts for the number of rows and columns of menu area 4, press Enter:

```
Enter the number of columns for menu area 4, 0 to 5004: <25>
Enter the number of rows for menu area 4, 0 to 1407: <7>
```

14. After digitizing the corners for menu area 4, you get the following prompt:

```
Do you want to respecify the Fixed Screen Pointing Area? <N>
```

15. Enter **Y**, then digitize the upper left, lower left, and lower right corners of the fixed screen pointing area.

16. Continue to designate the screen pointing area in the following prompts:

```
Do you want to respecify the Floating Screen Pointing Area? <N>
```

17. Enter **Y**, after which you see the next prompt:

```
Do you want the Floating Screen Pointing Area to be the same size as the
Fixed Screen Pointing Area? <Y>
```

18. When prompted, digitize the lower left and upper right corners of the screen pointing area, then you will see the final prompt:

```
The F12 key will toggle the Floating Screen Pointing Area ON and OFF. Would
you like to specify a button to toggle the Floating Screen Area? <N>
```

19. Enter **Y** or **N**. If you respond Yes, press any non-pick button on the digitizing cursor that you want to designate as the toggle button.

After configuration is complete, choose a few commands from the tablet and draw in the screen pointing area to test the configuration. The standard AutoCAD tablet menu is configured for your digitizer, and the configuration parameters are stored on your disk in a file.

N OTE

The floating screen-pointing area takes precedence over the fixed screen-pointing area, which in turn takes precedence over the tablet. Some Wintab drivers allow access to button commands only if the cursor is outside the screen-pointing area. If you notice that the buttons on your digitizing puck are not responding appropriately, move the puck anywhere outside the fixed screen pointing area and press the desired button.

The TABLET.DWG Drawing

AutoCAD LT comes with a drawing file, TABLET.DWG, that reproduces the plastic template menu included with AutoCAD LT for Windows 95. You can use this drawing to create a custom template drawing for your digitizer.

If you know how to edit drawings and customize the tablet menu, you can make your own tablet drawing, supporting the menu with your own tablet menu programs. If you customize your tablet menu drawing, make a backup copy of TABLET.DWG (call it MYTABLET.DWG) and make your changes to the copy, not to the original.

Other Installation Considerations

Some of you might have a previous version of AutoCAD LT on your computer and are upgrading to LT for Windows 95. Others might want to reinstall or uninstall AutoCAD LT for Windows 95. This section takes you through each of these topics.

Updating to AutoCAD LT for Windows 95 from an Earlier Version

If you have an earlier version of AutoCAD LT on your computer and have updated your operating system to Windows 95 or Windows NT, it is recommended that you uninstall the earlier version of LT before installing AutoCAD LT for Windows 95.

The best reason to uninstall an earlier version of LT is to free the hard disk space on your computer. After uninstalling the earlier version, it would also be advisable to run Windows 95 Scandisk and Defragmenter. These programs can be run by choosing Start from the Taskbar, then Programs, Accessories, System Tools, ScanDisk or Disk Defragmenter. These programs optimize the space on the hard disk in preparation for an AutoCAD LT for Windows 95 installation.

Reinstalling AutoCAD LT for Windows 95

If you find it necessary to either reinstall or add components you opted not to install initially, you can run the installation setup program again. The simplest way to reinstall is to go back through the steps given in the earlier exercises of this chapter, beginning with Installing the AutoCAD LT Software section.

To add components previously unselected, simply choose the Custom installation type at the appropriate setup dialog box, then choose the desired components you want to add.

If you find it necessary to reinstall AutoCAD LT, it might be to your advantage to uninstall the existing version, optimize the hard disk, then reinstall AutoCAD LT.

To restate an earlier note regarding existing installations, if the setup and installation process detects an existing version of AutoCAD LT on your computer, you will be prompted to create backups of existing data files. To save the previous version of AutoCAD LT, *do not* accept the default name displayed in the dialog box. Install AutoCAD LT for Windows 95 into a new folder with an appropriate name.

Uninstalling AutoCAD LT from Windows 95

The Windows 95 operating system includes a sequence by which you can select the existing application you want to uninstall. The following exercise takes you through this process for uninstalling AutoCAD LT for Windows 95.

USING WINDOWS 95'S REMOVE PROGRAM TO UNINSTALL AUTOCAD LT

1. Choose Start from the Windows 95 Taskbar, then choose Settings, Control Panel to open the Control Panel dialog box.

2. Double-click on Add/Remove Programs to open the Add/Remove Programs Properties dialog box shown in figure E.19.

Figure E.19

*Uninstalling AutoCAD LT
using the Windows 95
Remove program.*

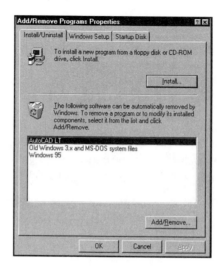

3. From the Install/Uninstall tab, choose AutoCAD LT in the list of programs, then choose Add/Remove.

4. From the Confirm File Deletion dialog box, choose Yes or No.

Should you opt to uninstall AutoCAD LT, the AutoCAD LT for Windows 95 program files will be removed from your computer. Any drawing or data files remain. To relocate data files, use the Windows 95 Explorer before deleting the AutoCAD LT folder(s).

RELATED COMMANDS

TABLET

GLOSSARY

3DPOLY:
426

Enables drawing a 3D version of a polyline.

ARC:
82-83

Creates a circular arc by specifying a combination of the start point, a point on the circumference, endpoint, center, and included angle that defines an arc.

AREA:
142

Calculates the area and perimeter of an object or defined area.

ARRAY:
130, 417

Creates a regular arrangement of objects, in a rectangular or circular pattern.

Associative dimension:
308-322

An associative dimension is a dimension whose extension line(s), dimension line, and dimension text are treated as a single object and is considered an unnamed block. Using grips, the DDEDIT command, or by changing the settings of its dimension style can easily edit the associative dimension.

If a dimension is exploded, it loses all associativity and its elements become individual objects.

ATTDISP:
215-216

Controls the visibility of all attributes in a drawing. Pulldown: Choose Options, Display, Attribute Display.

ATTEDIT:
218-220

Edits the attribute text values or characteristics of one or more attributes or one or more blocks. Pulldown: Choose Modify, Objects, Attribute, Global. Toolbar: Choose Attribute, Edit Attribute Globally.

BASE:
202

Changes the base insertion point of the current drawing.

BHATCH:
47, 172-174

Fills boundaries with patterns (dialog box method).

BLOCK:
230-235

Is the command line version of the BMAKE command. Toolbar: Choose Draw, Block, Block.

BMAKE:
188, 204, 213

Defines block definitions. Pulldown: Choose Draw, Make Block.

BOUNDARY:
186

Creates a polyline boundary from surrounding objects.

BREAK:
137

Deletes part of an object or cuts an object in two.

CHAMFER:
140-142

Places a bevel cut at the intersection of two objects.

CIRCLE:
484-485

Draws circles by using nearly any geometric method. The most common method (the default) is to specify the center point and radius.

COMPLEX LINETYPE:
463-464

The complex linetype contains dashes, dots, and spaces as well as shapes or text objects. The LTYPESHP.LIN linetype file contains several sample complex linetype definitions. See *Linetype Definition.*

CONTAINER APPLICATION/FILE:
475-477

The container application or file is that file to which an external file is linked or embedded. This is sometimes referred to as an OLE client application or receiving application.

COORDS:
93

Controls the updating of the coordinate display on the status bar.

COPY:
130, 217, 417

Duplicates a set of objects.

CUSTOMIZED LINETYPE:

Any linetype not contained in the default ACLT.LIN linetype file is considered customized. A customized linetype can be either simple or complex. See also *Complex Linetype, Simple Linetype.*

DDATTDEF:
210

Draws attribute objects. Pulldown: Choose Draw, Define Attribute. Toolbar: Choose Attribute, Define Attribute.

DDATTE:
218-220

Edits the attribute text values in insertions. Pulldown: Choose Modify, Objects, Attribute, Single. Toolbar: Choose Attribute, Edit Attribute.

DDATTEXT:
220

Extracts the attribute values from the drawing file to a text file.

DDCHPROP:
144, 416

Changes the properties of objects using a dialog box.

DDCOLOR:
56

Enables setting the current color. Pulldown: Choose Format, Color. Toolbar: Choose Object Properties, Color Control.

DDEDIT:
217, 260-261,
318, 456

Edits text lines, paragraphs, dimensions, and block attribute definitions.

DDEMODES:
472

Enables setting the current object properties. Pulldown: Choose Format, Current Properties. Toolbar: Choose Object Properties, Current Properties.

DDGRIPS:
114

Enables the selection set grips and modifies colors.

DDIM:
32

Opens the Dimension Styles dialog box. Additional dialog boxes found within include Geometry, Format, Annotation, and Primary Units. Dimensioning Toolbar: Dimension Styles, Pulldown: Choose Format, Dimension Style.

DDINSERT:
47, 191, 204-206,
214-215

Inserts defined blocks into the current drawing. It can also be used to insert drawings as blocks. Pulldown: Choose Draw, Insert Block. Toolbar: Choose Draw, Block, Insert Block.

DDLMODES:
335, 472

Dynamic Dialog Layer MODES uses the Layer Control dialog box to manage layer settings. Enables making new layers and assigns states, colors, and linetypes to existing layers. DDLMODES also provides an easy way to check layer status. Pulldown: Choose Format, Layers. Toolbar: Choose Object Properties, Layers.

DIMCENTER:
269

Places a center mark at the center of a circle or arc. The type and size of the center mark can be set in the Geometry dialog box.

DIMCONTINUE:
289-290

Continues a dimension from the last linear dimension placed. By default, the continued dimension is measured from the second extension line origin of the last dimension. Selecting an extension line of another dimension from which to continue overrides the default.

DIMDIAMETER:
295

Returns the diameter value for the circle or arc selected.

DIMLINEAR:
285-287, 386

Creates a linear dimension between any two points. Any two points in the current coordinate systems can be picked to define the linear dimension; or Enter to select the object to be dimensioned.

DIMORDINATE:
301-302

Returns ordinate (along the X or Y axis) dimensions from the datum point for the features selected, after the UCS Origin has been positioned at the desired datum (0,0) point.

DIMRADIUS:
294-295

Returns the radius value of the selected circle or arc. The arc can be a separate object or part of a polyline, such as a fillet. The radius dimension text can be positioned anywhere about the radius of the defined arc or the perimeter of a circle.

Dimension block:

You also can refer to an associative dimension as a dimension block. See *Associative dimension*.

Dimension override:
308-311

Manually entering the desired value for the dimension variable supersedes or overrides the individual settings of a dimension style. Because the settings found in the Dimension Style dialog boxes are stored in dimension variables, changing the variable manually overrides the setting in the dialog box. You also can override a setting by changing the value in the dialog box and electing to *not* save it to the current dimension style.

Dimension Style:
265-268, 276-278

A dimension style is a named set of dimension variables. Using the Dimension Styles dialog box (*see DDIM*), you can use several element-specific dialog boxes to configure the style of the dimension. Similar to the concept of text styles and layers, only one dimension style can be current, though you may have many dimension styles in a drawing.

DIST:
142

Calculates the distance between two points.

DIVIDE:
155

Adds points or blocks along an object path for a specified number of segments.

DLINE:
163

Creates double (parallel) line segments.

DONUT:
86

Creates polyline circles that can vary in width by specifying an inside and outside diameter.

DSVIEWER:
66-67

Displays the Aerial View window. Pulldown: Choose View, Aerial View. Toolbar: Choose Standard Toolbar, Aerial View.

DTEXT:
85, 240

Places text objects in a drawing by specifying the insertion point, text style, justification, height, and rotation, and places one or more lines of text, either directly below the first, or at other locations selected. Preview text appears on the screen as it is entered.

DVIEW:
404-411

Enables setting the line of sight used to generate the view in the current viewport, or invokes clipping planes and perspective mode. Pulldown: Choose View, 3D Dynamic View.

ELLIPSE:
379

Creates a true, mathematical ellipse or a polyline approximation.

Embedded:
481

When a file from a source application has been embedded in a container application, any edits to the source file are made in a temporary file from the source application; there is no automatic linkage to the originating source file.

ERASE:
87

Deletes a selection set from the drawing database.

EXIT:
38-39

Ends the current drawing session. If changes to the current drawing are detected, then the user is given the option to save the changes prior to exiting LT. Pulldown: Choose File, Exit.

EXPORT:
203

Exports a portion of the current drawing or the entire drawing using a variety of file formats. Pulldown: Choose File, Export.

EXTERNAL REFERENCE:

Any drawing can be referenced externally from within another drawing. The externally referenced file does not become part of the "host" drawing (as does an inserted drawing) but is attached or overlaid using the XREF command. Because the host drawing does not retain the entirety of the Xref, its file size is smaller than if the file had been inserted. See *XREF*.

FILLET:
140-142, 294-295

Places a smooth arc at the intersection of two objects.

HATCH:
184, 186

Fills closed areas with patterns (command line method).

HATCHEDIT:
181

Modifies an existing hatch pattern insertion.

HELP:
38

Displays help information. Pulldown: Choose Help, AutoCAD LT Help. Toolbar: Choose Standard Toolbar, Help.

HIDE:
400-401

Enables removing the hidden lines from the view in the current viewport. Pulldown: Choose View, Hide.

INSERT:

Is the command line version of the DDINSERT command. See *DDINSERT*.

LEADER:
299

Creates a leader line whose beginning point is represented by an arrowhead by default, and whose linework can be either linear or a spline. The termination point information may be single or multiline text, a tolerance or a dimension.

LENGTHEN:
133

Changes the lengths of objects and the included angle of arcs.

LIMITS:
15, 49, 79

Defines the current drawing area. LIMITS is also used to turn the limits on, preventing the drawing of any objects beyond the drawing limits. Pulldown: Choose Format, Drawing Limits.

.LIN:

Files having the .LIN extension are linetype files that contain simple or complex linetype definitions. These files are ASCII files that are editable by using a text editor such as the Windows 95 Notepad. See *Simple Linetype and Complex Linetype*.

LINE:
96-97, 106, 142,
378, 393

Draws one or more straight 2D or 3D line segments.

LINETYPE:
460, 472

By default, AutoCAD LT creates a solid, continuous line when drawing objects. By changing an object's *linetype*, you can change the look of the object's linework.

**LINETYPE
DEFINITION:**

A linetype definition contains the pattern code that defines the look of the linetype. All linetype definitions consist of two lines:

the first contains the linetype name and an optional description; the second contains the linetype pattern descriptors. Simple linetype definitions descriptors specify the values for the dashes, dots, and spaces. Complex linetype definitions expand on a simple linetype by including transformation variables for shapes and text objects. See also *Complex Linetype, Simple Linetype*.

LINKED:
481-484

When a file from a source application has been linked to a container application, the container file is automatically updated with any edits made to the source file.

When a source file (such as an AutoCAD LT drawing) is linked to a container file (such as a WordPad document) or when the source file is edited in the source application (AutoCAD LT), the graphic image in the container file is automatically updated with the edits.

LIST:
142

Displays the database information of a set of objects.

MEASURE:
155

Adds points or blocks along an object path at intervals of a specified length.

MOVE:
128, 217, 391, 416, 440

Repositions a set of objects.

MSLIDE:
438

Creates a slide file. Pulldown: File, Slide, Create.

MTEXT:
240

Creates paragraph-style text.

NEW:
39

Starts a new drawing. Pulldown: Choose File, New. Toolbar: Choose Standard Toolbar, New.

Object Application/File:
474

The object application or file is the source of linked or embedded information. This is sometimes referred to as the originating, native, or OLE server application.

OFFSET:
131

Creates parallel lines or arcs.

OLE:
489-490

Object Linking and Embedding is the process in which information from one Windows 95 application (the source or server) is linked or embedded into another Windows 95 application (the container).

OOPS:
87

Undeletes the most recently erased objects.

OPEN:
35-47

Opens an existing drawing. Pulldown: Choose File, Open. Toolbar: Choose Standard Toolbar, Open.

OSNAP:
104-106

Provides methods of specifying locations based on geometric points on objects.

PAN:
69

Enables panning the current display. Pulldown: Choose View, Pan, Pan Point. Toolbar: Choose Standard Toolbar, Pan, Pan Point.

PEDIT:
160-161

Edits polylines globally or vertices individually.

PICKBOX:
119

Assigns the object selection target height, in pixels.

PLAN:
397

Enables generating a plan view in the current viewport. Pulldown: Choose View, 3D Viewpoint, Plan View.

PLINE:
158

Creates a polyline.

PLOT:
152

Generates output from AutoCAD LT in the form of hard-copy paper plots or plot files.

POINT:
152

Adds a point object to the drawing.

POLYGON:
83

Creates multisided polygons (polylines) consisting of from 3 to 1,024 sides. There is no associated width value.

PREFERENCES:
42-69

Customizes the LT drawing environment for the individual user. Pulldown: Choose Tools, Preferences.

QTEXT:
257-258

Displays text entries as approximate rectangular outlines.

RAY:
168-170

Creates a construction line, anchored at one end and infinite in the other direction.

REDRAW:
65

Enables refreshing the display. Pulldown: Choose View, Redraw. Toolbar: Choose Standard Toolbar, Redraw View.

REGEN:
65, 400

Enables forcing LT to redo all the calculations needed to display the drawing. Pulldown: Choose View, Regen.

SPLINEDIT: Edits a NURBS (spline) curve.
166-168

STRETCH: Moves, elongates, or compresses objects along one axis.
133, 229, 311, 416

TBCONFIG: Opens the Customize Toolbars dialog box (Tools, Customize
445-446 Toolbars).

TEXT: Creates a single line of text.
240

TRIM: Cuts objects back to selected edges.
136-137

U: Reverses the most recent operation.
128, 189

UCS: Provides for the creation of User Coordinate Systems.
54, 92, 98-99, 417, 419

UCSICON: Positions the UCS icon or turns it on and off.
417

UNDO: Reverses the results of a series of commands.
189

UNITS: Sets the system of units and precision for linear and angular
14, 16-18 measurements. UNITS can also be used to set the direction of zero
degrees and the direction that positive angles are measured.

UPDATE: Issued from the Dim: prompt, the UPDATE command enables the
279-280 user to select existing dimensions to be updated with the current
dimension style.

VIEWTOOLBAR: Opens the Toolbar dialog box, from which the user may choose
26 which toolbar to show, and whether the buttons are to be Color
Buttons, display as Large Buttons, or Show ToolTips. You may also
reset the toolbars to the factory default setting.

VPOINT: Enables defining the line of sight used to generate the view in the
395-397, 403-404 current viewport. Pulldown: Choose View, 3D Viewpoint. Toolbar:
Choose Standard, View.

VPORTS:
71-73, 328, 399

Enables defining multiple viewports. Pulldown: Choose View, Tiled Viewport. Pulldown: Choose Format, Units.

VSLIDE:
438

Displays a slide file. Pulldown: File, Slide, View.

XLINE:
168

Creates a construction line, infinite in both directions.

XREF:
226-227, 234-235,
345

Enables external referencing, or attaching, an existing drawing file from within a host drawing. Once attached, it maintains a link to the external reference file (see External Reference).

ZOOM:
67-68, 346

Enables magnifying or shrinking the current display. Pulldown: Choose View, Zoom. Toolbar: Choose Standard Toolbar, Zoom In. Choose Standard Toolbar, Zoom Out. Choose Standard Toolbar, Zoom flyout.

I N D E X

N-O

Check Us Out Online!

New Riders has emerged as a premier publisher of computer books for the professional computer user. Focusing on CAD/graphics/multimedia, communications/internetworking, and networking/operating systems, New Riders continues to provide expert advice on high-end topics and software.

Check out the online version of *New Riders' Official World Wide Web Yellow Pages, 1996 Edition* for the most engaging, entertaining, and informative sites on the Web! You can even add your own site!

Brave our site for the finest collection of CAD and 3D imagery produced today. Professionals from all over the world contribute to our gallery, which features new designs every month.

From Novell to Microsoft, New Riders publishes the training guides you need to attain your certification. Visit our site and try your hand at the CNE Endeavor, a test engine created by VFX Technologies, Inc. that enables you to measure what you know—and what you don't!

http://www.mcp.com/newriders

WANT MORE INFORMATION?

CHECK OUT THESE RELATED TOPICS OR SEE YOUR LOCAL BOOKSTORE

CAD

As the number one CAD publisher in the world, and as a Registered Publisher of Autodesk, New Riders Publishing provides unequaled content on this complex topic under the flagship *Inside AutoCAD*. Other titles include *AutoCAD for Beginners* and *New Riders' Reference Guide to AutoCAD Release 13*.

Networking

As the leading Novell NetWare publisher, New Riders Publishing delivers cutting-edge products for network professionals. We publish books for all levels of users, from those wanting to gain NetWare Certification, to those administering or installing a network. Leading books in this category include *Inside NetWare 3.12*, *Inside TCP/IP Second Edition*, *NetWare: The Professional Reference*, and *Managing the NetWare 3.x Server*.

Graphics and 3D Studio

New Riders provides readers with the most comprehensive product tutorials and references available for the graphics market. Best-sellers include *Inside Photoshop 3*, *3D Studio IPAS Plug In Reference*, *KPT's Filters and Effects*, and *Inside 3D Studio*.

Internet and Communications

As one of the fastest growing publishers in the communications market, New Riders provides unparalleled information and detail on this ever-changing topic area. We publish international best-sellers such as *New Riders' Official Internet Yellow Pages, 2nd Edition*, a directory of more than 10,000 listings of Internet sites and resources from around the world, as well as *VRML: Browsing and Building Cyberspace*, *Actually Useful Internet Security Techniques*, *Internet Firewalls and Network Security*, and *New Riders' Official World Wide Web Yellow Pages*.

Operating Systems

Expanding off our expertise in technical markets, and driven by the needs of the computing and business professional, New Riders offers comprehensive references for experienced and advanced users of today's most popular operating systems, including *Inside Windows 95*, *Inside Unix*, *Inside OS/2 Warp Version 3*, and *Building a Unix Internet Server*.

Orders/Customer Service **1-800-653-6156**   Source Code **NRP95**

New Riders Publishing   201 West 103rd Street ◆ Indianapolis, Indiana 46290 USA